IN MY END IS MY BEGINNING

Burns: A Biography of Robert Burns
Vagabond of Verse: A Biography of Robert Service
William Wallace: Brave Heart
The Eye Who Never Slept: A Life of Allan Pinkerton
Michael Collins: A Life
Sounds Out of Silence: A Life of Alexander Graham Bell
Little Boss: A Life of Andrew Carnegie
The Man Who Invented Himself: A Life of Sir Thomas Lipton
I Have Not Yet Begun to Fight: A Life of John Paul Jones

IN MY END
IS MY BEGINNING

A LIFE OF
Mary Queen of Scots

JAMES MACKAY

MAINSTREAM
PUBLISHING

EDINBURGH AND LONDON

For Helen

First published in Great Britain in 1999 by
MAINSTREAM PUBLISHING COMPANY (EDINBURGH) LTD
7 Albany Street
Edinburgh EH1 3UG

ISBN 1 84018 058 7

A catalogue record for this book is available from the British Library

Typeset in Berkeley
Printed and bound in Great Britain by Butler & Tanner Ltd

CONTENTS

INTRODUCTION

In his memoirs, *The Way the Wind Blows*, Lord Home recalled an evening with Andrei Gromyko (the then Soviet foreign minister) and his wife at the play *Vivat Regina* in London. At the end of the second act, in which David Riccio was brutally murdered in the presence of his queen, Gromyko turned to Alec Douglas-Home and said: 'Do I not find myself in very dangerous company?' When Lord Home queried this, Gromyko replied: 'Did I not hear Mary Stewart say, as the dagger went into Riccio, "And you, Douglas, too?"' In the real-life drama of the Scottish queen there was a Lord Hume (*sic*) and Douglases aplenty. The prevalence of certain names, recurring over the centuries, is one of the few things that give stability and coherence to the aurora borealis of Scottish history. This is immediately countered by the permutations and combinations of alliances, factions and cliques, ever-changing, as traditional enemies draw together for mutual interest, and just as rapidly fall apart again. This factor is vividly and most forcefully exposed by the late Professor Gordon Donaldson in his brilliant study *All the Queen's Men: Power and Politics in Mary Stewart's Scotland* (1983) which unravels the tangled knot of politics, religion and family which bedevilled Mary at every turn.

Scottish history was never more kaleidoscopic than it was during the four and a half decades of the life of Mary Queen of Scots, nominally queen from the age of six days until her execution in 1587, but in fact monarch for little more than six years (1561–67) and only in real command of her destiny for a very few months at that. The first nineteen years of her life were mostly spent far from her own kingdom, when she was being groomed at the French court for eventual marriage to the Dauphin; and the last nineteen years were spent in captivity in England. The period of her personal rule was not only brief, but beset by problems and circumstances largely outside her control. Few people would share the view of Dr Jenny Wormald that Mary was the worst, most incompetent ruler that Scotland ever had. In justifying this sweeping condemnation she has produced a book which is worth reading if only as a powerful corrective to so much of the earlier hagiography dripping with uncritical adulation of the saintly martyr for her faith.

The volume of literature devoted to Mary is truly prodigious. Lady Antonia Fraser, the author of the best-known biography in modern times (1969), noted that the Collection Blis in the Bibliothèque Nationale in Paris contained about 20,000 books that touched on the subject. Of these, probably more than a thousand are biographies, novels or plays dealing with her life. It might have been thought that Lady Antonia's monumental volume, published almost thirty years ago, would be the last word on the subject, but the ink was scarcely dry when Gordon Donaldson's *First Trial of Mary Queen of Scots* appeared, followed by the same author's *Mary Queen of Scots* (1974).

To Professor Donaldson, Mary was an intelligent, able and energetic queen, with a sense of religious tolerance that was beyond the grasp of her contemporaries, guilty not of crimes but lacking in judgment at times, leading to a downfall unfortunate for being on the whole undeserved. In 1988 Dr Jenny Wormald produced *Mary Queen of Scots: A Study in Failure* which painted an unrelievedly black picture of Mary as negligent, irresponsible and incompetent at best; at worst guilty of complicity in the murder of Darnley. The previous year, the quatercentenary of Mary's execution, witnessed a spate of publications, including Rosalind Marshall's *Queen of Scots*, D. Breeze's *A Queen's Progress* and Ian Cowan's *Mary Queen of Scots*. Even David and Judy Steel got in on the act with *Mary Stuart's Scotland*, none of which shed fresh light on the subject. The one really bright spot in this Marian Year was the appearance of Margaret Sanderson's *Mary Stewart's People*, a fascinating collection of essays on a broad spectrum of people, from a humble tailor to Cardinal Beaton's mistress Marion Ogilvy, who lived during Mary's reign.

Most recently there has been *Mary Queen of Scots: The Crucial Years* by the Duke of Hamilton (1991). Apart from the unique qualification of being an actual descendant of Queen Mary, the Duke advanced our understanding of his tragic ancestress by concentrating on the two years between her marriage to Darnley and her enforced abdication, and backed this with a hundred biographical sketches of the chief personalities of Mary's reign. I have to admit that, of all the recent writings on Mary, this has been for me by far the most useful, not only distinguishing persons of the same or very similar names but also pinpointing what they were doing, and with whom they were allied, at any given juncture. While many other books include family trees, this book thoughtfully included charts and diagrams analysing, for example, the minority reigns that so often bedevilled the Stewart dynasty, and particularly the overlapping lists of those complicit in the murders of Riccio and Darnley. For a more detailed analysis of the wheeling and dealing, the power-play and the positively Byzantine background to Mary's personal rule, Gordon Donaldson's *All the Queen's Men*, previously referred to, is essential reading.

Reflecting the much more objective approach to Scottish history in recent years, as the sectarian propaganda and political polemics have given way to a more systematic, scientific examination of the facts, a clearer picture of Mary is beginning to emerge. Hand in hand with this process has been a re-appraisal of some of the other major actors in the drama, notably a volume in the Studies in British History series, William Blake's masterly exposition of William Maitland of Lethington (1990), and Caroline Bingham's biography of Darnley (1995) which re-examines the crucial years of 1565–67 from the standpoint of the principal victim of Kirk o' Field. To all of these writers, and very many more, especially those scholars who concentrated on specific aspects such as the Casket Letters and the Kirk o' Field affair, I owe an immense debt. One could, in fact, produce a volume many times the size of this book dealing with the diametrically opposing opinions, attitudes and interpretations of Mary's life and times, but for a concise survey of the extraordinary scope of Marian literature I can commend Ian Cowan's *Enigma of Mary Stuart* (1971).

I make no apology for offering this fresh look at Mary. Writing in the aftermath of the devolution debate and referendum, I have been forcibly struck by the application of so much that was happening in the 1560s to the present time. I had not fully appreciated, for example, the extent to which Queen Elizabeth, both personally and through her ministers, agents and ambassadors, manipulated and controlled the affairs of Scotland. Despite Schiller and Hollywood,[1] Mary and Elizabeth never met; yet their lives were inextricably woven together. Essentially this was a power struggle between two of the outstanding figures in British history. The fact that they were both women adds a feminist dimension: the one married only to her country and the other married all too often to men who failed her.

Ironically, Elizabeth (unlike her father) had no territorial ambitions in Scotland, whereas Mary was determined to secure the succession to the English throne, if not for herself then certainly for her son. In 1603, when James VI became James I of England, Scotland lost her resident monarch. Little more than a century later, 'a parcel of rogues' sold their nation's political independence. With the restoration of some measure of autonomy now imminent, a fresh look at the reign of Mary becomes vital to a better understanding not only of what happened long ago but where we stand today.

The title of this book is a literal translation of Mary's French personal motto, *En ma fin est mon commencement*. These curious words were embroidered on the chair of state which accompanied Mary throughout the long, dreary years of her captivity. It was noted by Nicholas White, a friend of William Cecil (later Lord Burghley, Elizabeth's Secretary of State for forty years and one of the more remarkable political survivors of Tudor times). Writing to Cecil from Tutbury in the spring of 1569, White described Mary's cloth of state and commented that it was 'a riddle I understand not'. Then he went on: 'Fame might move some to relieve her, and glory joined to gain might stir others to adventure much for her sake; then joy is a lively impetuous passion, and carrieth many persuasions to the heart, which moveth all the rest.' These words have proved all too true, for right down to the present day there have been many moved to relieve her, whether by the wish for fame, glory or impetuous passion, or simply from a desire to set the record straight (as they saw it) or to re-interpret the well-worn facts.

Few lives have been held up to such detailed scrutiny as Mary's. Every document, every fragment, every scrap of gossip has been picked over and over again, examined from fresh angles perhaps, or made to fit old prejudices. Mary is at one and the same time well known and little known, the substance and reality so often obscured by the prejudices of the individual writer. Only one thing may be said with certainty, and that is that today, more than four centuries after her death, Mary continues to exert her fascination over each succeeding generation and in every literary medium, from the polemics of Bishop Leslie to the historical romances of Jean Plaidy and Reay Tannahill, from the dramas of Schiller and Swinburne to the films of Hal Wallis and Meryl Streep. The tragic, romantic figure of the Scottish queen stirs the emotions not only in her native country but to the farthest ends of the world. In that sense alone Mary's motto could not have been better chosen.

In the course of my studies I have made use of the facilities of many libraries at both local and national level, and my thanks are due to the staff of the new British Library and the Bibliothèque Nationale in Paris, the National Library of Scotland, the Mitchell Library and the university libraries of Cambridge, Edinburgh and Glasgow. I must also commend the staff of the Langside Public Library, Glasgow, which actually stands on the site of the battle that brought Mary's rule to an end and, apart from an interesting collection of Marian literature, boasts a fine mural by Maurice Grieffenhagen depicting the battle itself. Elizabeth J. Brown, Margaret C. Lumsdaine of the Marie Stuart Society, Miss C. Reynolds, Assistant Keeper of the Muniments in Westminster Abbey Library, and my old friend John Holman, a Scotsman *manqué* and ardent Marian, have helped in many ways. Finally I must pay tribute to Jean Marshall, whose enthusiasm for those parts of Glasgow (Crookston, Darnley and Langside) with which Mary was connected has been infectious.

James Mackay
Glasgow, 1999

1. ROUGH WOOING

1542–47

Unhappy is the age which has o'er young a King.
Sir David Lyndsay of the Mount, *The Satire of the Three Estates*

At the beginning of the sixteenth century relations between Scotland and her much larger and infinitely more powerful neighbour were better than they had been since the death of Alexander III in 1286. England, under its first Tudor monarch, was still recovering from the effects of the Hundred Years' War and the prolonged civil conflict known as the Wars of the Roses. Henry VII not only restored internal stability but sought to create equilibrium externally and to this end he arranged the marriage of his son to Katherine of Aragon, daughter of the King of Spain, and his daughter Margaret to James IV, King of Scots. The romantically named Union of the Thistle and the Rose in 1503 seemed set to secure Henry's northern frontier and usher in an era of peace within the island of Britain; but within a decade the Scots invaded England. The immediate cause of the war was a bitter dispute between Queen Margaret and her brother, Henry VIII, over a legacy. Nevertheless Queen Margaret did everything in her power to prevent her headstrong husband going to war, but to no avail; the Scots would have gone to war anyway, under the obligation of their age-old alliance with France which was then at odds with England.

This would be the last time that the Scots would serve as cannon fodder for French interests. At Flodden King James IV and the flower of Scottish chivalry were slaughtered, and the crown passed to a seventeen-month-old baby. There is something ironical about Queen Margaret, Guardian of James V, being the heiress to the English throne, in default of issue to her brother. Apart from the quarter of a century between the birth of Elizabeth Tudor (1533) and the death of her half-sister Mary (1558), the heir presumptive to the crown of England was a Scot. Despite Flodden, there was a strong feeling that, sooner or later, a Stewart would succeed to the English throne. This, in turn, tended to bring the Scots closer to their southern neighbours. Conversely, when a Scottish succession was less likely, the Scots tended to pursue a more independent policy. This was the situation by 1540: not only was King Henry in the prime of life, but he had a son and two daughters. Of course, no one could foresee that all three would follow him on the throne, and that all three would be childless, thus bringing the Tudor dynasty into jeopardy.

The minority of James V lasted till his eighteenth year. For much of that period the reins of government were in the hands of his mother who, naturally, would have been expected to act in her brother's interest at all times. In point of fact she often let her heart rule her head, regardless of political considerations. Eleven months after the death of James IV, Margaret married Archibald, Earl of Angus, invariably dismissed as 'a young witless fool'.[1] This alienated many of the nobility, particularly the powerful earls of Arran and Home, and made her utterly dependent on the house of Douglas. Margaret's headstrong actions gave the Council the excuse for removing her from the regency and guardianship of the king in July 1515, in favour of John Stewart, Duke of Albany, the young king's cousin and next in line to the throne. Albany was actually born and brought up in France, and only returned to the land of his fathers after Flodden at the urgent request of the Council. Not surprisingly, he favoured closer ties with France. Henry VIII perceived Albany as a major stumbling-block to his plans for gaining control of Scotland though ironically Albany was fettered by the devious policies of France which, when it suited her, was only too ready to abandon him and his adopted country. Indeed, when Albany made what he intended to be a flying visit to France in 1517, the French went so far as to oblige Henry by revoking Albany's passport and holding him for four years.

In September 1515 Margaret fled to England where, a month later, she bore to Angus a daughter, Margaret, who later became Countess of Lennox and mother of Henry, Lord Darnley. In 1516 Margaret went to her brother's court, having parted from her husband who returned to Scotland, made his peace with Albany and was restored to his estates. Thereafter Angus was Margaret's implacable enemy. The rivalry between the French and English factions in Scotland was exacerbated and complicated by the private feuds of the Hamiltons and the Douglases, the respective heads of whose houses, Arran and Angus, contended for the supreme power during the enforced absence of Albany in France. Returning to Scotland, Margaret quarrelled with her estranged husband over money matters and began to agitate for a divorce. In this she was aided by Albany, who found an unexpected ally when she was temporarily alienated from the English faction by her brother Henry's strenuous opposition to her divorce. When Albany returned from France in 1521 his association with the Queen Mother gave rise to rumours that he intended marrying her himself, once she had obtained her divorce. At that time, however, Albany's star was in the ascendant, and it was Angus who found it prudent to leave the country and seek refuge in France till 1524.

During these years there was constant warfare along the Anglo-Scottish border. In May 1524 Albany was obliged to retire to France, but Henry's attempts to gain control of his little nephew were thwarted when James was proclaimed a reigning sovereign in July that year. Immediately after her divorce from Angus in 1527 Queen Margaret married Henry Stewart, second son of Lord Avondale, and her new husband, now created Lord Methven, became for a time the chief adviser to the boy-king. Margaret's last meddlesome act came in 1534 when she tried to arrange a meeting between her brother and her son, but was frustrated by the Council and the Scottish clergy. In her anger and disappointment, she betrayed certain state secrets to Henry. The last remaining links with her son were shattered when he accused her of betraying him for English gold. Margaret died at Methven Castle in October 1541.

Despite the prolonged campaign of intimidation waged by Henry VIII against his young nephew, the Scots in general were moving closer to England and drifting away from France. In 1517 Albany had negotiated the Treaty of Rouen which, among other things, envisaged a marriage between King James and a French princess, but the Scots, still reeling from the disaster of Flodden, no longer had the same zest for major cross-border wars in support of the Auld Alliance. Among the common people, there was a growing feeling that closer ties with England, a country which had prospered immensely under the strong rule of the Tudors, would be no bad thing.

These political developments went hand in hand with radical changes in religious outlook. By 1527 the Lutheran reform movement reached Scotland and struck an immediate chord in a country whose Church was notoriously corrupt. Within a decade many of the most powerful and influential noblemen and clergy had espoused reform. From 1534 onwards, when Henry VIII finally broke with Rome, the clamour for religious change gathered momentum. Many of the reformers, in fact, found shelter in England from persecution, and in due course would return to Scotland, stronger in their reforming zeal than ever. At the same time, those on the conservative wing of the Church were driven more deeply into the pro-French camp.

For centuries Scotland had been a pawn in the power struggle between France and England, but in the period of James V's personal rule the international situation was in a state of flux. France now felt infinitely more threatened by the rise of the Habsburg dynasty which, under the Emperor Charles V, controlled not only the Holy Roman Empire but also Spain and the Netherlands. Both France and the Emperor sought English support and while Henry astutely exploited this situation, keeping them at arm's length with vague promises, whichever continental power was temporarily at odds with England would seek accommodation with the Scots. Even the Papacy was drawn into this diplomatic manoeuvring, especially after Henry set up his own Reformation. James briefly enjoyed the rare experience of being courted on all sides. He favoured a continuation of the French connection, ably conducted by Albany on his behalf. Albany, related by marriage to Pope Clement VII, also facilitated closer ties with the Papacy. By contrast, James was violently hostile towards his stepfather Angus, who had actually kept him in close confinement for more than two years (1525–27). When James escaped from Edinburgh and assumed the reigns of government at the beginning of 1528, Angus was toppled from power and fled to England, a fact which did nothing to endear England to the King.

Albany hoped to marry James to his niece, Catherine de' Medici, a ward of the Pope, but Clement VII had other ideas on the matter and eventually secured her marriage to the son of Francis I, the future Henry II of France. The Pope compensated the Scots by granting James a tenth of the revenues of all ecclesiastical benefices in Scotland for three years, to be followed by £10,000 per annum, although in the end the annual payment was compounded into a lump sum of £72,000. In return James promised to uphold the Church of Rome and later on he secured for his illegitimate sons lucrative bishoprics. Meanwhile the quest for a suitable bride (that is to say, one whose dowry would give Scotland's precarious finances a much-needed boost) went on apace. Although an imperial princess was briefly considered, and even Mary Tudor, elder daughter of Henry VIII, was not ruled out, the obvious choice would be some relative of the French monarch. Overtures were made concerning Madeleine, the sickly daughter of Francis I, but the latter was loath to let her endure the uncertain rigours of the Scottish climate. James was fobbed off with vague promises of some more robust princess, together with the Order of St Michael.

The marital saga took a leap forward in 1535 when France and the Empire were at war and relations between France and England had been severed. Suddenly Scotland was back in the limelight, and it was at this point that a marriage between James and Mary, daughter of the Duke of Vendôme, head of the rival House of Bourbon, was seriously contemplated. The chief attraction – indeed, the only attraction, for the girl herself was ugly and deformed – was a much larger dowry than usual. When James went to France in 1536 to pledge his troth he was immediately repelled by the ill-favoured hunchback who had been selected as his bride; instead he was drawn to the frail but exquisitely beautiful Princess Madeleine and she to him. This was a genuine love match, and Francis I did not have the heart to oppose it. On 1 January 1537 the young couple were wed. In May the consumptive Madeleine accompanied her husband to Scotland but within six weeks she was dead.

With indecent haste a second French marriage was promptly arranged by David Beaton, nephew of Archbishop James Beaton of St Andrews and the rising star of Scotland's French faction as well as the bitterest opponent of the reformers. The replacement bride was Mary, daughter of Claude, Duke of Guise, a lady noted for her grace and great stature. She had lately lost her husband, the Duke of Longueville. The young widow was briefly considered as a bride for Henry VIII who had recently lost his third wife, Jane Seymour. The story goes that Henry proposed marriage, saying that as he was a well-built man he should have a well-built wife. Mary retorted, 'Yes, but my neck is small!'[2] Besides, Francis I had no desire to see the power of the Guise family (actual rulers of Lorraine and often virtual rulers of France itself) increased by marriage to the king of England;

but the king of Scots was another matter altogether, and so the proposed union received the royal blessing.

Mary of Guise was married by proxy in Notre-Dame, Paris, on 18 May 1538, Lord Maxwell standing in for the groom. In the company of Maxwell and a vast number of Scots nobility, Mary crossed the North Sea and landed at Crail in Fife on 10 June, barely twelve months after Madeleine. Shortly afterwards she went through a second marriage ceremony in St Andrews Cathedral. Thus was the Auld Alliance reaffirmed, just when relations between France and the Empire were cordial once more. Alarmed at the way his continental enemies seemed to be ganging up on him, Henry VIII made a desperate effort to detach Scotland from the threatened campaign. A meeting between James and Henry was planned at York, and the English king actually made the fatiguing journey north for that purpose; but James did not keep the appointment, fearing that Henry might abduct him. Henry, angered at James's failure to turn up, vented his spleen by ordering all-out war.

By and large, however, the Scots had no appetite for this conflict. Scotland was now more or less evenly divided between the Catholic pro-French party and the reformers who felt that James should follow his uncle's example and join forces with England against the papal crusade. When war broke out in July 1542 James could no longer rely on the mass of his subjects and was compelled to raise an army paid for out of his Church revenues and commanded by David Beaton who had succeeded his uncle as Archbishop in 1539 and was now a cardinal. He tried unsuccessfully to imbue the conflict with the nature of a holy war. The Scots' enthusiasm for the campaign evaporated even further when the field command was entrusted to the King's current favourite, the hopelessly inept Oliver Sinclair. At first the Scots, under the Earl of Home, succeeded in checking the English at Haddonrig in August, but when the main army crossed the border in the autumn it was decisively defeated on 24 November by the English under Sir Thomas Wharton, deputy warden of the West March, at Solway Moss. Twelve hundred prisoners were taken, including many prominent noblemen who were immediately hustled off to London for a stormy meeting with King Henry who cajoled, browbeat, bullied and finally bribed them to this way of thinking. The bulk of the Scottish army threw away their arms and fled back across the border in total disarray.

Hitherto James had been regarded as a vigorous young man, possessed of great personal courage; but as a result of the humiliating defeat at Solway Moss he suffered a complete mental and physical breakdown. He withdrew to Edinburgh (where he made his will and drew up an inventory of his personal wealth), and thence to Hallyards in Fife where he gloomily predicted that he would be dead within fifteen days. From Hallyards he journeyed to Linlithgow where he spent a few anxious days with Queen Mary, now heavily pregnant. In May 1540 Mary had borne a son, James. A second son, Robert, Duke of Albany, was born in April 1541 but died two days later. This tragedy was compounded by the death of little Prince James within the week. Queen Mary was distraught, though she showed remarkable fortitude, 'telling the King that they were young enough to expect to have many more children'.[3]

The King had six surviving sons and two daughters, all born out of wedlock, and what faith he still had in a legitimate succession was pinned on the babe now kicking in the Queen's belly. James had apparently been suffering acute depression for some time, and on that score had not been able to accompany his army. The news of Solway Moss tipped him over the edge. From Linlithgow he went to his favourite retreat, Falkland Palace, where he took to his bed. When informed that the Queen had given birth to a daughter on 7 December,[4] he cried out, 'It cam wi a lass and it'll gang wi a lass' – a reference to Marjorie Bruce whose marriage to Walter the Steward had started the Stewart dynasty. In this regard, James's gloomy prediction was not fulfilled, for through this latest lass the dynasty would go on to rule England as well as Scotland. James, in fact, was more deeply affected by the news that his favourite, Oliver Sinclair, had been taken prisoner. 'Oh fled Oliver! Is Oliver ta'en? Oh fled Oliver!'[5] And with a mournful sigh he turned his back on the world and expired around midnight on Thursday, 14 December. He was just thirty, and his successor was a sickly baby girl a week old who was not expected to live.

A document signed by James, and dated on the day of his death, may have been drawn up posthumously in order to name a regency consisting of Cardinal Beaton, the Earl of Huntly, the Earl of Argyll and the Earl of Moray (the King's illegitimate step-brother James Stewart – not to be confused by the later, and better-known person of the same name and title who was the eldest of James V's sons born out of wedlock). The eldest surviving descendant of James II's daughter Mary, James Hamilton, Earl of Arran, had been heir presumptive since the death of the Duke of Albany in 1536. As such, he had a virtual right to be Governor of the Realm in the event of a minority, but as leader of the reforming faction he was expressly excluded by this document. Not surprisingly, within days of the King's death, Arran is said to have drawn his blade and threatened the Cardinal, accusing him of being a 'false churl' who told many lies in James's name. Arran and his followers denounced the regency document as a forgery. This unseemly squabble was soon over-shadowed by the repatriation of the noble prisoners from London, now forming the core of a new pro-English faction under the Earl of Angus, returning to Scotland for the first time since he was ousted in 1528. This party, bolstered by English gold, were pledged to work towards an eventual marriage between the new-born infant and the five-year-old Prince Edward, Henry's son and heir. Rumours that the baby was either dead, or not expected to live, were rife,[6] and some at least of this English party were even prepared to help Henry or his son obtain the Scottish throne.

Cardinal Beaton appointed himself Chancellor on 10 January 1543. A fortnight later, however, the pro-English nobles had a meeting with Arran and within forty-eight hours the Cardinal had been deposed and taken into custody. In March parliament met briefly and solemnly declared Arran 'Second Person in the Realm and Governor until the Queen's perfect age' (her twelfth birthday). Those who knew him best, however, were not impressed by this weak, vacillating figure who had now thrust himself into the most powerful position. For the moment, however, he acted decisively, pressing ahead with ecclesiastical reform. Under his direction, and taking their cue from England, parliament sanctioned the reading of the Scriptures in the vernacular. The Catholic Church was now, for the moment, in retreat; when King Henry's special envoy, Sir Ralph Sadler, reached Edinburgh, he participated in a reformed com-munion ceremony alongside Arran. Afterwards commissioners were appointed to begin talks for the proposed marriage of Mary and Edward.

Sadler very quickly learned that while the Scots might be anxious for some sort of accommodation with Henry, they were a proud people who would react swiftly to any suggestion of subjection to England. Henry might have got his way regarding the proposed marriage if he had not coupled it with a demand that the castles of Dumbarton, Dunbar, Edinburgh, St Andrews, Stirling and Tantallon be surrendered and that all treaties and agreements with France be nullified. This was tantamount to the complete subjugation of Scotland and the admission of Henry's suzerainty. Even Henry's staunchest partisans on the Council baulked at these high-handed terms. Sir George Douglas, numbered among the most steadfast of Henry's supporters, stated bluntly: 'There is not so little a boy but he will hurl stones against it, the wives will come out with their distaffs and the commons universally will rather die'.[7] Reporting this verbatim to his royal master, Sadler was at pains to point out that the Scots might welcome a royal marriage that bound their country more closely to England, but they were adamant that Scotland's identity must be preserved. Consequently they insisted that Mary should continue to be brought up in her own realm, and that Scotland was to retain its independence.

Sadler's careful diplomacy was almost set at naught by King Henry who failed utterly to grasp the delicacy of the situation and insisted, rather heavy-handedly, that the baby queen should be sent to England as soon as she was weaned. This alarmed the Scots who felt that once Henry had obtained custody of the little girl, all the guarantees of Scotland's sovereignty would be worthless. With a bad grace Henry backed down, although his belligerent attitude could have done nothing to allay Scottish suspicions. The parallels between the behaviour of Henry in 1543 and Edward I in 1290 were too awful to contemplate. For the time being, however, Henry gave way, and the Treaties of Greenwich, signed on 1 July, provided that young Mary would remain in Scotland till the age of ten when she would be expected to 'complete marriage' by going to England.

The ink on these documents was scarcely dry when opinion in Scotland veered away from England and back to France once more. Cardinal Beaton, released from captivity at the end of March, though continuing under house arrest in St Andrews, openly condemned the compact with England, while the Queen Mother, outraged at the manner in which she was not consulted on her daughter's future, contrived to drive a wedge between Arran and King Henry. As the pro-French faction regrouped and consolidated behind Cardinal Beaton, the latter felt strong enough for a showdown with Arran. On 26 July Beaton mustered an army of about seven thousand men, advanced to Linlithgow that night and took charge of the little queen whom he conveyed to Stirling Castle, that impregnable bastion which, so often over the centuries, had been the very key to the kingdom.

This move was opposed half-heartedly, if at all, by Arran who, influenced by his half-brother John, Commendator of Paisley, was beginning to question the wisdom of too close an association with Henry VIII. Undoubtedly self-interest lay at the heart of these doubts, for he would have been extremely reluctant to agree to anything that might jeopardise his own prospects in the event of Mary dying childless. So he acquiesced in the transfer to Stirling, reasoning that a lot could happen in the ensuing years. Besides, if the arrangement with Henry broke down and the proposed marriage with Edward was called off, there was always Arran's own son and heir, the Master of Hamilton, who would make an excellent substitute.

At this juncture another factor entered the reckoning. Matthew Stewart, Earl of Lennox, was prevailed upon by the pro-French party to return from France. He was next in line of succession to the throne, after Arran, the legitimacy of whose own claim was often challenged. Beaton was in a strong position to pronounce one way or the other on Arran's legitimacy and a word to this effect from brother John had the desired effect. On being advised of Arran's change of heart, Henry VIII countered with the proposal that his daughter Elizabeth might wed the Master of Hamilton. This was backed by the offer of five thousand English soldiers, should military action be required to suppress the opposition. Henry overstepped the mark, however, with his final offer: if he was compelled to invade Scotland to achieve his goals, he was prepared to let Arran reign as king north of the Forth-Clyde isthmus. Arran did not relish the prospect of a Highland petty kingdom, and suggested that five thousand pounds in gold would be more useful than an expeditionary force. In the end he was persuaded to ratify the treaties on 25 August, but eight days later he went back on his word. As John Knox put it pithily:

> The unhappy man . . . quietly stole away from the lords that were with him in the palace of Holyroodhouse, passed to Stirling, subjected himself to the Cardinal and his counsel, received absolution, renounced the profession of Christ Jesus his holy Evangel and violated his oath that before he had

made for observation of the contract and league with England.[8]

The sacrament of absolution on 8 September was witnessed by Argyll and Patrick, Earl of Bothwell, who held the towel over his head. Arran's defection was completed by the ceremony, the following day, in Stirling Castle when the nine-month-old queen was crowned 'with such solemnitie as they do use in this country, which is not very costlie', as Sir Ralph Sadler duly reported back to Henry.[9] At the coronation, Arran bore the crown, Lennox the sceptre and Argyll the sword of state. The pro-English faction pointedly boycotted the affair.

The date could not have been less auspicious: 9 September was the thirtieth anniversary of Flodden.

Arran's sudden turnaround was subsequently endorsed by the Council in which the consensus was that Henry's arrogant, bullying tactics gave the Scots good cause to regard the treaties as null and void. In particular they took exception to Henry's peremptory demand that they repudiate the Auld Alliance. The offer of five thousand troops was seen as a provocative threat, and the Scots countered by saying that if such an army crossed the border, twenty thousand Scots would take up arms to oppose them. Henry retaliated by ordering the seizure of Scottish ships in English ports or on the high seas. By 11 December, when the Westminster parliament had failed to ratify the Treaties of Greenwich, and the English government continued to refuse to release the Scottish ships, the Scottish parliament repudiated the agreement with England, restated the alliance with France and confirmed Beaton as Chancellor.

Furthermore, to ensure that Arran would not swing back in favour of Henry, the Council had ordered that the Master of Hamilton be held in the Cardinal's castle at St Andrews to guarantee his father's compliance. Furthermore, Arran was compelled to take advice from a committee headed by Beaton and Mary of Guise. Beaton had already escorted Arran to Dundee, so that he might personally put down the mob attacks on monastic buildings. In December parliament, under Beaton's firm hand, now passed an Act for the ruthless punishment of heretics and Arran was urged to implement it without delay. Later the same month news arrived from

France that Catherine de' Medici, wife of King Henry II, had given birth to a son. In baby Francis, a year younger than little Mary, the Scots now had a viable alternative to Prince Edward.

Arran's dramatic change of heart signalled the first major turning-point in the life of the baby queen. Hitherto Henry VIII had tried to coerce the Scots with threats, bribes and harassment. Now the gloves were off and he would have to resort to force to bring the Scots to heel. For the moment, however, he watched and waited with mounting impatience to see how matters would develop in Scotland itself. Angus, Glencairn, Cassilis and a few other great magnates continued to protest their steadfast loyalty to Henry. The English party soon received a welcome though not wholly unexpected addition in the form of the Earl of Lennox. Hitherto a staunch member of the French party, he was first and foremost an enemy of Arran. Ergo, when Arran defected to the French party, Lennox must join the English party.

His change of allegiance, immediately after Mary's coronation, was so sudden that when he encountered Cardinal Marco Grimani, Patriarch of Aquileia and Papal Legate, together with an important French delegation headed by Jacques de la Brosse and Jacques Mesnaige, just landed at Dumbarton about 8 October, they were completely fooled by him and gladly handed over the artillery, ammunition and a thousand crowns in cash supplied by the King of France and the Pope. This valuable accretion of money and *matériel*, despatched from the Continent to ensure that the Scots joined the impending crusade against England, thus fell into the wrong hands. Even though Lennox failed to detain Grimani (who was worthy of a king's ransom), this coup put new heart and muscle into the English faction. With the money and military equipment unwittingly supplied by the French they were now in a strong position to dictate terms. In desperation, Cardinal Beaton produced a last-ditch but rather ludicrous plan for reconciliation between the opposing factions: Arran was to divorce his wife and marry the Queen Mother, while Lennox, then a bachelor of twenty-six, was to marry baby Mary. On 15 December 1543 the Scottish parliament endorsed these proposals and, to the relief of Brosse and Mesnaige, re-affirmed the 'auld bands' that tied Scotland to France.[10]

When Henry VIII learned that the Scots had swung back once more into the French camp and had unilaterally repudiated the marriage agreement, he ordered that series of vicious punitive expeditions which the Scots, with wry understatement, would later call the Rough Wooing. Henry's drastic action, intended once and for all to crush the enemy at his back, was also dictated to some extent by dramatic developments on the European front. The Emperor Charles V repudiated Henry while the Papacy summoned the great Council of Trent that would launch the Counter-Reformation, directed against England in particular. As a preliminary to a full-scale invasion of Scotland, Henry redoubled his efforts to secure the loyalty of Angus, Cassilis, Glencairn and Lennox. At one stage he got into a rather unseemly auction, whereby the Scottish earls were, in effect, ready to sell themselves to the highest bidder. In 1543 he had bribed them with relatively small sums of a hundred or two hundred pounds; a year later he was obliged to up the ante to a thousand pounds apiece. In the interim what then passed for the Scottish government (with continuing subsidies from France) made counter offers and, in the end, topped Henry's bid, so that some semblance of national solidarity, albeit cash-induced, was briefly restored by the end of 1544.

If English gold was the carrot, the expedition led by the Earl of Hertford in May 1544 was the stick. It gives us an insight into Henry's muddled thinking at this time that he convinced himself that he could best secure the loyalty of the Scots by systematically burning and pillaging throughout the Borders and the Lowlands. Scottish military opposition to this ruthless campaign was weak and ineffectual. On Sunday, 4 May, a 16,000-strong English force landed close to Edinburgh, virtually unopposed, while the main army crossed the Tweed and advanced overland. Towns and villages along the way were burned, but particular attention was paid to the great religious houses of Melrose, Dryburgh and Roxburgh. The wanton destruction of these abbeys was but the prelude to the onslaught on Edinburgh itself. The burning of the city occupied two days, during which the English soldiery went on an orgy of murder and rape. The Abbey and Palace of Holyroodhouse were sacked and extensively damaged. From the nauseatingly self-righteous tone of the report to Lord Russell, the Lord Privy Seal, it is clear that the English regarded this campaign as a crusade. 'In these victories,' wrote an anonymous correspondent, 'who is to be most lauded but God, by whose goodness the English hath had a great season, notable victories.'[11] Hertford then swung south-east and returned to England, leaving a trail of destroyed towns in his wake. There would be no let-up for the Scots, however; armies led by Sir Ralph Eure and Sir Brian Layton continued to ravage the Border districts throughout the rest of the year. The one crumb of comfort came on 26 May when Lennox and his ally Glencairn (who had gone over to the English) were routed in a ferocious battle near Glasgow. Glencairn took refuge in Dumbarton Castle, while Lennox sailed off to England.

Shortly after arriving in London about the middle of June, Lennox had a meeting with Henry as a result of which he concluded a marriage treaty. On 26 June, he formally bound himself to hand over Dumbarton Castle and the Isle of Bute as an English base, in exchange for Lady Margaret Douglas, the daughter of Margaret Tudor by her second husband, the Earl of Angus. As the ward and niece of Henry VIII, Lady Margaret Douglas was also next in line, after little Queen Mary, in the succession to the English throne. For thus nailing his colours to the English mast Lennox was rewarded not only with the lady's hand but appointed Lieutenant for the northern counties of England as well as the whole of southern Scotland, with the promise of the governorship of the entire northern kingdom if his mission to deliver Scotland into Henry's hands were successful. This Scottish quisling carried out a number of military sweeps with the avowed aim of securing the girl-queen and handing her over to Henry, but to no effect. His main achievement was to impregnate his bride who, on 7 December 1545, gave birth to a son, obsequiously named Henry after his royal godfather. Lennox, briefly considered as a potential groom for Queen Mary, would live to see his son, Lord Darnley, succeed where he had failed.

As Hertford's marauders came within six miles of Stirling, laying waste everything in their path, Queen Mary herself had been whisked off to Dunkeld, at the edge of the Highlands, for greater safety. In this hazardous undertaking Mary of Guise had the moral support of Cardinal Grimani, who was greatly impressed by her courage and fortitude. At all times she kept up a cheerful countenance, all the more remarkable in view of the desperate situation of such a divided kingdom as poor Scotland. 'I say poor Scotland,' wrote Grimani, 'because it is so divided and disturbed that if God does not show his hand and inspire these nobles to unite together, public and private ruin is clearly to be foreseen.'[12]

Instead of closing ranks in face of the English depredations, the Scots predictably were more divided than ever. Even the pro-French government was split into various factions. Arran was discredited, while Beaton was blamed for all the woes which beset the kingdom. Out of this confusion Mary of Guise emerged as the one resolute and stable figure. Now the mercurial nobles began shifting their allegiance and argued that the Queen Mother should have some say in the administration, a decision taken by the Council on 3 June 1544. Though not displacing Arran, she now played a significant part in the Privy Council. When she let her wishes be known that she favoured a French marriage for her daughter, however, the Scottish nobles recoiled. Arran, who still entertained ambitions about wedding little Mary to the Master of Hamilton, and now also Beaton, strenuously opposed a French match. Public opinion, such as it was, tended to favour Arran's son, and by the beginning of 1545 many of the influential nobles had come round to that way of thinking. For the time being Queen Mary would remain in her own country and in a brief resurgence of national feeling the Scots braced themselves for a further English invasion. Ironically, one of the commanders of the Scottish army which met the English and defeated them at Ancrum Moor on 17 February 1545 was none other than the Earl of Angus, ex-husband of Margaret Tudor and one-time tool of King Henry. Among the eight hundred English dead was Sir Ralph Eure himself.

There was now stalemate; Henry, who could think of no way out of this impasse, tried to revive the Treaties of Greenwich but when the Scots remained obdurate he again despatched Hertford to wreak havoc on the Lowlands. This time the expedition coincided with harvest-time, with the deliberate aim of burning the crops before they were gathered in. In this campaign of systematic rapine, Hertford was ably assisted by Lennox, whose cohorts ravaged Ayrshire and Renfrewshire. Interestingly, about this time several of the clan chiefs in the West Highlands agreed to a form of regional autonomy under English auspices; but, as the nominal head of this government was killed shortly afterwards, this curious state within a state never got off the ground. With the onset of winter Hertford and his army retreated south, having succeeded only in antagonising former sympathisers and potential allies by their brutal tactics, and stiffening the resolve of those who had always opposed Henry. The only positive achievement, so far as the English were concerned, was the removal of Beaton, and even that was something attained by factors other than Henry's bribes.

Beaton's popularity had dipped sharply as a result of the Rough

Wooing; after all, it was his pro-French policy that had precipitated it in the first place. As well as getting the blame for the misery endured in the Lowlands over two summers, Beaton was widely perceived as the very worst kind of churchman: a cardinal who amassed a personal fortune, who practised nepotism on a grand scale, and whose lascivious personal life was scandalous in the extreme. Henry had long sought to eliminate Beaton but in the end the Cardinal's assassination was triggered off by local events. In 1543 the reformer George Wishart had returned to Scotland from Cambridge ostensibly to assist in the drafting of the Treaties of Greenwich, but he also took the opportunity to preach the gospel of reform. Unlike John Knox, George was a gentle soul, possessed of other-worldly, almost saintly, qualities, and it seems highly unlikely that he was 'the Scottish man callit Wishart' who allegedly had complicity in plots to murder the Cardinal. On 1 March 1546 he was seized by Beaton's agents and burned at the stake in the castle forecourt of St Andrews while the Cardinal and his cronies spectated in comfort from the castle walls. To add some excitement to the spectacle, Beaton ordered that bags of gunpowder be sewn into Wishart's clothing at strategic points. At each explosion Beaton and his cronies cheered as if watching a fireworks display.

Wishart's death provoked a bloody response from the Protestant lairds of Fife who, disguised as the stonemasons hired by Beaton to strengthen his fortifications, entered the Cardinal's castle on the night of 29 May 1546 and seized the prelate in bed with his long-term mistress, Marion Ogilvy. The terrified Cardinal was dragged from his chamber at sword-point, asked to repent for shedding the blood of Wishart, and then savagely put to death. Afterwards, his horribly mutilated corpse, grotesquely clad in archiepiscopal vestments, was dangled from the foretower of the castle, that the common people might jeer, taunt and insult him further. According to one eye-witness account: 'Ane callit Guthrie loosit done his ballops' poynt and pischit in his mouth that all the pepill might sie'.[13] Later the body was preserved in salt like pork and kept in a barrel in the notorious Bottle Dungeon of St Andrews for fourteen months, while Beaton's murderers held the sea-girt castle against government troops.

The Castilians, as the defenders were nicknamed, hoped that King Henry would send a seaborne expedition to raise the siege, but no help from that quarter was forthcoming. Arran, still Governor of

Scotland, vacillated. Unable to condone the murder of a prince of the Church (especially as his brother John was now Bishop of Dunkeld) but loath to summon French assistance lest it jeopardise his son's chances of a royal marriage, he did nothing. The fact that the Master of Hamilton was being held hostage by the Castilians also had some bearing on his resolution, or lack of it. Although the Governor's troops made several attempts to tunnel their way into the castle, the fact that this episcopal fortress was washed by the waves meant that supplies of food and ammunition could easily be sent in. The siege dragged on, and was only brought to an end with French help on 31 July 1547. The more prominent Castilians were promptly shipped off to French dungeons, but the smaller fry, including the preacher John Knox, became galley-slaves. The great reformer would remained chained to his oar for the next two years.

On 31 March 1547 Francis I of France died and was succeeded by his son Henry II, a monarch who was under the influence of the powerful Guise family and therefore more amenable to doing something positive to help Mary of Guise and her daughter. This help soon materialised in the form of the taskforce that captured St Andrews Castle. This success brought Arran and his government more firmly back into the French fold again. Arran, now discredited for placing family before national interest, strove to retrieve his position. Having been fobbed off with the possibility of a daughter of the Duke of Montpensier as a bride for his son, he gave way and agreed to a French marriage for Queen Mary. As Governor, he had had the care of King James V's considerable personal wealth and what clinched the deal for him was a guarantee that no questions would be asked regarding his handling of this fortune. In January 1548 he finally undertook to persuade the Scottish parliament to sanction the marriage of Mary to the Dauphin, her immediate transfer to France, and the surrender of the principal Scottish fortresses to French garrisons.[14] As a reward for effectively handing over his country to France, Arran was given the French duchy of Châtelherault, a title proudly borne by his descendants to this day.

Meanwhile, on 28 January 1547, Henry VIII died and was succeeded by his son Edward VI, a boy of ten. This produced no change in English policy; if anything, the situation became much worse, for the Earl of Hertford had now been elevated and, as Duke of Somerset, was Lord Protector of England. With the experience of two seasons' campaigning in Scotland under his belt, Somerset laid his plans with sadistic skill. In addition to a well-trained army of about 25,000 English troops, he had enlisted 2,000 of the 'wildest and most savage' Irishmen, many of them veterans of the western raids led by Lennox. The Scots, well aware that retribution was at hand, made plans to meet this catastrophe. The fiery cross was sent into every parish and, as a result, the first truly national effort since Bannockburn in 1314 was organised. Over 36,000 men converged on Edinburgh from all over the country. On hearing that the English had landed, the Scots army marched out of the capital under the command of Arran.

At Pinkie Cleugh, on the escarpment known as Edmonstone Edge south of Musselburgh, they encountered the English army on 10 September. Unfortunately for the Scots, Arran was no Wallace or Bruce and he seems to have been singularly lacking in their qualities of generalship. To be sure, he doubted the reliability of his lieutenants, especially the flamboyant Earl of Huntly, only recently ransomed from England, but he had little control over his troops whose ferocious courage was no substitute for the most elementary discipline. At the sight of the English, the Scots abandoned their commanding position and swooped down the steep slopes in a headlong charge, to be skewered on the pikes and lances of Somerset's highly trained army. When Arran himself, closely followed by Angus, fled the field, the surviving Scots threw away their arms and tried to outrun the pursuing cavalry, only to be cut down in swathes. In five hours of ferocious combat, some 14,000 Scots were killed while the rest fled in headlong rout back to Edinburgh.

Only five years after Solway Moss, the Scots had suffered another crushing defeat. Somerset's men now ravaged the Lothians at will and it was the day after Pinkie, when the English seized the port of Leith, that the little queen and her mother were transported by Lord Livingston from Dunkeld to the even more secure priory of Inchmahome, on a picturesque little island in the Lake of Menteith, sixteen miles west of Stirling. Robert Erskine, Commendator of Inchmahome, was one of the fatal casualties of Pinkie so he could not have met Mary, far less taught the four-year-old Latin, French, Spanish and Italian, history, geography, horticulture and embroidery as the legends maintain. To this day one may visit the impressively atmospheric ruins on the heavily wooded island and see Queen Mary's Garden, Queen Mary's Bower and Queen Mary's Tree, the tangible if highly unlikely mementoes of the royal toddler's three-week sojourn. Mary and her mother returned to Stirling as soon as the English recrossed the border on 29 September. The next four months were spent in the castle which was the only real home she had ever known. Shortly after returning to Stirling she was struck down by a serious illness which Sadler claimed was smallpox, but from the fact that she contracted this disease later in life, it seems more probable that the dread malady late in 1547 was chickenpox. Word that an English army under Lord Grey de Wilton had invaded Berwickshire and seized Haddington determined the Queen Mother on 21 February 1548 to move her daughter to the relative safety of Dumbarton Castle. A few days later, the little queen, now fully recovered from her illness, was transferred to the impregnable fortress on the Firth of Clyde.

In the aftermath of Pinkie, the Scots were forced to the conclusion that French protection was the lesser of two evils. As if to emphasise the ease with which the English could invade the disunited country whenever they chose, there was the constant reminder of Lord Grey's English garrison at Haddington, disconcertingly close to the capital and occupying a strategic position on the main south-east trade route. At a meeting of the Council in November the Scots bowed to the inevitable, and a few weeks later a mission consisting of fifty officers arrived from France. These military advisers were but the advance guard for the well-equipped army of six thousand men, under André de Montalembert, Sieur d'Essé, which landed at Leith on Saturday, 16 June 1548. In their train came German artillerists, Italian engineers, Swiss pikemen, Dutch arquebusiers and other military specialists, as well as two squadrons of crack light cavalry. This expeditionary force wasted no time in besieging Haddington, in whose abbey, on 7 July, it was formally agreed that Mary, as the future bride of Dauphin Francis, should go to France at the earliest opportunity.

This huge military build-up was almost nullified by a sudden turn of events. In March 1548 the little Queen of Scots fell violently ill again, this time with measles. For several days she hovered between life and death, and rumours that she had actually succumbed circulated widely. The nation held its breath, and the Council (with dire memories of the Maid of Norway in 1290) must have lamented the fact that, once again, the fate of Scotland relied on the uncertain health of a little girl. Eventually the high fever abated and the immediate crisis passed on 23 March. That spring she recuperated from her illnesses, and by the second week of July she was restored to health and fit enough to undertake the most arduous journey of her life. Meanwhile King Henry II had sent a French fleet with his personal galley to bring the little queen to safety. On 29 July Mary went aboard the flagship of Admiral Villegaignon and took a highly emotional farewell of her mother. Mary's departure was something of an anticlimax, however, for the galleys were delayed in the firth for nine days awaiting a favourable wind.

Although Mary of Guise was left behind – the government of Scotland was now in her hands, backed by Montalembert's formidable army of occupation – the little girl was accompanied by a vast retinue suitable to her exalted station. They included at least two of her half-brothers, Robert and John Stewart, and possibly also James Stewart (later Earl of Moray), her eldest half-brother, proving that royal blood, even if tainted by bastardy, was still thicker than water. This principle even extended to Mary's governess, Janet Stewart, an illegitimate daughter of James IV by the Countess of Bothwell. Janet was recently widowed, her husband Lord Fleming being among those slain at Pinkie. Lady Fleming, regarded as a great beauty marred by a short temper, created a fuss before the little armada had even set out. Chafing at the delay waiting for a suitable wind, she demanded that the ship's captain allow her to go ashore 'to repose her'; but the French skipper retorted that Lady Fleming, 'so far from being able to go on land, could go to France and like it, or drown on the way'.[15]

Among the assorted lords and ladies aboard ship were the four little girls of noble birth known to posterity as the Four Maries: Mary Fleming, Mary Seton, Mary Beaton and Mary Livingston. The first was the daughter of the irascible governess, Lady Fleming, and therefore a distant kinswoman of Queen Mary herself. Mary Seton was the daughter of George, sixth Lord Seton, and his French wife Marie Pieris who had come to Scotland as a maid of honour to Mary of Guise. Mary Beaton was the daughter of Robert Beaton of Creich and a distant relative of the late Cardinal David Beaton and his brother, the future Archbishop James Beaton. She, too, had a French mother, yet another of the Queen Mother's ladies-in-waiting. Mary Livingston was the daughter of Lord Livingston, Queen Mary's guardian at Stirling and Dunkeld.

The flotilla finally weighed anchor on 7 August. The feelings of

Mary of Guise at being parted from her daughter can be imagined. Once before, she had been forced, for reasons of state, to abandon a child, the son of her first marriage, when she departed for Scotland. Now she was wrenched from the daughter with whom she had shared so many adventures in a few short years. Henry Jones, an English spy, reported to Somerset that 'The Old Queen do lament the young Queen's departure, and marvelleth that she heareth nothing from her'.[16] The Queen Mother's anguish was compounded by the uncertainty of the voyage down the west coast of Scotland, through the channel between Ireland and the Isle of Man to Wales. Then giving the tip of Cornwall a wide berth they beat up the Channel for the French coast. The westerly wind for which they had prayed turned out to be too stiff for comfort. By the time they were thirty miles off the Lizard, mountainous waves pursued them and the galley's rudder was smashed. Queen Mary alone seems to have been immune from seasickness and quite oblivious of the dangers of shipwreck.

Six days after leaving the Clyde, the battered fleet anchored off the French coast and Mary stepped ashore at Roscoff, the fishing port near Brest where, 198 years later, her great-great-great-grand-son, Bonnie Prince Charlie, would disembark after the collapse of the Forty-five Rebellion. The little Chapel of St Ninian at Roscoff is said to mark the very spot where Mary landed.[17] According to the anonymous compiler of the *Diurnal of Occurrents* she went to France to be brought up under the fear of God. John Knox, inevitably, had a different view: she had gone 'to the end that in her youth she should drink of that liquor, that should remain with her all her lifetime, for a plague to this realm and for her final destruction'.

2. FRANCE

1548–60

> O little did my mother ken,
> The day she cradled me,
> The lands I was to travel in
> Or the death I was to die!
>   *The Queen's Maries*, a traditional ballad

After spending a few days at Roscoff recovering from the arduous voyage, Mary and her entourage sailed southwards to the estuary of the Loire, then upriver to Orleans. Thence she travelled overland in easy stages, arriving at Paris on 16 October 1548, more than two months after landing in France. King Henry II, absent at Moulins for the wedding of Antoine de Bourbon to Jeanne d'Albret, daughter of King Henry II of Navarre, left detailed instructions for the proper reception of the girl-queen in his absence. Thoughtfully, Henry arranged that Mary should share quarters with his daughter, Princess Elisabeth, sumptuous apartments being prepared for them in the Château de Carrières Saint-Denis near Saint-Germain-en-Laye on the north-west outskirts of the capital.[1]

The King was captivated by the little girl when he met her for the first time on 9 November: 'The most perfect child I have ever seen' was his immediate reaction. And Catherine de' Medici was equally fulsome in her praise: 'This small Queen of Scots has only to smile in order to turn all French heads.'[2] Little Mary was like a breath of fresh air at the French court. Even her speech, which the courtier and historian Pierre de Brantôme described as 'very rustic, barbarous and harsh', was spoken, he conceded, 'with such fine grace and formed in such a manner, that she made it seem quite beautiful and agreeable in her, though not in others'.[3] Even allowing for the fact that Mary was believed to be bringing her kingdom as a gift to France, and therefore everyone was well disposed towards her from the outset, and discounting some of the lavish praise showered on her from all directions, there is no doubt that young Mary was extra-ordinarily attractive, charming, lively and intelligent. Well above average height for her age, she was quite free of the gawkiness often associated with tall children. She had a grace and commanding presence which she never exploited as she might so easily have done.

Among her peers, the young Valois princes and princesses, her Guise cousins and the other children of the court, she stood out as their natural leader, not only because she was the eldest but because of her forthright personality. She had a natural ability to get on with people of all ages and classes. Her generosity of spirit and affability were developed early and remained with her throughout her turbulent life. She treated everyone, high and low alike, with the same warmth and sincere interest. There is ample evidence, in her letters to her mother, of her detailed and genuine concern for the welfare of her retainers. Even, many years later, during her confinement in different parts of England, her solicitude for friends and servants was an enduring and endearing characteristic. At the same time Mary was inclined to be headstrong and self-willed, and there is no doubt that her passionate nature was the key to so many of her later misfortunes. A bit of a tomboy even as a small child, Mary developed an easy, boisterous camaraderie but this, too, would become one of her most striking social accomplishments.

It was at Carrières that Mary met her future husband for the first time. The physical contrast could not have been greater: Mary was tall, robust and vivacious, with a zest for life and a lively mind, whereas the Dauphin, almost two years younger, was small for his age, a puny, sickly child, pasty-faced, slow, clumsy and lethargic in his movements. He had been in poor health since the day he was born; malicious tongues wagged that the trouble with little Francis stemmed from the assortment of pills and potions which his mother had guzzled in her desperate bid to conceive. The boy's parents fretted over him constantly, watching like hawks for any symptoms, any ailments, which might destroy his frail constitution. No one was more tender in ministering to the sickly Dauphin than Mary. Whenever he was ill or miserable he naturally turned to her for comfort and she invariably responded with a loving care that touched the hearts of all who witnessed them together. Truly, this seemed a match made in heaven, rather than the formal arrangement arising out of political expedience.

It was an unlikely match, yet Mary was from the outset drawn to this ailing, undersized boy. She was like a little mother to him, fiercely, passionately loving him and sticking up for him; and he, in turn, was besotted and utterly devoted to her, the docile and compliant companion in all her escapades. Even the hard-bitten courtiers were agreeably surprised at the genuine warmth and love between these children who might some day be king and queen of France.

Mary could not be regarded as beautiful in the conventional sense. In adulthood she attained a height of six foot; overcoming a teenage tendency to hunch her shoulders, she had grace and elegance to match her stature so that the overall effect was truly majestic. Her complexion was pale and delicate, setting off her piercing, deep-brown eyes and light auburn hair. Her mouth was on the small side while her nose was long and her cheekbones high. With her long, pointed nose and slight squint, by no stretch of the imagination could she be regarded as pretty, as even the most flattering of her portraits testify; yet she had an animation that lit up her countenance and an inner beauty that gave her a radiance of expression. Mary's attractiveness came from her vivacity and exuberance. She possessed a strength of character and individuality which, allied to her powerful histrionic talents, gave her a presence that was truly regal, yet at all times affable and warm.

These many and varied natural gifts would be keenly developed in her new environment. She was fortunate to grow up at the French court during a period when it was renowned for its dazzling splendour. There was a hedonistic quality about it in which the consumption of good food and fine wines was allied to an appreciation of music and proficiency in the arts of the dance-floor and the card-table. The social graces were cultivated in a high degree. This was a period when jousts and tournaments and other amusements from the age of chivalry past were still very much in fashion, but newer forms of amusement were coming into vogue. Archery, tennis, hunting and falconry vied with horseracing, while ballets, banquets and masked balls were all the rage. Mary entered enthusiastically into the spirit of the age and would become an accomplished all-round sportswoman with a fondness for horses, dogs, birds and pet animals of all kinds. Particular importance was attached to dancing, and in this Mary became not only a highly skilled and versatile performer but an extremely competent choreographer of the elaborate ballets which had been introduced to France by Catherine de' Medici. Envy of her cousin's far-famed balletic achievements was one of the factors that, quite early on, turned Elizabeth Tudor against Mary. If Elizabeth was a more competent performer on the virginals, an early form of harpsichord, Mary, by all accounts, possessed the sweeter singing voice. Brantôme records that Mary 'sang excellently, accompanying herself on the lute, which she touched deftly with her beautiful white hand and her finely shaped fingers'.[4]

In one respect the newly arrived little Queen of Scots was sadly deficient in the eyes of King Henry: despite her French mother, she could not speak a word of French. He immediately gave orders that she was to begin learning the language and to facilitate progress he insisted that all her servants and companions should be French. The four Maries were bundled off to a convent at Poissy where Henry would have them properly educated. Only when the King tried to have Lady Fleming replaced by a French governess did opposition come from Mary's Guise relatives. Alarmed at some possibly sinister motive on the part of the King, Mary's uncles interceded on her behalf. While they appreciated the need for her to be properly educated in French, their own natural talents for intrigue made them highly suspicious that Henry aimed to alienate Mary from her relatives and bind her more closely to the Valois family. It must never be forgotten that the little girl was a queen *regnant* in her own right, and this enhanced their standing. These apprehensions were shared by the girl's mother, Mary of Guise, who, from the relative remoteness of her adopted land, refused point-blank to have Lady Fleming dismissed. In the end, Henry gave way. Lady Fleming remained in her position and Henry conceded that Queen Mary should take precedence over his own daughters at court. For the time being, therefore, the Guise family were satisfied. In place of the four Maries, the little Queen of Scots had the close companionship of Henry's daughters, Elisabeth and Claude.

Late in September 1550, when Mary had been in France just over two years, she received a surprise but welcome visit from her mother. Mary of Guise, alarmed at the way in which the Reformation was gaining ground in Scotland, aided by the subversive tactics of the

English, desperately sought military reinforcements from France. The situation, in fact, was by no means as dangerous as she implied. Recent Franco-Scottish success had forced England to the negotiating table and had resulted in the conclusion of a peace treaty between France and England the previous April. Under the terms of this treaty the integrity of Scotland was guaranteed. Anxious to press home the advantage, Mary of Guise was determined to make more permanent arrangements for consolidating French influence in Scotland. To this end, the Queen-Dowager was attended by a large retinue of the Scottish nobility who were lavishly entertained and bedazzled by King Henry. Mary of Guise was in no hurry to return to Scotland and, in fact, remained in France until November 1551. She took full advantage of her prolonged sojourn to renew her relationship with her son by her first marriage, the teenage Francis, Duke of Longueville, as well as the eight-year-old Mary. The bond between mother and daughter grew even stronger when, as the former was about to depart for Scotland, fifteen-year-old Francis suddenly took ill and died. This tragedy, and her mother's departure, had a traumatic effect on young Mary, compounded by the peremptory dismissal of Lady Fleming who was sent home in disgrace in April 1551 after her torrid affair with King Henry came to light. Queen Catherine joined forces with the King's principal mistress, Diane de Poitiers, to eject Lady Fleming when her indiscretion with His Majesty became so obvious in the size of her belly. In due course she produced a son, ever afterwards known as the Bastard of Angoulême. She was replaced as governess by Françoise d'Estamville, Madame de Parois, an excitable and temperamental Frenchwoman, invariably at odds with the governesses of the princesses and a disruptive element in the royal household.

While Mary of Guise was still in France, a strange conspiracy to poison her daughter was exposed. The chief perpetrator of the plot was Robert Stewart, a confederate of the men who had murdered Cardinal Beaton. When St Andrews Castle fell, Stewart had been consigned to the French galleys, but was subsequently released from his oar when he agreed to enlist in the *Garde d'Ecosse*, the élite bodyguard of the French king. While on furlough, he went to London and intrigued with the Privy Council. The plot was later exposed by a fellow Scot, John Henderson, then residing in London. In fact, the Council thought so little of Stewart's murderous intentions that they had promptly clapped him in the Tower; and had it not been for Henderson's denouncing Stewart to the French authorities the matter might never have come to light. King Henry was indignant when informed of Stewart's treachery and demanded his extradition to France, which was promptly granted. The wretched plotter was handed over in chains at Calais and conveyed to Angers on 5 June 1551 where he was hanged, drawn and quartered shortly afterwards.[5]

In spite of these upsets, Mary made rapid progress in French, while the uncouthness of her native speech was eliminated by an extensive course of elocution. On one occasion King Henry paid a visit to her quarters to see how she was progressing and was astonished to find a child mature beyond her years, who conversed with him on a wide range of topics for upwards of an hour. Mary's uncle, the Cardinal of Lorraine, commented admiringly that Mary, at ten, could converse like a woman of twenty-five. Along with the French royal children she took part in masquerades and little dramatic productions for the entertainment of the court. From this arose Mary's passion for theatrical performances and poetry. The latter accomplishment was particularly esteemed, and, following in the footsteps of her ancestor James I, Mary herself dabbled in verse. In this she had the instruction of none other than the celebrated poet Pierre de Ronsard who had accompanied Mary of Guise to Scotland as her page. Apart from Ronsard, Mary's favourite poets were Joachim du Bellay and Maisonfleur; all three of them returned the compliment by composing flattering verses extolling her charms in extravagant terms. Mary's own verse, if not exactly inspired, was at least technically competent, rhyming and scanning well. The excellence of her literary education is demonstrated in her letters which are characterised by grammatical correctness, an easy style and elegant turn of phrase reflecting the high cultural attainments of the writer.

Mary also excelled in the outward trappings of courtly life. This was an age of extravagant personal decoration, and both sexes revelled in the lavishness of their dress and jewellery. Mary in maturity was arguably the best-dressed lady of the French court, her great height enabling her to carry off the sumptuousness of her costume – a very striking combination. In the autumn of 1554, with a royal wedding imminent, Mary caused a stir with the magnificence of her costume in cloth of gold embroidered all over with her royal cypher and topped off by a stunning necklace of pearls and rubies. She outshone Queen Catherine and the princesses, and thereafter was the undisputed arbiter of *haute couture*. In such matters as interior decoration and the appreciation of beautiful furniture, costly furnishings, fine paintings and sculpture, Mary exhibited exquisite taste.

It must not be imagined that Mary's interests and attainments were entirely frivolous, the pursuit of amusement for its own sake. Her devotion to music, painting, poetry, dancing and the arts went hand in hand with the development of a formidable intellect. Under the direction of Princess Marguerite, sister of Henry II, Mary and the royal children were rigorously instructed in French literature, history and geography. As well as French and her native Scots, Mary, along with the young princes and princesses, got a good grounding in Spanish, English and Italian as well as the rudiments of Latin and Greek. Several Latin essays by Mary are extant, revealing a punctiliousness of grammar and nobility of thought inculcated by her education. A Latin letter to her cousin Elizabeth Tudor gives the flavour of this:

> The true grandeur and excellence of a prince, is, my dear sister, not in splendour, in gold, in purple, in jewels, and the pomps of fortune, but in prudence, in wisdom and in knowledge. And so much as the prince ought to be different from his people in his habits and manner of living, so ought he to have nothing to do with the foolish opinions of the vulgar.[6]

At the age of thirteen Mary declaimed a Latin oration in praise of learned women in the hall of the Louvre before the assembled French court. This earned her a standing ovation, not so much on account of grammar or sentiment as the charming manner in which this address was delivered and the beauty of her diction.[7] Mary was never so accomplished a linguist as her rival Elizabeth, but she persevered with her Latin studies, the prerequisite of international diplomacy, and after her return to Scotland she continued under the guidance of George Buchanan. The Queen's tutor, the greatest Scottish humanist of his era, would later turn against her. If not the actual forger of the Casket Letters (as some have averred), he was certainly the willing tool of Moray in the charges against Mary.

The French court under Henry II was a curious blend of the moral and amoral, of an elaborate protocol and etiquette on the one hand that admitted no transgression, and, on the other, a certain moral laxity which not only turned a blind eye to adultery but accorded a position of some eminence to the King's mistress. To be sure, Diane de Poitiers was an exceptional woman; despite the fundamental impropriety of her position she, more than anyone else, strove to ensure that the court maintained an outward semblance of respectability.

Unlikely though it seems, Diane was aided and abetted by the Cardinal of Lorraine. This prince of the Church, like his Scottish counterpart Cardinal Beaton, was not a religious man in the modern sense, but more like the chief executive of a vast corporation. It is impossible to determine what were his personal views on religion, or the precise role of religion at the French court. The Cardinal, a member of the powerful Guise family, was as fervent a prince of the Church as Beaton, but in his personal conduct he was more blatantly immoral. In politics and diplomacy he was ruthless and unscrupulous, with a seemingly inexhaustible talent for the mean and base, the treacherous and dishonest. His Eminence wielded enormous influence over Diane de Poitiers and thus, in turn, manipulated King Henry. Diane enjoyed a remarkably cordial relationship with Queen Catherine who even went so far as to entrust her with the supervision of the royal children's education. Diane not only superintended their formal studies but 'likewise caused them to be instructed by good and learned preceptors, as well in virtue and wise precepts, as in the love and fear of God'.[8]

Mary's detractors, including many nineteenth-century biographers, seized on Diane's role as an unsavoury influence over the impressionable young Queen of Scots, but this is belied by Mary's letters to her mother in which she invariably speaks of Diane's kindness. At one point she went so far as to suggest that a marriage might be arranged between the young Earl of Arran and Diane's daughter, Mademoiselle de Bouillon.[9]

Although the Huguenot brand of Protestantism had made considerable inroads in France by the middle of the sixteenth century, the great majority of the population at all levels of society still adhered steadfastly to the Catholic Church. Great care was taken to ensure that Queen Mary was not tainted by Huguenotism, and one of the reasons for the selection of the mercurial Madame de Parois as governess was that she was a devout Catholic on whom Cardinal de Lorraine could rely to instil sound Catholic values in her young charge. At first Mary meekly accepted the zealous harangues of her governess, but her natural exuberance rebelled against this as she approached womanhood. Relations between the Queen and her governess deteriorated when Mary discovered that Madame had been filing bad reports of her conduct to Queen Catherine and Mary of Guise. Eventually Mary begged her mother to replace Madame de Parois with Madame de Brêne, a close friend of Diane de Poitiers. It is probable that Diane herself engineered this proposal, but it certainly had the unanimous approval not only of the Queen Mother, but of Queen Catherine, King Henry and the Guise family in general. Diane's influence was further consolidated when her daughter, Mademoiselle de Bouillon, was appointed to carry Mary's train, while a niece of Madame de Brêne was appointed a lady of her bedchamber.

On or shortly after her eleventh birthday, Mary took rank at court and acquired her own separate household by 1 January 1554 when she entertained the Cardinal to supper. At the instigation of Henry II, the parliament of Paris decreed that, in accordance with French tradition, Mary's majority should date from the beginning, and not the end, of the year of her majority, and that from the beginning of her twelfth year her kingdom should be governed in her name by the advice and counsel of persons chosen by the French king who was now her guardian. This was in effect a flagrant violation of Scotland's sovereignty, for no Act of the French parliament could be regarded as binding on the Scots. The Scottish regent, formerly the Earl of Arran and now known as the Duke of Châtelherault, was persuaded to acknowledge this arrangement, although he did so with the utmost reluctance and only as a result of substantial financial inducements and the promise of a French princess for his son. Fearing that the Duke would go back on his word when the opportunity arose, the Queen-Dowager and Henry II plotted together to engineer Châtelherault's resignation, even fabricating a date for this a year earlier than reality.

This deplorable chicanery was an unwarrantable interference in the domestic affairs of Scotland, but Mary of Guise operated so skilfully that Châtelherault was completely outflanked. When the convention of nobles met at Stirling, they were presented with a *fait accompli* and could do little other than agree to Henry's recommendations. Mary being deemed to have reached her majority, she had the power to appoint a regent. On the advice of her counsellors, Queen Mary appointed her mother as regent, 'at the pleasure of the

French king'. Châtelherault did nothing to help himself by boycotting the convention; but when letters were sent to him by Huntly and others, his nerve failed and he finally agreed to terms for his resignation. It is probable that the erstwhile regent only gave way when his half-brother and arch supporter, now the Archbishop of St Andrews, was incapacitated by a stroke that robbed him of the power of speech. When the Scottish parliament met on 12 April 1554, the Duke meekly tendered his resignation.

When the Archbishop recovered his speech he was quick to condemn his half-brother, dismissing him as 'but a very beast given over of the government'.[10] John Knox pithily commented that a crown had been placed on the head of the Queen Mother, 'as seemly a sight (if men had eyes) as to put a saddle upon the back of an unruly cow'.[11] Of course, Knox was bound to be biased against Mary of Guise. Only someone as ruthless, clever, devious and extremely skilled in diplomacy as Mary could have beaten the scheming and self-serving Scottish nobles at their own game. Mary of Guise might have been successful at winning the power she coveted, but unfortunately it soon transpired that she was far less successful at using it wisely. Many historians and biographers have adopted a sexist attitude in commenting on the regency of Mary of Guise, taking their cue from John Knox. He set the tone with his infamous diatribe against the 'monstrous regiment of women', alluding not only to the regency of Mary of Guise but also to the accession to the English throne of Mary Tudor on 6 July 1553. Of course, Knox was viewing the reign of Mary Tudor from his ultra-fanatical Protestant standpoint. When she married Philip II of Spain on 25 July 1554 the balance of power in western Europe changed dramatically. If this marriage produced an heir to the English throne, the likelihood of the Queen of Scots inheriting that throne would be greatly diminished, if not eliminated. But, more importantly, her position in Scotland would be seriously undermined, while France, faced with the united power of Spain and England, might be forced to relinquish its hold over Scotland.

As it happens, the marriage proved barren and fate dealt Mary Tudor a cruel blow when what she fondly believed was a child growing in her belly proved to be a malignant tumour. Her untimely death in 1558 brought her Protestant half-sister Elizabeth to the English throne. The Counter-Reformation of Bloody Mary was immediately brought to a halt, and England henceforward was aligned with the forces of Protestantism, wherever they might be, in France, Germany, the Low Countries or Scotland. The dying Mary Tudor would have preferred to see her legitimate cousin Mary of Scotland succeed her, rather than her half-sister whom she regarded as an incestuous bastard (Anne Boleyn was widely believed to have been the illegitimate daughter of Henry VIII). Ironically, the succession of Elizabeth was engineered by King Philip and the Catholic nobility of England, mainly on the grounds that Philip had hopes of marrying Elizabeth himself.

This topsy-turvy situation was compounded by a confusion in the ecclesiastical policies of Europe. Pope Paul IV, the nominee of Henry II, supported France both against Spain, the traditional bastion of Catholicism, and England which under Mary Tudor was hell-bent on rooting out Protestantism with fanatical ruthlessness. Conversely, Mary of Guise, sister of the Cardinal of Lorraine, was pursuing a policy of expedience in Scotland. As part of her plans to destabilise the English government, the Queen Mother was actually intriguing with the English Protestants against Mary Tudor in order to gain Protestant support in Scotland against the Hamilton faction (headed by the Duke of Châtelherault). The high point of this policy came when Mary of Guise went so far as to allow Protestant refugees to return to Scotland. At the same time, she tried to embroil Scotland in the war which had broken out again between France and England, but in this regard she was much less successful. The increasingly Byzantine convolutions of the Queen Mother's religious and foreign policies would eventually lead to disaster, both for her adopted country and for the interests of her daughter.

The complex and inherently unstable nature of European politics was closely monitored by the powerful Guise family. Anxiety about the way things were going induced them to press Henry II for the consummation of their ambitions to marry their ward to the Dauphin. Although Mary and Francis had been affianced from a very early age, a marriage was by no means a foregone conclusion, especially in the event of the King dying. The Guise family had to contend with a powerful and dangerous rival in the Duke of Montmorency, Constable of France. Nevertheless, there does not seem to have been any serious doubt that Mary and Francis would eventually wed.

The nearest thing to a fear on that score came in a statement allegedly made by the French ambassador to Venice that in the event of Philip of Spain arranging a marriage between the Archduke

Ferdinand of Austria and Elizabeth of England, Henry II would give Mary Stewart to a complete nonentity called Lord Courtenay 'to prevent the House of Austria establishing itself in that kingdom'.[12] This preposterous idea was without foundation. The Queen of Scots was not the ward of King Henry, to be married off at the merest whim; and even if she were, Henry never wavered in his intention of marrying his son to the Scottish queen.

There is ample evidence that Henry viewed the relationship between his sickly son and the very flower of European princesses with mawkish sentimentalism. In particular, he was deeply moved by Mary's tenderness towards the puny boy and the latter's doglike devotion to her. As children they were inseparable; one may cite the charming description by one diplomat of the way in which the youthful lovers used 'to retire by themselves into a corner of the apartments, in order that they might be able to communicate to each other their small secrets'.[13] As Mary developed into a handsome young woman, Henry warmed to her even more than ever, and it is impossible to contemplate a political scenario which would have been so dire as to compel him to alter his intention.

Nevertheless, real or imagined, the Guise family had their moments of doubt, and would never rest easy until the matter was resolved. At last, on 8 April 1556, the Cardinal of Lorraine joyfully told his sister that Henry had decided that Mary should wed the Dauphin during the next winter. Even then, however, the Cardinal had his doubts of Henry's intentions unless the Queen Mother paid a personal visit to France. Mary of Guise felt that the political situation in Scotland by that time precluded her absenting herself from the kingdom, but she compromised by despatching her secretary, William Maitland of Lethington, instead. Maitland crossed to France in July 1556 but could not pin Henry down. The King was then greatly preoccupied with fears for his wife's health in the last stages of pregnancy, but as soon as she was safely delivered of a baby Henry departed on an extensive provincial tour. By the time he returned to Paris, the Queen of Scots had succumbed to a 'persistent fever' brought on by the unusually hot weather, perhaps an early intimation of the porphyria that was to dog her in later years. She had no sooner recovered, in October, when the Dauphin fell ill of a 'quartan fever'.

The following spring the Convention of the Estates (the Scottish parliament commonly called the Estates) recommended to the Queen Mother that she should either go to France herself or send a diplomatic mission to complete the arrangements for the marriage. Again, Mary of Guise found it inconvenient to leave Scotland, and wrote to Henry and the Constable of France requesting that they communicate with her on the matter. Henry was too preoccupied with the war against Spain and did not address himself to this matter until after the defeat and capture of the Constable at St Quentin on 10 August 1557. The ignominy of this defeat was a severe blow to the prestige of the Constable and his faction. By contrast, the spectacular victories of the Duke of Guise, campaigning in Italy and Picardy, put his family in the ascendancy. The Spanish victory at St Quentin made Henry fully aware of the need to bolster the Scottish connection against England, and a new-found desire to reward the Guise faction finally made the long-looked-for marriage imminent.

On 30 October 1557, therefore, Henry wrote to the Scottish Estates, formally inviting them to send a deputation to discuss the terms for the marriage. On 14 December the Scottish parliament selected nine men, representative of each of the three estates (the nobility, clergy and burgesses) as well as Protestant and Catholic viewpoints. They were James Beaton, Archbishop of Glasgow; David Panter, Bishop of Ross; Robert Reid, Bishop of Orkney; the earls of Cassilis and Rothes; Lord James Stewart; Lord Fleming; Lord Seton; and John Erskine of Dun. As a preliminary, the Estates wrote to Henry demanding guarantees of the continuing independence of Scotland. Both Henry and the Dauphin were to bind themselves and their successors, in the case of Mary's death without issue, to support the succession to the Scottish throne of the nearest heir by blood.

When the Scottish deputation landed in France in March 1558 they found Henry affable and amenable, readily agreeing to all their terms. In addition, it was agreed that the Dauphin should, after marriage, bear the title of King of Scots. On his accession to the French throne, the two kingdoms were to be united under one crown; that in the event of the death of her husband, Queen Mary should have the option of remaining in France or returning to Scotland; that, should there be male issue of the marriage, the eldest surviving son should inherit both crowns; and that should there be only female issue (which in France was debarred from the succession), the eldest surviving daughter should get the Scottish throne.[14]

The only demand at which the Scottish deputies baulked was that the Scottish crown be sent to France so that the Dauphin could be crowned with it as King of Scots. While refusing to let the crown out of their sight, the Estates conceded that Francis should have the crown matrimonial, although this was clearly understood to refer only to the duration of the marriage, 'without any manner of prejudice to her highness's self, the succession of her body, or lawful succession of her blood whatsomever'. This was supported by Henry granting Letters of Naturalisation to Scotsmen, ratified by the Paris parliament on 8 July; in November the Estates granted reciprocal naturalisation to all subjects of the King of France. In this manner the Auld Alliance was reinvigorated, with the promise of happier connections between the two countries than in the recent past.

The Scottish commissioners would have been far less sanguine had they been aware of Henry's real plans. Before signing the public marriage contract Mary had already signed three secret protocols. By the first, in the event of her death without issue, Mary assigned to Henry her rights and claims to the English throne as well as her Scottish kingdom. By the second, Scotland was specifically mortgaged to the French king and his successors until France was reimbursed for the money expended in Scotland's defence. By the third, Mary renounced any agreement to which the Estates might induce her to consent if it were to interfere with these promises. These documents indicated that King Henry, the Queen Mother and the Guise family were actively conspiring against Scottish independence. As it happened, Mary of Guise failed to execute her part of the bargain, thanks to the efforts of the Protestants; but it is questionable whether Henry could ever have realised his ambitions, with so many other imponderable factors, such as the Dauphin dying childless.

Mary's motives in signing these protocols have been endlessly debated. At best she was singularly naïve; at worst, guilty of high treason in signing away her country's sovereignty. In mitigation, it should be remembered that she was still a young girl, that she had spent the greater part of her life in France and that, with her marriage to the Dauphin imminent, she could not imagine a future existence that precluded her continued residence in France. By contrast, the country over which she nominally ruled was no more than a distant memory. It never entered Mary's head for a moment that the only issue of her body would be a Protestant son by a second marriage. By signing these articles Mary, in effect, robbed her son James of his birthright.

An unexpected concomitant was that, in disowning her son, Mary was obliged to nominate as his successor none other than Philip II of Spain, the implacable enemy of Henry II and the Guise family. By default, Philip, as widower of Mary Tudor, was next in line. The French and Spanish dynasties were then, and for many years thereafter, locked in a deadly struggle for supremacy, much of which pivoted on the twin kingdoms of Scotland and England. Both Mary and her cousin Elizabeth were thus objects of desire, not so much for their own sakes but on account of the kingdoms they ruled. In truth, Mary (and to a lesser extent Elizabeth) were mere pawns in this great power game.

Mary probably never gave these weighty matters a thought as she made her preparations for the elaborate marriage ceremony. On Tuesday, 19 April 1558, several days before the wedding, there was the ancient ceremony of hand-fasting or formal public betrothal, superintended by the Cardinal of Lorraine in the grand hall of the Louvre. This culminated in a grand ball at which King Henry and Queen Mary led off the first dance. The marriage itself was held the following Sunday, 24 April, in the Cathedral of Notre-Dame, extravagantly decorated for the occasion. The Bishop of Paris received the bridal couple at the doorway under a canopy of fleurs-de-lis and preached a sermon to them before the marriage ceremony was performed, amid great pomp and circumstance, by Cardinal Charles de Bourbon, Archbishop of Rouen. The Duke of Guise, as Grand Master of Ceremonies, endeared himself to the Paris mob by moving aside lords and ladies so that the common people could get a better view.

Then the bridal couple entered the cathedral itself to hear Mass. This was the first marriage of a Dauphin in Paris in over two centuries, and the event naturally excited the greatest interest. It was widely regarded as setting the seal on French diplomacy, and there was widespread optimism that the marriage of the Dauphin and the Queen of Scots would usher in a new and even more splendid era for France. Brantôme waxed lyrical as he captured the mood of the moment:

> She appeared a hundred times more beautiful than a goddess of heaven . . . so that the universal voice of the court and the great city was that a hundred and a hundred times happy must be the Prince who went to join himself in marriage with this Princess – that if the Kingdom of Scotland was anything of a prize, the Queen was far more precious than it, for even

if she had had neither sceptre nor crown, her person alone
was worth a kingdom.[15]

Significantly, Brantôme was silent regarding the bridegroom. Mary,
tall, stately and stunning in her blue and white velvet robes richly
studded with diamonds and rubies, a golden coronet encrusted with
sapphires, pearls and rubies setting off her Titian coiffure and a
breathtaking diamond necklace flashing at her throat, must have
seemed a strange contrast alongside the gaudily costumed runt with
his beady little eyes almost buried in his pale, puffy face.

For the moment, however, everyone was blinded by the magnificence of the spectacle. In the evening the newly-weds headed a
grand royal cavalcade through the main streets of Paris to the Palais
de Justice where a sumptuous banquet was staged in their honour
by the assembled aristocracy of France. The Dauphin and
Dauphiness passed through the jubilant crowds on a magnificent
litter. The Dauphin's little brothers trotted along at their side,
followed by King Henry, princes and prelates on richly accoutred
chargers, then the ladies of the court no less richly equipped with
ponies clad in crimson velvet embroidered in gold thread. The
brightly lit windows of the palace were left uncurtained so that the
ordinary Parisians could crowd round and gaze upon the costly
spectacle, feasting their eyes if nothing else. After the banquet came
the dancing far into the night, and, as always, the Queen of Scots
was the belle of the ball. Entertainment in the interludes was
provided by masques, mummeries, tableaux and a triumphal march.

The *pièce de résistance* was a flotilla of six galleons gorgeously
draped with cloth of gold, their sails of silver cloth billowing, which
glided across the ballroom floor and simulated the motion of ships
on a turbulent ocean. In each ship sat a masked prince dressed in
gold. As the galleons passed before a marble table where the Queen
and princesses sat, each of the princes invited one of them to fill the
seat beside him. Queen Catherine, the Dauphiness, the Queen of
Navarre and the Princesses Elisabeth, Marguerite and Claude were
borne away amid the sustained applause of the assembled nobles.
Afterwards the bridal pair were escorted to their bedchamber by the
entire royal family and principal guests, who put the embarrassed
teenagers to bed amid a great deal of coarse ribaldry. The celebrations continued for several days, with an endless round of fêtes,
tournaments and spectacles.[16]

Greater attention than usual was paid to royal amusements that summer and the festive atmosphere lingered on into the autumn. Then Mary came down to earth with a bump, stunned by news of the tragedy that had befallen her commissioners as they journeyed back to Scotland in September. They were taken ill with food poisoning and four of them, Cassilis, Rothes, Fleming and the Bishop of Orkney, died. Lord James, Mary's half-brother, was also stricken but survived both illness and the dreadful remedy of being hung upside down by his ankles to let the malevolent humours drain from his body. Rumours were rife that the commissioners had been deliberately poisoned, and it seems surprising that no attempt was made at the time to get to the bottom of the mystery. The ever-superstitious Scots took this calamity as an ill omen, and their fears were not allayed when King Henry wrote again, insisting that the Scottish crown be sent over to Paris so that the Dauphin could be properly crowned as King of Scots. To the Scots the crown was the tangible symbol of their sovereignty. Doubtless mindful of the removal of the Stone of Destiny by King Edward I centuries earlier, they shrank at the prospect of letting the precious symbol of their independence leave the country. The Estates did not refuse Henry outright but temporised for several months. In the end fate would intervene to remove this threat.

Meanwhile, the Dauphiness was settling down to her new status. In reality life was little changed, except that Mary and Francis now lived together as man and wife, with their own court at Villers-Coterets. Mary, now approaching sixteen, was in the first flower of womanhood, and in other circumstances would have been engaged in the serious business of making babies; but Francis, at fourteen, was weedy, undersized and almost certainly immature for his age. Rumours abounded that the Dauphin suffered from syphilis, though there is nothing to substantiate this. Nevertheless, Francis suffered from the rare deformity of undescended testicles and the probability is that the marriage was never consummated.

Mary now spent an increasing amount of time in the company of her mother-in-law, though the two women had little in common. Where Mary was tall, handsome and majestic, Catherine was small, dumpy and swarthy. Apart from the generation gap, there was a vast difference between them in temperament. Mary wore her heart on her sleeve, while Catherine had the Medici talent for intrigue and malice. Poles apart in looks, temperament and attitudes, the two queens were only as one in their concern for and utter devotion to the Dauphin. Had the marriage of Mary and Francis been a torridly physical affair, Catherine would have been mad with jealousy and bitterly resentful of the younger woman; but, as it turned out, Catherine saw Mary as nothing more than a close ally in the chief aim of her life, the welfare of her sickly first-born. Catherine and Mary endlessly discussed the Dauphin's health and shared their worries over his illnesses and ailments, real or imagined. By the same token, they pounced eagerly on any shred of evidence, however slight, that Francis was on the mend or showed signs of maturity.

Mary's sense of her divine purpose was given a considerable boost before the year was out. On 17 November Mary Tudor died; when the news reached the French court Henry ordered that his daughter-in-law should be proclaimed in Paris as Queen of Scotland, England and Ireland, and she and Francis promptly incorporated the English quarterings in their arms. This has been condemned as a rash act, but with the benefit of hindsight. In November 1558 Mary could not have done otherwise. Her claim to be the legitimate heir of the English throne was widely recognised not only on the Continent but also among the staunchly conservative Catholics of England who regarded Elizabeth as illegitimate since they did not recognise Henry's divorce and remarriage. Moreover, a formal protest against the accession of Elizabeth soon became part of the ongoing power struggle between France and Spain. Not only did the grieving widower Philip II of Spain rush to congratulate his sister-in-law on her accession, but he followed this up with a proposal for a secret peace, and hard on the heels came a proposal of a much more personal nature. The assumption of English titles and arms by Mary and Francis seems outrageous at this remove in time, but it should not be overlooked that Elizabeth, like her predecessors and successors right down to George III, blatantly proclaimed herself monarch of France and flaunted the fleur-de-lis emblem in her arms.[17]

Mary's claims to the English throne were therefore not as impudent as has often been implied, nor indeed did they play any part in the intense diplomatic manoeuvring that took place over the ensuing months, culminating in the Treaty of Cateau-Cambrésis on 2 April 1559 which brought the war between France and Spain to an end. The Treaty was signed by representatives of France, Spain and England, the pivotal role being played by Philip II who, having failed to interest the recently crowned Queen Elizabeth in matrimony, now settled for her namesake, the Princess Elisabeth of France. On 21 April, only days after the treaty was signed, Mary wrote to Elizabeth in the most cordial terms, expressing her personal satisfaction at the successful outcome of the diplomatic negotiations which led to the Treaty of Cateau-Cambrésis and expressing the hope of an alliance between 'her very dear and loved sister and cousin'. Elizabeth dutifully replied in similar vein, and Mary concluded the correspondence with a second letter on 25 May in which she affirmed her desire for an increase in their friendship, which she would do everything in her power to promote.[18]

At midsummer the Duke of Alva, on behalf of Philip II, journeyed across the Pyrenees and took part in the proxy wedding in Paris on 22 June 1559 to Princess Elisabeth. This lavish spectacle, accompanied by widespread rejoicing, was followed a few days later by the equally sumptuous wedding of the Duke of Savoy to Princess Marguerite. The high point of the joint celebrations was a grand tournament in which King Henry himself played a prominent part. Henry, one of the finest horsemen of the period and a master of sword and lance, distinguished himself in jousts with the dukes of Guise and Savoy, but met his match in his first encounter with the captain of his guard, Jacques de Lorges, Comte de Montgomerie. Against the advice and pleas of both Queen Catherine and Diane de Poitiers, Henry decided to have a second joust with Montgomerie. He also wished to try out his new war-horse, Le Malheureux, a gift from the Duke of Savoy.

The two heavily armoured knights charged towards each other, lances lowered. As they collided, Montgomerie's lance shattered on impact with the visor of the King's helmet, and splinters of it penetrated deeply into Henry's left temple and eye. Severely injured, he was carried to a nearby house. Septicaemia set in and on 10 July King Henry died, attended by the entire royal family including his adoring daughter-in-law.

Suddenly, in her seventeenth year, Mary Queen of Scots found herself queen-consort of France. Now she rose nobly to the occasion. The French royal family, indeed the entire court, was demoralised by Henry's tragic death. It was Mary who consoled and comforted Catherine, and when the Spanish ambassador presented King Philip's condolences, it was Mary who replied on Catherine's behalf when the widow was too overcome by grief to speak for herself. Mary also had the presence of mind to order an immediate inventory of the royal jewels, especially those which Henry had lavished all too freely on his mistress. It was Mary who made sure that Diane de Poitiers disgorged these jewels, on the grounds that she had more need of them herself.

The Guise faction was now in the ascendant. On 18 September Francis was crowned at Rheims, but the real power lay in the hands of the Duke of Guise and the Cardinal of Lorraine. Mary trusted her uncles implicitly, and Francis, in his devotion to Mary, was as putty in their hands. Moreover, the boy showed not the slightest aptitude for statecraft. Morose, taciturn, dull-witted, lethargic, obstinate are the adjectives most frequently applied to Francis. The only thing that motivated him was hunting, which he pursued with uncharacteristic passion. Soon he tired of even the most elementary of official observances and effectively delegated all his powers to the Guises.

One of their first acts was to dismiss their old *bête noire*, the Constable, Montmorency. The Duke of Guise as commander-in-chief of the army and his brother the Cardinal as controller of finance between them wielded enormous power. Francis rather touchingly continued to defer to his mother, the Queen-Dowager Catherine, but she was soon elbowed out of the decision-making by the Guise brothers. Her attitude towards the new queen now turned to hatred. In due course the canard would arise that this was due to some jibe of Queen Mary about Catherine de' Medici being only 'a merchant's daughter', but the truth is that she blamed Mary for the usurpation of her son's powers by the Guise family.

France was in turmoil as religious sectarianism began to assume dangerous proportions. Nevertheless, the Guise brothers made the most of the situation to consolidate their personal power and advance the fortunes of their niece and themselves. There was a brief period of elation mingled with unease, caused by a mysterious illness of Queen Mary. She was assailed with bouts of sickness, which, it was widely assumed, were evidence that she was pregnant at last. Mary went along with this supposition, perhaps through ignorance, even for some time adopting the loose-fitting gown habitually worn by pregnant ladies. There is a curious parallel between Mary Stewart and the late Mary Tudor, both of whom buoyed themselves up on the groundless gossip of their respective courts and fooled themselves into believing that they were pregnant. Mary came to her senses about the end of September 1560 when her delusion evaporated and she returned to her fashionable, tightly waisted robes. The Guises, who had believed the rumours, were crestfallen when the truth emerged, though they concealed their chagrin by saying that a king of sixteen and a queen of seventeen had still a future before them.[19]

There is a distinct possibility that Mary's phantom pregnancy was induced by some form of hysteria arising from the greatest tragedy that had so far befallen her. On 11 June 1560, exhausted in body and mind by her long and wearisome labours to govern Scotland, Mary of Guise died at Edinburgh Castle. Her daughter was beside herself with grief when the news reached her; but the dire situation in Scotland left her precious little time for grieving. On 27 February 1560 Queen Elizabeth had put her seal to the Treaty of Berwick, promising military assistance to the Protestant Lords, led by Lord James Stewart, who were now in open rebellion against the regent and her French forces. As Mary of Guise lay dying in Edinburgh Castle, English artillery were pounding the fortifications of Leith, and she expired to the sound of cannon.

Queen Mary dried her eyes and gave instructions to the emissaries from Scotland to negotiate a peace with England as soon as possible. On 6 July the Treaty of Edinburgh was concluded. Thousands of English and French troops would evacuate the country immediately, leaving only sixty on either side. As part of the deal, Mary and Francis agreed to relinquish their claims to the English throne, and to remove the English lions from their arms. A month later the self-styled Lords of the Congregation, a group of Protestant noblemen, consolidated their position by pushing through the Estates a series of Acts introducing a Protestant Confession of Faith. Papal authority was abolished and the observances of Catholicism, including the confessional and the Mass, were declared illegal.

The Catholic Mary might be Queen of Scots, but Scotland was now effectively a Protestant republic governed by a powerful oligarchy of noblemen under the spiritual thumb of an ayatollah. The situation was intolerable, and the Guise brothers addressed the problem of finding a suitable replacement for their sister as regent. Before the matter could be resolved, however, fate intervened. With his new-found passion for hunting and outdoor activities, *Le Petit Roi*, as Francis was popularly known, suddenly grew taller; but his rapid growth, coupled with his poor physique and indifferent health, was a bad sign. On 16 November, after a day on the hunting field near Orleans, Francis returned to his quarters complaining of severe earache. No one was unduly worried; it had been a cold day with a biting wind and it was said that Francis only took to his bed to placate his over-anxious mother. A week later, the Venetian ambassador reported that 'everyone feels that His Majesty's illness is not dangerous . . . there is no doubt that in two or three days he will have quite recovered'. By 1 December, however, his despatches told a very different story: 'Although they endeavour to conceal the malady more than ever, the Queen Mother cannot suppress the signs of her sorrow, which is increased by the recollection of the predictions made by many astrologers, who all prognosticate his very short life.'[20] An infection of the left ear had spread to the brain; Francis developed a high fever, with attacks of delirium and fainting fits.

The court was thrown into turmoil. Mary and Catherine momentarily sank their differences and maintained a constant vigil at the dying king's bedside. His apartments were sealed off, and armed guards were given strict orders to admit no one, other than the two women and the Guise brothers. No servants were permitted to attend him, the women dealing entirely with his most basic needs. As she prayed beside her dying husband, Mary must surely have pondered on the fickleness of fate. The wretched youth with his waxen pallor was a poor specimen of manhood. He had nothing to commend him; and only an accident of birth had placed him in a high position for which he was totally unsuited, physically, temperamentally or intellectually. He was quite unfit for the role in which he had been cast, and his life was of no intrinsic value to his family, to his country, or to the world at large.

As Francis sank into a coma he may have been spared the unedifying spectacle of his mother and his wife engaging in bitter slanging matches like a pair of fishwives. The Guises were far too preoccupied with the precariousness of their own position to intervene and restrain the Italian harridan from her vituperative diatribe against their niece. Instead, the Duke of Guise reserved his invective for the luckless physicians, threatening them with the most barbarous execution imaginable should their incompetence and neglect lead to Francis's death.

The doctors, in sheer desperation, prescribed a series of massive enemas on 2 December and, for a brief hour or two, this brutal treatment seemed to be having some beneficial effects; but that night Francis's condition took a further turn for the worse. He lingered on, comatose, till the evening of 5 December when he breathed his last.

The hopes of a powerful few had been pinned on this poor worthless body: the Catholic hierarchy in their struggle against the Huguenots, and the Guises against Montmorency and Louis, Prince of Condé, brother of the King of Navarre and leader of the French Protestants. By the death of Francis II, however, his mother Catherine de' Medici regained her power and influence, immediately ousting the Guise brothers and becoming regent on behalf of her second son, Charles IX.

The one who truly lost the most by the death of *Le Petit Roi* was his grieving young wife. Her affection for Francis was deep and sincere. He had been her constant companion for more than a decade, and ever afterwards, though she was to be married twice more, she would always think fondly of Francis as the one great love of her life and her one true husband.

3. WIDOWHOOD

1560–61

A weary lot is thine, fair maid,
A weary lot is thine!
To pull the thorn thy brow to braid,
And press the rue for wine!
   Sir Walter Scott, *Rokeby*

While Mary donned the white robes of mourning and locked herself away for forty days in a darkened room draped in black as etiquette demanded, Catherine de' Medici moved swiftly to protect the interests of her son Charles and oust the Guises. The latter were far too busy saving their own necks and salvaging what they could from the disaster to waste much time on their grieving niece. Mary, who had never got over the death of her mother the previous June, was drained physically and mentally by her bedside vigil. Now she suffered a nervous breakdown, prostrate with grief, refusing food and weeping uncontrollably. An eye-witness was Michiel Surian, the Venetian ambassador, who reported back to his masters on 8 December:

> Everyone will forget the death of the late King, except the young Queen, his widow, who, being no less noble-minded than beautiful and graceful in appearance, the thought of widowhood, at so early an age, and of the loss of a consort who was so great a King, and who so dearly loved her, and also that she is dispossessed of the crown of France with little hope of recovering that of Scotland, which is her sole patrimony and dower, so afflict her that she will not receive any consolation, but brooding over her disaster with

constant tears, and passionate and doleful lamentations, she universally inspires pity.[1]

And this description is borne out by the poignant letter which Mary herself wrote to Philip of Spain, saying that, without the aid of Heaven, her misfortunes would be unsupportable.[2] There is absolutely no foundation for the canard, repeated by some nineteenth-century writers, that even before Francis was cold in his grave, Mary was casting around for another husband. This was derived from a statement of the English ambassador, Sir Nicholas Throckmorton, to William Cecil on 6 December that 'so far as he could learn, she more esteemed the continuance of her honours and to marry one that might uphold her to be great, than she passed to serve and please her fancy'. Sir William Cecil, later Lord Burghley, was Elizabeth's principal adviser for forty years, from her accession in 1558 till his death in 1598. He was the archetypal bureaucrat, a private secretary who became, in effect, Secretary of State. Throckmorton, Cecil and naturally Queen Elizabeth herself had, of course, more than a passing interest in Mary's future, especially the choice of husband which could alter the political situation dramatically. But the object of this speculation, robed in her widow's weeds, remained incommunicado for several days, so there is no way in which Throckmorton could have had any first-hand knowledge of Mary's feelings at that time, whether voiced or not. A poem by Mary in French, composed during this period, summed up her sense of bereavement: 'Without ceasing, my heart feels only pangs of regret for an absent one'.

A week after Francis's death, Mary was eventually persuaded to see her closest relatives. The first to be allowed into her chamber were her brother-in-law, the eleven-year-old Charles IX, accompanied by King Antoine of Navarre, the Duke of Guise and the Cardinal of Lorraine. Some time afterwards she was seen by her closest friends, but it was not until early January 1561 that she admitted any of the foreign ambassadors. In the interim, speculation as to the future of the young widow was rife, and there was a flurry of diplomatic activity. First off their marks as potential husbands were Frederik II of Denmark and Erik XIV of Sweden, closely followed by the Archduke Charles, younger son of the Emperor Ferdinand. The Duke of Finland and Henry of Béarn (the future Henry III of Navarre and Henry IV of France) were among the other contenders. The young Earl of Arran, who, as the Master of Hamilton, had been in love with

Mary since early childhood, was pressing his suit within weeks, at the instigation of his father, the Duke of Châtelherault, and John Knox and through the mediation of King Antoine of Navarre and the Constable of France. Trailing the field was Lady Lennox who had begun 'to be of good hope' concerning her son, Lord Darnley. A natural choice would have been Charles IX, and it seems that Mary herself was not averse to this suggestion, even if the young king were seven years her junior and she would have to wait a considerable time before such a marriage could take place; but there was the insurmountable and implacable obstacle of Catherine de' Medici.

The next best thing, in Mary's opinion, was a Spanish marriage, although the prospect of Don Carlos, the nominal heir to the throne, was even less attractive than the poor, miserable alliance with Francis had been. Two years younger than Mary, he was a scrawny youth weighing less than six stone, with a twisted, deformed body. He suffered from epileptic fits, slobbered incessantly and had a serious speech impediment. Despite these handicaps, as Infante of Spain he was potentially the most powerful ruler in Europe and immensely wealthy to boot. Misshapen, dribbling oaf or not, Don Carlos seemed a dazzling prospect to the young widow.

Philip himself, only recently married to Mary's closest confidante, Elisabeth of France, calculated that such an alliance between Spain and Scotland would at one stroke thwart French ambitions in Scotland and England, as well as strengthen his hand. He lost no time, therefore, in opening negotiations, through his ambassador, Perrenot de Chantonay, with the Cardinal of Lorraine. In helping to procure this Spanish marriage, of course, the Cardinal was working against the interests of France; but with that country now in religious turmoil, Lorraine placed the interests of his Church before his country. King Philip would be an exceedingly powerful ally in the coming religious struggle, so the Cardinal went to work with a will to arrange for his niece a marriage that was as grand and grotesque as her previous one. Late in January, Philip despatched his special envoy, Don Juan Manrique. After presenting his credentials to Charles IX, Don Juan went to pay his respects to the Queen of Scots with whom, according to the Venetian ambassador, 'in the presence of the Duke of Guise and the Cardinal of Lorraine, he held very confidential communications, and, I am assured that, besides his other concerns, Don Juan is also empowered to treat a marriage between Her Majesty and the Prince of Spain'.[3]

Don Juan's mission was common knowledge, and the Venetian ambassador in the same report noted the reaction of Throckmorton who forecast that if such a marriage were to take place, 'the friendship subsisting between the Queen his mistress, and the King Catholic, would be converted into a no less enmity'. No doubt Queen Elizabeth and her advisers took due note of the fact that English opposition to the match would negate Philip's present goodwill. So far, he had been using his influence with the English Catholics so that Elizabeth would not be embarrassed by religious problems, while also giving her a free hand in Scotland to prevent French ambitions to take over that kingdom.

This policy had been governed solely by political expedience, and the death of Francis, in fact, meant that it was no longer necessary. French influence in Scotland had died with him, and there was therefore no longer any reason for Philip to give Elizabeth his support. Besides, the English Catholics, outraged at Elizabeth's restoration of Protestantism, had been pleading with Philip to withdraw his support from her. Even before the death of Francis, therefore, relations between Elizabeth and Philip were strained to breaking point. Elizabeth's position was seriously undermined by the mysterious death of Amy Robsart, wife of Lord Robert Dudley, and rumours were flying around that the Queen had a hand in this business. Elizabeth shrugged aside the innuendo and continued to show her personal favour for Dudley who was her Master of Horse. The situation had deteriorated to the point at which Alvaro de Quadra, the Spanish ambassador in London, was assuring Philip that the English were disgusted with their queen and were ready to rise in favour of Mary. Ironically, on 22 February De Quadra forwarded to Philip a petition from Dudley no less, seeking the King's support in his bid to marry Elizabeth; in exchange, Dudley promised to support the restoration of Catholicism.

Philip cynically endorsed this petition, not because he had any trust in Dudley or Elizabeth, but because he sensed that such a marriage would be Elizabeth's downfall. It is against this background that the proposed marriage between Mary and Don Carlos seemed highly desirable. At one stroke the balance of power in western Europe would be altered and Spain, rather than France, would emerge as the dominant force, with Scotland and England firmly in the Spanish sphere of influence. The fact that Don Carlos was even more physically challenged than the late King Francis was a matter which seems never to have been brought to Mary's attention.

Elizabeth, however, was always one jump ahead. Whether she seriously entertained a marriage with Dudley or not, the important thing was to delude Philip into thinking that this was her intention. In the meantime, she sent the Earl of Bedford to Paris to negotiate an alliance with the Huguenots and to do everything in his power to prevent the marriage of Mary to a European prince.

Catherine de' Medici had her own reasons for throwing a spanner in the works. Had she had the interests of France at heart she would have sanctioned the marriage of Mary to her son Charles IX, and a papal dispensation allowing Mary to marry her brother-in-law would have been easily obtained. But Catherine could not see beyond the fact that this move would lead to the reinstatement of the Guises and her own political eclipse. For the same reason she opposed the Spanish match, having in mind a marriage between Don Carlos and her youngest daughter. (Her daughter Elisabeth, of course, was already married to Philip himself.) In her desperation to secure this match Catherine was prepared to place Charles IX under Philip's guardianship and to force the King of Navarre to renounce his throne. Navarre, still nominally an independent kingdom though effectively a French protectorate since 1516, had had a succession of French princes as its rulers. Currently, the titular sovereign was Antoine de Bourbon, husband of Jeanne d'Albret, who had gained the crown matrimonial through the death of his father-in-law, Henry II of Navarre, in 1555. The eldest son of this union, Henry III of Navarre, would succeed his friend and namesake as King of France in 1589 when the Valois dynasty died out, taking the title of Henry IV.

When Catherine's overtures to Philip came to nothing, she resorted to threats. She was even prepared to forge an alliance with Elizabeth of England if he persisted in marrying his son to the Queen of Scots. Faced with the appalling prospect of an alliance of two such formidable and unscrupulous women as Catherine and Elizabeth, Philip had second thoughts. By now Elizabeth had changed her mind about marrying Dudley, so the prospect of a Catholic insurrection in England seemed remote. Conversely, Philip feared that an alliance between Catherine and Elizabeth would immeasurably strengthen the hand of the Huguenots, and as a good Catholic, first and foremost, he shrank at the prospect. What clinched the matter was a reminder from his wife (at the instigation of her mother Catherine) that by marrying his son to Mary he would be committing himself to an expensive military adventure in Scotland and surely this was not what he had in mind. Philip took the hint and, by the end of April 1561, let Mary know through his intermediaries that there would be no marriage with Don Carlos.

According to some modern writers, Mary was bitterly disappointed at this news, although Brantôme, writing at the time, noted that Mary 'desired a hundred times more to remain in France a simple dowager, and content herself with Touraine and Poictou for her dowry than to go to reign in her savage country; but messieurs her uncles, at least some if not all of them, counselled her to go'.[4]

Mary may have been disappointed, but she was sufficiently hard-headed to appreciate the inevitable. Moreover, her Guise uncles were no longer in a strong position, and were being pressed by Catherine to send Mary out of the country. So long as she remained on French soil she was, at best, an embarrassment; at worst she was a dangerous adversary. Mary now gave serious thought to going back to Scotland. The last thing she desired, however, was a return backed by foreign troops. If she went back, it would have to be because the Scots themselves welcomed her. Her reputation as a devout Catholic, of course, was a major obstacle, but Mary naïvely considered that religion was not such a big issue. Surely some *modus vivendi* could be worked out, satisfactory to all concerned. Mary was at pains to reassure her subjects that she would be coming home without French strings attached. Above all, she was the Queen of Scots, appointed by divine right. Perhaps Mary did not appreciate the subtle distinction between Queen of Scotland and Queen of Scots. That she ruled the people and not the land was inherent in the Scottish constitution all the way back to the Declaration of Arbroath in 1320 whereby the Scots had made it clear that they would only tolerate a ruler who governed them wisely and in their best interests. By inference, any ruler that failed to come up to that standard could soon be replaced by another.

Furthermore, the reality of the situation in 1561 was that for more than a year the royal prerogative had ceased to have any meaning. Even before the death of Mary of Guise in June 1560, real authority in Scotland had passed into the hands of a powerful oligarchy who styled themselves the Lords of the Congregation, headed by the Duke of Châtelherault whose own position had been strengthened as a result of the Estates naming him as heir-apparent to the crown. He was now effectively in more or less the same position as he had enjoyed during Mary's infancy. In truth, however, the Duke was little more than a puppet in the hands of more ruthlessly determined men than himself, namely the dourly singleminded reformer John Knox and his powerful supporter, Lord James Stewart, the illegitimate eldest brother of the Queen. Châtelherault had recently made a great profession of his adherence to the new religion, and was, at this point in time, dusting off the proposal of his son, the young Earl of Arran, as a husband for Queen Elizabeth. In this ambition he had the solid backing of the Protestant Lords who saw such a marriage as paving the way to the union of the two kingdoms under staunchly Protestant rulers. Elizabeth was not interested in gaining the Scottish crown, by marriage or otherwise, and she was not particularly interested in Protestantism either, at least the Calvinist brand being practised in Scotland. At that stage she was mainly concerned with restoring political, economic and religious stability to her own kingdom.

In 1560, before Francis died, it was more probable that Mary, now firmly settled as Queen of France, might be deposed, or at least persuaded to abdicate her Scottish throne. In that case the crown would have passed to her half-brother Lord James Stewart, rather than the Duke of Châtelherault, for the Scottish nobility would never have settled it on any of the Hamilton family. The Duke's position as heir-apparent was purely nominal and could quite easily be set aside when it no longer suited Lord James. He was twenty-nine and a bachelor. But for the taint of bastardy, he would have succeeded his father James V. In the unstable climate of 1561 the prospect of electing Lord James as King of Scots seemed increasingly attractive to many influential Scotsmen. Matters were not helped by the package of measures rushed through the Scottish parliament the previous autumn, transforming the country into a Protestant theocracy. At that time King Francis, as titular King of Scotland, had expressed his great displeasure and promised to send two envoys to summon a proper parliament for the express purpose of revoking the anti-Catholic legislation, but his death had prevented such a provocative measure.

By the spring of 1561 Scotland was effectively ruled by a triumvirate. Posterity has adjudged John Knox to have been the out-standing figure of the period. Small of stature and unprepossessing in appearance, with his long beard and piercing eyes, he resembled the popular image of a biblical prophet. In addition to his colossal self-assurance he possessed vivid eloquence, a shrewd insight into human nature, a large measure of pragmatism and a strong intellect. He had immense oratorical gifts which electrified peasantry and bourgeoisie alike, but he also possessed an uncanny ability to manipulate, magnetise and motivate the nobility and gentry – the people who really mattered in the mid-sixteenth century. A self-publicist who was centuries ahead of his time, it is mind-boggling to speculate what he might have achieved, or how far he might have gone, had he had the resources of the modern media at his disposal. That he achieved so much, and in such a short space of time, with nothing more than word of mouth, testifies to his charismatic qualities. Shrewdly gauging that religion was about power, he first targeted the nobility in a series of face-to-face house parties. Having persuaded the nobility, he imposed Protestantism with an iron will, harnessing the instincts for self-interest and exploiting to the fullest the external support of England. He even organised the mob, channelling its nihilist passions into the destruction of churches and chapels, abbeys and monasteries, as well as priceless works of religious art. It is a matter for regret that there was no superior force in Scotland to hold Knox's intolerant, fanatical zealotry in check, but in the power vacuum of 1560–61 he was virtual dictator, his powers direct and boundless.

The third figure in the triumvirate, after Knox and Lord James, was William Maitland of Lethington. Where Lord James was candid and open, a man of principle who sincerely believed that he had the best interests of Scotland at heart, Maitland was devious, unscrupulous, a consummate diplomat in an age when diplomacy was marked by chicanery and skulduggery. It was not for nothing that the Scots nicknamed him 'Mitchell Wylie', a corruption of the Italian Macchiavelli. At their first meeting, at a dinner in 1555 hosted by the Laird of Dun, Maitland got the better of Knox in a sharp debate over attendance at Mass. At that time Maitland was still a staunch Catholic and it was as such that the Cardinal of Lorraine recommended the brilliant young lawyer to Mary of Guise as her personal secretary, a position which brought him immense influence and power. He continued in that capacity till 19 October 1559 when he deserted to the Lords of the Congregation. No turnaround was ever more dramatic or more thorough than Maitland's, bringing with him invaluable intelligence on French intentions. Three days after Maitland's defection, the Queen Mother was suspended from the regency. Maitland's talents for negotiation and persuasion were soon put to good use. His greatest coup was to win over the unreliable, self-seeking Earl of Huntly to the Protestant cause. Subsequently he brought over the powerful earls of Morton and Home, Douglas of Drumlanrig and the Kers of Ferniehirst and Cessford as well as a score of lesser nobility and gentry. This was an important accretion to the Protestant party, but it also laid the foundation for the Morton-Maitland combination which, off and on, dominated Scottish politics for good or evil over the coming years.

The turncoat Maitland, more than any other single figure, secured the ultimate triumph of the Lords of the Congregation. Where Knox was the ayatollah of the movement, Maitland was the apparatchik working quietly behind the scenes, putting the organisation on a sound footing and rallying a vast number of supporters whose interest in the religious aspects of the movement was very much subordinate to the political benefits. For a time, therefore, Maitland wielded a political power as supreme as Knox's in the ecclesiastical field. In his hands, the Scottish nobility were easily manipulated. Cecil shrewdly observed to Queen Elizabeth that Maitland was 'disposed to work the nobility to allow whatever your Majesty determine'.[5]

This alluded to the diplomatic activity then afoot whereby the Lords of the Congregation sought the military support of Elizabeth. Only three weeks after changing sides, Maitland was chosen to head a delicate mission to England which resulted in the substantial armed assistance that tipped the balance in favour of the Protestant faction. Both Cecil and Elizabeth were dazzled by his brilliant intellect, emotional eloquence and personal magnetism. Elizabeth was impressed by his obvious sincerity, but it was his fervent belief in promoting permanent goodwill between Scotland and England that affected her most of all. Subsequently it was Maitland who engineered the Treaty of Berwick (a pact for Anglo-Scottish defence against France) signed on 27 February 1560, and it was chiefly due to him that the Scots accepted the terms of the Anglo-French Treaty of Edinburgh the following July. Potentially his greatest coup was his proposal to Cecil before leaving London that if Mary could be persuaded to recognise the legitimacy of Elizabeth's rights, Elizabeth should reciprocate by naming Mary as her heir. Elizabeth's ambiguous reply did not rule out such an agreement, although she hinted that she would be happier if the Queen of Scots returned to her native land and gave up any plans of marrying a foreign prince. Maitland concealed his disappointment and replied later that he would do his utmost to keep the Scots in touch with England, for the sake of both countries.[6]

Where the French were concerned, Maitland was on less sure ground. When he heard that an emissary was coming from France to negotiate a renewal of the Auld Alliance, he feared that this would be followed by another military occupation. The Protestant Lords countered by sending Lord James to France 'to grope her mind' and try to persuade Mary to trust her subjects. The spectre of French annexation receded, and by the end of February 1561 Maitland was cautiously optimistic that, if Mary could be detached from the baneful influence of her uncles, her return to Scotland might be turned to advantage. There was some residual fear that Elizabeth's attitude might alienate Mary; it was in Maitland's best interests that Elizabeth and Mary come to some sort of agreement. Being a politician and pragmatist, and not a religious fanatic, Maitland did not share Knox's gloom at the prospect of a Catholic queen. On the contrary, after some initial apprehension, he regarded the prospect of dealing with Mary as a challenge to his diplomatic skills.

The attitude of Lord James to his half-sister's return was philosophical, and the prospect roused neither fear nor despondency in him, as it affected Maitland and Knox. After the proposal of a marriage between Elizabeth and the Earl of Arran fell through, Lord James felt that Mary's return was inevitable. From her viewpoint, it was in his favour that he had made no attempt to seize power for himself. Throckmorton reported to London as early as 31 December 1560 that Mary 'holds herself sure of the Lord James, and of all the Stewarts. She mistrusts none but the Duke of Châtelherault and his party'.[7]

By the Convention of January-February 1561 it was resolved that Lord James should cross to France and visit Mary. In general Lord James was given a free hand; only the overweening Knox saw fit to impose instructions on him:

> That if ever he condescended that she should have Mass publicly or privately within the Realm of Scotland, that then betrayed he the cause of God, and exponed the religion even to the uttermost danger that he could do.[8]

To this Lord James responded tactfully that he would never

consent that she should attend Mass publicly, but that he considered it impossible to prevent her hearing Mass in private.

Mary seems to have been just as apprehensive about Scotland as the Lords of the Congregation were about her. Even before her forty days of official mourning were completed, she was making arrangements to despatch to Scotland a delegation consisting of four Scots. Reporting on this mission on 18 January, Throckmorton stated that the commissioners had been charged with the task of persuading the Estates to remove the clause in her marriage covenant by which she could marry again only with their consent. They were also commanded to exert their influence to put a halt to the proposals of the Convention to press ahead with sweeping religious reforms, but Mary quickly backed down and countermanded these instructions. Shrewdly she realised at this early stage that 'least said, soonest mended'. Mary's discretion and tact in the matter caught the Protestant extremists, Knox included, on the wrong foot. The tenor of both her public declarations and the numerous private letters entrusted to the commissioners for the leading figures of Scotland was that she wished for reconciliation. Past offences and indiscretions were to be swept aside. She hoped for a renewal of the alliance with France; she wished the Estates would keep her informed of their deliberations; and she hoped to come back to Scotland as soon as she had wound up her affairs in France.

The only matter likely to cause disquiet was the proposed renewal of the Auld Alliance, but this soon proved to be a non-starter anyway. When Mary had expressed that hope, she had been optimistic of a marriage with Charles IX, but as that prospect receded Mary's interests in ties with France likewise evaporated. When the Estates reconvened in May, they had had reports from Lord James that allayed their fears. Consequently they could reply to King Charles diplomatically 'as to the renewal of the old friendship between the realms, for which they will not be ungrateful, consistent with their duty to their sovereign'.[9]

As soon as her period of seclusion was over, Mary accompanied her grandmother, Antoinette de Bourbon, to a small *château* near Orleans. When the court moved to Fontainebleau she went with it, specifically to meet with the English commissioner, Bedford. This interview was delayed by Throckmorton's illness until 16 February 1561. On that date the English envoys had an audience with King Charles and his mother before being conducted by the Duke of

Guise to Mary's chamber. There they found Mary with the Bishop of Amiens, various other prelates and a large gathering of ladies and gentlemen.

When they conveyed the condolences of Queen Elizabeth, Mary responded that she would 'endeavour to be even with her in goodwill'. She also expressed a wish that she and Elizabeth 'might speak together, and then she trusts that they would satisfy each other much better than they can do by messages and ministers'.[10] Mary was absolutely sincere in her desire to be on good terms with her cousin, and would quite happily have acknowledged Elizabeth's title so long as the offensive arrangement of Henry VIII debarring Mary, though next in line, from the English succession, was annulled. That Elizabeth could never see her way to concede this point lay at the heart of Mary's later plots and intrigues against her, with the most tragic consequences for Mary. Elizabeth's failure to make this concession is baffling at this remove in time. In the summer of 1561 it was widely taken for granted that the matter had been settled to the mutual advantage of the two queens. As late as 30 August, the Papal Nuncio was reporting confidently to Rome that, on the authority of the Duke of Guise no less, the matter was 'a settled thing, though not finally sanctioned'.[11]

Mary left Fontainebleau for Rheims about 18 March 1561, travelling via Paris on 20 March to inspect her robes and jewels. She reached Rheims six days later and took part in the first Guise family council since the death of King Francis. On 14 April, while travelling to stay with her grandmother at Joinville, Mary was met at Vitry by John Leslie, Parson of Oyne, Aberdeenshire, and later Bishop of Ross, who had been despatched by the Earl of Huntly and other Catholics of the north-east to invite her to return to Scotland via Aberdeen, where they promised her an army of twenty thousand Catholics who would convoy her south to Edinburgh. Sensibly Mary declined this invitation, though she softened her refusal by asking Leslie to join her retinue. Mary's chief reason for turning down the offer was that it would place her at the mercy of Huntly, who had betrayed her mother in 1554. This was a prudent move, for Huntly was one of the most volatile and least trustworthy of the Scottish nobles. With the Spanish marriage still in contention, Leslie's offer was premature.

The following day Lord James Stewart caught up with his half-sister at St Dizier. Mary, who had happy memories of her brother in her early childhood, must have entertained bitter and resentful feelings towards him, acutely aware of the political and religious barriers that now existed between them. Details of this first meeting are confused and contradictory. There seems no substance to the oft-repeated assertion that Lord James demanded the earldom of Moray as the price of his loyalty (as Leslie later asserted), or that Mary offered him a cardinal's hat if he would renounce Protestantism and return to the true faith. That Mary remonstrated with him over his religious stance is not disputed, but he apparently took this in good part. After some preliminary sparring they got down to serious business. Lord James subsequently reported to Throckmorton that Mary had agreed to be guided by the Estates in ratifying the treaty with England, that she was anxious for an improvement in relations between Scotland and England, that she was hoping that the Estates would agree to her marriage with a foreign prince, and that she was as indifferent to the friendship of France as she was to that of England.

It is surprising that Lord James, the Scottish emissary, should have been so ready to communicate with the English ambassador (and thus with Elizabeth herself); indeed, to pass on vital intelligence to a foreign power before informing his own government. On the face of it, this smacks of treachery; but neither his instructions from the Scots, nor Mary's own wishes, precluded him from revealing the gist of his conversation to the English. As Lord James hoped that Queen Elizabeth would adopt a conciliatory attitude to her cousin, he was quite prepared to bend over backwards to co-operate with her government. In any case, James shrewdly surmised that Mary was not telling him everything, or revealing her true intentions. This was borne out by her refusal to allow him to accompany her to Nancy, the principal seat of the Guises in Lorraine, and he suspected that she wished to conceal from him the details of the negotiations over the marriage to Don Carlos which were now at a crucial stage. Lord James parted company with his sister and returned forthwith to Paris, arriving there on 23 April and having a full discussion with Throckmorton the following day.[12] Mary herself wrote to Throckmorton from Nancy on 22 April, saying that she had met her brother, but that his visit was of a private and personal nature and not official in character.[13]

Lord James tarried at Paris till 4 May, waiting for letters from Mary. When this correspondence duly arrived, he was disappointed that it did not contain the coveted commission appointing him regent until her return to Scotland. By hinting to this effect, Mary had sought to delay James until the matter of the Spanish marriage was resolved. By 9 May Throckmorton learned that Mary was sick of an ague at Nancy, but this may have been some sort of psycho-somatic ailment induced by the shock that the negotiations with Philip II had fizzled out. Throckmorton, unaware of this Spanish development till 23 June, reported to London on 9 May his suspicion that Mary was only feigning illness in order to delay ratifying the treaty with England. Throckmorton hoped to seize the opportunity of the boy-king's coronation at Rheims on 15 May to pin down Mary on this matter. But Mary was still prostrate with disappointment by mid-May and did not get farther than her grandmother's *château* at Joinville where she remained till after the court had returned to Paris. She did not go on to Rheims until 28 May. On 10 June she went back to Paris, joining the French court at the Louvre. Brantôme has left a vivid account of the appearance of Mary, her beauty heightened by her pallor and the white robes which signified her great grief. He adds that the young King Charles was so entranced by the frail beauty of *La Reine Blanche* that Catherine could not hustle her away from the court fast enough.

Throckmorton had his audience with Mary at the Louvre on 18 June. To his pressing question about ratifying the treaty she replied that she would not make up her mind until she had had the advice of the Estates, though she added 'that she meant to retire all the French out of Scotland, so that she would leave nothing undone to satisfy all parties'.[14] On the subject of religion she was disarmingly candid. 'She was none of those who would change her religion every year; she did not mean to constrain any of her subjects, but trusted they would have no support at the Queen's hands to constrain her.' Subsequently Mary sent her personal envoy, Henri Cleutin d'Oysel, to Scotland via England to prepare the way, diplomatically and politically, for her return to her kingdom. Throckmorton, unfortunately, supposed that d'Oysel, while seeking a safe conduct for Mary through England to Scotland, would do everything in his power to dissolve the incipient alliance between Scotland and England and bind the Scots more closely to the French. In view of this misunderstanding it is hardly surprising that Elizabeth refused to let d'Oysel proceed to Scotland, but sent him back to France with the message that as soon as Mary had ratified the treaty, she would give her cousin a safe-conduct pass as well as arrange 'a friendly meeting for corroboration and perfection of their amity'.[15]

Some historians blame Mary for throwing away a golden opportunity to settle her differences with Elizabeth; but so long as Elizabeth refused to admit the validity of Mary's claim to the succession, a meeting between the two queens seemed pointless. Nevertheless, it is one of those might-have-beens of history. Had Elizabeth and Mary met in the summer of 1561, and taken the measure of each other, the course of Anglo-Scottish history might have been radically different. As it was, they never met, though Mary must often have regretted this. In mitigation of Elizabeth's obduracy, it should be noted that she genuinely feared that, once she acknowledged Mary's claim to be her successor, she would effectively be signing her own death warrant.

Mary's deference to the wishes of the Estates, while it may have been intended mainly to temporise with Elizabeth, put her in good standing with the Scottish parliament, which took a similar line in dealing directly with the English government. The tone of the letters from the Scottish Council to Queen Elizabeth was courteous but ambivalent, though Cecil was privately assured by Maitland of Mary's good intentions and desire for closer accord with England. On 14 July Cecil wrote to Throckmorton in confidence, stating that if Mary surrendered her claims to the English throne, Elizabeth would acknowledge her 'in default of heirs of the English Queen'. Cecil said that Elizabeth knew of this proposal and considered it feasible, though he hoped that she would resolve the matter by marrying and producing a son and heir.

Maitland was hopeful that some accommodation between the two queens would be speedily arranged. On 10 June Lord James wrote a friendly letter to Mary, tantamount to an invitation from the Lords of the Congregation to her to return to Scotland. A letter from Maitland to Mary about the same date hints that he would do his utmost to promote her interests. Finally Lord James himself wrote to Queen Elizabeth in July respectfully reminding her that 'by the law of all nations' his sovereign lady was next in lawful descent 'of the right line of King Henry the seventh your grandfather'.[16] Over the ensuing six weeks he and Maitland travelled extensively all over the north of Scotland, 'advancing the religion and the common cause', as Maitland reported to Cecil on 10 August.

Maitland continued to work feverishly to improve relations

between the two queens. Sensing the impasse over the ratification of the treaty, Maitland tactfully suggested to Elizabeth the creation of a Protestant league including Scotland and England. While Maitland and Lord James conceded that, until Mary and Elizabeth were on more cordial terms, Mary's departure from France should be delayed, they would have been horrified if they had seen the instructions from the Privy Council to Throckmorton, stating bluntly that the longer the Scottish queen's affairs were uncertain the better should Queen Elizabeth's affairs prosper, 'especially as long as she thus forbeareth to confirm the treaty'.[17] This obsession with ratifying the treaty bedevilled Anglo-Scottish relations at this sensitive time. Neither Maitland nor Lord James wished Mary to sign the treaty at this juncture, and continued to stress to Cecil the advisablility of conciliating Mary. Maitland's fears as to Elizabeth's good intentions were intensified when he discovered from d'Oysel that she would do everything in her power to prevent Mary going home.

There is ample evidence that Elizabeth planned to intercept Mary, on the high seas if need be, and prevent her reaching Scotland, but Maitland reasoned that a couple of swift galleys might easily evade the English vessels patrolling the Channel and the North Sea. In the event, Elizabeth bowed to the inevitable. Realising that her cousin remained adamant, common sense took over, and she did nothing further to stop her. When even Throckmorton expressed to Cecil his astonishment at Elizabeth's refusal to grant a passport to Mary, his views were doubtless conveyed to the Queen who may have realised how petty and pointless her action had been. Finally, Mary herself wrote a very conciliatory letter to Elizabeth on 8 August. Although this has not survived, we get the gist of it from Elizabeth's reply of 15 August saying that as Mary proposed to be guided by her Council she had suspended her 'concept of all unkindness'. And with this letter she enclosed the long-desired passport; but before it reached Paris Mary had already set sail for Scotland without it.

On 21 July Mary again saw Throckmorton and hoped that she would get a favourable wind that would steer her well clear of the English coast; but if not, she was quite resigned to placing herself in Elizabeth's hands. She even joked that if Elizabeth were so hard-hearted as to desire her end, 'she might then do her pleasure and make sacrifice of her'.[18] That evening Mary went to Saint-Germain for the start of a four-day farewell fête in her honour. On 25 July, accompanied by her six Guise uncles and other friends, she set out for the coast. At Beauvais she waited for several days for the return from England of the secretary of the King of Navarre. What news he was expected to bring is not known; but whether she was influenced by this or not, she despatched her envoy Lord St Colme to Elizabeth with a special message, and in this connection she requested Throckmorton to call on her at Abbeville, which he did on 8 August. That evening Mary continued her journey to Calais and after sending St Colme off on his vital mission, she boarded ship on 14 August.

The Duke of Guise and the Cardinal of Lorraine dared not accompany her, for the preservation of their interests was now uppermost in their minds, but at least they would give their niece a good send-off. On the quayside the Cardinal suggested that she should entrust her valuable collection of jewellery to him for safe-keeping. Mary gave him a quizzical half-smile and retorted that if he was willing to trust her to the high seas, then surely her valuables would be safe too. The Queen and her extensive retinue took passage aboard two of the fastest rowing-galleys belonging to her uncle, the Grand Prior. It was confidently believed that these ships, commanded by Villegaignon and Octavio Bosso, could outrun the fleetest English warships, but as an added precaution, they were escorted out of Calais by two of the largest battleships in the French navy.

Mary was accompanied by three of her Guise uncles, Claude, Duke of Aumale, Grand Prior Francis and René, Marquis of Elboeuf. Among the large retinue of French and Scottish courtiers were Brantôme, Castelnau and Pierre de Châtelard, the recently elevated Bishop Leslie, and the four Maries who had been her companions on the outward voyage twelve years earlier. Mary's sombre mood as she embarked was not helped by an accident in which a boat capsized in the harbour with the loss of all hands. 'What augury is this!' she exclaimed dolefully. This tragedy visibly affected her throughout the homeward voyage, so that she seemed quite impervious to the perils of the sea and the ever-present danger of interception alike. So long as the French coast was in sight, she stood on deck repeating endlessly and almost hysterically, 'Adieu! Adieu, France!' and as the land sank beneath the horizon she renewed her wailing, 'Adieu, France! C'en est fait! Adieu, France, je pense ne vous revoir jamais plus!' The premonition that she would never see France again, the only place in which she had ever been truly happy, only deepened her depression.

Despite the issue of the safe-conduct pass, Elizabeth never rescinded the orders to her navy whose warships continued to scour the North Sea for the French expedition. On 17 August the Earl of Rutland, Lord President of the North, reported to Cecil that at three o'clock that morning the two French galleys had been sighted off Flamborough Head and he was confident of capturing them. They were so close to the shore that people could discern their flags and highly distinctive livery. Intriguingly, Rutland also mentioned two squadrons of thirty-two and twenty sail some way behind the galleys. It can only be assumed that if the sightings were accurate these ships were either merchantmen, in no way connected with Mary's galleys, or warships of Elizabeth's own navy. Castelnau's description of the voyage corroborates the latter theory, for he says that these round-bottomed sailing ships could not overtake the galleys on account of their speed. The trip was otherwise uneventful, a providential fog having descended on the galleys as they neared Berwick, forcing them to anchor offshore until the evening of 18 August. The fog lifted at nightfall, enabling them to continue without further trouble. During the night they entered the Firth of Forth and anchored off Leith early the following morning. There was a typical east-coast haar that morning, a far cry from the superstitious nonsense penned by John Knox about the 'dolorous face of the heavens' foreshadowing the 'sorrow, dolour, darkness and all impiety'[19] which the arrival of this young queen was to bring into Scotland, giving the impression that a summer fog was almost as rare an occurrence as a solar eclipse.

As for Mary herself, we can imagine that her first impressions of her kingdom were not very favourable. In addition to the dour, dreich weather, her arrival was greeted with total silence. The summons to the nobility and magistrates of Scotland to assemble at Edinburgh to greet their sovereign in a fitting manner presupposed an arrival towards the end of August; so when the galleys berthed at Leith a week ahead of schedule (and early in the morning at that) and fired a salute, the Queen was greeted only by a straggle of curious dockers and other common people. Instead of being whisked off in a triumphal procession to Holyrood, Mary repaired straightway to the residence of Andrew Lambie, a Leith merchant with whom Mary of Guise had had some business dealings. There, in the most modest of surroundings, Mary received the Duke of Châtelherault, closely followed by Lord James and the Earl of Arran.

As Holyroodhouse had not been made ready for her occupation, it was not until evening that Mary set off up the long hill towards Edinburgh. Brantôme, inevitably, has left a tragi-comic account of the proceedings, with a wry description of the shaggy ponies, crudely saddled, that formed her cavalcade. The sumptuous costumes of the Queen and her mainly French retinue contrasted sharply with the drab appearance of the 'sundry noble men and the town of Edinburgh' who accompanied her to her palace. As the ragged cavalcade set off, bonfires were lit on Calton Hill and the Salisbury Crags. Knox describes how 'a company of the most honest, with instruments of musick, and with musicians, gave their salutations at her chamber window'.[20] Brantôme, however, is probably nearer the truth when he describes Knox's company of honest men as 'five or six hundred *marauds*', scroungers who, accompanied by out-of-tune fiddles and rebecs, chanted doleful psalms in a crazy cacophony.

To this tuneless, tasteless serenade Mary responded tactfully. According to Knox she affirmed 'that the melody liked her well; and she willed the same to be continued some nights after'. On the whole, however, she got a warm and heartfelt reception, and if the welcome from the Catholics was the more joyful, that of the Protestants was no less sincere; for they were patriots first and foremost, and their hearts went out to their beautiful young queen, the daughter of their proud dynasty, who had braved the elements and the threats of her mighty cousin to trust herself to the goodwill of her people. Her youth, her beauty, her personal magnetism and her courage endeared her to everyone. Her popularity was as immediate as it was widespread.

4. MARY AND ELIZABETH

1561–62

The daughter of debate
That discord ay did sowe
Shall reape no gaine where former rule
Hath taught stil peace to growe.
    Queen Elizabeth on her cousin Mary

Mary arrived in her capital on a Tuesday. The widespread rejoicing and euphoria at the return of this beautiful young queen, so warm, affable and radiant, lasted all of four days. Any delusion she may have nurtured about winning back her loving subjects to the old faith was dramatically shattered on her first Sunday, however, when she attended Mass in the Chapel Royal at Holyrood, accompanied by her uncles and her personal household. This insensitive outrage 'pierced the hearts of all' in the words of John Knox, though, to be sure, these sentiments were confined to the religious extremists like himself. In no time at all a vicious mob had been whipped up by Knox's henchman, the thuggish Master of Lindsay. As the sixth Lord Lindsay of the Byres, he would later become Mary's bitterest and most implacable enemy, but on this fair Sunday morning he contented himself with leading the cries for the lynching of the 'idolatre Priest'. The ugly situation was only saved from total disaster by Lord James who, having promised his sister that she could worship in her own way so long as she did it in private, pointedly stood on guard at the chapel door. Afterwards, as Lindsay's bullies pushed and jostled the terrified French priest, it was Lord James and his stalwart brothers Robert and John who escorted him back to his quarters.

Word of the incident spread like wildfire and by evening an unruly crowd of several hundreds had congregated at the entrance to Holyroodhouse and screamed their disapproval. Mary acted swiftly to defuse the situation. The following morning she issued a proclamation forbidding everyone, until the Estates convened, from making any change or innovation in the religious situation which she had found 'publictlie and universallie standing at her Majestie's arryvell in this her Realme, under the pane of death'. At the same time all the lieges were ordered not to molest or trouble 'in wourd, deed or countenance' any of the Queen's French servants or attendants. This proclamation, intended to take the heat out of the situation, only exacerbated it. It inferred that the recently established Protestant faith was merely a temporary arrangement effected by an irregular convention when Scotland was virtually in a state of civil war. Effectively it put the religious dispute on hold until Mary's argument with Elizabeth was settled. In the meantime Mary, as sovereign, claimed the right to determine what religion she herself should profess.

As the dust settled, it became evident that Scotland was sharply divided between the Protestants (in the ascendancy) and the Catholics (momentarily in disarray). In England, Protestantism had come to imply a certain measure of religious freedom, the excesses of the clergy being held in check by the secularity and self-interest of the monarch. In Scotland, during what had effectively been an interregnum, the only obstacle to Knox and his fanatical cohorts had been the worldly ambition of the nobility and their innate suspicion and jealousy of clerics. Mary was at a disadvantage; while her kingdom had been practically ungovernable in the past two years, Elizabeth, by contrast, had moved quickly and decisively to overturn and undermine the intolerance and bigotry of her own predecessor. Protestantism triumphant was more benign in England and the power and prestige of the monarchy were only enhanced as a result. In Scotland, however, the monarchy had never enjoyed such ascendancy, the sovereign being first among equals rather than set apart from the nobility.

Previous rulers of Scotland only had to contend with factiousness among the great nobles. Now Mary had to deal with something entirely novel, an ecclesiastic whose power far exceeded that previously wielded by any cardinal or archbishop. It was Mary's misfortune to be confronted by the towering personality of Knox, overwhelming even more by virtue of his defects than by reason of his merits. His practical wisdom, his strident eloquence, his dour adherence to principle, his unflinching integrity and incomparable self-assurance would have been a powerful enough combination, but they were enhanced rather than diminished by his negative qualities. The narrow-minded bigot possessed a shallow intellect and a curiously blinkered outlook. Knox never questioned his own beliefs or entertained a single doubt concerning his infallibility. He was firmly convinced that he had been appointed by God Almighty. On his broad shoulders had fallen the mantle of Elijah and his divine mission was to lead Scotland to true enlightenment. Mary's sense of her own divine right, well developed though it was, was as nothing compared with Knox's almost mystical belief in his own God-given powers. While Knox paid lip service to the notion of being one of Mary's subjects, he never wavered for one minute in his claim to ecclesiastical superiority more powerful and infinitely more far-reaching than that of any pope, because his claims were both political and ecclesiastical. Sooner or later, therefore, there was bound to be a clash. There is abundant evidence that Mary, far from being a ruthless fanatic for the old religion, was pragmatic and tolerant, always seeking an accommodation with the new faith and doing rather little to protect her fellow Catholics. But even if Mary had meekly given way and conformed wholeheartedly to the Protestantism which had now been imposed on her subjects, Knox would never have rested until he had effectively robbed her of every vestige of her temporal sovereignty.

The first round in the battle of wills came on Sunday, 31 August, when Knox thundered from the pulpit that even a single celebration of the Mass was 'more fearful to him than gif ten thousand armed enemyes were landed in any pairte of the Realme, of purpose to suppress the haill religioun'.[1] Outwardly Mary was calm, shrugging off the immoderate language of the fiery sermon, but inwardly she was seething with anger. As soon as an opportunity presented itself, she would lock horns with this unruly cleric.

For the moment, however, she was preoccupied with settling in, testing the water rather than flexing her muscles. On the very evening that Knox delivered his first counterblast, Mary and her uncles were entertained by the provost and magistrates of Edinburgh at a sumptuous banquet. Two days later she paid a formal visit to her capital, travelling in state from her palace, along the Royal

Mile thronged with cheering crowds, and up the hill to the castle where she dined at noon. Elaborate preparations were made to mark the Queen's first official entry into the city, although Knox, in his usual sour-grapes manner, dismissed the jollification alliteratively as 'in farces, in maskings and in other prodigalities, fain would fools have counterfooted France'.[2]

After dining in fine style with the leading citizens and nobility, Mary made a formal progress back down the Castle Hill and the High Street to her palace in a stately litter surmounted by a pall of fine purple velvet borne over her head by twelve representatives of the magistrates, followed by a procession of fifty young men dressed as Moors, and leading burgesses uniformly attired in a colourful costume which had been designed specially for the occasion. As she approached the Butter Tron she heard an angelic choir composed of young children. As she passed through the richly ornamented gateway a beautiful child disguised as a cherub descended from the arch like some pantomime fairy and gracefully presented Mary with the keys of the city, 'together with a bible and a psalm book covered with fine purple velvet'.[3] Knox was a grim eye-witness of this charade and dourly recorded:

> The verses of her own praise she heard and smiled. But when
> the Bible was presented and the praise thereof declared, she
> began to frown: for shame she could not refuse it. But she did
> no better, for immediately, she gave it to the most pestilent
> Papist within the Realm, to wit to Arthur Erskine.[4]

Mary was merely passing the gifts of the vernacular bible and Protestant prayerbook in all innocence to the captain of her guard for the sake of convenience, but we may be sure that nothing less than a dramatic renunciation of Catholicism on the spot would have satisfied the self-appointed spiritual leader of his country.

If the counterfeit angels of the Butter Tron, like some over-ambitious, under-rehearsed school nativity play of modern times, failed to produce the desired instant conversion, the next spectacle was even less likely to have had this effect. At the Salt Tron Mary was confronted by a tableau in which the biblical idolaters Coron, Nathan and Abiron were burned at the stake. This was bad enough, but when the performers made to burn the effigy of a priest in his vestments, as if about to say Mass, the Earl of Huntly intervened to suppress the pageant. Nevertheless, the damage was done, and it was a grim-faced Mary who proceeded down the Canongate towards her palace. There, before the gates, she was buttonholed by a gaggle of children who chanted to her an exhortation to put away the Mass. Knox does not record how Mary received this unwarranted intrusion, though she was apparently mollified by the presentation of the city's gift, a beautifully gilded cupboard which had cost Edinburgh two thousand marks, or about half of the sum expended on the entire celebrations.

What should have been a joyful occasion was marred by the crudely propagandist elements masterminded by John Knox. Within forty-eight hours he was summoned to Holyrood for a right royal reprimand. Regrettably the audience was private, and neither Mary nor any of her closest aides left a record of it, though John Knox more than made up for that, in his own manifestly biased account. Lord James was present throughout the interview, but characteristically he remained in the background and said nothing. Two ladies-in-waiting were also present, but they might have been articles of furniture, for all that their presence served.

It is clear, even from Knox's one-sided account, that Mary had been spoiling for a confrontation with him for some time. He had been a tiresome thorn in her mother's flesh for several years, and Mary, who had loved her mother intensely, probably blamed Knox directly or indirectly for the Queen-Dowager's untimely death. Mary went straight for the jugular, upbraiding Knox for fomenting civil disturbances and inciting her subjects to rebellion. One is left with a clear impression that the religious aspect of the struggle was very much secondary to the question of law and order. Mary's first-hand experience of religious disturbances in France gave her the firm impression that Protestants came in two categories: those who whipped up the people to question the rightful authority of the sovereign, and the decent, honest people who were led astray by demagogues and the harangues of unprincipled rogues. There was no doubt in which category she placed John Knox.

With all the skill of the veteran debater, Knox let the young queen make her spirited speech and when she had paused for breath he immediately leaped in with a tirade on his favourite topic, the monstrous regiment of women. There was the question as to whether Mary, as a woman, had any right of sovereignty at all. Condescingly, he answered the question himself saying that provided Mary did as he desired, and on the supposition that the realm found no inconvenience from the government of a woman, that which the people approved of he would not 'farther disallow than within my own breast'.

The insolence of the fellow almost took her breath away, but Mary seems to have given as good as she got. Even Knox, in his biased account, could not conceal this fact. Mary maintained her position with a dexterity and skill which were the equal of Knox's assertiveness.

'Conscience, Madam,' said he, 'requires knowledge and, I fear, right knowledge ye have none.'

'But I have both heard and read,' she riposted.

So the argument raged on. Both were equally convinced of the rightness of their respective cause. It was a case of an infallible Church pitted against an infallible Book. Both were forced to retreat into entrenched positions bolstered by their respective faiths, and nothing would budge either of them. Mary seems to have had a certain sneaking admiration for the courage and integrity of her opponent, although she was well aware of his ambitions. At one stage in the argument she summed this up pithily: 'Well, then, I perceive that my subjects shall obey you and not me; and shall do what they list, and not what I command: and so must I be subject to them and not they to me.'

Without batting an eyelid, Knox replied, 'This subjection unto God, and unto his troubled Church, is the greatest dignity that flesh can get upon the face of the earth, for it shall carry them to everlasting glory.'

'Yes. But ye are not the Kirk that I will nourish. I will defend the Kirk of Rome for, I think, it is the true Kirk of God.'

With that, Knox realised that he was dealing with a hopelessly incorrigible female. 'If there be not in her a proud mind, a crafty wit, and an indurate heart against God and His truth, my judgment faileth me,' he wrote. By this, of course, Knox meant his own interpretation of God's truth.

In the end he graciously conceded that he was 'well content to live under your Grace, as Paul was to live under Nero, so long as that ye defile not your hands in the blood of the saints of God'. When he likened a Catholic monarch to a mad father whose children restrained him to prevent him killing them, and observed that it was the duty of subjects to disobey a Catholic monarch because he was dangerously wrong, Mary exploded with wrath at his intemperate language. According to Knox, she was rendered speechless for upwards of a quarter of an hour; but it was not astonishment at the treasonable rudeness of his speech that silenced her. She was so angry that she could not trust herself. With superhuman willpower she restrained herself, and her brother, sensing her distress, rushed to her side, but already Knox was off at a tangent with a long and extremely convoluted sermon. At length he wound up his tedious peroration and Mary looked down on him sardonically, saying simply, 'Ye are ower sair for me.' Now it was her turn to state in simplistic terms the doctrines in which she had believed since early childhood. This verbal duel dragged on, leading nowhere, until they were interrupted by a courtier with the welcome news that the Queen's dinner was ready. Needless to say, the turbulent priest was not invited to the dinner-table.

To his immediate impression of the proud mind, crafty wit and an indurate heart, Knox, on reflection a few weeks later added that 'In communication with her I espied such craft as I have not found in such age.' He recognised in this girl a dangerous adversary; ever afterwards he would use every device to undermine her authority.

On 6 September 1561 Mary appointed her Privy Council from the leading nobles of the kingdom regardless of their political or religious outlook. Six of them were to live with her, a kitchen cabinet to assist her with the routine business of government. This admirable system soon fell into abeyance, however, and the administration remained firmly in the hands of Lord James and Maitland. On 2 September the Duke of Aumale had sailed back to France with the two galleys, but the other Guise uncles remained for some weeks. They were at her side when she set off with a large party of the Scottish nobility to visit her royal residences and some of the country's main towns.

Leaving Holyrood on 11 September, Mary reached Linlithgow by evening and spent the night in the palace in which she had been born. Two days later she set off for Stirling Castle which had also played a dramatic role in her early life. There, on Sunday, 14 September, her chaplains began to sing High Mass in the Chapel Royal, immediately precipitating an unpleasant incident. According to the English ambassador, Thomas Randolph, 'Argyll and Lord James so disturbed the choir that some, both priests and clerks, left their places with broken heads and bloody ears.'⁵ Such a fracas would have been upsetting enough, but the spectacle of Lord James, who had hitherto protected Mary, now belabouring her clerics with a cudgel, unnerved her completely. To make matters worse, Mary came very close to death that evening when she fell asleep with a lit candle at her bedside. This set alight the heavy drapes of her four-poster and she only narrowly escaped asphyxiation. Having survived this fire, she set out the following morning for Perth. Along the route her entourage passed the dismal blackened ruins of several monasteries which had recently been put to the torch, and one may imagine Mary's feelings of anger and disgust at the wanton destruction, all in the name of religion. At Perth she was received cordially enough, but the gift of a gold heart stuffed with gold coins did little to improve her mood.

That afternoon, as she rode up the main street, Mary was suddenly assailed by yet another of those mysterious ailments which may have been psychosomatic, induced by stress, or may even have been induced by the gene disorder porphyria from which many of her descendants (most notably George III) also suffered. Fortunately her lodgings were near by, and after a good night's rest she was ready to go on, the following day, to Dundee. After crossing the Tay she rode on to St Andrews where the handiwork of the reformers was all too evident in the fallen masonry of the once-magnificent cathedral. Thomas Randolph relates a story (which he did not fully believe himself) that a priest had been murdered there the previous Sunday. Either along the road, or in St Andrews itself, there was an unseemly quarrel between Lord James and the Earl of Huntly, sparked off by the latter's assertion that, if the Queen commanded, he would set up the Mass in three counties. Mary, however, had more sense than to order such folly. From St Andrews she went on to Falkland Palace near the Lomond Hills, where her father had wasted away after the débâcle at Solway Moss.

Fighting the temptation to go hunting in the extensive game forest adjoining the palace, Mary hurried back to Edinburgh on 29 September. No doubt she had by this time got wind of the activities of her enemies in her absence. This time the challenge to her authority came from Edinburgh's town council which issued a proclamation on 2 October. The provost, bailies and council, having perceived the priests, monks, friars 'and others of the wicked rabble of the antechrist [sic], the Pope', resorting to the town, now ordered 'all monks, friars, priests, nuns, adulterers, fornicators and all such filthy persons' to remove themselves from the area, 'under the pain of carting through the town, burning on the cheek and banishing the same for ever'.[6] This was a restatement of a proclamation of March 1561, but the timing was calculated to offer the maximum insult to the Queen, besides being much more offensive in its wording. Significantly, while the earlier proclamation had been made in the name of 'our Soverane Ladie', this document was published by authority of the town council, itself a direct challenge to Mary's authority.

To her credit, Mary did not act in the white heat of the moment, but evidently gave long and careful consideration to what she should do, for it was not until 5 October that she sent a summons to the council, requesting their attendance at the Tolbooth three days later, when the provost and bailies were summarily stripped of their offices. This was promptly followed by a royal proclamation announcing that the town would be 'patent to all lieges', that is to say, free and open to all law-abiding subjects. Needless to say, Knox (who seems to have had a hand in drafting the offensive proclamation) dismissed Mary's decisive action as being motivated by 'pride and maliciousness'. It merely reinforced his view 'that the Cardinal's lessons ar so deeply printed in her heart, that the substance and the quality are liek to perish together',[7] but what annoyed him most of all was that Mary had the wholehearted support of Lord James and Maitland.

Knox was not the only person to tackle Mary regarding her religion. The English ambassador, Thomas Randolph, tried to show her the error of her ways, albeit in a far more diplomatic and respectful manner than Knox, by proffering her tracts on the subject. Commenting on Randolph's well-meaning interference, Mary told Lord James that she could not reason, but she knew what she ought to believe. Interestingly, Mary's response to Randolph himself was cleverly couched in the jargon so beloved of the reformers. According to the ambassador, Lord James continued to deal with the Queen 'rudely, homely and bluntly', and Maitland 'more delicately and finely' while Mary was 'patient to hear and beareth much'.[8] Disturbed by the Queen's obduracy, Knox even wrote to his friend Calvin in Geneva on 24 October seeking his advice on how to deal with a monarch who maintained that it was unlawful for 'ministers of the Word' to prohibit her from openly professing her religion. In point of fact, Protestantism was, at that time, on thin ice, legally speaking. It had been authorised by a parliament which had not been properly summoned and whose proceedings had never had the royal assent. Calvin, who headed a theocratic republic, was not the most disinterested party to consult on such a ticklish matter, for he held the robust view that rulers should either be reformed or expelled 'by them by whom they were chosen'. Scotland did not quite come into this category, despite Knox's fervent wish that it did.

On All Hallows Day (1 November) Mary celebrated a choral Mass in her chapel at Holyroodhouse, but one of her priests was beaten up by a servant of Lord Robert Stewart who had taken grave exception to this musical celebration. This incident brought matters to a head, the Protestant ministers now openly raising the question of whether it was right to obey such an idolatrous ruler any longer. At a meeting of the Council with the leading Protestant divines at the home of James MacGill, the Clerk Registrar, Knox offered to write to Geneva to seek advice on the point, omitting to add that he had already taken this step. Maitland neatly sidestepped this by saying that he himself would write to Calvin on the matter. This was no more than a feint, for shortly afterwards it was resolved that the Queen and her household should be allowed to practise their faith in her own chapel. In 1564 when the matter was again raised, MacGill was under the impression that Knox had written to Calvin in 1561, to which Knox retorted that Maitland had refused his consent. Clearly Knox was being economical with the truth. He never mentioned a reply from Calvin and it can only be assumed that Calvin's advice was far too moderate for Knox's liking.

Lord James had already given his promise to Mary regarding the private practice of her religion, so he could hardly go back on his word now, though he recognised the danger in such an unsatis-factory arrangement. Pragmatist that he was, he hoped that the matter would quietly resolve itself in due course, seeking a solution to the religious and political impasse through a closer accord with Elizabeth. That unfortunate business over the passport, com-pounded by the hostile activities of the English navy during her voyage to Scotland, made it very difficult for Mary to make friendly overtures to her cousin. For her part, Elizabeth could not now climb down without some loss of face. So the situation between them remained deadlocked. Mary's initial reaction to Thomas Randolph, when he presented his credentials two days after her arrival, was to ask him suspiciously what he was doing there and when was he leaving Scotland. Mary thawed visibly when the ambassador explained Elizabeth's last-minute change of heart and apologised over the delay in sending the passport which St Colme brought from Paris soon afterwards.

On 1 September, therefore, Mary despatched Maitland to London to announce her safe arrival and to reaffirm her wish for improved relations between the two kingdoms. Maitland hoped that Elizabeth would now recognise Mary as her heir, and then the treaty could be ratified. Elizabeth, however, insisted on ratification first, and then she would consider the matter of the succession. Elizabeth made her father's mistake of treating Mary and the Scots not on equal terms but with the condescension of a suzerain to a satellite, a habit deeply engrained in most English monarchs since William the Conqueror. Maitland gently pointed out to Elizabeth that the good conceit she had of herself was not necessarily shared by the world at large which had quite a different perspective on Scotland and England. In short, he felt that Elizabeth had as good, and probably better, reasons for reaching an understanding with Mary, as Mary had for coming to an understanding with her. His blunt speech was tempered by the assertion that he spoke only as the friend of both countries and both queens, and could not speak personally for Mary.

Maitland's argument had both logic and justice on its side, but these are factors that fly out of the window where international relations are concerned. It was expedient for the two rulers to make common cause, but however much the interest of both might have been served by some amicable agreement, this was found to be impossible. Had the monarchs been men, so the traditional argument runs, such an accord might have been possible; but because they were women there was 'the incalculable element of feminine idiosyncrasies'.[9] The plain truth, however, is that Elizabeth was extremely reluctant to settle the matter of the succession. Aside from the ever-present fear of assassination, this matter was complicated by the possibility that Mary, as a Catholic, would always pose the threat of a Catholic insurrection in her favour. Conversely, as long as Elizabeth left the question unresolved, her position was strengthened. It is probable that, even by this early date, Elizabeth had already made up her mind never to marry. Consequently, at the back of her mind, was the probability that the day would come when either Mary or her offspring would get the English throne; but that, hopefully, was a very long way off. For the moment, therefore, Elizabeth was content to let the matter ride. So she quipped to Maitland, 'Think you that I could love my own winding-sheet? Princes cannot like their own children.' Even if Elizabeth would not go so far as to name her successor, Maitland felt that the least she could have done was to rescind the clause in her father's will disqualifying Mary from her rightful inheritance; but Elizabeth was not inclined to take any step that might diminish her own status, however indirectly.

Each queen also had a very different set of goals. Elizabeth, unlike her father, had no territorial ambitions in Scotland, and it was of little consequence what happened to England or Scotland after her death. She was solely concerned with governing England to the best of her ability and raising her country to the dignity and status of a great mercantile and political power. Her own career was inextricably bound up in England's glory, and there is more than a measure of truth in her oft-repeated assertion that she was married to the realm of England.

Mary, on the other hand, had recently suffered an incalculable loss. From being the queen-consort of one of the most powerful nations, she was reduced to going back to a country she hardly knew and barely remembered, a country which was in turmoil, and in which her future was uncertain. Against this background, her ambition to see Scotland and England united under her rule is understandable. The religious question was not a major issue so far as she was concerned. She started out with a desire for general toleration: let every man worship according to his own conscience. Sadly, she soon discovered that in the real world tolerance was a rare commodity, and she was hard-pressed to win a measure of toleration for herself.

Maitland wrote to Robert Dudley on 13 November 1561 in the hope of getting him to influence Elizabeth in his aim of bringing the two queens together: 'such a couple of ladies, as I think the world did never see the like in our age'. And he went on to state that in Queen Mary he had discovered 'a reciprocal goodwill double more and more increased, which of late hath taken so deep root that her Majesty doth now wish nothing more earnestly than that she may once have occasion to see her good sister'.[10] It seems likely that the outcome of this letter was a proposal from Elizabeth herself that she and Mary should commence a private correspondence. Although she dropped more than a hint that some explanation for the non-ratification of the treaty was desirable, she added grandly that 'we will require nothing but that which in like honour, justice and reason you ought to grant'. It was all so sweetly reasonable; given the mutual goodwill of two such intelligent monarchs, both uniquely motivated, how could they fail to reach an agreement?

Elizabeth's initial letter to her cousin was delivered to Mary by Randolph on 12 December 1561. Randolph wrote to London five days later that, following a subsequent meeting with the Queen, he had elicited the reason for her delay in answering. Mary revealed that she had waited till a meeting of the Convention. Another reason was caution on Mary's part. Until she knew why her cousin had had a change of heart she could not respond fully. Accordingly, Maitland wrote to Cecil on 15 December, saying that he had advised Mary to defer an answer for a few days. In the meantime he would be glad to have Cecil's opinion 'how the same may be so framed, so as neither be pained nor miscontented'. And he took the opportunity to reassure Cecil that Mary was willing to do anything if 'made sure of her title' but that 'to enter into a demand and find a repulse, it would much offend her, being of such courage'. When no reply from Cecil was immediately forthcoming, Maitland wrote again on 26 December, to the effect that he was delaying Mary's answer until he had received this advice. Cecil replied on 3 January 1562 ignoring the main points in Maitland's letters and merely stating that he was 'something offended' that Maitland had sought his advice. It is possible that Cecil had not been privy to Elizabeth's initial letter and was somewhat annoyed on that score; but this exchange of letters alone would have put Maitland on his guard respecting an early outbreak of frank cordiality between the two queens.

When Mary eventually answered Elizabeth's opening letter she did so fully and frankly. Even setting aside the value of the treaty in the changed circumstances, far less its legal validity, Mary answered her cousin's question with one of her own. Was it reasonable, she asked, to expect that she could willingly ratify a treaty so deeply prejudicial to her own interests and prospects? She was ready to do everything concerning the treaty that might be reasonably expected of her, although she would prefer that an entirely new treaty be drafted. She ended in the hope that she and Elizabeth might meet soon, when she would 'mair clearly perceive the sincerity of her good meaning' than she could express in writing.[11] This reveals a refreshingly conciliatory spirit. Elizabeth may have been hard, cold and calculating, but the warmth of Mary's vibrant personality shines through. That her motives in cultivating this friendship lacked the sinister character with which some nineteenth-century historians imbued her is clearly demonstrated by her letter to the Duke of Guise on 5 January 1562. A sincere wish to be on good terms with the Queen of England was uppermost in her mind. By contrast, Catholicism, and the restoration of the old religion to her own kingdom, were now very much of secondary importance. In this respect she differed quite radically from her namesake, Mary Tudor, whose devotion to Catholicism was the be-all and end-all of her existence, and who had made the restoration and advancement of her faith the principal plank of her political platform.

Elizabeth, on the other hand, was unsure how to respond to such a candid letter. Having maintained a high-handed approach previously, it was very difficult for her to retreat from that position. In the end, Cecil came to the rescue with a hint that a meeting between the queens would be desirable and mutually advantageous. In the interim, there were rumours that the Cardinal of Lorraine had urged his niece to embrace the Anglican form of Protestantism which would have represented a compromise between the extremes of Catholicism and the Calvinism of John Knox and his adherents. Randolph, reporting this to London, observed that these rumours had thrown the religious fanatics into a fury. To them, Anglicanism was every bit as bad as Catholicism, and to emphasise this Knox had preached a savage sermon the previous Sunday giving 'cross and the candle such a wipe' that Randolph could have wished that Knox had held his tongue. Knox had concluded his harangue with a prayer for the continuance of 'amity and hearty love with England', though the united kingdom which Knox envisaged would have nothing to do with anything so idolatrous as crosses and candles.

Lord James Stewart, sworn in as a member of Mary's new Privy Council in September 1561, rapidly became his sister's right-hand man. Over the ensuing three and a half years he was, effectively, Mary's chief minister, formulating the policies of her government. James was betrothed to Christian Stewart, Countess of Buchan in her own right, but instead of marrying her he had her shut up in his castle in Lochleven, his mother, Lady Margaret Douglas, being the unfortunate countess's gaoler. On 8 February 1562 he married Agnes

Keith, daughter of William, Earl Marischal, John Knox officiating at the ceremony. The previous day, Mary created him Earl of Mar.

By the end of February Randolph had come round to the view that a face-to-face meeting of the queens would be positively beneficial. On the last day of that month Maitland wrote another of his frank letters to Cecil. He admitted that it had been his ambition to promote friendship between Scotland and England during the reign of Mary Tudor. More recently, he had worked tirelessly to the same end, despite the fluctuations in Elizabeth's attitudes. As he put it colourfully, 'as one occasion doth fail me, I begin to shuffle the cards off new, always keeping the same ground'.[12]

Four weeks later Randolph handed over a letter from Elizabeth to Mary. What it contained, far less the actual text, is not known as neither Randolph nor Cecil seem to have been privy to its contents. But Randolph duly reported back to Cecil that though Mary did not discuss the letter with him she laughed heartily all the time as she read it. At the end she told the ambassador that she was beholden to Elizabeth for sending her such a long letter, and she hoped that when they saw each other, she would better know her heart than she judged from her writings.

In ensuing weeks there was a steady exchange of correspondence, though the contrast between the warm, generous and flattering letters of Mary to Elizabeth and the cool, reserved responses of Elizabeth reveal the vast differences in the character and attitudes of the protagonists. Mary wooed her cousin (in the circumstances, that is not too strong a word) not only with fulsome letters but with verses of her own composition, written from the heart, as well as costly gifts. When Mary sent Elizabeth a heart-shaped diamond ring in the summer of 1562 Elizabeth eventually responded with a ring which Randolph delivered a year later. Subsequently he reported back that Queen Mary was well pleased with this ring which she 'marvellously esteemed, oftentimes looked upon, and many times kissed'. On another occasion Mary joked with Randolph that at times like this she wished she were a man, so that the marriage between the two monarchs could be properly consummated. Indeed, there must often have been times when their respective courtiers shared this sentiment. Instead, they had to face the reality of two strong-willed women, the obstinacy in their Tudor blood an obstacle rather than a bond.

Through his Guise contacts, Throckmorton learned late in March that the Scottish Council did not favour a meeting between the queens. The Duke of Guise, however, felt that such a meeting could do no harm and might well do much good, so he suggested that it should go ahead, preferably somewhere in the Borders. Although the Cardinal of Lorraine had some reservations, the Guise family in general welcomed the proposal. The Bishop of Amiens wrote prematurely to Mary on 21 April warmly congratulating her on the proposed meeting: 'I think that the Queen of England has so much good judgment, and is so well advised, that therein she will not forget anything.' Some time was lost as a result of a serious riding accident sustained by Mary while residing at Falkland Palace, and it was not until 19 May that she was fit enough to confer at Edinburgh with her Council on the matter. After a great deal of argument the Council now gave way to the Queen and agreed in principle to the meeting taking place. It seems that, aside from the lingering fear that Elizabeth might kidnap Mary and hold her against her will, the Council was worried about the likely expense of such an important mission. Interestingly, both Protestant and Catholic factions were concerned about such a meeting, the one fearing that any amity between the queens would diminish Elizabeth's support and protection, the other afraid that Mary, who had so far been disappointingly lukewarm in furthering their cause, might be corrupted and converted to Anglicanism by Elizabeth.

Mary despatched Maitland to London on 25 May to clinch the deal and make preliminary preparations for the meeting. Following his arrival there on 31 May Maitland not only found Elizabeth enthusiastic about the meeting, but that even Cecil had been won round to perceiving the positive advantages for both countries that would come out of it. Like their Scottish counterpart, the English Council was appalled at the estimated cost of the venture, put at around £40,000.

Unfortunately, the summer of 1562 turned out to be the wettest in living memory, rendering the unmetalled roads of both kingdoms quite impassable for weeks on end. In the hope that the heavens would look kindly on such an important venture, plans went ahead for the meeting to take place at York between 20 August and 20 September. Subsequently the venue was changed several times; ironically, one of the proposed sites was Sheffield House, the seat of the Earl of Shrewsbury where Mary would be held captive in the 1570s. Eventually Nottingham was settled upon. On 10 June

Elizabeth wrote a relatively affectionate letter to Mary saying how much she looked forward to their meeting. Mary was overjoyed and rapturously tucked the cherished epistle into her bosom. When Randolph brought Mary a miniature portrait of Elizabeth, Mary's first reaction was to enquire whether it was a good likeness, to which the ambassador replied that she would soon be able to judge for herself.

Elaborate plans were laid in London regarding the masques and other entertainments which would be staged during the month-long meeting. The highlight was to be an allegorical tableau illustrating the punishment of False Report and Discord by Jupiter at the request of Prudence and Temperance. This wordy performance was scheduled to be spread over three evenings, and Cecil himself vetted the script minutely, checking the words against any hidden meanings, *double entendres* and possible misinterpretation. In the end fate intervened yet again. This time it was not the unseasonable elements but a dramatic deterioration in the political situation in France which caused the meeting to be aborted.

In 1560 a Huguenot conspiracy to seize Francis II at the royal *château* of Amboise failed, and over twelve hundred Protestants were cold-bloodedly slaughtered as a consequence. Ruthless though it had been, the massacre at Amboise had failed to curb the growing power of the reform movement in France. There were political overtones to the religious struggle; as the Valois dynasty teetered on the brink of extinction, the rivalry between the Guise and Bourbon factions intensified. While the Guise family were staunchly Catholic, the scion of the Bourbons, King Antoine of Navarre, had married a Huguenot and their son Henry had been raised in the Protestant faith. Even worse, Antoine's brother Louis, Prince of Condé, was the avowed leader of the Huguenot party, instigator of the failed coup at Amboise and now spoiling for a showdown again. On 1 March 1562, henchmen of the Duke of Guise shot up a Protestant prayer-meeting at Vassy and this triggered off the violent civil war that engulfed France within weeks. Mary, naturally enough, sympathised with her Guise relatives and the French Catholics, whereas Elizabeth's sympathies lay with the Huguenots. The French civil war ended in an uneasy truce which came into effect on 25 June, and on 6 July Elizabeth gave instructions for the meeting with Mary to go ahead as planned. On 8 July Cecil prepared Mary's safe-conduct but four days later the civil war broke out anew, more bitter and ruthless than ever, and as the prospect of Spain and other powers being sucked into the conflict grew more likely, Elizabeth reluctantly decided that she could not afford to be so far from London while war raged on the other side of the Channel.

On 15 July Mary sent out letters to all her nobility, summoning them to Edinburgh as a preliminary to the meeting. The very same day, Elizabeth sent Sir Henry Sidney north to inform the Scottish queen that the proposed meeting was off. Sidney reached Edinburgh a few days later, but was unable to deliver the news till 23 July. The shock of this announcement was not mitigated when Mary learned that Elizabeth affirmed that the renewal of the war was due to an act of treachery on the part of the Duke of Guise. According to Sidney, Mary showed her disappointment not only in words 'but in countenance and watery eyes'. Mary's reaction would have been infinitely more dramatic had the news not already been broken to her gently by Maitland immediately Sidney reached Edinburgh. She is said to have collapsed in a dead faint and her confinement to her bed for several days delayed the audience with Sir Henry to receive the formal details of the postponement. Mary tried to take some crumb of comfort from Sidney's promise that the meeting was not cancelled, only delayed on account of the French war, and that Elizabeth hoped that they would be able to meet the following summer, between 20 May and the end of August, at York, Pontefract, Nottingham or some other suitable venue. Mary would have assented immediately to this, but Maitland advised her to delay answering until the Council had been consulted.

On 15 August 1562 the Council met and after due deliberation decided that Mary herself should decide if and when the meeting should take place. Mary thereupon decided to comply with Elizabeth's suggestion, and at Perth on 20 August she confirmed the existing arrangements, recommending that the meeting take place at York on 20 June 1563. She could not have imagined that, within a few months, Elizabeth would be embroiled in a war against her Guise relatives.

5. HAMILTONS AND GORDONS

1562–63

It is a strange desire to seek power and to lose liberty.
Francis Bacon

Shortly after her arrival in Scotland, Mary had run into a great deal of trouble from the staunchly Protestant Hamilton family. The outstanding feature of Mary's dealings with her nobles and officials was her affability and friendliness. She could chat and joke easily with them without actually flirting with them. There was a fine line, however, between putting men at their ease and leading them on, and it was inevitable that some men read more into the Queen's free and easy manner than she ever intended. John Knox, who professed to be impervious to her charm, was not alone in claiming that she possessed powers of enchantment, 'whereby men were bewitched'.[1] One of those who was bewitched by her was James Hamilton, third Earl of Arran, eldest son of the Duke of Châtelherault. He had been proposed by Mary as a suitor for the daughter of Diane de Poitiers, but shortly after the death of Francis II, Arran had proposed marriage to Queen Elizabeth and had been promptly rejected. Nothing daunted, within weeks of this rebuff, young Arran (who had been in love with her since childhood) was being promoted as a possible husband for Mary, in a plan concocted by the Duke and John Knox with a view to binding the Queen to the Protestant cause. Not surprisingly, Arran's offer was turned down before Mary even left France.

So much rejection was hard for a temperamental young man like Arran, who used Mary's adherence to the Mass as an excuse to stay away from her court. While Arran was posing as a dissident, there was a rumour on 16 November 1561 that he had crossed the Firth of Forth with an armed band, determined to seize the Queen by force and marry her. The kidnap plot seems to have been more imaginary than real, and largely based on some intemperate remarks of Arran about seizing Mary from Holyrood, 'as once was to have been done unto her mother'.[2] The truth is that Arran was half-mad, but before he could be brought under control, there was an ugly incident involving one of Mary's younger Guise uncles, the Marquis of Elboeuf, her half-brother Lord John Stewart and the unruly James Hepburn, Earl of Bothwell. These three young bloods forced their way into an Edinburgh merchant's house in pursuit of Alison Craik, a 'good, handsome wench', allegedly Arran's mistress. This was little more than a drunken frolic that got out of hand, but it was sufficient to rouse the Protestant extremists who loudly demanded that Elboeuf should be expelled. It was out of the question that Mary should punish her uncle so harshly, but she reprimanded his companions. Unabashed, Bothwell and Lord John let it be known that they would repeat their performance, regardless of the Queen's reproof. Learning of this, the Hamiltons formed up with clubs and spears and set off towards Bothwell's lodgings. The Earl, apprised of their approach, mustered his friends and prepared to take on the Hamiltons. A pitched battle in the streets of Edinburgh was only averted by the timely intervention of Lord James Stewart, accompanied by the earls of Argyll and Huntly who, issuing a proclamation in the Queen's name, ordered the armed men to disperse on pain of death. This had such an effect that within half an hour the streets were totally deserted.

The following day the Duke and Bothwell were summoned to the court, the Protestants turning out in strength to support the one, and the Catholics, just as numerous and well armed, to support the other. Bothwell had the good sense to withdraw quietly before the rival factions could come to blows. Arran now planned to leave Scotland for France where the Huguenots momentarily had the upper hand; but on 17 January 1562 he suddenly changed his mind and went to Linlithgow where he was reconciled to Queen Mary in an emotional scene.[3] On 8 February he was present at the marriage of Lord James Stewart and Agnes Keith, but fell ill the following day. Randolph, who had numerous conversations with both Châtelherault and his unstable son, records that while the father was so inconstant, save in greed and covetousness, 'that in three moments he would take five purposes', young Arran was 'so drowned in dreams and so feedeth himself with fantasies, that either men fear that he will fall into some dangerous and incurable sickness, or play, one day, some mad part what will bring himself to mischief'.[4]

Incredibly, Arran was soon afterwards reconciled to Bothwell who not so long before had been his deadliest enemy. Credit for initiating this must go to Mary and her Council in the interests of national security. While Bothwell was prepared to meet Arran halfway, Arran was at first not inclined to make friends with anyone, least of all Bothwell for whom he entertained the deepest and most irrational hatred. In truth, all that he could be persuaded to do was to keep the peace with him; but Bothwell, determined on the restoration of amity, sought the good offices of John Knox whose family had been feudal dependants of the Earl's father and grandfather. Knox eventually engineered a meeting between the two men at Hamilton House, Kirk o' Field, a name which would shortly earn a dubious place in Scottish history. At this meeting Arran, without waiting for Bothwell's apology, rushed forward and embraced him warmly, saying, 'If the hearts be upright few ceremonies may serve and content me.'[5] Bothwell was completely won over by Arran's impetuous cordiality and this oddly matched couple thereafter became the closest of friends, invariably seen together on the hunting field, in church or at public functions, to the wonder and incredulity of all who witnessed their familiarity.

On Thursday, 26 March, they dined together, as was now their wont, and afterwards Bothwell, accompanied by Gavin Hamilton, titular Commendator of Kilwinning, went to the Duke's house at Kinneil. The following day, however, Arran came to Knox in great distress, claiming that Bothwell had proposed a plot for abducting the Queen, holding her in Dumbarton Castle and killing Lord James, Maitland and her other advisers. Knox, realising that Arran was babbling incoherently and behaving irrationally, tried to calm him down and urged him to do nothing further, but the obsessive Arran would not let things rest. After writing a letter to Mary at Falkland exposing the plot, he rode to Kinneil. There, after an ugly confrontation in which he accused his father of complicity in Bothwell's plot, he retired distraught to his bedroom where he was locked in. This prudent precaution was insufficient to detain him, for he tied the bed-sheets together and escaped through the window. Clad only in doublet and hose, he reached the home of Sir William Kirkcaldy, laird of Grange near Burntisland, where he unburdened himself of the conspiracy between his father and Bothwell, all the while shouting incoherently and gesticulating wildly.

It was painfully obvious that the Earl was demented. Normally, the ravings of such a madman could be discounted, but it was common knowledge that Châtelherault and his son had been acting subversively, while Bothwell's propensity for hare-brained schemes was likewise well known. In due course both Arran and Bothwell were apprehended and brought before the Council. Now Arran changed his tune, dropping the charge against his father and placing the blame for the kidnap plot entirely on Bothwell. His words might have had more weight had it not also become embarrassingly obvious that, by implicating his erstwhile friend, Arran now sought once more to bolster his ambitions of marrying the Queen. Arran was manifestly insane, so the Council decreed that he be confined for his own good, though indirectly this would also effectively hold the unruly Hamiltons in check.

As for Bothwell, under interrogation (but not with the customary forms of torture) he conceded that some sort of plan to hold the Queen had occurred to him. This admission was sufficient for him to be kept in custody, pending trial for treason. On 14 May he and Gavin Hamilton were taken under close arrest from St Andrews to Edinburgh Castle from which, a few months later, Bothwell made his escape, his half-formed intentions towards Mary being left to mature some other day. Arran was also conveyed from St Andrews, but bound and closely confined in Mary's personal carriage, due to his madness. Though he lived till 1609, outliving all the other players in this tragedy, he never recovered his wits. The Duke himself, brought before the Queen and Council at St Andrews, was a pitiable sight, lamenting the fate of his son with tears streaming uncontrollably. He was a broken man, his dynastic ambitions crushed. Though he was never again to cause trouble to the throne, he lingered on long enough to experience the bitter chagrin of seeing Mary married to the son of his enemy Lennox.

This affair, tinged with farce, broke the power of the Hamiltons, a family of which, on account of its ramifications and relationships, Mary had had to be extremely careful in her dealings. Never again would they pose a threat to her, but next in importance to the Hamiltons were the Gordons, as much a threat to the stability of the kingdom by their espousal of Catholicism as the Hamiltons had been in their adherence to the new religion. The manner in which their power was broken was bloodier and more dramatic, and occurred in the autumn of 1562.

Mary was devastated by the cancellation of her meeting with Elizabeth, and for several days those closest to her feared for her health as she suffered a severe bout of depression. After a week, however, she snapped out of her despair. Fundamentally resilient, she decided that if she could not go south, she would head north and make an extended tour of her Highland dominions. This would be a mixture of business and pleasure, part fact-finding tour and vacation, with the hunting season in full swing. There was also a more sinister aspect of the trip which would gradually develop into a punitive expedition.

On 11 August 1562 Mary and her extensive entourage left Edinburgh and reached Stirling two days later. Mary held meetings of her Council there on 14 and 15 August to discuss the postponed meeting with Elizabeth. Before leaving Stirling, Mary also had an urgent consultation with Lord James, now the Earl of Mar, Maitland and Randolph to consider a proposal from Elizabeth to send military assistance to the Prince of Condé, the leader of the Huguenots. This was backed by John Knox who insisted in presenting the Queen with a petition from the Kirk recommending the endorsement of Elizabeth's military expedition. Mary, who had only three weeks previously declined the overtures of the Pope to send a deputation to the Council of Trent by which the Counter-Reformation was organised, steadfastly maintained a neutral stance and declined to get involved in such continental adventures.[6] Mary's reluctance to commit herself to a Catholic *coup d'état* also stemmed from the fact that she now had no confidence in the Earl of Huntly, without whose wholehearted support such an attempt to overthrow the Protestant régime was impossible. Huntly, who now found himself supplanted in the Queen's good grace by her half-brother, the recently created Earl of Mar, took his rejection very badly. Thereafter relations between the Queen and the leading Catholic nobleman deteriorated sharply.

On 18 August Mary left Stirling for Perth where, two days later, she ratified the revised plans for a meeting with Elizabeth. The following day she was at Coupar Angus, while a meeting of the Council took place at Edzell on 25 August. She was at Glamis the next day and rode north, reaching Aberdeen on 27 August where she visited the university.[7] Here she was met by Elizabeth, Countess of Huntly, who interceded on behalf of her wayward son, Sir John Gordon, then a fugitive from justice; but Mary insisted that Sir John give himself up to answer for his crimes. On 31 August he surrendered to the court of justiciary at the Tolbooth of Aberdeen and was ordered the following day to ward himself in Stirling Castle within seven days.

Mary left Aberdeen the same day, expecting Sir John to obey her command, but when she subsequently learned that he had broken his bond, she hastily changed her plans. Instead of proceeding to Huntly's mansion as expected, she gave Strathbogie, the Huntly stronghold, a wide berth and went on towards Inverness, staying at Darnaway Castle where she conferred the earldom of Moray on Lord James. At the same time she issued orders for the apprehension of Sir John Gordon. In retaliation, when she reached Inverness on 11 September, entrance to the castle was barred to her by its keeper, Alexander Gordon, despite the fact that Inverness was a royal castle. This was a treasonable act and, suspecting that the Earl of Huntly himself (as Sheriff of Inverness) was responsible, Mary's fears of abduction had she stayed at Strathbogie as planned were confirmed. The townspeople and many from the surrounding countryside flocked to her side and Alexander Gordon was eventually persuaded to open the gates, being promptly seized and hanged from the ramparts for his impudence.

After a few days' rest in Inverness, her forces now augmented by large numbers of horsemen and retainers on foot, Mary proceeded to Spynie, a residence of Patrick Hepburn, Catholic Bishop of Moray and a great-uncle of the young Earl of Bothwell. Previously the bishop had been a staunch ally of Huntly but now he found it prudent to throw in his lot with Mary although he had no love for Lord James, the new Earl of Moray. Mary, enjoying the fresh air, had colour in her cheeks and was in splendid form as her burgeoning entourage advanced eastwards into Gordon territory.[8] Her temper, however, was not improved by the actions of Sir John Gordon whose light cavalry constantly harried the flanks of her baggage train in the finest traditions of guerrilla warfare.

George Gordon, fourth Earl of Huntly, was not only Scotland's leading Catholic layman but also one of the most powerful magnates in the kingdom. He was a grandson of King James IV and therefore

Mary's cousin. The man who had promised her an army of twenty thousand Catholic troops was potentially a powerful ally in any struggle against the Protestant extremists. Regrettably, Huntly soon proved unreliable. Apart from the generation gap – at forty-eight, he was old enough to be Mary's father and, indeed, had been reared with James V – Huntly had a long track record of deviousness and double-dealing, his intrigues with England amounting, at times, to high treason. Apart from their religious differences, Huntly and Lord James Stewart were political rivals and implacable enemies. Soon a clash of personalities would escalate into a virtual civil war, in which armed factions fought each other ferociously.

The immediate bone of contention had been the powerful and lucrative earldom of Moray, vacant for several years since the death of the last earl, an illegitimate son of James IV. In default, the lands and revenues of Moray had, for some years past, been administered by Huntly. Lord James Stewart had set his heart on this rich earldom and eventually persuaded his half-sister to confer it upon him in exchange for the earldom of Mar. She agreed rather reluctantly and only on condition that the appointment remain a close secret for the time being. Inevitably James's elevation would become public; and it may be that Mary was apprehensive about Huntly's reaction when he was forced to disgorge the Moray estates and account for their revenues in due course.

At first Mary had entertained high hopes of Huntly, but she soon tired of his arrogant manner. He was becoming almost as tiresome as John Knox, continually criticising her religious policies and mistaking her liberal, tolerant attitude for a bias towards Protestantism at the expense of her co-religionists. As a result, a coolness developed between Mary and Huntly, exacerbated by the fact that he arrogantly conducted himself as the head of an independent fiefdom, a dangerously destabilising influence in the north. Gradually, and doubtless with the advice and encouragement of Lord James, Mary came to the conclusion that she would have to take measures to bring Huntly to heel. Fortunately, Huntly soon provided her with a pretext for military action.

On 27 June 1562 Sir John Gordon, third son of Huntly, gravely wounded Lord Ogilvy of Airlie in a brawl in Edinburgh and was imprisoned in the Tolbooth as a result. The fracas had arisen because of a dispute in the Ogilvy family involving Gordon who had formed a scandalous liaison with Lord Ogilvy's stepmother, robbed Ogilvy of his inheritance and then falsely imprisoned his erstwhile mistress when he could extract no further lands from her.[9] After a few days in prison, he had escaped and fled to the safety of his father's extensive estates. Extraordinary as it may seem, the swashbuckling Sir John, as handsome as he was hot-headed, had at one stage even been considered as a possible husband for the widowed Mary.

Mary had several excellent reasons for bringing the fugitive to justice. Not only had he flouted the law by his escape, but he had seized the lands of her Master of the Household, James Ogilvy of Cardell, who had been dispossessed by the perjury of his step-mother. Now, Mary's entourage included James Ogilvy, seeking revenge from the unrepentant Sir John. From Mary's viewpoint, the Gordons were to be taught the lesson that they were not above the law. On the advance into Huntly territory Mary felt an exhilaration compounded with grim determination. Her scouts brought the disconcerting news that over a thousand Gordon men were concealed in the woods near the Spey, intent on ambushing the royal party, but they had vanished by the time the Queen's column approached the river-banks. She passed Findlater Castle and called upon its garrison to surrender. They refused, and Mary, lacking artillery and siege-engines, passed on to Old Aberdeen without further incident, arriving there on 22 September. The following day she entered the New Town where she received a tumultuous welcome from the townspeople.

Mary intended to remain there for some time, until the Huntly disturbance was settled. To this end she mustered 120 musketeers and sent south for such veteran commanders as Lord Lindsay, Kirkcaldy of Grange and James Cockburn, the 'Black Laird' of Ormiston, together with the heavy artillery required to reduce Findlater and other Gordon strongholds by force. While these warlike preparations were in train, Huntly sent his eldest son, Lord George Gordon, south to confer with his father-in-law, the Duke of Châtelherault. Simultaneously he played for time, sending a message to Mary that he was quite prepared to bring an armed force to her assistance in apprehending his own son. Without this armed band, however, he declined to answer her summons, and retreated into his vast dominions, keeping well away from Strathbogie and not daring to sleep more than a night in any one place. When he relaxed his vigil, to the extent that he felt it safe enough to visit his home during daylight, Mary's staff devised a plan to seize him. Kirkcaldy, with the Tutor of Pitcur and twelve hand-picked men, set out from Aberdeen early on the morning of 9 October, in order to reach Strathbogie at noon when the Earl would be taking his midday meal.

Kirkcaldy reasoned that a handful of men would not arouse suspicion, but would suffice to seize the entrance to the house and secure it until the arrival of a much larger force under Lord John Stewart. Unfortunately, the advance party of Lord John's army had galloped too quickly and appeared on the horizon, about a mile distant, just as Kirkcaldy was arguing on the doorstep with Huntly's porter. The lookout in the watch-tower immediately raised the alarm, and the Earl, in his stockinged feet and without sword or pistols, escaped out of a back window and across a low wall where his horse was tethered. He was off and away before the Tutor of Pitcur (who had ridden to the rear of the building) could detain him. Pitcur and his men gave chase, but Huntly's fresh mount soon outran them. By the time they returned to the house, Countess Elizabeth had opened gates and doors to admit the Queen's men. They found that Huntly's retainers had virtually stripped the mansion of its contents, leaving only the family chapel intact; it was still elaborately decorated in anticipation of Mary's visit.

Huntly's flight gave the lie to his promise to assist in the capture of his son. Now he was regarded as an accomplice. When the Council met on 15 October it was decided that unless Huntly gave himself up the following day he would be 'put to the horn' as an outlaw. This drastic step was forced on Mary by an incident two days earlier when Sir John Gordon, accompanied by about 150 men, had taken a company of the Queen's men by surprise in a village near Findlater and relieved them of fifty-six firearms. When a messenger from Huntly brought the keys of Findlater and Auchendown to the Queen, saying that these strongholds had been evacuated, Mary retorted that she did not require keys as she now had other means to open these doors.[10]

Huntly and his followers had by now retreated into the wilds of Badenoch. Countess Elizabeth, on 20 October, got as far as the outskirts of Aberdeen in the hope of personally interceding with the Queen for her husband and son, but Mary refused to see her. On her return to Strathbogie the die was cast, for Huntly now decided to march on Aberdeen at the head of his own army, 'with purpose,' according to Randolph, 'to apprehend the Queen and to do with the rest at his will'. Had he remained in Badenoch he could have eluded his enemies indefinitely, but by going on the offensive he signed his own death-warrant. Estimates of the numbers of armed men at his disposal range from 700 to 1,200, but it is generally agreed that his only hope of success was in the treachery of the Queen's followers, many of whom wore a sprig of heather in their caps to show that they were secretly Huntly's men. Instead, desertion occurred in the Earl's ranks, as the rebels encamped on the summit of the Hill of Fare at Corrichie on 27 October.

Huntly, obese and in poor health, did not rise till ten o'clock the following morning, but when he looked out of his tent he was staggered to find the Queen's forces drawn up at the foot of the hill. He dropped to his knees and prayed. 'Oh Lord! I have been a bloodthirsty man, and by my means has much innocent blood been spilled. But wilt Thou give me victory this day, and I shall serve Thee all the days of my life!'

Huntly's position, on top of a hill 500 metres in height, should have been well-nigh impregnable. It was well chosen to enable him to strike at his opponents from any direction, should the anticipated defections from the Queen's ranks occur; but Mary's troops held firm, and it was Huntly who now found himself in a trap. The steep slopes left the Gordon men exposed with no room to manoeuvre. Many of them were picked off by the Queen's arquebusiers and those who escaped the initial gunfire were driven into a swampy tract where Mary's light cavalry made mincemeat of them. About 220 were slain and 120 taken prisoner, including Huntly himself.[11] His hands bound, he was put on a horse and brought before Mary's generals, whereupon he suffered a massive stroke and toppled dead from his horse – a dramatic end to a life noteworthy only for its deviousness and inconsistency. Sir John Gordon and his brother Adam, a boy of seventeen, were taken alive. Huntly's corpse was embalmed and shipped off to Edinburgh, along with the more valuable pieces of furniture from Strathbogie which Mary had confiscated. The cadaver was carefully preserved until the Estates met the following year when, in time-honoured tradition, it was trotted out before the bar of parliament in order that the act of forfeiture and attainder might formally be passed upon it. Huntly's place as Chancellor was promptly taken by James Douglas, Earl of Morton.

The immediate instigator of this rebellion confessed under torture and on 2 November was executed at Aberdeen in the Queen's presence. Mary, who had a lifelong aversion to human suffering in any form, would have given anything to avoid attending such a gruesome spectacle; but her presence was vital in order to defuse the widespread suggestions that the Earl of Moray had undertaken the expedition against the Gordons without her approval. The headsman botched the job and as the life was horrifyingly snuffed out of the bold, beautiful Sir John, Mary fainted and was carried away weeping hysterically, utterly distraught by such a shattering experience. Young Adam, on account of his age, was pardoned and lived to become the hero of the popular ballad 'Edom o' Gordon' and to fight for his queen after her escape from Lochleven. The eldest of Huntly's sons, Lord George Gordon, being still in the south when the battle of Corrichie was fought, had no direct part in the affair, but in due course he was captured, tried for treason and sentenced to be hanged, drawn and quartered, but this barbaric execution was commuted to a term of imprisonment. Having spared his life, Mary had him set free after her marriage to Darnley. Like his brother, he would be closely involved with the Queen in her later tribulations.

Mary was sufficiently recovered from the ordeal of Sir John's execution to depart from Aberdeen three days later. Travelling via Dunnottar, Craig, Kincardine, Arbroath, Dundee, Perth, Tullibardine, Drummond, Stirling and Linlithgow,[12] she reached Edinburgh on 21 November and promptly succumbed to influenza, an epidemic whose novelty was signified by its quaint Scottish name of the New Acquaintance. Moray and Maitland went down with this illness about the same time.

The Huntly affair created a much greater stir in Catholic circles abroad than at home. Nicholas de Gouda, the Papal Nuncio whose clandestine mission to align Mary with the Council of Trent failed, left Scotland on 3 September 1562, some time before the showdown with the Gordons, but he was not far short of the mark when he commented that Huntly's downfall was due simply to the 'heretical bastard-brother of the Queen'.[13] Alvaro de Quadra, the Spanish ambassador in London, reported to King Philip that Huntly had planned to 'seize the Queen of Scots and turn out Lord James and other heretics that govern'.[14] Mary herself blamed no one but Huntly himself and Sir John Gordon for the tragedy that befell them, and minimised the religious aspects of the conflict. Regrettably, Mary's full account of this episode which she sent to her uncle, the Cardinal of Lorraine, has not survived, but the gist of it was reported in a letter from the Cardinal to the Emperor soon after he had heard from Mary. She herself wrote to the Pope on 30 January 1563, at pains to point out that she had not failed her religion but had taken appropriate action to deal with a rebellious subject. More importantly, this letter indicated that Mary would, henceforward, be more fully committed to the Catholic cause than ever before.[15]

This decision, to re-establish Catholicism in Scotland 'at the peril of her life', marks the beginning of a new phase in her policy. Her change of heart was dictated by the devastating news that her cousin Elizabeth was now engaged in military action against Mary's Guise relatives. This was bad enough in itself, but it also implied a shocking breach of faith on Elizabeth's part. It is ironic that on the very day after Mary decisively defeated Catholicism in the northeast, she received news of Elizabeth's crusade against her uncles. Randolph brought her the letter from Queen Elizabeth announcing that, as a result of Guise treachery, the religious war in France had resumed and that she intended supplying military aid to the Huguenots. Randolph records that Mary burst out laughing as she read the letter, but this may have been no more than a hysterical reaction, as there can be no doubt that Mary was deeply mortified by the contents.[16] Nevertheless, she had not given up all hope of a *rapprochement* with Elizabeth; when she learned a few days later that her cousin had been struck down by smallpox but was now recovering, she let Randolph know how delighted she was to learn that 'her beautiful face will lose none of its perfections'.[17]

Mary, in fact, was walking a tightrope: anxious at all costs to maintain good relations with Elizabeth; but at the same time concerned that this friendship would alienate her Guise uncles, more especially as they controlled her dowry and the revenue from her French estates on which, to a large extent, she depended. What she needed was some reassurance from Elizabeth that she would stop meddling in matters that did not concern her. Moreover, the fact that Elizabeth had been recently so close to death as a result of smallpox that her Council had had to take responsibility for important decisions without her, merely reinforced Mary's frustration that Elizabeth had so wilfully refused to put the question of her succession in order. During Elizabeth's illness, her Council had seriously debated the matter. According to the Spanish ambassador, reporting to Philip, the sixteen men of the Council had produced almost as many suggestions regarding the succession. The

Catholic members were divided in allegiance between the Queen of Scots and Margaret, Countess of Lennox, the latter being preferable because she was considered 'devout and sensible' – implying that Mary was not.[18]

Poor Mary, to be so distrusted by the Catholics, at home and abroad; yet, at the same time, condemned by Knox and the Protestant extremists. Randolph, who frequently conversed with Knox, reported to Cecil that as far as Knox was concerned the Queen was a hopeless case, doubting whether she would ever see the error of her ways and 'come to God':

> He is so full of mistrust in all her doings, words and sayings, as though he were either of God's privy council, that knew how he had determined of her from the beginning, or that he knew the secrets of her heart so well, that neither she did or could have for ever one good thought of God or of his true religion.[19]

What worried Knox most of all was that, even if Mary abjured Catholicism, she would never submit to him in spiritual matters. By this stage Maitland, Moray, Morton and other prominent figures were beginning to tire of the dictatorial pronouncements of Knox and the Protestant divines, and were ready to accept the modified form of English Protestantism. Knox retaliated characteristically, thundering from the pulpit against the Queen's love of dancing, particularly a recent occasion when she had danced excessively till after midnight which, he alleged, was her way of rejoicing at the beginning of the persecution of the Huguenots in France. This was partly true, except that the occasion for Mary's rejoicing was the fall of Rouen to the Catholics in December 1562, and not the outbreaks of the previous spring. When Mary summoned him to answer for his ill-humoured conduct, he claimed that he had not been criticising her behaviour in general, but her specific joyous reaction to news of the Guise victory. That mollified her to some extent. Disarmingly, she told him that she was quite well aware that he and her uncles differed sharply in religious matters, but that if he heard anything about herself that displeased him he should come and tell her of it, and she would listen to him.

He was taken aback at this, especially as he wished to continue the privilege of rebuking her publicly rather than privately. To this end, therefore, he suggested that she should attend his public services, so that she could personally hear him denouncing her from the pulpit, rather than get his strictures second-hand. Then he added, rather lamely and rudely, that he declined to be taken away from his book 'to waite upon her chalmer-doore'. Mary sweetly countered this by saying that she was sure he was not always at his book. Knox says that she then turned her back on him and walked away, but the truth is that he probably could not come up with a suitable riposte.[20] This confrontation marked another turning point; henceforward Mary would adopt quite a different tack in dealing with her upstart cleric.

6. MARRIAGE PROSPECTS

1563–65

The marriage of our Queen was in all men's mouths.
    John Knox

As 1562 closed, and the Huntly affair faded into the background, there was widespread speculation concerning Mary's matrimonial intentions. She had been a widow for twelve months and it was time for her to take another husband. By now it seemed less and less likely that Elizabeth, eight years Mary's senior, would marry, and therefore the question of Mary's remarriage, and the prospect of producing an heir, became all the more important not only for Scotland but for England as well.

In February 1563 the Council decided to despatch Maitland to England again, ostensibly to offer Mary's intercession between England and France in order to bring the religious war to a speedy conclusion. Maitland was also given a free hand to negotiate with Elizabeth on other matters, unspecified but clearly referring to the succession. This was precipitated by growing concern that the English Council might choose Lady Margaret Lennox in preference to Mary, thereby blocking the latter's pretensions to the English crown. Maitland was even prepared to go before the English parliament to argue Mary's case, adding that if her just claim was denied she would be injured and offended and would therefore feel free to take appropriate steps to remedy the injustice. The debate in parliament was unfavourable to Mary's claim, but Maitland prudently decided not to make an issue of it. Nevertheless, the highly unsatisfactory manner in which Elizabeth and her parliament had failed to resolve the matter induced him to pursue an independent policy, one which he had no intention of revealing to Elizabeth directly or indirectly.

In the spring of 1563, about the time Maitland was preparing for his delicate mission, Mary suffered the first of a series of traumatic experiences which caused her considerable anguish while providing salacious tittle-tattle for the gossip-mongers. Among Mary's French courtiers was the poet Pierre de Boscotel de Châtelard. He had impeccable aristocratic connections, being descended on his mother's side from the Chevalier Bayard; but he was highly accomplished, a good musician and an agreeable poet, all of which gave him a good conceit of himself, besides placing him high in the esteem of his patrons. In common with other poets at the French court, he was inspired by the radiant beauty of the Queen-Dauphiness to compose the fulsome, high-flown verses which were fashionable at the time, and Mary returned the compliment from time to time with verses of her own.

Châtelard had returned to France with his patron, the Sieur Damville, son of the Constable of France, but some time later he returned to Scotland. In November 1562 he appeared suddenly at Montrose while the Queen was at supper on her journey south from Aberdeen. He delivered a letter from his master which Randolph observed she read with great satisfaction.

Apparently Châtelard, passing through London a week or two earlier, had confided in a friend that he was on his way to see his lady love.[1] Though the name of the lady was not revealed at that time, hindsight would supply the answer. Mary received him warmly and not only lent him a sorrel gelding (a gift from Lord Robert Stewart) but may also have given him money to enable him to dress himself in a manner befitting a French gallant; and, as was her custom, she was free and easy with him, delighting in his company and conversation. Later, of course, Randolph and others would write that Mary had been unduly familiar with 'so unworthy a creature and abject a varlet', a familiarity 'too much to have been used to his master himself by any Princess alive'.[2] Randolph, however, was unaware of the esteem in which poets were held at the French court, or that Mary was particularly fond of poetry. To Mary, Châtelard was something of a protégé to be petted, and this in all innocence. Had she ever been guilty of undue familiarity with other courtiers, the charge of scandalous conduct might have had more significance. As it happens, the highly coloured version of what happened is that given by John Knox, hardly the most impartial of observers.

By now Knox nurtured an ill-disguised hatred of his queen, who made an easy transition from idolater to fornicator and adulterer in his mind. Moreover, the way she gently poked fun at his ecclesiastical pretensions was more than he could tolerate. Thus he was only too ready to listen to any calumny against her, hungry for the slightest morsel of uncorroborated scandal which he could transmute into hard fact, suitably garnished with all the rhetoric at his command. From other sources, notably Randolph and Maitland, one forms the impression that if Mary were guilty of anything it could only have been that she failed to realise how infatuated the boy was with her. The fault was almost entirely Châtelard's. He was so besotted with Mary that he easily mistook her gracious kindness for love and affection. Thus emboldened, the poor deluded fool entered the Queen's apartments very late one night, while Mary was closeted with Moray and Maitland. As she was giving her minister last-minute instructions before he set off for London, the love-sick poet slipped into the Queen's bedroom and hid under the bed. He was discovered shortly afterwards by two manservants, during a routine search of the tapestries and tester, and dragged out unceremoniously. Mary was not informed of this incident till the following morning when she peremptorily banished Châtelard from her presence.

Having got off so lightly, the foolish boy was encouraged to follow her on her journey towards St Andrews. On 14 February he suddenly burst into her presence while she was resting at Rossend Castle near Burntisland. It later transpired that he merely wished to apologise for his previous indiscretion, but his dramatic appearance, just as Mary was about to disrobe to go to bed, evidently alarmed the Queen who was accompanied only by two of her gentlewomen. Randolph's first impression of this incident was that Châtelard had jumped on the Queen with intent to ravish her. Her screams had brought her brother Moray rushing to her aid, his dagger drawn. His first impulse was to despatch the impudent poet there and then, but he put up his blade, deciding that so heinous a crime should be dealt with according to the full rigour of the law. This was the version that Knox got hold of and subsequently embellished so shamelessly, painting a dramatic picture of a bloodthirsty queen ordering her brother to run him through and Moray on his knees imploring Mary not to insist on him killing the boy:

'Your Grace has entreated him so familiarly before, that ye
have offended all your Nobility; and if he shall be secretly
slain at your own commandment what shall the world judge
of it? I shall bring him to the presence of Justice, and let him
suffer by law according to his deserving.'

'Oh,' said the Queen, 'ye will never let him speak?'

'I shall do,' said he, 'Madam, what in me lyeth to save your
honour.'[3]

This account is self-evidently false, for if Moray had really said
those things he would never have betrayed his sister's honour to the
hostile Knox. Later, Randolph discovered that this was Châtelard's
second offence. Instead of mitigating the earlier crime, however, it
merely aggravated it. Even so, it did not warrant being despatched
on the spot by Moray as Knox would have us believe. It seems more
likely that the Queen herself ordered the young man's arrest. He was
sent in chains to St Andrews where he was tried, convicted and
hanged in the market-place on Monday, 22 February 1563, the very
next market-day. Poetic to the last, on the scaffold he recited
Ronsard's hymn to death. As the life was throttled out of him he
rolled his eyes heavenwards and cried out, as best he could, 'Adieu,
the most beautiful and cruel princess in the world!'[4]

Later it transpired that Châtelard, under interrogation, had
confessed that he was a Huguenot, and had been sent back to
Scotland for the express purpose of compromising Mary. According
to Maitland, the poet had identified the instigator of this plot as a
Madame de Curosot (or Cursolles). This was independently cor-
roborated by Chantonnay, Spain's ambassador in Paris, to King
Philip, and the nineteenth-century French historian Alexandre
Teulet identified this as a code-name for the first wife of Admiral
Coligny, the Huguenot leader.[5] Thereafter the Queen took the
precaution of sleeping with Mary Fleming.

Mary was still recovering from the shock of the Châtelard affair
and its singularly unpleasant aftermath when news reached her on
15 March that her favourite uncle, Francis, Duke of Guise, had been
assassinated on 24 February. The Duke had been shot at close range
by a young Huguenot terrorist named Poltrot. Not long afterwards
Mary suffered a second blow when she learned that her uncle, the
Grand Prior, had died of influenza. The delivery of a letter of
condolence from Queen Elizabeth, on news of the Duke's death,

touched Mary so greatly that she was reduced to tears. Thereupon she unburdened herself to Randolph, the bearer of the letter, recounting all the woes and sorrows she had suffered since her husband's death, remarking pathetically that she had virtually no one she could call a friend. Warming to her subject, she told the ambassador that it was 'most needful' that she and Elizabeth should be friends, 'and I perceive it to be God's will it should be so: for I see now that the world is not that, that we do make of it, nor yet are they most happy that continue longest in it'.[6]

Randolph was moved by Mary's obvious sincerity, but his report to London did not produce any reciprocal feelings in Elizabeth who, as usual, wished to have everything her own way: to avoid any recognition of Mary as her successor, while also preventing Mary from remarrying, or at least settling for a bridegroom who would not endanger Elizabeth's sovereignty. The death of the Duke of Guise eliminated a major obstacle to friendship between Mary and Elizabeth, but at the same time it weakened Mary's position; without her uncle's powerful backing she had little to bargain with in her attempts to bring Elizabeth to a reasonable compromise. To this end, therefore, Mary now began to look elsewhere for an ally in the ongoing struggle for her due recognition. Consequently, Maitland entered into discussions with Bishop Alvaro de Quadra, the Spanish ambassador in London, with a view to reopening negotiations for the marriage of Queen Mary to Don Carlos. Maitland reasoned that Mary would never marry a Protestant, and that she would never accept a husband of Elizabeth's choosing, whether Catholic or Protestant. Such a choice could only have been one of Elizabeth's subjects, like Lord Robert Dudley previously proposed, and that would be most unsuitable because Mary would be brought down by such a husband to the level of a subject of Elizabeth, and her hopes of winning recognition would be greatly diminished as a result.

Some nineteenth-century historians, notably Hume Brown, considered that Maitland (and Moray) supported the Spanish marriage, not from any desire to see it take place, but because such a possibility would be sufficient to force Elizabeth's hand. The fact that Maitland took great care to conceal these negotiations from Elizabeth gives the lie to that notion. In point of fact, neither Maitland nor Moray were in a position to act independently; in humouring or manipulating Mary as an alternative to a desperate political crisis, they were between a rock and a hard place. To what extent Maitland really had his heart set on the Spanish match is debatable. It is more probable that, realising how fervently Mary cherished this ambition, he was prepared to go along with it, knowing that there was little chance of it succeeding. And if it should succeed, there was the probability that Mary would go off to Spain, leaving Protestant Scotland under the regency of her brother, Moray. In this matter, Moray probably concurred; it certainly presented an attractive proposition so far as he was concerned.

Maitland put a lot of effort into securing the Spanish marriage. When he heard that the Cardinal of Lorraine, on his own initiative, was negotiating with the Emperor to marry Mary off to the Archduke Charles of Austria, Maitland sent a furious despatch to the Cardinal begging him not to negotiate this marriage 'as the Scottish people could not consent to it and it would cause confusion'.[7] This marriage would never have been acceptable to Mary anyway. Quite apart from her cherished ambitions to be the greatest queen-consort in Europe, she would never marry a foreign prince who was incapable of upholding her position in Scotland. It was important that whoever she married must be in a position to assert her right to the English throne, by armed force if need be, should Elizabeth die without issue. The Cardinal of Lorraine, however, had a different perspective, regarding his niece merely as a useful pawn in his grand designs to further the cause of France in general and his own interests in particular. Previously the Cardinal had been keen to further the Spanish marriage, but now he was just as resolutely opposed to it, much to Mary's distress.

These matrimonial intrigues were further complicated by the interference of Catherine de' Medici. One of her ambitions was the restoration of French influence in Scotland, but that would require the marriage of Mary to Charles IX and inevitably the Guise faction would once more be in the ascendant. Clearly that was the last thing she wanted, and for that reason she gave her backing to the Cardinal's Austrian proposal. That, in itself, was enough for Mary to shy away from the prospect. While never seriously entertaining this proposal, however, Mary and her advisers used it to keep Elizabeth guessing. To that end an elderly courtier of vast diplomatic experience, Philibert du Croc, was appointed to treat with the Emperor and his son. Mary even suggested that Du Croc travel to the Continent via London where he could report his business in person to Elizabeth. Whether he did is not known, but certainly his intentions were revealed to Elizabeth in mid-June when the English diplomat Henry Middlemore sent word from Paris of Du Croc's mission. At the same time, Mary hoodwinked Randolph into believing that she was seriously considering the Austrian match. It was not until 26 June that the Cardinal of Lorraine was apprised of Mary's true feelings in the matter and was nonplussed as a result. Nevertheless, he took it upon himself to press on with the Austrian proposal in the hope that it would at least scupper the Spanish alternative.

When the Spanish negotiations appeared to have stalled, Maitland, the master intriguer, on his own initiative put about a rumour of a French marriage. Indeed, Maitland went so far as to tell De Quadra, on his return from a visit to France, that 'a person of rank in France had told him that if his Queen could only wait a couple of years she could no doubt marry the King'.[8] This prospect so alarmed De Quadra that he wrote to King Philip immediately, but Philip coolly replied that although he had decided to 'entertain negotiations', quite frankly he would have preferred to support the Austrian marriage.[9]

These comings and goings had the effect of frightening Elizabeth into meddling in the matter by embarking on a course of alternately threatening and cajoling Mary with hints regarding the succession. In turn, Maitland used this to play off Philip against Elizabeth. De Quadra went to inordinate lengths to get a special envoy, Louis de Paz, sent from Spain via Ireland, to convey Philip's best intentions to Mary. She was overjoyed at the prospect, so long deferred, now coming to fruition. De Paz returned to London to report to De Quadra but found the ambassador dying from the plague. Shortly before De Quadra died he received a letter from Philip, written on 15 August, giving his formal consent to negotiations. Had De Quadra lived, it is not improbable that the Spanish marriage would have taken place; but without De Quadra to spur him on, Philip lost interest once more.

Meanwhile, Mary had sent her French secretary, Augustine Raullet, to London to confer with De Quadra who was already dead by the time the Frenchman arrived. On the advice of Diego Perez, who had succeeded De Quadra as Spain's ambassador to England, Raullet went to Brussels where he conferred with Cardinal de Granville, the Duchess of Parma and Chantonnay, Philip's ambassador in Paris. Despite Raullet's energy and persistence, he was constantly thwarted by Catherine de' Medici and the Cardinal of Lorraine. Catherine allayed Philip's fears of a French marriage, while making him uneasy at the possibility of an Anglo-French alignment. The Cardinal of Lorraine sought the intervention of the Pope regarding the Austrian match, but the Pope, ignorant of the Cardinal's plan, supported the Spanish match. Philip, at the behest of Diego Perez, wrote to the Duke of Alba on 12 October, seeking his advice on the proposed marriage. The Duke replied at great length on 21 October, concluding that Philip should now do everything to support the Austrian marriage. His main objection to the Spanish match was that it would drive France into the arms of England.

By this time, too, Philip realised how unfit his son was, if not to rule Spain, certainly to handle the responsibility of facing the combined might of France and England. This view was reinforced by the serious illness which befell Don Carlos about this time. Now, with the Pope coming round to the Austrian match, Philip finally made up his mind. The Spanish deal was off. Though he continued to prevaricate for some time, Mary herself eventually got wind of his decision. Early in December Randolph found that Mary was ill, and on 21 December he reported to London that 'some think the Queen's sickness is caused by her utterly despairing of the marriage of any of those she looked for'.[10] She soon recovered, but thereafter the memory that her Spanish ambitions had been thwarted by the Pope and her very own uncle, the Cardinal of Lorraine, soured her. While her personal faith remained as deeply engrained as ever, she would never again be the unquestioning upholder of Catholicism.

Indeed, she now had little alternative. Without the moral and material help of France and Spain she stood no chance against the fundamentalism of John Knox on the one hand and the selfish rivalry of Elizabeth on the other – 'the two portentous dragons guarding the entrance to her political paradise', as her biographer Thomas Henderson puts it so colourfully.[11] Though neither Knox nor Elizabeth was aware of the renewal of the Spanish negotiations, they both had knowledge of the Austrian proposal, and both, for their own selfish reasons, were extremely apprehensive about it.

Having wielded almost dictatorial powers (for religious matters overrode the temporal), Knox suddenly found his position undermined in many ways. He was alarmed to note, when the Estates reconvened in May 1563, that the drab, sombre clothing previously affected by the nobility had given way to bright colours, while their ladies now paraded their finery as never before, dramatic evidence of how far the Queen's 'joyusitie' had contaminated her court. Mary herself was at the height of her personal popularity, neatly encapsulated in the cries of the Edinburgh mob as she rode to the parliament: 'God bless her sweet face!' Her brilliant speech at the opening of the parliament brought rapturous applause. Sourly Knox recorded the occasion:

> The first day she made a painted orison; and there might have been heard among her flatterers 'Vox Dianae!' The voice of a goddess (for it could not be *Dei*) and not of a woman! God save that sweet face! Was there ever orator spoke so properly and so sweetly![12]

The colourful spectacle was marred by the gruesome charade of the forfeiture of the late Earl of Huntly. By contrast, the actual proceedings of parliament were noted only for the watering-down of the legislation concerning adultery, and little was done to settle the burning question of a national religion. Scotland, much to Knox's disgust, was by no means committed definitely and irrevocably to his extreme brand of Protestantism. Indeed, the fate of Protestantism and Catholicism still hung in the balance. The increasingly luke-warm attitude of Moray and Maitland, with other nobles taking their cue from them, angered and alarmed Knox, just as the likelihood of the Austrian marriage and the growing popularity of Queen Mary filled him with foreboding. Knox himself claims that so annoyed had he become with Moray that he did not speak to him for more than a year and a half. Desperately clinging to the moral high ground, he used his pulpit to vent his spleen on Mary. Before parliament rose, he preached an extremely violent sermon which concluded:

> Dukes, brethren to Emperors, and Kings, strive all for the best game: but this, my Lords will I say (note the day and bear witness after), whensoever the Nobility of Scotland professing the Lord Jesus, consents that an infidel (and all Papists are infidels) shall be head to your sovereign, ye do so far as in ye lyeth to banish Christ Jesus from this Realm; ye bring God's vengeance upon the country, a plague upon yourself, and perchance ye shall do small comfort to your sovereign.[13]

Even Knox was forced to admit that this immoderate language gave offence to Catholics and Protestants alike. It is hardly surprising that, when he was summoned before the Queen as a result, he found Mary 'in a vehement fume'. When Mary indignantly asked him, 'What have ye to do with my marriage? What are ye within this Commonwealth?', Knox smoothly replied, 'I am a subject, born within the same.' Knox's champions have seized on this as an early assertion of democratic rights, but in the context of the time and place where he said these words, they must have been delivered with mock humility. It was not in his capacity as a mere subject that he had taken it upon himself to rail against the Queen's marriage, but as the self-appointed spiritual leader of Scotland, a latter-day Elijah.

So far as the danger besetting Mary from her cousin, this now entered a period of alternate threats and promises. When Maitland was in London in May 1563 Elizabeth suggested that Mary should seriously consider Lord Robert Dudley as a husband. The widower, and probable murderer, of Amy Robsart, he was commonly regarded as Elizabeth's lover. The suggestion of a match between Mary and Dudley was as preposterous as it was immoral and the very idea that Mary should accept her cousin's cast-off paramour was both ludicrous and insulting. The notion was even more grotesque, for Elizabeth sincerely believed that in offering the lover she held so dear she was giving Mary the sincerest pledge of her friendship. One has to wonder whether Elizabeth was living in a dream world of her own.

Elizabeth remarked to Maitland that it was a pity that the Earl of Warwick, Dudley's elder brother, 'had not the grace and good looks of Lord Robert, in which case they each could have had one'. To this staggering comment Maitland, thinking on his toes as usual, responded jocularly that Elizabeth should first marry Dudley herself and then Mary, if she survived Elizabeth, could have the reversion of him and the English crown after Elizabeth's death.[14]

A few months later, when Elizabeth learned of Du Croc's mission, she warned Maitland that if Mary married either Don Carlos or the Austrian archduke, 'she could not avoid being her enemy'. As well as the stick, she held out a carrot: if Mary married 'to her satisfaction she would not fail to be a good friend and sister to her and make her heir'. Maitland could afford to discount Elizabeth's threats; the trouble was that he could put no faith in her promises either. On 20

August Elizabeth instructed Randolph to warn Mary against a Habsburg marriage. Furthermore, Randolph was told that if Mary asked him what would be considered a suitable marriage, he was to suggest 'some person of noble birth within our realm' and to hint at the possibility of 'such as she would hardly think we could agree unto'.[15] In view of her earlier suggestion to Maitland, this could refer to no one else than her lusty lover, Dudley. If that powerful argument failed, Randolph could 'descend further' and suggest 'some other noble person of any other country, being not of such a greatness, as suspicion may be gathered that he may intend trouble to this realm, might be allowed'.[16]

This argument smacks of desperation. If Mary were assured of the English succession she would be unlikely to trouble Elizabeth's realm. Why should Mary sacrifice her own interests simply for the preservation of Elizabeth's peace of mind? As Mary listened to Randolph, the poor man was acutely aware of how ludicrous the message sounded. Mary was, as usual, perfectly charming to him, but she bombarded him with so many pointed questions that he was confused, and to add to his confusion Mary peremptorily told him to put 'his sovereign's mind shortly in writing'. Randolph formed the dismal conclusion that Mary 'was more Spanish than Imperial', which was the worst scenario he could imagine. At a somewhat lower level, Moray, in response to some 'friendly advyce' from Cecil, pointedly observed that it was not to Mary's honour to 'impede and stop' the suit of princes, nor could he advise Her Highness to do so.[17] Mary herself submitted to Randolph a questionnaire so that Elizabeth could give her some definite answers as to whom she could allow to marry Mary and whom she did not like, with the reasons for her answers, of course. This was followed by the vexed question of the succession: 'by what way she intends to proceed to the declaration of our right to be her next cousin'.

By the end of the year, however, when Randolph returned from London with formal protests against Spanish, Austrian or French marriages, Mary was less inclined to entertain such a notion. She had, by that time, come to the conclusion that a foreign marriage was impractical, and not so desirable as she had hitherto imagined. Although she had no faith in Elizabeth's promises, she was now less scornful of her offers and more disposed to play her at her own game.

When Randolph came north in December 1563 he ran into

Maitland at Haddington. Maitland told him that the Queen was unwell, having exhausted herself dancing too long at her twenty-first birthday party. When he reached Edinburgh, Randolph was concerned to find that Mary's illness was much more serious, and that she wept suddenly and for no apparent reason. It seems that she was suffering a bout of that severe depression which dogged her all her adult life. She was no longer keen to discuss her matrimonial prospects; indeed, her conversation was lacklustre and confined to generalities. It is probable that this latest depression was brought on by bad news from Madrid, though the exact nature of that is not known. Certainly, in January 1564, she sent Raullet back to Flanders to try to resume negotiations through Cardinal de Granville. Raullet returned to Scotland early in May without accomplishing anything positive. The gist of this may be gleaned from a letter of Sir William Kirkcaldy of Grange to Randolph on 5 May summarising the present position. Raullet had not been welcomed by Catherine de' Medici, and as a result Queen Mary's dislike of her former mother-in-law intensified. More serious was Mary's growing antipathy towards her remaining Guise uncles who, she suspected, were trying to do her out of her revenues. In February Mary sent Stephen Wilson to Rome in the vain hope of getting the Pope to put pressure on King Philip, but the diplomat returned with nothing more that a bland statement in which Pius IV exhorted Mary to do her best for the preservation and maintenance of the Catholic religion.

Mary's dislike of Catherine was intensified when the latter sent Castelnau de Mauvissière to London to offer Elizabeth the hand of Charles IX. He then went to Edinburgh to offer Mary the hand of the Duke of Anjou, the French king's little brother (and future Henry III of France). Both proposals were patently absurd; but Mary replied charmingly and with perfect sincerity that while 'all the kingdoms and countries of the world did not touch her heart so much as France' she could not go even there as a secondary personage and that, 'grandeur for grandeur, she preferred the Prince of Spain'. Even at that time, she had not lost all hope of a Spanish match, although in this context it is more probable that she used this as a ploy to frighten Catherine into agreeing that she should marry King Charles.

That the proposed Spanish marriage was definitely off became common knowledge shortly after 6 August 1564. On that date Philip wrote to Cardinal de Granville stating that as the Cardinal of Lorraine had offered Mary's hand to the Emperor for Archduke

Charles, the proposal to marry her to Don Carlos must be considered at an end.[18] Philip also informed the Cardinal that his son was unfit to marry anyone. While chasing a serving wench, the boy had tripped and fallen headlong down a staircase. As a result of his head injuries he was blind and paralysed for several weeks until a piece of his skull was removed to relieve the pressure on his brain. This gradually restored his sight and locomotor powers but left him prone to sudden and severe bouts of homicidal mania. Remarkable though it seems, King Philip did not absolutely rule out the possibility of a marriage between Don Carlos and Mary, but this desperate measure was only to be trotted out if there seemed any likelihood of Mary marrying Charles IX of France.

For this reason, as late as September 1564, Mary made one last attempt to resuscitate the Spanish negotiations through James Beaton, Archbishop of Glasgow. The right-hand man of Mary of Guise, he had left Scotland after her death and spent the rest of his long life in France where he died in 1603. Unlike his uncle, the Cardinal, James was as honest as he was devout, and his long years of devoted service abroad to his native country were eventually rewarded by the restoration and dignities of his office five years before his death. In Mary's lifetime, James loyally served as her ambassador in Paris, and in this capacity he tried to persuade Don Francisco de Alava to raise the matter of the proposed Spanish match, but to no avail.

Although Mary regarded Elizabeth's offer of Robert Dudley as beneath contempt, it gave her the germ of an idea which was eventually to bear fruit. On 14 April 1564 Randolph had written to Cecil saying that a friend 'of good knowledge and judgment' had expressed to him an opinion concerning Mary's marital intentions. This he couched in colourful nautical metaphor: 'Where somever she hover, and hoe many times somever she double to fetch the wind, I believe she will at length let fall her anchor between Dover and Berwick, though perchance not in the port, haven or road that you wish she should.'[19] This shrewd comment indicates that the possibility of another of Elizabeth's subjects had occurred to at least one courtier and probably to many. Yet this obvious choice was not mentioned in any of the correspondence between Elizabeth and Mary, and is an indication of how little faith the one had in the other by the summer of 1564.

The rival claim of Margaret Douglas, Countess of Lennox, to the

English throne has already been mentioned. She was a veteran intriguer who, over the course of many years, never lost sight of her ambitions of winning the English throne, if not for herself, then for her elder son Henry, Lord Darnley, godson of King Henry VIII. Following the death of Francis II, Lady Margaret realised that Mary's chances of winning the support of the English Catholics were greatly enhanced. As a result, she suggested that she and Mary should sink their differences and combine through a marital union. At that stage, however, Mary was still very much under the Guise influence, and had her sights set on marriage with Charles IX or Don Carlos. Nevertheless, there was always at the back of her mind the possibility of Lord Darnley if all else failed, for she was confident that Lady Margaret had no better prospect than such a marriage for her son. When Elizabeth got wind of Margaret's negotiations with Mary, as far back as November 1561, compounded with the Earl of Lennox allegedly plotting with English Catholics, Elizabeth detained the Earl in the Tower of London, while Margaret and her son were placed under house arrest in the home of Sir Richard Sackville at Sheen near Richmond, west of London. By the end of 1562, however, all three were set free. When Mary's matrimonial negotiations with France, Austria and Spain became public, Elizabeth made a great play of taking the Lennox family under her wing.

In May 1563 Elizabeth raised the subject of restoring Lennox to his Scottish estates, and followed this on 16 June with a letter to Mary herself on the subject. Elizabeth kept up her high-profile patronage of the Lennoxes for more than a year, extravagantly praising Lord Darnley for his lute-playing. It is doubtful whether Mary was taken in by Elizabeth's posturing, and so long as there remained the slightest chance of a continental marriage she kept her own counsel. By February 1564 Maitland seemed to Randolph to favour a match between Mary and Dudley, and this view was endorsed by John Knox who, in October 1563, had gone so far as to write to Elizabeth's lover asking him to use his influence with the Queen to further the true (Protestant) religion. Even Moray seemed in favour of the Dudley marriage. In view of this, Randolph was crestfallen when the proposal by Elizabeth (made at his suggestion) to revive the meeting between the two queens met with a singular lack of enthusiasm. The Scottish Council decided, on 4 June 1564, that 'for divers reasons' unspecified, the meeting should not take place. Evidence of Scottish mistrust of Elizabeth was the letter which Maitland gave to Randolph to deliver to Cecil at that time, saying that 'gentle letters, good words and pleasant messages be good means to begin friendship among princes, but I take them to be too slender bands to hold it long fast'.[20]

This scepticism, along with the news that Mary had given permission for Lennox to return to Scotland to seek restitution, gave Elizabeth pause for thought. Clearly her much-vaunted cultivation of the Lennox family had not produced the effect she had intended. Mary's action was a severe blow to Elizabeth's carefully laid plans. Now she compounded the problems of her own making. For all her feline deviousness, Elizabeth could be blundering at times. Writing to Moray and Maitland, she proposed that Mary should rescind the permission granted to Lennox on the grounds that his return to Scotland might give offence to some of Elizabeth's Scottish friends. Furthermore, she wished it to appear that Mary was acting on her own initiative. One may imagine Mary's annoyance at this bare-faced effrontery; but Moray replied blandly to Elizabeth that he was quite unaware of any animosity in Scotland towards Lennox. He suggested that if Elizabeth, for reasons of her own, wished to detain Lennox in England, then it was up to her to prevent his movements.

Maitland backed this up with a letter to Cecil, reminding him that the recall of Lennox had been suggested by Elizabeth herself. And he added a nice touch when he said that Moray, as a Stewart, would be pleased to see his kinsman Lennox restored. He himself and Queen Mary too had simply desired to oblige Queen Elizabeth. Whether Lennox came or not he regarded as of no importance one way or the other, and he added that the Queen, his mistress, saw no danger in the matter to 'move her to put her reputation in doubt before the world by breach of promise'.[21] This implied reproof was all the more unpleasant to Elizabeth because it showed that the Scots were having a quiet chuckle at her expense. Mary herself wrote to Elizabeth on the matter; this being unanswerable, Elizabeth had dismissed it angrily as 'so despiteful that she believed all friendship and familiarity had been given up'.[22]

On 18 September 1564 Mary sent Sir James Melville of Halhill to London to mend fences. Sir James was instructed to apologise to Elizabeth on Mary's behalf should anything she had written on the recall of Lennox have given pain to the Queen. He was to make arrangements for a conference at Berwick on the subject of the Dudley marriage, to sound out the English parliament regarding

Mary's succession claim, and to induce Elizabeth, if possible, to declare publicly in favour of Mary as her successor. Melville was chosen for this delicate mission because he was an experienced diplomat, having served Mary, man and boy, from the age of fourteen when he was appointed her page at the French court. Charming, suave and urbane, he had a razor-sharp intellect; but his chief asset for the task was that he was an unknown quantity to Elizabeth who would be less on her guard than she would with Maitland, of whose formidable negotiating powers both she and Cecil were in awe. The real purpose of Melville's mission, however, was to keep up the pretence of goodwill between the two queens, so that Darnley might be allowed to visit Scotland.

Elizabeth used all the weapons of deception, deviousness and dissimulation in her arsenal to pull the wool over Melville's eyes, but the result was hardly what she had expected. On the contrary, she so exhibited her feminine foibles that his record of his interview with her is by far the most graphic and amusing description of her personality in existence. It was during this bizarre meeting that she introduced Melville to Robert Dudley whom, on the spot, she created Baron Denbigh and Earl of Leicester. She gave the game away, however, by unthinkingly putting her hand on Dudley's neck 'to tickle him smilingly'. She prattled on about giving her former lover to Mary as a special token of her favour and even suggested that after Mary and Robert married they should come to London and live with her as part of her household! Melville kept a suitably straight face throughout this grotesque performance but he had no illusions about Elizabeth and her preposterous behaviour. In subsequent interviews over succeeding days Elizabeth constantly plied Melville with questions about Mary: which of them was the taller, the more beautiful and so on. When she discovered that Mary played the lute and the virginals, she contrived, whenever Sir James came into her presence, to be playing a musical instrument of some sort or another.

By contrast, when Melville reported back to Mary she asked him, in her usual forthright manner, whether Elizabeth was sincere in her profession of friendship. Melville gave a straight answer, saying that 'there was neither plain dealing nor upright meaning, but great dissimulation, emulation and fear, that her princely qualities should all too soon chase her out and displace her from the kingdom'.[23] As if to underline this, Melville reported how the newly created Earl of

Leicester had taken him into his confidence on the boat journey down the Thames. When Leicester asked Melville what Queen Mary thought of the proposed match, Melville replied very coldly, as he had been instructed to do. Leicester's self-esteem was stung by this response and he realised that his dilemma was both absurd and dangerous. Leicester admitted that he never had any ambitions to marry the Queen of Scots, that the scheme had been concocted by his arch-enemy Cecil, and that if he showed any enthusiasm for the marriage he would lose the favour of both queens. He wished the farce could be ended as quickly as possible.

Melville's full and candid report disabused Mary of any residual notion regarding Elizabeth's sincerity. She was now convinced that Elizabeth had no intention of letting her marry Leicester and that, so far as the English succession was concerned, she would get no satisfaction either. The conference at Berwick between Scottish and English commissioners on 18 November 1564 was allowed to go ahead, although both sides knew that the grave deliberations over the forthcoming marriage between Mary and Leicester were non-sensical. The only person taken in by this charade was Randolph who earnestly believed that such a marriage was on the cards. Moray and Maitland both wrote to Cecil on 3 December 1564 saying that a decision on the matter was urgent, in view of parallel negotiations for a foreign marriage which were now coming on quickly. While they did not approve of a foreign marriage, and were anxious to accommodate Elizabeth as much as possible, it was necessary that she deal frankly with them. In such a case they would do everything in their power to assist her plans; but if she persisted in the course she was following, she need not find it strange 'if we thereafter change our deliberations as cause shall be ministered, and seek to save ourselves the best way we can'.[24]

What precisely they meant by a satisfactory course of action on Elizabeth's part probably neither of them was clear. Cecil replied that Leicester was the ideal choice because he 'was dearly and singularly esteemed of the Queen's Majesty'. The word 'beloved' (Cecil's first choice) was crossed out on second thoughts, as this might have been misconstrued. There was more unconscious humour in this burlesque epistle which Cecil, with tongue in cheek, probably did not intend to be taken too seriously. Moray and Maitland replied in similar vein, coming straight to the point and saying that if Elizabeth was determined to do nothing about the succession then they would never allow Queen Mary to marry an Englishman. Had Mary married Leicester she would have made herself a standing joke all over Europe. On 1 February 1565 Maitland, on his own account, wrote candidly to Cecil, appealing to his vanity and sense of his own destiny by saying that if they succeeded in the union of the two nations, posterity would judge them to have been more honourable than even those who 'did most valiantly serve King Edward the First in his conquest, or King Robert the Bruce in the recovery of his country'.[25] Even if Cecil could have been inspired by Maitland to a higher form of patriotism, he was hamstrung by the selfish caprice of Elizabeth.

Meanwhile, poor Randolph was still going about his fool's errand, fondly believing that Leicester and Mary would soon be heading for the altar. At the beginning of February he visited Mary at St Andrews, finding her living quietly and modestly in a merchant's house. She was in high spirits and showed Randolph how like a bourgeois wife she could live with her little troupe of lap-dogs, while she merrily rebuked him for interrupting her simple pleasures with his great and grave matters. A day or two later they went riding together and Mary reminisced about her happy years in France, of her many friends there and of the close ties between that country and Scotland. She hinted that her Guise relatives were pressing her hard with their views on re-marriage. How could she ignore their wishes, she asked rhetorically. Randolph clumsily brought up the matter of the Leicester marriage and Mary, with a straight face, said that she was ready to place herself in his mistress's will, if only Elizabeth would remove that obstacle of the succession. She would be happy that, inhabiting the same island, they should live together like sisters, instead of being hurt and estranged; but she warned him that unless they came to a definite friendly agreement, it would pass the power of both of them to live as friends, whatever she might say or do. In furtherance of her plans, she instructed Archbishop Beaton in Paris to convey the impression that a marriage with King Charles might, after all, be imminent.

Randolph dutifully reported back to Elizabeth who promptly fell into the trap. If Mary was hell-bent on some foreign suitor, then she would complicate the situation and embarrass Mary into the bargain. She now gave her permission for Lord Darnley to pay a visit to Scotland. Elizabeth had as little inclination to let her rival marry Darnley as she had of relinquishing Leicester to her. If she wanted

Mary to marry Darnley she had only to say so, and Mary would not have cavilled at that, whether the succession question was settled or not. Maitland would have approved, for no other marriage would have rendered the succession more secure. Even Moray, who had his own ambitions to the Scottish throne, could not have demurred because such a marriage would have been acceptable to the majority of Protestants.

On 10 February 1565, Lord Darnley crossed the border and entered the land of his fathers.

7. AN IDEAL HUSBAND

1565

If languor makes me light
I am for evermore
In joy, both even and morrow.
> Henry, Lord Darnley, to Queen Mary, summer of 1565,
> Bannatyne MSS II, p.227

Immediately after investing Dudley with his earldom, Queen Elizabeth had turned to Sir James Melville and asked him how he liked the new earl. Sir James made a suitably complimentary reply, to which Elizabeth responded slyly: 'Yet you like better of yonder long lad,' and she nodded across the room to the tall young man who had borne the sword of honour before her when she entered the chamber. Melville seems to have formed an immediate but uncanny impression of the youth. 'No woman of spirit would make choice of such a man that was more like a woman than a man,' he replied, and by way of explanation he added in his *Memoirs*, 'for he was very lusty, beardless and lady-faced' – although that was written with the benefit of hindsight.

Henry Stewart, Lord Darnley, was eighteen at the time. Though born and brought up in England, he had impeccable Scottish antecedents. His father, Matthew Stewart, Earl of Lennox, was descended from a Stewart princess (Mary, daughter of James II) and on this was based his own claim to the Scottish throne, ahead of the Earl of Arran (later Duke of Châtelherault). When Arran allied himself with Cardinal Beaton, Lennox turned to England to bolster his own position. In 1544, seeking to marry Lady Margaret Douglas, the niece of Henry VIII, he tried to seize Dumbarton Castle with the aid of English troops and had suffered forfeiture and banishment as a result. In England, the traitor married Lady Margaret, daughter of Archibald Douglas, Earl of Angus, and his second wife Margaret Tudor, sister of Henry VIII and widow of James IV. The Countess of Lennox was therefore half-sister to James V, niece of Henry VIII, first cousin of Queen Elizabeth and aunt of Mary Queen of Scots. Her own claim to the English throne was second only to Mary's. The elder son of this marriage was Henry, given the courtesy title of Lord Darnley after one of the Lennox estates near Glasgow. There is considerable doubt regarding his date of birth. All biographers and historians till the late-nineteenth century gave this as 7 December 1545, making him exactly three years younger than Mary, but David Hay Fleming (1897) was the first to point out that Knox's Continuator said that he was not yet twenty-one at the time of his death (10 February 1567), and in March 1566 he was precisely stated by Mary's envoy to the Cardinal of Lorraine to be nineteen years old. On that basis he must have been born some time after 10 February 1546, and if we accept that people may be hazy about the year of their birth but never their actual birthday, then 7 December 1546 seems the most probable date.

Having agreed to let the Earl of Lennox return to Scotland, then tried at the last moment to prevent it, Elizabeth gave way. Making the best of it, she even recommended to Mary that his estates be restored, and it was on this score alone that Mary suggested to the Council his reinstatement, formally proclaimed at the Cross of Edinburgh on 9 October 1564. Ostensibly also to show good faith to 'her good sister, the Queen of England', Mary arranged tastefully furnished lodgings for him and entertained him at a series of banquets and masked balls organised in his honour. In turn, he hosted a number of dinners at which he entertained the Queen, 'the four Maries and some other delicate dames', as well as showering costly gifts (which he could ill afford) on the more influential courtiers. On one occasion he entertained Mary to supper at which she displayed her accomplishments as a dancer. Afterwards they played dice, the Queen losing a costly jewel to him. The Lennox Jewel, an elaborate piece which was at one time thought to have been designed as a memento after the Earl's death, belongs on stylistic grounds to an earlier period and is now believed to have been ordered by Lady Margaret at her husband's behest, and sent to him by the hand of Sir James Melville from London so that he could present it to Mary in exchange for the jewel she had gambled away.

On 27 October Mary set up a meeting at which Lennox and his old adversary Châtelherault were publicly reconciled, although in fact they would remain implacable foes. A life-long Catholic, Lennox now made a great show of his conversion to the new religion, and attended Protestant services regularly; with rapt attention he hung on every word that dropped from Knox's lips. By the end of the month it was widely rumoured that the Countess herself would soon be coming back to Scotland with her two sons. Randolph noted approvingly that there was a 'marvellous good liking of the young lord' and that many wished to see him in Scotland, though the public regarded the return of his mother as about as welcome as a visitation of the plague.

Darnley, born and brought up in England, was raised in the Catholic faith. Doubtless he was well aware, all his life, of his high position in regard to both the English and Scottish thrones, for through him his mother hoped to realise her own unfulfilled dynastic ambitions. Next to securing recognition for her son, Margaret Lennox worked ceaselessly to have her husband reinstated. When Francis II was crowned at Rheims she despatched her son thither for an audience with Queen Mary to try to have the family's estates restored. In this he failed, but he was back in France a year later to offer his condolences at the King's funeral. As early as December 1561, his ambitious mother regarded him as the ideal replacement for Francis. For her part, Mary must have been impressed by this boy. After they met for the third time, at Wemyss Castle on 17 February 1565, Mary confessed to Sir James Melville that he was 'the lustiest and best proportioned lang man she had seen'.[1]

After crossing the Tweed at Berwick on 10 February, Darnley had travelled via Dunbar and Haddington, reaching Edinburgh three days later. He spent three days in the capital as the guest of Randolph who lent him horses and otherwise went to such trouble on his behalf as leads us to suppose that Darnley's visit to Scotland was at Elizabeth's instigation. He was entertained, in the Queen's absence, at Holyroodhouse by Lord Robert Stewart on whom he made a very favourable impression. Thus encouraged, Darnley mounted one of Randolph's horses and rode over to Fife where Mary was hunting. Exactly one week after crossing the border, Darnley encountered his future wife at the home of the laird of Wemyss.

In four years Darnley had grown enormously in stature; estimates of his height (based on his skeleton) put him between six foot one and six foot three. He was slender without being skinny, well proportioned and exceptionally good-looking – too good-looking perhaps, for there was a hint of effeminacy about him. The two portraits by Hans Eworth – a three-quarter length on his own at the age of ten and a full length at the age of seventeen standing beside his little brother – reveal an oval face with perfect features framed by golden-brown curls. The earlier portrait seems to show a maturity beyond his years, but the later portrait hints at sensuality in the full lips. The eyes are oddly expressionless, though some commentators, notably Antonia Fraser, have remarked fancifully on the hint of cruelty which they betray. Mary, who was well aware of Darnley's potential as a suitor, seems to have been greatly taken with him from the outset, although it cannot be said by any stretch of the imagination that it was love at first sight. They met as cousins and at first Mary was inclined to be reserved with him, on account of Lennox having previously broached the subject of marriage with her, much to her annoyance at the time. But Mary was impressed by Darnley's elegance and impeccable manners. He was courteous, charming and suitably deferential without being subservient, and Mary soon found herself warming to him. Besides, apart from his girlish beauty, he was one of the few men she had met who was taller than herself.

Darnley seems to have been especially groomed for his future exalted position. He was accomplished in music, dancing and the arts, a competent scholar and no mean versifier; but he was also an excellent horseman, a crack shot and master swordsman. He was a good athlete and sportsman, while his experience in ceremonial duties at Elizabeth's court must have stood him in good stead. Superficially at least he seemed perfect in every respect, but appearances were deceptive. Despite his Renaissance education he was intellectually shallow. His head was turned by his ambitious mother and adoring father and he had been brought up to believe that he was the only person of real importance. His over-indulgent parents never inculcated a sense of self-discipline; instead, he developed a passion for all the pleasures of the flesh amounting to an obsession, his teens being devoted to all manner of dissipation and debauchery.

On this first encounter Darnley had the good sense not to

overstay his welcome. After a brief interview, he set off for Dunkeld to pay his respects to his father who was residing there with his old friend, the Earl of Atholl. With the Queen's good wishes ringing in his ears, Darnley was back within the week, joining the royal entourage at North Queensferry and riding back to Edinburgh in the Queen's company. Thereafter he was never out of Mary's sight. He was urbane and fitted in well with Mary's assortment of foreign courtiers, forming an especial attachment to David Riccio, Mary's Italian secretary. Darnley had a veneer of culture and aesthetic sensibility that was singularly lacking in the Scottish noblemen and this in itself would have commended him to the Queen. Soon he was her constant companion, dancing with her and relaxing with her in the evening over cards or dice. A brilliant lutanist, he often accompanied her while she sang her favourite French ballads. He also shared her passion for hawking, hunting and other outdoor pursuits.

Although it was widely rumoured that the Queen was enamoured of her handsome young cousin, Mary herself seems not to have given him any encouragement so long as the marriage to Leicester was likely; but Mary's enthusiasm for this match evaporated as soon as she realised that Elizabeth would not recognise her as her heir, even if she did marry him. In truth, even if Mary did not 'weap her full' when Randolph broke the news to her, she probably only heaved a sigh of relief now that the charade with Leicester was seen to be no more than a meaningless sham. Strangely enough, Randolph, who had been cultivating a close friendship with Darnley, as one Englishman to another, seems to have been exceptionally naïve in thinking that Mary had no thought of marrying Darnley, and that her frequent and friendly intercourse with the boy was due entirely to 'her own courteous nature'.[2]

Opinion as to Scottish attitudes towards a marriage between Mary and Darnley is sharply divided and Henderson was alone in assuming that such a union 'specially appealed to a Scottish sentiment that was deeper than the religious contention of the hour'.[3] Mary assumed that Elizabeth would approve, because she had virtually thrown the boy at her; but the capricious Elizabeth was outraged when she heard the rumours. To be sure, Elizabeth's emotions were in turmoil at the time and she does not appear to have known her own mind. It is probable that she had played with Mary and Darnley on the grounds that such a marriage would be demeaning to Mary and make of her a laughing-stock throughout Europe. Doubtless she knew Darnley well enough to realise that this young fop would sooner or later show his true colours.

Love was never more blind than in this case, and Mary rapidly became so infatuated by Darnley as to be totally insensible to his shortcomings. As Mary's infatuation increased, so Darnley's attitude towards her became more casual, at times almost indifferent – which only served to intensify her passion for him. Friends and courtiers were correspondingly alarmed at these developments, but she was deaf to their advice and entreaties. Soon, Mary's intentions upset virtually everyone with whom she came in contact; she even quarrelled with the four Maries that spring, and fell out with her closest advisers. Others, of course, had their own selfish reasons for opposing the match. Moray was particularly upset because such a marriage destroyed his own ambitions on the throne. The nobility, on the whole, opposed the match because it advanced the house of Lennox at the expense of rival factions, notably the Hamiltons. Randolph observed prophetically, 'What shall become of him I know not, but it is greatly to be feared that he can have no long life amongst this people.'[4] By now, Randolph himself was aware of Darnley's shortcomings, and of the efforts Mary was making to change him: 'The Queen herself, being of better understanding, seeketh to frame and fashion him to the nature of her subjects,' though even Randolph had to concede that it was an impossible task. 'He is counted proud, disdainful and suspicious. A greater plague to her [Mary] there cannot be, a greater benefit to the Queen's Majesty [Elizabeth] could not have been chanced.'

In the face of so much adverse opinion and contrary advice, Mary exhibited a fatal obstinacy. The more people opposed the match, the more she favoured it. Then, as so often happened, fate lent a hand. In April, when the court was at Stirling, Darnley went down with an attack of what was believed at the time to be measles, but was more probably secondary syphilis. The tender-hearted Mary was constantly in attendance in his bedchamber, a reprise of those bedside vigils for the sickly Francis. Lady Lennox assured Diego Guzman de Silva, the Spanish ambassador in London, that the Queen had spent the entire night in her son's sickroom, but it is more probable that Mary had only gone there late at night in order to avoid being seen.

Inevitably the 'fond tales and foolish reports' of gossiping servants magnified these ministrations into something more prurient. Mary might have been flouting convention by her thoughtless, generous behaviour, but with Darnley racked by high fever it is impossible that her nightly visits were for the purpose of amorous dalliance. Darnley's pathetic gratitude at her attention soon gave way to general peevishness which Mary mistook for a symptom of his illness and accordingly made allowances for his petted behaviour. The more tongues wagged, the more Mary drew towards Darnley, partly due to her own waywardness and partly through her instinct to protect him. But Darnley's violent tendencies became manifest in May, while he was still recovering in bed. One day Châtelherault, a long-time enemy of Lennox, paid the young man a visit, with a view to a reconciliation between their families. His reward was a threat from the vindictive youth that when recovered he would knock the Duke's pate.

Interestingly, Mary and Darnley were not the only targets of the gossip-mongers that spring. In March John Knox, whose first wife, Marjory Bowes, had died, married seventeen-year-old Margaret Stewart, daughter of Lord Ochiltree. Knox, with his patriarchal beard of biblical proportions and physically exhausted by his super-human exertions in reforming his fellow-countryman, looked much older than his fifty-odd years and, indeed, within eight years he would have gone to his Maker.[5] The match was as sudden as it was bizarre. Margaret, a kind of religious groupie, may have been motivated by morbid religiosity, but Knox was probably actuated by ambition rather than love, seeking to recover the status that was slipping away from him since Mary's return to Scotland. It was this marriage which was the last straw so far as Moray was concerned. Outraged that Knox should have married a Stewart, Earl James refused to have any contact with the elderly bridegroom for upwards of eighteen months. Mary herself was horrified and outraged when she was apprised of his intentions, regarding Knox as a sanctimonious old humbug and threatening to expel him from Scotland for presuming to marry one of her own 'blood and name'.[6] Nevertheless, she must have had good cause to be thankful towards the old goat, for his amorous adventure took some of the limelight away from herself. An eye-witness described Knox riding to his wedding accompanied by his numerous henchmen and mounted on a trim gelding, 'not like a prophet or an old decrepit priest, as he was, but boy like as had been one of the blood royal, with his bands of taffeta fashioned with golden rings and precious stones'.[7]

While Darnley was laid low by his mysterious ailment, Maitland was in England. Randolph, who accompanied the diplomat as far as Berwick, was unaware of the true nature of his mission, and supposed that it was with a view to finalising the negotiations for the Queen's marriage to Leicester. In fact Maitland was engaged on the rather delicate business of securing Spanish approval for the Darnley match while, at the same time, continuing to press Elizabeth about a settlement to the long-running problem of the succession. He also had the unenviable task of breaking the news to Elizabeth about Mary's impending marriage to Darnley. The first objective was readily attained, De Silva warmly approving of Darnley as a husband for Mary after reassuring Maitland that there was now absolutely no prospect of a marriage with the homicidal Don Carlos.

Elizabeth was another matter. She herself had been making approaches to Charles IX, Don Carlos and Archduke Charles on her own account, not from any real hopes of marrying one of them but merely to spike her cousin's guns. Officially, the engagement of Mary to Leicester was still her avowed aim, although she was behaving in a very peculiar manner if that were the case. In addition to the neck-tickling incident at Leicester's elevation, there was a curious incident in April 1565. Leicester and the Duke of Norfolk were playing tennis one day while Elizabeth looked on. Leicester, sweating profusely, had absent-mindedly taken the handkerchief from the Queen's hand and wiped himself with it, whereupon Norfolk swore to thrash him with his racket for his impudence. Elizabeth separated them before they came to blows and expressed herself 'offended sore with the Duke'.[8] When Leicester had a serious riding accident shortly afterwards and was confined to bed for several days, Elizabeth ministered to him exactly as Mary was doing for Darnley about the same time.

Nevertheless, when Maitland informed Elizabeth of Mary's intentions regarding Darnley, Elizabeth flew into a rage. The luckless Lady Lennox was put under house arrest and Sir Nicholas Throckmorton was despatched hot-foot to Scotland with instructions to bring Darnley back to London immediately. Before he reached his destination, however, Elizabeth recalled Throckmorton. At the end of April he was back in London where he met with Cecil and Maitland to discuss the matter at length before it was put before the Privy Council. On 1 May the Council met and declared the Darnley marriage to be 'unmeet, unprofitable and perilous to the sincere amity between the Queens and their realms,' but compromised by offering 'a free election of any other of the nobility either in this whole realm or isle, or in any other place, being sortable for her state, and agreeable to both the realms'.[9] This was quite meaningless, for the Council retained the right to veto any other marriage proposal. Elizabeth issued a fresh set of instructions to Throckmorton which promised that if Mary persisted with the Darnley marriage she could forget the succession. If she chose Leicester, however, she *might* consider the matter. In her heart of hearts Elizabeth knew that Mary would not now agree to the Leicester proposal.

Mary was so confident of Maitland's success in bringing Elizabeth round that she was in an unusually perky mood. On Easter Monday she and the ladies of her court dressed themselves as 'bourgeois wives' and went through the streets of Stirling lightheartedly begging money off passers-by for a banquet which she organised for her servants. Mary herself presided over this feast, much to Randolph's surprise. Her exuberance was severely dented when the express messenger arrived the following Saturday with despatches from Maitland conveying Elizabeth's extreme displeasure. Fun and frolic flew out of the window that weekend.

Mary was only momentarily downcast. Suddenly flinging discretion to the wind, and without waiting for Maitland's return or the arrival of Throckmorton with Elizabeth's own formal message, she resolved to announce her forthcoming marriage. When Moray came to Stirling the following day she put before him a document which she asked him to sign. It was, in fact, a promise to do his best to promote the marriage. Taken aback at the suddenness of this, James asked for time to consider the matter, whereupon Mary flew into a rage with him. On 5 May she sent off John Beaton, brother of the Archbishop, to intercept Maitland as he headed north. Beaton had orders in Mary's own hand instructing Maitland to turn around and let Elizabeth know, in no uncertain terms, that Mary was perfectly capable of choosing a husband for herself, with the advice of her own Council. Throckmorton was present when Maitland received this letter, and managed to peruse it for he wrote to Cecil afterwards that he wished that he and Leicester could have read it: 'You would have said that there had neither wanted eloquence, dispite, anger, love nor passion.'[10]

Beaton also had orders for Maitland that, as soon as he had

delivered this impassioned outburst to Elizabeth, he was to cross over to France to win the backing of that country for the marriage. Beaton met Maitland on the road between Newark and Grantham, but Maitland ignored Mary's orders and hurried north as quickly as possible, catching up with Throckmorton at Alnwick. Throckmorton recorded that the usually self-possessed Maitland was beside himself with anxiety, and wondered what had agitated him so uncharacteristically. He assumed from this that Maitland had little relish for the marriage, but Maitland's anguish ran much deeper, for he had a sudden vision of all his carefully laid plans for the ultimate union of the kingdoms set at naught by Mary's rash actions. He was terrified that Scotland would be plunged into civil war as a result. There can be no question as to Maitland's motives, putting the good of his country above his own future. By disobeying Mary's orders he not only jeopardised his career and the prospect of marrying his fiancée Mary Fleming (one of the four Maries), but put his life in danger. Furthermore, in striving to keep Mary on her throne at all costs, even if it meant her backing down and adopting a conciliatory approach to her duplicitous cousin Elizabeth, Maitland was alienating his former allies, Knox and Moray. Knox had been the Queen's implacable enemy from the outset, and now Moray, who still entertained notions of becoming regent if not King of Scots, was becoming estranged from his half-sister as a result of her proposed marriage.

Maitland fervently believed that the only way out of this mess was to patch up the quarrel between the two queens and, by adopting a cautious and conciliatory policy, to persuade Elizabeth to accept with a good grace what it was beyond her power to prevent. He realised the folly of giving Mary's rash letter to Elizabeth; this would have opened up a rift that could never have been healed. With a heavy heart and mounting apprehension, he travelled on to Edinburgh which he reached on 13 May. Here he was instructed by Mary to delay Throckmorton for several days before going with him to Stirling, on the grounds that his accommodation was not yet ready. Maitland passed on the message to Throckmorton but left him to his own devices and hurried on to Stirling alone to face the music. He arrived on the evening of 14 May, but the following morning Throckmorton himself arrived. To his consternation he found the castle gates locked. Demanding that the porter open the gate and admit him immediately, he fumed and fretted for several minutes before two members of the Council appeared and ordered him, in the Queen's name, to retire to his lodgings, saying that Mary would grant him an audience once he had suitably rested himself.

That afternoon Throckmorton was finally admitted. Accompanied by Lord Ruthven and Lord Erskine, he was escorted to the audience chamber where he found Mary and the leading men of her Council – Châtelherault, Argyll, Moray, Morton and Glencairn. Unabashed by such an august gathering, Throckmorton delivered an offensive harangue on his mistress's behalf, complaining bitterly not only of Mary's hasty proceeding with Darnley but the manner in which she had erred 'by unadvisedness and rashness'. Mary responded with remarkable restraint and dignity, saying blandly that she had done as she had because she thought that no marriage could have been so agreeable to all parties, Elizabeth and England as well as her subjects and the realm of Scotland. Throckmorton discovered that although the marriage was virtually settled, it would not actually take place for three months, during which time Mary hoped to do everything possible to reach an amicable understanding with her sister queen. Somewhat mollified, Throckmorton hoped that Elizabeth could be persuaded to agree.

In pursuing this marriage, however, Mary was to find the odds stacked heavily against her. Quite apart from Darnley's increasingly negative personal qualities, there was the religious aspect to contend with. Lennox was now at least a nominal convert to Protestantism, and Darnley himself would have blown whichever way suited him best; but Lady Margaret was a high-profile Catholic and that in itself damned the marriage in the eyes of the religious extremists. If Mary had been better advised she might have perceived the danger in persisting with this marriage; but at the end of the day Mary would have gone her own way regardless of the advice she got. Her immediate reaction to Throckmorton's message from Elizabeth was to create Darnley Lord Ardmarnock and Earl of Ross, thus keeping him on par with Leicester. Mary would also have created him Duke of Albany – an elevated title hitherto confined to heirs to the throne and virtually the Scottish counterpart of Prince of Wales – but prudently she decided to hold that in reserve until she saw what Elizabeth's reaction would be. When the coveted dukedom was withheld, however, Darnley flew into a furious rage, drawing a dagger and lunging petulantly at the Justice-Clerk, bearer of the bad news, which Randolph gleefully reported to Leicester, of all people.[11]

Mary tried to retrieve the situation by sending John Hay, a prominent Protestant, to London on 14 June with the task of smoothing Elizabeth's ruffled feathers. Mary feigned surprise that Elizabeth should be so vehemently opposed to a match that she had done so much to engineer. While she could hardly go back on her word to her fiancé, she now suggested that the matter be referred to an Anglo-Scottish commission whose Scottish members she proposed would be Moray, Morton, Glencairn, Ruthven, Maitland, Bellenden and Carnegie of Kinnaird, a body of men so irreproachably Protestant that Elizabeth's interests were bound to be guaranteed. Elizabeth, apprised of Hay's mission, did not wait for him to reach London but sent a courier north with letters to Lennox and Darnley peremptorily recalling them to London. On 24 June, the day of Hay's arrival, Elizabeth sent Lady Lennox to the Tower. Hay was granted a brief interview, during which Elizabeth ranted and raved at him and cut him short. He was sent packing with a curt, arrogant note to Mary. Before leaving London he had a meeting with De Silva who assured him that King Philip favoured the marriage and seems to have given some kind of guarantee that Spain would take all steps necessary to prevent Elizabeth interfering by armed force. De Silva also cautioned that Mary should act as prudently as possible, and not aggravate the situation by raising the question of the succession at this moment.

This was some crumb of comfort to Hay, still smarting from his interview with Elizabeth. It seemed to him that Elizabeth, in her violent rejection of any compromise after luring Mary into this marital trap, was behaving towards the Scots with her father's duplicitous arrogance. Elizabeth's extremely high-handed behaviour now roused in the Scots the old hostility, dormant for several years but never far from the surface, and these anti-English feelings were far stronger than any attachment to Protestantism. There was a certain animosity against Darnley, particularly among the more prominent noblemen who had a chance to observe the youth at close quarters; but Elizabeth's foolish behaviour now obliged them to close ranks and accept Mary's wishes.

On 26 June commissioners from the Kirk presented Mary with a set of proposals. The first urged that the Mass should be abolished throughout the kingdom, 'not only in the subjects' but also in the Queen's own person'. Mary refused to answer this, although a compromise was effected on 12 July when it was announced that she had no intention of molesting any of her subjects in 'the quiet using of their religion'. On 29 July Mary finally got around to answering the commissioners, saying that she could not, in all conscience, abandon the faith 'wherein she had been nourished and brought up'. To have done so would have lost her the friendship of princes abroad. She had no desire to press the conscience of anyone and hoped that no one would seek to press her conscience. The formal establishment of religion, she maintained, would be deferred until the Three Estates were agreed.

On 30 June Mary received word from Charles IX that he approved of her proposed marriage. Catherine de' Medici had her own good reasons for seeing her rival settled in a marriage that did not interfere with her own interests. By contrast, the Cardinal of Lorraine wrote to Mary at the end of May trying to talk her out of a marriage with such *un gentil huteaudeau*, a rather coarse slang expression whose equivalent today would be 'a complete prat'. When he learned that Mary was determined on this marriage, he had the good grace to give way and undertook to write to the Pope for a dispensation enabling the cousins to wed.

Chief among those who continued to oppose the marriage was the Queen's half-brother, Moray. On 18 July he and a group of malcontents met secretly at Stirling to formulate a request to Elizabeth for military intervention as she had done in the time of the Queen Mother. They may have been thus emboldened by an assurance from Elizabeth a week earlier that she would not be found wanting if they required her assistance. Meanwhile Mary, having got wind of what the conspirators were up to, brought forward the date of her wedding. In fact Randolph reported to London on 16 July that Mary and Darnley had married clandestinely on 9 July and had consummated their marriage that very night at Seton House. Two days later, he added, the bridal couple had gone to Edinburgh in disguise (Mary in male attire) and had promenaded through the town after dinner at the castle. Whatever the truth of this, Mary on 22 July mobilised her subjects to withstand possible invasion from England and on the same day created Darnley Duke of Albany, the banns of marriage being proclaimed simultaneously in St Giles and the Chapel Royal.

About nine o'clock on the evening of 28 July a proclamation was read at the Mercat Cross, stating that Prince Henry, Duke of Albany, was henceforth to be named and styled as King. All royal letters would be in the names of 'the said illustrious Prince our future husband and us as King and Queen of Scotland conjunctly'. A well-armed body of troops was on hand lest this proclamation provoke a disturbance, but it passed off without incident. Adam Zwetkovich, the Imperial ambassador to England, later told the Emperor that he had heard that Mary created Darnley king before her marriage because she had previously been married to one of the greatest kings in Christendom and therefore intended to wed no one unless he were a king. This was a wilful act, reflecting Mary's concern for her own dignity, but it was strictly illegal, without the advice and consent of her Council or the Estates.

The marriage took place in the Chapel Royal on Sunday, 29 July, the sacrament being performed by John Sinclair, Dean of Restalrig, later Bishop of Brechin and Lord President of the Council. The necessary dispensation from the Pope did not reach Edinburgh till some months afterwards, indicating Mary's disregard of papal authority when it clashed with her own wishes. She who had defied her nobility and Elizabeth was quite prepared to defy the Pope if need be.

The wedding was a magnificent affair by Scottish standards, though well below the sumptuous level of Mary's marriage to Francis in Notre-Dame. The only detailed account of it was penned by Randolph who was not actually an eye-witness. According to this account, she was clad in her widow's weeds and led into the chapel at six in the morning by the earls of Lennox and Atholl. There she waited until the groom was brought in by the same lords. Vows were exchanged and Darnley solemnly placed three rings on the Queen's finger, then the bridal couple knelt while numerous prayers were said over them. When Darnley was referred to as King Henry the congregation was silent, except the bridegroom's father who loyally cried out, 'God save his Grace!' Darnley, demonstrating his new status, and his indifference to his wife's religion, refused to remain for Mass. Kissing his bride, he went to her chamber where, a few minutes later, Mary followed after receiving the sacrament on her own.

There was a quaint ceremony in which Mary, after a nominal show of reluctance, was divested of her black garments (the Scottish, as opposed to French, colour of mourning) and robed in raiment more suited to such a joyful occasion. After resting till noon the bridal couple were conveyed to a wedding breakfast by the assembled nobility amid the rejoicing of the ordinary people.

Trumpets sounded and largesse, in the form of gold and silver coins, was scattered to the crowd. At the banquet itself Atholl, Morton, Crawford, Eglinton, Cassilis and Glencairn performed the tasks of carvers, cupbearers and attendants on the royal couple. After the meal they danced together before retiring to rest before an equally lavish supper, followed by more dancing, 'and so theie go to bedd', according to Randolph.

With a powerful militia at her back, Mary now took decisive action against her rebellious brother. The following day the Council issued a summons to Moray to appear before them within six days 'or be pronounced rebel and pursued under the law'. Letters were also directed to Châtelherault and Argyll, ordering them not to assist Moray or his confederates. A number of suspects were rounded up in the north of Scotland as a precaution. Moray prudently withdrew to Argyll to watch events, doubtless hoping that English military intervention would not be long in coming.

Moray's principal backers were Châtelherault, the earls of Argyll, Glencairn and Rothes, Lord Boyd and Lord Ochiltree and the veteran general Kirkcaldy of Grange. With the exception of the last-named, they were all prominent nobles whose power lay mainly in the south-west of Scotland. Theoretically they posed a serious threat. Unlike the time, five years previously, when the Scots had united against Mary of Guise, however, there was little enthusiasm among the common people for an uprising against a queen who, despite her marriage, was still immensely popular in the country at large. Elizabeth, perceiving this to be the case, was not minded to send the military assistance which Moray and his friends so desperately needed.

On the other side Mary could count on powerful backing from her father-in-law and his close friend, the Earl of Atholl, but the earls of Caithness, Erroll, Montrose, Cassilis and Home, beside lords Fleming, Lindsay and Ruthven, also supported her. Her half-brother Lord Robert Stewart sided with her. Darnley himself had powerful connections, not only with Stewarts but with the Douglas faction headed by the Earl of Morton. Lord George Gordon, in prison since Corrichie, was now liberated, and Bothwell recalled from exile in France. While Gordon, now created Earl of Huntly, never quite forgave Mary for the cruel barbarity towards his father, he was even more violently opposed to Moray whom he would have cheerfully torn apart if he had got his hands on him. Similarly, Bothwell, who had suffered on account of his connection with the insane Arran plot and who had said many bitter things against Mary while in exile, was the implacable enemy of Moray. So he swallowed his pride, came home and joined in the campaign that would hopefully effect the downfall of his deadliest adversary.

While this odd assortment of noblemen were mustering their forces in defence of their queen and her effete husband, an envoy named John Tamworth arrived from England with a message from Elizabeth. She was pained at Mary's rejection of Leicester, expressed her astonishment that Mary was now treating her so strangely, and warned her against any attempt to suppress the new religion. Tamworth was instructed to entreat Mary to receive Moray and his supporters back into her favour and, lastly, to procure 'a continuance of peace and amity' between the two kingdoms. Tamworth's work was rendered difficult by an instruction that he was to ignore the marriage and if required by Mary to address Darnley as her husband he was to refuse to do so. This curious muddle of menace and cajolery, pretence of friendship and insult was the desperate act of a queen who was worried lest Mary enlist the help of France and Spain. She was alarmed to find that the Scottish Protestants were not so opposed to Mary's marriage as she had supposed. Now her only chance of maintaining a strong Protestant party in power in Scotland lay in inducing Mary to end her quarrel with Moray who, she hoped, would then be in a position to hold Mary's foreign policies in check.

Mary told Tamworth that she had offered to delay her marriage until the conditions had been considered by the Anglo-Scottish commissioners, but after Elizabeth refused to countenance such a commission there was no point in waiting any longer. She marvelled at Elizabeth's objection to her marriage, especially as Darnley and his father had been specially recommended to her goodwill by Elizabeth. Besides, her marriage should not be seen as an obstacle to their sisterly friendship. She had no desire to act with foreign powers against England, and expected Elizabeth to treat her and Scotland in the same vein. She had no intentions of making any changes in religion 'but that most convenient for the state of herself and her realm'. As regards Moray, she wished that Elizabeth would not interfere in Scotland's domestic affairs.

To these answers she added some counter-proposals of her own. She and King Henry undertook to do nothing to the prejudice of Elizabeth's title, they would not meddle in England's internal affairs nor harbour fugitives from English justice and they would not join any foreign league against England. On the contrary, they wished to form an alliance with England. Finally, if Mary should be called to the succession, she would make no changes in the religion, laws and liberties of England.

There were conditions attached, notably that Elizabeth should enact the proper succession to the English throne, naming her and her issue first, and failing that Lady Margaret and her lawful issue, that she would not meddle in Scotland nor join any league against Scotland. These were fair and reasonable proposals; the pity is that Mary was not dealing with a fair and reasonable person when she made them. By now even Elizabeth's own Council were urging her to settle the vexed question of the succession. Mary probably realised the futility of her argument, but saw no harm in making her counter-proposals anyway. Matters were not helped by the stiff-necked Tamworth refusing a passport for his return journey, signed by King Henry. This refusal earned him several days' detention, thereby triggering off a diplomatic incident that threatened to disrupt Anglo-Scottish relations altogether.

As the crisis deepened, King Henry, now posing as a staunch Protestant, made a point of attending Knox's services and listening intently to his sermons. Interestingly, the only verbatim transcript of any of these long sermons is one made by Henry and was written down from memory immediately after hearing it from the pulpit on 19 August. It was a vicious personal attack on the young king who worked off his anger by writing it down rather than taking his dinner. Had Henry not been in church that day from purely political motives, he would certainly have stormed out of the building in high dudgeon. After writing out as much of the tirade as he could recall, Henry went hawking to work off his spleen. In the sermon Knox likened Mary to 'that harlot Jezebel'. At Mary's behest Knox was barred from preaching for fifteen days, an extremely lenient punishment in the circumstances, though Mary had no wish to offend Protestants at such a crucial time. Unabashed, Knox spent the enforced idleness of the ensuing two weeks preparing his offensive sermon for publication.

On 15 August the rebels began mobilising near Ayr, with the intention of going on the offensive nine days later. As soon as Mary was apprised of their plans she issued a summons on 22 August, calling up the men of the middle shires. On Sunday afternoon, 26

August, Mary left Edinburgh for Linlithgow, with a strong force consisting of 600 arquebusiers and 200 spearmen close behind. As she journeyed westwards, armed men flocked to her standard, and by the time she had reached Glasgow her army had swollen to over 5,000. Moray and Châtelherault, however, outflanked her and entered Edinburgh on 31 August with 1,200 horsemen. Argyll, with a similar number of cavalry, was expected to join them two days later. Moray's strategy was quite simple. He and the Duke would control the capital, raise as many recruits as they could from the townspeople, and hold out until a force of 400 English arquebusiers landed at Leith.

The citizens of Edinburgh, however, remained loyal to Mary and Moray failed to recruit more than a handful. Infinitely more serious was the non-appearance of the hoped-for reinforcements from England. John Erskine (whom Mary had created Earl of Mar on 23 June), held Edinburgh Castle in the Queen's name, and he now threatened to turn his artillery on the rebels. In fact, Mar's great guns began to bombard the city while John Knox was putting the finishing touches to his sermon which ended fittingly with a prayer amid 'the terrible roring of gunnes and the noyce of armour'. As the cannon thundered and masonry crashed around him, Knox was at the lowest point of his turbulent career. The plot to overthrow Mary seemed doomed, and with it Protestantism and Knox would perish together.

Moray reacted to the bombardment by dashing off a timid letter to his sister, urging her to lay off while he submitted to the justice of the Council. Mary, however, had the bit between her teeth and was determined to crush her brother's power for ever. She pressed on regardless, brushing aside with the contempt it deserved the well-meaning proposal of the French ambassador Castelnau that Elizabeth should mediate in the dispute. Some of her followers had no great enthusiasm for an armed showdown with Moray but they were now swept along with her. Randolph stood by, a helpless bystander, amazed and disgusted at Elizabeth's indecisiveness, when the relatively small sum of £8,000 or £10,000 in his estimation might easily have brought the Scots to their senses. But the cash never materialised, and matters went on their tragi-comic course.

In the face of Mary's rapid advance eastwards, Moray and his troops evacuated Edinburgh on the afternoon of Sunday, 2 September, under cover of a providential thunderstorm. They headed southwards to evade the Queen's forces and made for Dumfries where they would wait in vain for help from England. Mary went back to Glasgow via Stirling to monitor the movements of Argyll, but then returned to Edinburgh later in the month to organise a much larger army to deal with a possible invasion from the south. On 10 September the rebels sent Robert Melville to London to entreat Elizabeth to send them help in the form of 3,000 infantry, with field artillery and a battery of siege engines. Randolph endorsed this plea, exaggerating Mary's difficulties and maximising the half-heartedness of her supporters.

Elizabeth hinted that she would provide help, but, fearing possible intervention from France or Spain, she did nothing. Mary, having got the moral support of Spain and the Papacy, mustered a large force and took the field against her brother before help could reach him. A powerful addition to her army was the new Earl of Huntly, who brought with him a large contingent of Gordons from the north-east. The Earl of Bothwell also mustered a sizable contingent from the Borders. By the time this vast army had advanced on Dumfries, however, the rebels had dispersed, its leaders having fled into England. At Carlisle, Moray received a letter from Elizabeth, refusing military aid but 'out of her private love and clemency' offering him her protection.[12]

His humiliation was complete when he appeared before Elizabeth and was scolded by her for his folly, in the presence of the two French ambassadors, De Foix and Castelnau. As he bowed his head and half-listened to Elizabeth railing at him, he must have pondered what might have been the outcome if his bold venture had succeeded. Had he managed to capture his sister and her husband and delivered them over to Elizabeth, his achievement would have been rewarded by the regency at least, perhaps even the Scottish crown. Now browbeaten and shamed, he chose the insults of Elizabeth in preference to the wrath of his sister. Randolph provided the tailpiece to this episode, high drama tinged with farce. Writing to Leicester on 19 October, he reported that Queen Mary was 'now returned from her painful and great journey. She rode far with great expedition, much trouble of the whole country, and found not them whom she sought, when she came to her journey's end'.[13]

8. THE RICCIO AFFAIR

1565–66

Laurel is green for a season, and love is sweet for a day;
But love grows bitter with treason, and laurel outlives not May.
  Algernon Swinburne, *Hymn to Proserpine*

In the aftermath of the Chaseabout Raid, as the indeterminate campaign of 1565 came to be known, there was a lull in Scotland. Catholics and Protestants had reached some sort of peaceful co-existence as the easy-going attitude of Queen Mary percolated down to the lieges. Even the firebrand Knox was keeping a low profile. Despite his gloomy forebodings during the bombardment of Edinburgh, he had survived. He had not fled into England like so many of the leading Protestant figures, but sought refuge in the far west of Scotland where he put his time to good use in revising his *History*. Beyond the domestic scene, all was sweetness and light for the moment, and the correspondence between the two queens was resumed, dripping with insincerity, for each lady now had the measure of the other.

It would be an exaggeration to claim, as some biographers have done, that Mary was pre-eminently concerned with the attainment and exercise of power. She was robbed of that by the death of her first husband, and then thwarted in her ambitions to recover her exalted continental status. One tends to forget that although her personal rule of Scotland had only existed for four years, she was still little more than a girl. At the time of her marriage to Darnley she was only twenty-three, an age at which most women were engaging in matrimony for the first time. Despite living in wedded bliss with Francis it is probable that Mary was still a virgin. On account of his congenital deformity, general immaturity and poor physical condition, it is unlikely that penetrative sexual intercourse ever took place.

Now, probably for the first time in her life, Mary was aroused sexually and the effects appear to have been quite devastating. While Mary and Darnley doubtless had some sort of handfasting or betrothal at Seton early in May the canard of their sleeping together then can be discounted. Had intimacy taken place at that juncture it is unlikely that Mary would have proceeded with the marriage, but by saving herself till after a public wedding, she increased the intensity of her infatuation. After the wedding, the honeymoon phase lasted about eight weeks, a period during which Mary was consumed by ambition and passion, a devastating combination. There have been fanciful, if quite unsubstantiated, theories that Mary was in some sort of triangular relationship, that Darnley and Mary's foreign secretary David Riccio were both intimate with the Queen and with each other.

To be sure, Darnley and Riccio were on the most intimate terms, certainly in the period immediately preceding the marriage; and supreme sensualist that he was, with his girlish appearance and camp mannerisms, there was the suggestion that Darnley engaged in homosexual practices, though with whom was never specified. As for Mary's sexual relationship with her husband, this appears to have been confined to the two months immediately following the wedding. Prince James was born on 19 June 1566, and assuming a birth at full term it appears that conception took place during the Chaseabout Raid when Darnley, suitably dashing in his ornately gilded armour, rode at her side. Before the end of 1565, however, a disillusioned Mary had virtually separated from her poltroon of a husband. Although they continued to live under the same roof, they had quite separate apartments.

Mary's relations with David Riccio have been the subject of endless speculation, although there is no hard evidence that they were lovers in the carnal sense. Born in the mid-1530s of an ancient but by then rather indigent Savoyard family, he was the son of a musician at Pancalieri near Turin and came to Scotland in 1561 in the retinue of Count Robertino Solara di Moreta, the ambassador of Duke Emmanuel Philibert of Savoy. Riccio was a confirmed bachelor; significantly, while the English ambassador Thomas Randolph had plenty to say about Knox and Maitland falling in love with girls young enough to be their daughters, he is silent on the subject of Riccio. Contemporary accounts maintain that Riccio was deformed in some way, though they are vague as to the nature of his deformity. Certainly the Scots regarded him as an ugly little man, but that may have been nothing more than a northern prejudice against swarthy men with sallow complexions. Some say that he was in his fifties, though if he was born in the mid-1530s he would have been co-eval with Bothwell. Authentic portraits of Riccio show a generous, sensuous mouth and large, frank, twinkling eyes which betray a sense of humour. He was well bred, widely travelled and experienced in courtly manners. He was an accomplished musician, credited with the composition of the music of at least seven of Scotland's best-loved songs, including *The Lass of Patie's Mill*, *Auld Rob Morris* and *Down the Burn, Davy*, though it may be that he merely collected and mended traditional ballads, in much the same way that Robert Burns collected and restored lyrics more than two centuries later.[1]

Davy Riccio possessed a fine baritone voice and it was his singing skills that first brought him to Mary's attention. Needing a bass to complete her chapel quartet, she persuaded the Savoyard ambassador to let him remain behind when the embassy returned to Turin, and he was then appointed a valet of the chamber with a salary of twenty pounds a quarter. Rumours that he was a papal agent survived till the end of the nineteenth century, but a careful search of the Scottish papers in the Vatican archives by the historian Father Pollen failed to produce a shred of evidence to support this notion.

While Maitland was Mary's principal secretary of state, handling domestic matters as well as relations with England, she employed the Frenchman Augustine Raullet as her secretary for foreign correspondence. By December 1564, however, Mary suspected him of betraying state secrets. Randolph asserts that Raullet was dismissed because he was too intimate with himself,[2] but it is more likely that Raullet was reporting on Mary behind her back to the Cardinal of Lorraine, at a time when it was vital to the Queen to keep France in the dark regarding her plans. Randolph states that Riccio, aided by his fellow valet Mingo, was the chief broker of the Darnley marriage, even to the extent of organising the betrothal, but this probably overstated the position that he was doing no more than obeying his mistress's instructions.

From foreign secretary Riccio advanced rapidly in Mary's esteem. Not only was he a good Catholic but, as a foreigner, he was entirely free of Scottish prejudice. Maitland's Protestantism may have been lightly held but he was bent on the union of the kingdoms, and even if he and Mary did not differ in their aims they were beginning to disagree in their policies. After Moray's revolt, however, Maitland's position became increasingly precarious. Mary no longer trusted him, and the vacuum was immediately filled by Riccio. While he never became her political adviser in the full sense, he was certainly the repository of Mary's political secrets, which made him both a dangerous man and a danger to himself.

The fact that Mary spent a great deal of her time with Riccio, both on official business and relaxing of an evening, soon had tongues wagging. The Scottish nobility resented this base-born foreign inter-loper, but Mary contemptuously brushed their objections aside, claiming that 'a generous spirit and faithful heart' made up for a humble origin.[3] Indeed, the fact that Riccio was not a member of the Scottish nobility was one of his chief assets so far as Mary was concerned. In pursuing the policy on which she had embarked she was taking enormous risks, but these risks would have been infinitely greater and more complicated had her closest political confidant also been her lover. Mary and Riccio were both personally devout, and the ordeal of the confessional would have been sufficient to suppress any mutual carnal desires. Above all, Mary was always conscious of her sovereign dignity; while relatively free and easy with her courtiers, she was also adept at ensuring that such liberties never overstepped the mark. Nevertheless, Riccio's meteoric rise was the subject of endless malicious gossip.

Randolph articulated this gossip, insinuating that the breach between Moray and the Queen was due mainly to the fact that he had detected some impropriety between his sister and an unnamed courtier. 'Here is the mischief, this is the grief, and how this may be salved and repaired, it passeth, I trowe, man's wit to consider,' he wrote to Cecil on 13 September 1565.[4] For further details he referred Cecil to Tamworth who was returning to England shortly, and on the strength of this Elizabeth herself informed the French ambassador, Paul de Foix, that the reason Mary hated her brother so much was that she had been told that Moray would gladly have hanged an Italian named David that she loved and favoured, 'giving him more credit and authority in her affairs than was consistent with her honour'.[5] Of course, Moray had good grounds for wishing Riccio dead, whether he was having an affair with Mary or not. He was a

Catholic and an Italian upstart who was privy to state secrets which the Queen was at pains to conceal from her very own brother.

Whereas Moray's hatred of Riccio dates from August 1565, if not earlier, when the Italian was perceived as playing a leading role in the Darnley marriage, the animosity of Darnley towards Riccio did not develop till some time later. In the immediate aftermath of the marriage, Mary and her consort were apparently in harmony, but soon after their return to Edinburgh they began to drift apart. Although Mary made a great play of having their names together on state documents, the reality was that Darnley had little time or inclination for the business of government, and preferred the pursuit of his own pleasure to assisting his wife. His advice, on the rare occasions it was offered, was valueless; and Mary quickly realised that her love and affection were not returned. Disillusioned by this idle fop who was held in contempt by everyone, she resigned herself to ruling without him, and thereafter denied him access to matters of state. As for her political ambitions, she carefully concealed their real nature from her wayward husband.

One of the matters on which Mary and Darnley soon differed concerned the appointment of the Lieutenant-General, effectively the commander-in-chief of Scotland's military forces. Darnley proposed that his father should have this appointment; but while Lennox was undoubtedly well skilled in military matters, such an appointment was out of the question as Mary had no wish to offend the more fanatically Protestant nobles. Her preference, on purely political grounds, was the Earl of Bothwell. Although Mary was probably aware of the way in which Bothwell had slandered her during his exile in France, denouncing her as the Cardinal's whore and saying that she and her cousin Elizabeth together would not make a single decent woman, Mary now felt it politic to ingratiate herself with this powerful noble who would later play such an important – and disastrous – part in her life. So the Queen had her way and Bothwell got the appointment, but from then onwards the rift between Mary and Darnley was irrevocable. By Christmas Randolph was reporting that the original styling of 'the King and Queen or His Majesty and Hers' on official documents had now been dropped. Darnley was no longer referred to as King Henry but merely as 'the Queen's husband', if at all. Where he had formerly been placed first in all Mary's writings he was now placed second. Most significant of all, Randolph reported that the face-to-face coins with the inscription HENRICUS & MARIA, REX & REGINA SCOTORUM had been withdrawn from circulation and replaced by coins transposing the names and titles. From this, Randolph concluded that, while Darnley might still be king-consort, he was not to have the crown matrimonial which would have given him the power to interfere directly and independently in affairs of state.[6]

Conversely, of course, if Darnley were denied this, it would be a source of even greater bitterness between him and Mary. Moreover, as Darnley continued to go down in the Queen's estimation, the star of Riccio was more and more in the ascendant. Riccio foolishly flaunted his new position, ordering fine apparel and jewels which he could never have afforded on his official salary (still fixed at eighty pounds per annum). George Buchanan, Mary's Latin secretary, remarked that Riccio's equipage was now even grander than the King's. The suspicion that Riccio was receiving huge bribes from those requiring special favours was confirmed when over two thousand pounds in cash was discovered among his personal effects soon after his death. Unless Riccio's exalted position were due to yet another of the Queen's infatuations, it can only be assumed that he, and he alone, could be entrusted with Mary's most secret and dangerous plans.

All the evidence points to a restoration of Catholicism, with the corollary of Mary's seizure of the English throne by armed force. To these ends, therefore, secret despatches were addressed to King Philip and the new Pope Pius V.[7] Philip responded with a subsidy of 20,000 crowns which was entrusted to Mary's courier Francis Yaxley, but his ship was wrecked off Bamburgh and he was drowned. The cash was salvaged but never forwarded to Mary as it was deemed by the Earl of Northumberland to be his perquisite as the spoils of shipwreck. The letters which Yaxley was carrying from Philip to Mary were never found, to the annoyance of Cecil who would rather have had these potentially incriminating documents than the cash.

What advice Philip was tendering to Mary is implied in a letter which he wrote to Cardinal Pachero about 18 October 1565.[8] In this he speculated that Mary faced three hypothetical dangers: a rebellion in Scotland, English intervention to help the rebels, and the likelihood of Mary invading England to depose Elizabeth and take the throne by force. The first problem could be avoided by bribes, for which he was prepared to put up cash, the second would require considerable financial and military assistance, but the third was to be avoided at all costs – 'until the right moment came'. What he meant by the 'right moment' was never clear, though it would have to be of his choosing. By March 1566 the situation was slightly clearer than it had been six months earlier. Rebellion had been averted but not suppressed, and the exiled lords could now plot against Mary with impunity. To defuse a dangerous situation Mary instructed her parliament that Moray and the other rebel lords should be stripped of their lands and titles. The elderly Châtelherault alone got off lightly with five years' banishment to France. At the same time parliament, at the Queen's behest, was to enact that Catholics throughout Scotland should be allowed to exercise their religion freely.

In so doing, Mary had no immediate intention of persecuting or harassing Protestants, but she was hard-headed enough to appreciate that two such diametrically opposed creeds as Catholicism and the Knox brand of extreme Protestantism could not exist side by side for long. Secretly Mary hoped that if Catholicism were tolerated it would ultimately triumph. Her long-term ambitions were revealed in the letter she wrote to Pope Pius V on 31 January 1566,[9] congratulating him on his consecration and letting him know that she planned to restore Catholicism when the time was right – when her enemies were either in exile or in her power. Furthermore, she stated that the restoration of Catholicism in Scotland would be but a preliminary to its extension to England also, once she had secured the throne there. This was a very rash matter to commit to paper, and had this letter fallen into the wrong hands it could have destroyed Mary. Riccio, who wrote the letter at Mary's dictation, was thus privy to her most perilous endeavours.

At this time the complexion of Mary's government was decidedly Catholic. Bending with the wind, Darnley now made an ostentatious display of religiosity, celebrating High Mass on Christmas Day 1565. Mary, by contrast, had been up most of the night playing cards and did not get to bed till daybreak. Five weeks later, when he again celebrated Mass, Darnley boasted publicly that he would have Mass celebrated in St Giles itself. It is probable that this display of devotion was little more than pretence, designed deliberately to provoke a reaction from the nobility as well as show up the Queen, whose own devotions had been perfunctory of late. Only one Protestant nobleman of any stature remained at large and that was the Earl of Argyll, now a fugitive in the heather of the West Highlands. Moray and the other Protestant leaders were kicking their heels in Newcastle, such of their followers as had remained in Scotland being in disarray. Châtelherault was in France, the Hamilton faction behaving themselves to ensure his eventual comeback.

By contrast, the restoration of the earldom of Huntly and the downfall of Moray altered the balance of power in the north-east. In February 1566 Bothwell married Huntly's sister, Lady Jean Gordon, in the Canongate Kirk. She had previously been in love with Lord Ogilvie of Boyne but he had married Mary Beaton instead. It was Queen Mary herself who urged Bothwell to marry Jean and the resulting ties between the two earls were, for a time, the core of Mary's domestic policies. This alliance was also the basis for Mary's plans which, had she succeeded, would have altered the course of British history, the overthrow of Elizabeth no less and the restoration of the unified kingdoms to Catholicism. These twin goals were as preposterous as they were impetuous, and they were fatally flawed by Mary's wilful disregard for the overt hostility towards her Italian protégé, as much as for the colossal mistake of placing any trust in her husband.

A few days after the Bothwell marriage, Darnley was ceremonially invested with the order of St Michael, conferred on behalf of Charles IX by the French ambassador, the Sieur de Rambouillet. Admittedly, Darnley was at the end of the line, Rambouillet having been in England a few days earlier to confer the same knighthood on the Duke of Norfolk and the Earl of Leicester. The accolade was bestowed on 10 February, at the conclusion of Mass in the Chapel Royal, Darnley swearing before the assembled congregation that if he ever committed a fault which disgraced the order, he would surrender the collar to the sovereign. This brought a wry smirk to the faces of those who knew only too well that Darnley was already forsworn. When the question of what arms the new knight should assume arose in Council, Mary betrayed by her lukewarm attitude what she now thought of her husband. At a celebratory banquet for Rambouillet, Darnley not only drank to excess, but got at least one of the French guests, De la Roc Paussay, hopelessly plastered as well.

On the surface everything seemed tranquil, but by now the country was seething with hatred against the unfortunate Riccio. The Protestants loathed him as a papal agent, while the nobility resented his usurpation of their special privileges. And then there was Darnley, once his boon companion and now his deadliest enemy, motivated by jealousy, spite and pique. Denied the crown matrimonial and supplanted as the Queen's closest confidant by this ugly toad, Darnley even convinced himself that the Italian had cuckolded him, and to this end put about a story that he had caught Mary and Davy at midnight in a locked room, the Italian clad only in his nightshirt.[10] This was an affront to his honour, and, as such, should have been settled at rapier point, but Riccio being so far beneath the dignity of King Henry, the latter could not demean himself by fighting a duel. Had the story been true, it must be supposed that Darnley would have run the little Italian through on the spot.

The truth is that a conspiracy to murder Riccio had been in progress for several weeks before the deed took place, and for some time prior to that Darnley had been airing his grievances to those of his drinking companions who would listen to him. Of late, King Henry had taken to boozing and whoring in taverns and brothels, and in view of the very compact character of Edinburgh his profligacy was common knowledge. Even on those increasingly rare occasions when he deigned to accompany his wife to civic functions, he drank to excess and behaved abominably. At an entertainment one evening in the house of a prominent citizen, Mary gently remonstrated with Darnley who had reached the loudly loquacious stage of drunkenness. He responded in an extremely offensive manner, as a result of which she flounced out of the room in tears. Haughty, insolent and imperious in his manner, he seemed to go out of his way to give the Queen nothing but grief and pain. As his drunken querulousness became more pronounced, it was not long before certain disaffected persons were seeking to harness his personal gripes to their own ends.

In view of the fact that Mary's supposed infatuation with Riccio was one of the reasons for Moray's rebellion, it seems hard to believe that Moray should now try to bribe the self-same Riccio with a huge diamond, according to Sir James Melville.[11] Nevertheless, other sources tell how one of Moray's kinsmen, young George Douglas of Lochleven, approached Riccio with a bribe of five thousand pounds, only to be told that he would not take a penny less than twenty thousand pounds to secure Moray's re-instatement.[12] Moray was certainly intriguing with both Mary and Elizabeth at this time, seeking some sort of accommodation whereby he could be allowed to return to Scotland. In these negotiations he let it be known that whatever were the relations between Riccio and his sister, he was prepared to overlook them. When all these manoeuvres came to nothing Moray and his fellow conspirators decided to eliminate this Italian fly in their ointment, and to enlist the disreputable Darnley for their vile enterprise. Moray's conduct in this disgraceful affair is indefensible, though some historians have tried to enter a plea in mitigation by saying that Moray was won over by Darnley's promise to restore Protestantism. It can scarcely be believed that this was a good reason for Moray giving his support to a man whom previously he had loathed and for whom he had nothing but contempt. Had Darnley succeeded by this plot in gaining the crown for himself, it could only have been on terms that the real power remained in Moray's hands.

As the plot grew to maturity, Riccio seemed unstoppable. By now he was in control of virtually the entire machinery of government, with the help of Sir James Balfour who dealt exclusively with Scottish affairs. Maitland, though not formally dismissed, was completely sidelined. Acutely aware of Mary's rashness and impetuosity, he was alarmed at this development, but there was nothing he could do for the moment but bide his time and try to ingratiate himself with the Queen socially. He rightly perceived the way in which he was deliberately excluded from her councils as evidence of the dangerous policy she had now embarked on. Maitland saw the elimination of Riccio not in the same light as the self-serving conspirators, but as a prerequisite to saving Mary from disaster and the ruin of his own statesmanlike plans for the mutual benefit of Scotland and England.

When Maitland learned that Mary was pregnant, he became even more convinced that the best hope for the Scottish succession lay in cultivating the friendship of England. He was overjoyed, therefore, when, after a long silence, he received a letter from Cecil on 9 February and replied immediately to reassure him of his best intentions. Regarding the parlous state of Scotland at that moment he concluded, 'Mary! I see no certain way unless we chop at the very root. Yow know wheare it lyeth, and so far as my judgement can reach, the sooner all things be packed up the less danger there is of any inconvenience.'[13] So Maitland, too, felt that Riccio had to be got rid of, though to what extent he was implicated in the assassination plan is debatable.

John Knox also knew of the plan and gave it his blessing. His father-in-law, Lord Ochiltree, was one of those Protestant lords presently in exile in England. The exact relationship of the plotters with one another and their several degrees of responsibility for the deed cannot, by the very nature of the crime, be ascertained; but the consensus is that Darnley was at the very centre of the conspiracy. He alone had personal reasons, real or imagined, for killing Riccio. The others, while not concerned with Darnley's selfish motives, regarded the removal of Riccio as vital to their plans to recall the exiled lords. On the other hand, Darnley was less concerned with wreaking vengeance on Riccio as in winning the crown matrimonial, and it was only on this condition that he consented to help.

Interestingly, one of the best accounts of the plot and its execution was provided by none other than Randolph, who had quite a hand in the affair himself. On 25 February 1566 the English ambassador reported to Cecil details of the compact between Darnley and the exiled nobles. This intelligence was conveyed to Elizabeth who raised no dissent, despite her earlier resolution not to recognise Darnley's kingship. The Earl of Morton, Lord Lindsay and Lord Ruthven, all close relatives of Darnley, were the principal agents of the plot, and struck the bargain whereby Darnley would come to terms with the exiled rebels, not so long ago his own deadly enemies. Riccio was not actually named in this remarkable document, but neither Cecil nor Elizabeth could have been in any doubt as to who was 'to be tane away'.[14]

Argyll, Moray, Glencairn, Rothes, Boyd and Ochiltree were the exiles who put their names to the bond with Darnley, promising to support him 'in all his just and lawful acts' and to procure at the next parliament the crown matrimonial on his behalf. Among other things, they promised to intercede with Elizabeth for the liberty of Darnley's mother and brother. Darnley, on the other hand, promised to amnesty them and restore their estates, to support them in the exercise of the reformed religion and 'to maintain them as a good master should'.[15]

Moray and the other leading rebels had been ordered to appear before parliament on Tuesday, 12 March 1566, to answer for their transgressions. They acceded to this demand, in so far as they would arrive in a group in Edinburgh on the evening of Sunday, 10 March. This simultaneous arrival was nicely timed, for the seizure of Riccio was scheduled for the previous night. In that way they would have alibis and could be seen to have had nothing to do with the deed. Parliament had been in session since the previous Wednesday and

Edinburgh thronged with noblemen and their retainers. Atholl, Bothwell, Huntly and other supporters of the Queen were staying at Holyrood. According to Ruthven, it had been decided to assassinate Riccio in his own chamber or passing through the close. It was Darnley who, with feline vindictiveness, insisted that Riccio be 'taken at supper-time, sitting with her Majesty at the table, that she might be taunted in his presence, because she had not entertained her husband according to her accustomed manner as she ought of duty'.[16]

As night fell on the appointed day hand-picked followers of Lindsay, Morton and Ruthven sauntered in twos and threes towards the open spaces near Holyrood; by eight o'clock they had secured all the gates and doors to the palace. About the same time Darnley, well liquored up to give himself courage for the desperate enterprise, and his nerve steeled by his hatred for the Italian, slowly mounted the private stair to the inner boudoir where Queen Mary, her half-sister Jean Stewart (Countess of Argyll), Lord Robert Stewart, Bethune of Creich, Arthur Erskine and Riccio were seated at supper. Darnley had not dined with his wife for some time (and probably never with Riccio), so the Queen and her friends were surprised to see him. Mary quickly recovered her composure and moved to let him sit beside her. Darnley had scarcely sat down when the diners were startled at the sudden entrance of Ruthven, haggard from a serious illness (which was, in fact, terminal), his ghastly pallor heightened by the fact that he was clad in full armour. Mustering all his strength, he called out that Riccio must come forth of the Queen's 'privy chamber, where he had been over long'. Mary immediately turned to her husband and angrily demanded to know whether he knew anything of 'that enterprise'. Darnley hotly denied involvement, though the coincidence of his arrival was not lost on the supper party. Mary imperiously commanded Ruthven to leave her presence, but he had gone too far and could not retreat. Besides, he was well aware that armed men lurked on the staircase waiting to do their part. According to his own account he recited a long litany of Riccio's misdeeds, but in fact he probably kept this very short and to the point.

Then he turned to Darnley saying curtly, 'Take the Queen your wife and sovereign to you.' If Darnley had complied, the scene in the chamber might have been less chaotic and violent than it turned out, and Ruthven might have succeeded in hustling poor Davy out of the room. Without the Queen there, no one else would have come to his assistance. Characteristically, however, Darnley instead protested his innocence, stood aghast and did nothing. Mary got to her feet, resolute, cool and fearless, and stood in front of Riccio who drew his dagger and cowered in the embrasure of the window, clinging to the folds of her gown with pitiful cries of 'Save me, Madame! Save me!' Erskine and Lord Robert lunged at Ruthven who drew his own blade and cried, 'Lay no hand on me for I will not be handled!' The words were scarcely out of his mouth when the tiny chamber was filled with a band of armed men. The table and chairs were overturned in their wild scramble towards their target. The resultant mêlée would have taken place by firelight alone had not the Countess of Argyll the presence of mind to grab hold of one of the candles as it fell to the floor. There she stood, holding the spluttering flame aloft to illumine the horrific scene.

While the assassins attacked the luckless Riccio, Ruthven himself took hold of Queen Mary and thrust her into Darnley's arms, rather pointlessly exhorting her not to be afraid as the ruffians dragged her trusted confidant, kicking and shrieking, towards the ante-chamber. Later, Darnley would maintain that he had agreed only to Riccio's arrest; and Morton, Ruthven and contemporary writers agree that the plan was to have removed Riccio to a place where he could be formally tried and convicted before execution.[17] Ruthven himself says that he gave orders that Riccio was to be escorted downstairs to the king's chamber.

Violent events, however, have a momentum of their own and in a matter of seconds blood-lust took over. While Andrew Ker of Fawdonside prodded the Queen's swollen belly with a loaded pistol, Morton's half-brother George Douglas (Postulate of Arbroath and later Bishop of Moray) drew the dagger from Darnley's belt and struck the first blow, stabbing Riccio over the horrified Queen's shoulder, so close to her neck that she later claimed she felt the coldness of the steel. As the wounded Riccio was bundled through the door, a score of other conspirators fell upon him with their daggers. In their frenzy and in the confined space, some of them stabbed their fellow assassins by accident. Riccio's horribly mutilated body sustained at least fifty-six wounds before the murderers, on Ruthven's orders, hurled the mangled corpse down the stairs. It was then carried to the porter's lodge where it was stripped naked. According to Ruthven, the porter remarked 'that this was his destiny; for upon this chest was his first bed when he came to this place, and now he lieth a very niggard and misknown knave'. Finally George Douglas, who had struck the first blow, symbolically plunged Darnley's dagger into Riccio's heart as mute witness to Darnley's complicity in the crime.[18]

Ruthven's graphic account of the recriminations after the murder sheds an interesting light on the reactions of the various actors in this melodrama. Queen Mary comes best out of the ghastly affair. Considering that she was now seven months pregnant and highly strung by temperament, she kept her dignity. What is significant is that she did not behave as one would expect, had she actually been conducting a passionate affair with Riccio. Such a scenario would have had the Queen swooning with the intensity of her emotion. Instead, she remained dry-eyed, pulled herself up to her full height, and, with eyes blazing, soundly berated her faithless, treacherous husband. In contrast to her white-hot courage and steely resolve, the drunken Darnley babbled incoherently as he whined: 'Suppose I be of mean degree, yet I am your husband, and you promised me obedience at the day of your marriage, and that I should be participant and equal with you in all things; but you have used me otherwise, by the persuasion of David.'

'My Lord,' retorted Mary, 'all the offence that is done me, you have the wite [knowledge] thereof, for the which I will be your wife no longer, nor lie with you any more, and shall never like well till I cause you have as sorrowful a heart as I have at this present.'

Then Ruthven intervened sanctimoniously: 'I beseech your Majesty to be of good comfort, to entertain your husband and use the counsel of the nobility, and then your government will be as prosperous as in any King's days.' Worn out by his exertions, he then asked permission to sit down. 'For God's sake!' he cried out to a French servant, 'Bring me a cup of wine.'

Eyes blazing, Mary turned on the sick old man. 'Is this your sickness?'

'God forbid your Majesty had such a sickness,' he said wearily.

'If I die in childbirth as a result,' she spat, 'or my commonweal perish, I will leave the revenge thereof to my friends, to be taken of you, Lord Ruthven, and your posterity! I have the King of Spain and the Emperor my great friends, and likewise the King of France, my good-brother, with my uncles of Lorraine besides the Pope's Holiness and many other princes in Italy.'

'These noble princes are over great personages to meddle with such a poor man as I am, being your Majesty's own subject,' said Ruthven with mock humility, adding, 'If anything be done this night that your Majesty mislikes, the King your husband, and none of us, is in the wyte, which he confessed to be true.'[19]

All the screaming, shouting and commotion in the chamber alerted Mary's supporters led by Bothwell and Huntly, but when they realised what was afoot and how numerous the well-armed marauders were, they instinctively held back and went to their own apartments. Not long afterwards, Ruthven staggered to their chambers and, weak and wracked with pain but indomitable as ever, tried to explain what all the tumult was about. He and his friends, he said, had taken vengeance on Riccio at the King's behest. They shook hands and had a drink on it; but Bothwell and Huntly were secretly dissatisfied at Ruthven's explanation and on hearing that Moray and his friends were expected the following day they felt it prudent to make their escape, with the best possible motive of helping the Queen. Somehow they managed to get a message to her to this effect, but Mary decided that she should remain where she was, come what may. Afterwards Atholl, Sutherland, Caithness, Maitland and Sir James Balfour were allowed by Darnley (at Ruthven's suggestion) to leave Holyrood, the conspirators considering it better that they should have a clear field for negotiating with Queen Mary.

By now, news of the affray had spread to the town and a huge crowd, armed with spears and pikes, converged on the palace but dispersed in an orderly manner when Darnley came out to assure them that all was well. As a precaution, however, he now posted guards at the entrances, and also outside the Queen's bedchamber so that she had difficulty in keeping in touch with her servants. Sleep eluding her, Mary paced up and down all night. Fear for her own safety hardly entered her head, but she was beside herself with rage mingled with grief. Darnley, by contrast, immensely satisfied with the outcome of the evening's good work, slept soundly in his own bedroom below.

The following day a proclamation in the name of King Henry announced that parliament was prorogued and members of the Estates were ordered to disperse to their homes. All that day Mary remained a prisoner in her chamber. It being the Sabbath (as Sunday was now to be known in the Judaic jargon affected by the Protestant

Mary Queen of Scots around the age of nine;
(below) the Château of Chambord on the Loire,
where she spent part of her childhood

Francis II of France, *le petit roi*, whom Mary would always
consider to be her one great love and one true husband

OPPOSITE PAGE: Mary of Guise, queen of James V and mother
of Mary Queen of Scots; and *(below)* Francis, Duke of Guise

Mary Queen of Scots

OPPOSITE PAGE *(clockwise from top left)*: Henry II of France;
Charles IX of France; Don Carlos; Philip II of Spain

Henry Stewart, Lord Darnley; *(below, from left to right)*
Cardinal Beaton; David Riccio; James Hamilton, Duke of
Châtelherault

James Hepburn, Earl of Bothwell; *(below, from left to right)* James Douglas, Earl of Morton; Matthew Stewart, Earl of Lennox; Robert Dudley, Earl of Leicester

Mary Queen of Scots in her later years

extremists) it was not seemly or appropriate to discuss business, far less portentous matters of state. In any case, the conspirators were impatiently awaiting the arrival of Moray and his friends. After dinner, Darnley condescended to look in on his prisoner. Mary feared that she would miscarry, and protested bitterly at being denied the service of her gentlewomen. On Morton's orders they were now allowed in, but when it transpired that Mary planned to slip out of the chamber in the crowd of servants, additional guards were posted at the door to check that no one in disguise passed through. In view of the Queen's unusual height, this would have been impossible; but Mary's main purpose in getting access to her maids was to entrust them with letters to Bothwell, Huntly and her other supporters.

That evening Moray and his party reached Edinburgh and dined at Morton's house not far from Holyrood. On hearing that James had arrived Mary sent for him and, according to Ruthven, 'received him pleasantly'. Melville gives greater detail, saying that the Queen embraced and kissed her brother, exclaiming that if he had been there 'they would not have seen her so uncourteously handled'.[20] According to Melville, Moray was reduced to tears at this, and Mary herself confirmed that on account of her condition and treatment he was 'moved with natural affection towards us'.[21] Mary added that Darnley was to blame for the exile of the Protestant lords. Had it been left to her alone she would have recalled them long ago, but she had not wished to displease her husband. This implies that Darnley's jealousy of Moray and Châtelherault had much to do with the rift; but for Darnley's caprice Mary would not have been driven towards such a drastic course of action.

Moray swore that, until he reached Edinburgh, he had known nothing of Riccio's murder. Mary, who knew her brother to be a truthful and honourable man, had no reason not to believe him; although, in view of the fact that the general outline of the plot was known to Randolph, Cecil and Bedford, it would be surprising if Moray had had no inkling of it. No doubt Moray was aware of some vague plan to arrest Riccio, and was conveniently forgetting that the real reason he had fallen out with her was her allegedly shameless conduct with the Italian; but his horror at the actual deed and its effect on his sister seems genuine enough. At any rate Mary and James now sank their differences. In turn, Moray mediated between Mary and her husband who were persuaded to make up their quarrel. The conspirators even suggested that the King and Queen should retire to bed together to seal their new-found agreement, but Darnley, drunk as usual, fell immediately into a deep asleep and could not be roused.

It must by now have dawned on the conspirators that the man on whom their plan depended most for its success – Darnley – was virtually useless and wholly unreliable. The problem was that they needed a Darnley of sufficiently strong a character to withstand Mary's powers of persuasion, and at the same time a Darnley that was weak enough to be putty in their hands. All too soon it became clear that he was concerned solely with saving his own skin and grabbing as much power as he could for himself. Their only trump card was the enticing offer of the crown matrimonial which appealed to Darnley's overweening vanity. By murdering Riccio, they had unwittingly undermined their own position with Darnley for now his jealousy had nothing to focus upon. If they imagined they could use Darnley to manipulate Mary they were soon in for a shock.

Overcoming her loathing and disgust of her husband when he visited her on the Monday morning, Mary starkly pointed out to him his monumental folly, and how, in effect, he had been duped by the conspirators. Now Mary hoped that they would allow her, in her husband's custody, of course, to leave the palace. To this end she pretended that she was on the point of miscarrying. Her physicians and nurses backed her up, saying that she needed to get away 'to some sweeter and pleasanter air'. Still pretending to be ill, she received the conspirators in her outer chamber and formally pardoned them, offering 'to put all things in oblivion as if they had never been'. And, keeping up the charade, she asked them to draw up articles for their security, to which she promised to append her signature. With Darnley on one hand and Moray on the other, she took exercise in the outer chamber for more than an hour. There being no fly on the wall to record their conversation for posterity we can only guess at what took place. But as a result of this extraordinary meeting Moray was completely put off guard. On Mary's full and frank promise of a signed and sealed pardon for the conspirators Moray persuaded them to release her into the tender care of her husband for the night. The plotters had no intention of granting her liberty, even if they received the written pardon they demanded. From Darnley Mary discovered that they intended sending her under armed guard to Stirling Castle the following morning where, as Lindsay crudely put it, 'she would have plenty of pastime in nursing her baby and singing it to sleep' while King Henry, guided by his nobles, got on with the business of government.[22]

After supper Darnley came downstairs for the documents which the Queen was to sign. There and then he arranged for the conspirators to vacate the palace, taking upon himself the responsibility for keeping Mary closely guarded overnight. Incredibly, the plotters were foolish enough to believe this, and left the palace without the vital signature on the pardons. Darnley, the tool of the conspirators, was now duped by his wife into believing that if they were ever to succeed in their grand design of winning the English throne, they must henceforth co-operate closely. She even persuaded him of the enormity of his mistake in conspiring to bring about the death of such a good and faithful servant, the like of whom he was unlikely ever to possess again. In a penitent frame of mind, therefore, Darnley now obeyed her instructions, fooling the conspirators regarding the pardon and even managing to dismiss the palace guards. Mary could not be sure that the conspirators had not placed some of their own men round the perimeter but as it happened, through the mediation of the redoubtable Dowager Countess of Huntly who had been permitted by the conspirators to attend the Queen, Mary easily managed to get word to Arthur Erskine to have horses and attendants waiting outside the walls of the royal cemetery.

At midnight, Mary, who was nominally under the protection of her gallant husband but in reality was stealing him away from his late confederates, passed through Darnley's chamber and thence to the quarters occupied by her French servants – to the last man utterly loyal to her. With their assistance Mary and Darnley slipped out of a side door to the cemetery, passing close by the newly dug grave of the unfortunate Riccio. At the sight, Darnley let out a startled whimper. When Mary asked him what was the matter, he said that they had just passed her servant's grave. Thereupon, according to Claude Nau, Mary's French secretary, he delivered a pompous encomium filled with insincere remorse, which must have sorely tried Mary's temper.[23] Fortunately she had greater presence of mind than her dolt of a husband and in a moment they found Erskine and his helpers. Wordlessly they mounted up and rode through the night towards Dunbar. Darnley rode his own horse, but Mary rode pillion behind Erskine. John Stewart of Traquair, a gentleman of the King's bedchamber, led the party, while Anthony Standen and a couple of loyal soldiers brought up the rear.

In view of Mary's advanced pregnancy the little cavalcade moved off at a sedate trot which would not draw undue attention should supporters of the conspirators be in the vicinity, but as soon as they were clear of the city Darnley, panicking lest his double-dealing be discovered, spurred his horse into full gallop. Erskine, with the Queen clinging on behind him, could barely keep up. When Darnley espied some soldiers near Seton he panicked again, and wheeled round behind Erskine's steed to whip it on faster, until its violent motion caused extreme discomfort to the Queen. When Mary gasped at him to remember her delicate condition, he retorted brutally, 'Come on! In God's name, come on! If this baby dies, we can have more.'[24] Gritting her teeth, Mary glared at Darnley and sarcastically suggested that he should push on and save himself. Without realising the nature of her rebuke, Darnley was mean enough to do just that.

As she watched his horse disappear into the first grey light of dawn, Mary felt such a bitterness and disgust that she could barely look upon her husband again. At that precise moment, the last strand of affection for Darnley snapped. By that cowardly act, King Henry sealed his own fate.

9. BIRTH AND DEATH

1566–67

O hush thee, my babie, thy sire was a knight,
Thy mother a lady, both lovely and bright.
     Sir Walter Scott, *Lullaby of an Indian Chief*

Alerted by the resourceful Dowager Countess of Huntly, Mary's supporters were at Seton to greet her and convoy her safely on to Dunbar Castle, twenty-five miles east of Edinburgh. The nightmarish ride from Holyrood lasted five hours and Mary was exhausted and dishevelled but remarkably calm when she finally dismounted. During the long night she had had time to gather her thoughts, and revenge was now uppermost in her mind. Eyewitnesses marvelled at how this woman, now seven months pregnant, could coolly demand eggs and eat a hearty breakfast. After attending to her toilet, she got straight down to the serious business of dictating a series of long letters: to her cousin Elizabeth and to Archbishop James Beaton, among others. The Earl of Bothwell, who was now the staunchest of her supporters, was promptly rewarded with the wardship of Dunbar Castle, the previous incumbent, the Laird of Craigmillar, being stripped of his appointment because of his complicity with the conspirators. Mary's endurance and courage had amazed those who had accompanied her on the night ride; now she showed her true mettle by her decisiveness and single-mindedness in dealing with the conspiracy.

Correspondingly, the consternation of the plotters when they discovered that Mary had escaped their clutches may be imagined, but their dismay was compounded by anger at Darnley's betrayal. If they had ever had any illusions about the man in whose name they had supposedly staged their coup, they were certainly disabused of them now. Had the Queen merely fled without him, Darnley could still have been of some use to them; but by taking her husband Mary ensured that the conspirators had no basis on which to form an insurrection. She had robbed them of the puppet through whom they might have maintained some semblance of legality. Now Darnley had virtually disowned them. Their immediate reaction reveals the weakness of their case, for they sent Robert, Lord Sempill (who had played no part in the conspiracy), to Dunbar to intercede with the Queen on their behalf and obtain her signature on the articles of pardon. Mary reacted to this effrontery with customary composure. She held the luckless Sempill incommunicado for three days, while the conspirators agonised over her intentions. As panic spread through their ranks Mary rallied her supporters.

Her first step was to offer a full pardon to those nobles who had taken merely passive roles in the affair, but she let it be known that no mercy would be shown to those who had played an active part in Riccio's murder. At one stroke, therefore, she split the conspirators. Many of them, still suffering in the aftermath of the Chaseabout Raid, responded with alacrity to Mary's summons and, one by one, they made their way to Dunbar to make their grovelling apology and be received into the Queen's peace once more. Glencairn was the first, closely followed by Rothes and Argyll (whose wife Jean, it will be remembered, had been Mary's closest confidante, and a horrified onlooker at Riccio's brutal slaying).

Only Mary's brother, the Earl of Moray, remained obdurate at first. With the Laird of Pittarrow and Kirkcaldy of Grange, he stood by Morton and the active plotters, until Morton himself suggested that it would be politic for him to make his peace with the Queen. With Moray and Mary reconciled, the conspirators would have a powerful friend at court to argue their case. Sir James Balfour was the go-between, counselling Moray to make his peace with the Queen, especially as Darnley himself had repented for his part in the plot. Moray's change of heart was the last straw for the assassins who departed from Edinburgh on the morning of Sunday, 17 March. They left the capital in good order, a large, well-armed band who rode first to Linlithgow and then headed south for the border. They found an uncertain refuge in England, Elizabeth no longer so ready to avow them, far less give them financial and material aid.

Maitland was now at the nadir of his fortunes. Apparently

denounced to Mary by Darnley, and with his implacable enemy Bothwell (who detested and feared him) now in the ascendant, the Secretary of State fled to Dunkeld till things died down. In the meantime, Mary stripped him of his preferments, conveying his abbacy of Haddington to Bothwell as a reward for services rendered. John Knox fled the capital on the very same day, uncertain whether old family ties to Bothwell would save his skin this time. Lamenting the fate of the good and the godly, he took refuge in Argyll.[1] As the principals in the Riccio affair fled Edinburgh, Mary was issuing a proclamation from Dunbar, summoning the lieges to muster at Haddington the following day with eight days' provisions. On Monday, 18 March, Mary, despite her advanced pregnancy, rode into Edinburgh at the head of an army eight thousand strong. Only nine days after Riccio's murder and her headlong flight, Mary had triumphed yet again. At her side proudly rode Bothwell, Huntly, the Earl Marischal, Hume and Seton. Darnley was at her elbow, though anything less kingly in demeanour would be hard to imagine. Mary did not return to Holyrood, with its ghastly memories, but after lodging briefly in the High Street she took up quarters in the castle.

Two days later she issued a writ, summoning the fugitive assassins to answer for their crimes. On 21 March a proclamation at the market cross of Edinburgh declared King Henry's 'innocency' in connection with the murder, the conspiracy or the seizure of the Queen, although he had allowed the 'English lords' to return home 'without the consent and favour of our sovereign lady'. In absolving Darnley from the main charges, Mary was not so much protecting her husband as salvaging her own reputation. For the same reason it was important for Mary to uphold the fiction that Moray and the other returned exiles had as little to do with the affair as possible. Mary's immediate aim was to let bygones be bygones and to minimise factiousness. She persuaded Bothwell to tolerate Moray; and Moray, his henchmen demoralised and confused by the rapid turn of events, had no option but to tolerate Bothwell. No one was fooled for a single moment; the show of friendship between the deadly rivals was one of the more grotesque charades in the brief period of Mary's personal rule.

On the face of it, Mary was now more firmly in control of the government than ever before. The Protestant extremists were in total disarray, and the various political dissidents were either in hiding or had fled the country. Mary's personal popularity was at an all-time high, compounded by the nation's sympathy for her in the last stages of pregnancy. In reality, however, the picture was very different. Her ambitions had suffered a severe blow; she had sustained a deep personal misfortune as well as the humiliation of seizure, detention and flight; and, worst of all, she was saddled with a husband whose unfitness to rule was daily more apparent to everyone. As Darnley hastened to betray everyone with whom he had been associated in the plot, Mary had nothing but contempt for him. At the same time, his treachery ensured that his former confederates now became his deadliest enemies, and they took the malicious step of sending proof of Darnley's duplicity to the Queen herself. By 4 April Mary had the damning evidence of the bonds between Darnley and the conspirators, showing that he had perjured himself when he swore his innocence of the plot to murder Riccio. Any lingering doubt in Mary's mind, which had not been dispelled in the fateful supper-room itself during the exchange between Ruthven and Darnley, now vanished completely as she studied the incriminating documents.

For the moment she contained her anger and disgust; but as soon as Darnley's public declaration of innocence had served her immediate purpose she cast him aside. He was an embarrassment and a liability, not only to Mary but also to noblemen of all factions. Within weeks of Riccio's murder, Darnley found himself without a single friend of any influence. Despite his precarious situation, he seems to have been completely blind to reality. Hell-bent on obtaining the crown matrimonial, he now turned his animosity against the person who had supplanted him as the Queen's right-hand man. Within a matter of days he was as insanely jealous of Bothwell as he had been of Riccio. The hatred between the two was common knowledge by early April when the English agent Sir William Drury reported to London from Berwick that the 'displeasure abates not between the King and Queen, but rather increases, insomuch that Darnley had with thirteen or fourteen horse ridden towards Stirling with the purpose of renewing the conspiracy with Argyll and Moray'.[2] Drury adds that Darnley was foiled when Mary sent Robert Melville to warn her husband against a renewal of his treachery. In any case, Darnley was greatly mistaken if he thought that he could enlist Moray's support. Darnley, who had proved to be such a broken reed, was the last person anyone would trust. Randolph, writing to Cecil on 13 May, commented that Argyll and Moray had 'such misliking of their King as never was more of man'.[3]

As Mary neared her time, she tried to put a gloss on her fragile relationship with her wayward husband. At the same time she took the precaution of summoning Argyll and Moray and arranging that they should be lodged in Edinburgh Castle as her guests. They were well treated but they could not have been in any doubt that they were now virtually the Queen's hostages. Bothwell would have gone much further, and suggested to Mary that Moray be held under lock and key,[4] but Mary gambled that the most effective method of thwarting a conspiracy was to trust her brother implicitly – or, at least, to be seen to trust him. She was acutely aware of the bad feeling between her brother and Bothwell and Huntly, and just to be on the safe side she temporarily excluded these earls from her dinner table. Bothwell, at least, was mollified when Mary let him know that, under the terms of the will she was drawing up as her confinement drew near, she was appointing him a member of the council of regency. Darnley, on the other hand, was pointedly excluded from this commission.

The actual document has not survived, but appended to it was an inventory of her jewellery, and from this we learn of Mary's true feelings to those closest to her. This document reveals an extraordinary magnanimity on Mary's part; even Darnley as well as his father and mother were beneficiaries. So too were Argyll, Moray, Bothwell and Huntly, although the Queen's French relatives were especially singled out. Mary's will stipulated that if she died in childbirth, and the baby survived her, everything she possessed would go to the child; the various legacies would only take effect if she and her baby died simultaneously.

In the event, both mother and baby survived the ordeal. Sir James Melville records that, after praying for the Queen night and day, he received the good news from Mary Beaton between ten and eleven on the forenoon of Wednesday, 19 June, that Mary had been safely delivered of a son. Within the hour he was in the saddle, riding southwards to convey the good news to Queen Elizabeth. Elizabeth had written to Mary a week previously in friendly and sympathetic terms. The warmth and sincerity of this letter, praying that Mary would suffer as little pain as possible and would soon reach the happy hour of her delivery, indicates that, whatever rivalry there existed between them concerning the English throne, at a personal level Elizabeth bore her cousin no ill-will.[5] As it happened, the labour was exceedingly long and very painful, compelling the wretched Mary to cry out that she wished she had never been married. The midwives and attendants tried everything to alleviate her pain, from the solemn parade of the sacred relics of St Margaret to a piece of witchcraft by the Countess of Atholl who tried to transfer Mary's birth-pangs to Lady Reres who obligingly rolled in agony alongside the Queen; but all to no avail.

The confinement took place in a tiny chamber in the south-east corner of the old palace within the castle precincts, a side room to the much more impressive apartment known to this day as Queen Mary's Chamber. The date 1566 carved in wood above the fireplace is a reminder to this day of the birth of the baby who would one day unite the kingdoms of Scotland and England. Although exhausted by her labour, Mary insisted on her husband being summoned immediately after the baby was born. 'My Lord,' she gasped, 'God has given you and me a son, begotten by none but you.' Then drawing back the bed-sheet from the baby's face she cried out, before the assembled courtiers, 'Here I protest to God, as I shall answer to him at the great day of Judgment, that this is your son and no other man's son. I am desirous that all here, with ladies and others, bear witness.' Then she added bitterly, 'For he is so much your own son that I fear it will be the worse for him hereafter.'

Melville arrived in London the following Sunday and passed the news to Cecil who broke it to the Queen that evening when she was dancing after supper at Greenwich. In the twinkling of an eye Elizabeth's merriment gave way to anguish and despair. She slumped in a chair with her head in her hands and cried out to her ladies-in-waiting 'how that the Queen of Scotland was lighter of a fair son, and that she was but a barren stock'.[6] The birth of Prince James thus created a new heir presumptive to the thrones of both England and Scotland.

With the birth of his son it might have been supposed that King Henry was in a stronger position than before; but the converse was the case. Having produced a son and heir, Mary had no further need of her husband. Sir Henry Killigrew, the new English ambassador, reported to Cecil on 24 June that notwithstanding the birth of the young prince, there was small account made either of Darnley or his father, Lennox.[7] There was not much comfort there for Lady Lennox, still languishing in the Tower.

For the moment, the ongoing vendetta between the Moray and Bothwell factions gave Darnley some respite. According to Killigrew,

Queen Mary now put her faith in Bothwell whose credit with her was more than all the other nobles put together. Mary had no wish to see her brother come to harm and over the ensuing weeks strove to reconcile the two main factions, Moray, Mar and Atholl on one side and Bothwell and Huntly on the other. For this reason she turned a deaf ear to Bothwell's proposal that Darnley be employed one last time in persuading his kinsman George Douglas to denounce Moray, Maitland and others as the chief instigators of Riccio's murder. The idea of employing Darnley in any business was now utterly repugnant to Mary; but in any case her instincts rebelled against placing herself entirely in Bothwell's hands. She resolutely refused to countenance such a serious allegation against her brother, probably realising that any move against Moray might trigger off a civil war.

Shrewdly Mary also realised that, once Moray were eliminated, Bothwell would not be long in destroying Darnley as well. Her feelings at this point must have been very mixed. On the one hand she shrank from thinking of getting rid of her brother and husband; but on the other her determination to wreak vengeance on Darnley grew stronger day by day. There has also been some speculation that, as Mary felt herself inexorably drawn under the spell of Bothwell, she clung instinctively to the indirect protection of her brother. With Moray out of the way there would be nothing between her and complete submission to Bothwell. The historian Henderson seems to be overstating the matter, however, when he speculates that 'at this early stage of the enamourment she may have been vaguely fighting against her passion'.[8] Mary was the victim of her French upbringing, seeing in Bothwell a strong man who would also be her champion. He would be not so much a shoulder to cry on as the wise, capable and energetic troubleshooter to whom she could bring all her problems for ready solution.

Sadly for Mary, she was gravely mistaken. James Hepburn, the Earl of Bothwell, though typical of his class in many respects, was a cut above the other Scottish nobles of his generation. For one thing, he was much better educated than most, having been tutored by his uncle Patrick Hepburn, Bishop of Moray, and his letters and despatches reveal a higher than average degree of literacy. He possessed an excellent library which reflected his catholic taste in literature. He had studied the sciences so avidly that he was alleged to practise witchcraft, but as hereditary Lord High Admiral of

Scotland and one-time commander of the Scots Guard in France he had also studied military science. Born about 1536, he inherited the lands, titles and hereditary offices of his father at the age of twenty. He was one of the more cosmopolitan of the Scottish earls, having travelled extensively on the Continent. He first encountered Queen Mary at the French court in September 1560 whither he had gone in search of a subsidy to enable him to marry his Norwegian mistress, Anna Thorssen or Throndsen, in a manner befitting his exalted station. The marriage never took place, and in 1563 Anna pursued her lover to Scotland in the vain hope of obtaining redress.

Though a Protestant, he had staunchly supported Mary of Guise and was rabidly anti-English. He had spent some time in Denmark and France and was fluent in the languages of both countries. He was, in effect, an international adventurer, and had the unusual distinction of having been a prisoner in both Edinburgh Castle (May to August 1562) and the Tower of London (1564) before fleeing to the Low Countries. When Mary recalled him in the autumn of 1566 he journeyed back to Scotland aboard a fishing-smack from Flushing, narrowly eluding recapture by the English. He was the scion of one of the most powerful Borders families, and as his star rose he consolidated this power with the chief lands of the earldom of March and the wardships of Dunbar and the Hermitage, as well as the lieutenancy of the Borders, all of which made him by far the most powerful noble in Scotland.

Despite his numerous affairs of the heart, including some sort of irregular matrimonial entanglement with Janet Beaton of Cranston Riddell – she was sixty-one and he was twenty-four, when she is said to have ensnared him by witchcraft – his alliance with the Earl of Huntly was cemented by his marriage to the latter's sister, Lady Jean Gordon, in February 1566. Significantly, the marriage settlement reveals that the bride would use her wealth to cancel the groom's substantial debts. As Mary drew closer to Bothwell at Moray's expense, malicious tongues wagged that she and Bothwell were, in fact, brother and sister. This was based on the fact that, after the death of King James V in December 1543, Bothwell's father, Earl Patrick, had paid court to the widowed Mary of Guise. Whether Patrick the Fair and the Queen Mother were ever intimate is a matter for speculation, but the timing of their relationship is such that the future Queen Mary could not possibly have been the result as she was born before her father died. Nevertheless, the salacious rumours of incest would continue to surround the Queen during and after her third marriage.

For all his urbane outlook and polished manners, however, James Hepburn was a bit of a thug. There is an abundance of testimony, from Sir Nicholas Throckmorton down to the servants who provided evidence of misconduct at the time of Bothwell's divorce, that the earl was prone to violence. We have already seen how he was always ready to resort to physical force in an argument, when he was implicated in brawls and disorders in the streets of Edinburgh; but on one occasion he kicked his servant Nicholas Hubert (popularly known as French Paris) in the stomach and beat him to the ground. He was quick-tempered, boastful and vain, but lacked the vindictive petulance of Darnley. In appearance he could not have been more different from Darnley: swarthy, stockily built and no more than five foot six in height. While we may discount the comments by Bothwell's detractors, such as Brantôme and George Buchanan, that he possessed the charm and beauty of a gorilla, Bishop Leslie was probably nearer the truth when he spoke of Bothwell's great bodily strength and beauty, although adding that he was vicious and dissolute in his habits.[9] The only authentic portrait of him, the miniature in the Scottish National Portrait Gallery, shows rugged, saturnine features. Compared with the foppish effeminacy of Darnley, here was the face of a man who had overcome his ugliness to weave his spell over women, and his success on that score was well attested. Mary herself would come under his spell, although the process would be tumultuous, and characteristically violent.

As soon after the birth of Prince James as she was able, Mary decided that a change of air would greatly assist her recovery. She broached the subject with the Earl of Mar, governor of Edinburgh Castle, and as a result made arrangements to visit his seat near Alloa in Fife. This seems natural enough, but the manner in which Mary journeyed thither was curiously secretive. George Buchanan gives a graphic account of how the Queen slipped out of Edinburgh early one morning and boarded a small vessel at Newhaven whose crew, William and Edmund Blackadder, Leonard Robertson and Thomas Dickson, were notorious pirates, 'avowed men and dependants of the said Earl Bothwell' in whose company Mary crossed the Firth of Forth to Alloa, 'to the great admiration of all honest persons, that she should hazard her person among a sort of such ruffians'.[10]

Contrary to Buchanan's statement, Bothwell was not aboard the vessel on that fateful morning, although it is obvious that Mary had relied on him to make the necessary preparations for her journey. At all events, the voyage was uneventful, it being a beautiful summer's morning, a tonic in itself after the ordeals she had endured of late. At Alloa and subsequently in Stirling, Mary began living it up, with dancing, masked balls and other revels arranged for her entertainment. It was as if the Queen had acquired a new lease of life, a reaction against the misery and unhappiness of recent months. Perhaps this was evidence of mental perturbation, as some writers have speculated, or merely the natural reaction of a normal, high-spirited woman of twenty-four. When Darnley caught up with her at Alloa, she gave him short shrift, telling him curtly to 'depart or do worse'.[11] During the hunting season in August Mary spent much of the time at Meggatland and Glenartan in the southern parts of Peeblesshire, accompanied by Bothwell, Moray and Mar, but when Darnley again put in a drunken appearance, at Traquair, he was told by Mary in no uncertain terms that his company was entirely distasteful to her.

This confrontation was made no more pleasant when Mary told her brother that Darnley had threatened to kill him. In his customarily sulky fashion, Darnley had confirmed this. Why Mary should have made this stark revelation is a puzzle, but it seems most likely that she was now determined to prevent her estranged husband from winning the sympathy or friendship of the nobles. At this juncture also, Mary was ingratiating herself with her brother whom she was supporting against Bothwell's efforts to block Maitland from a return to her court. For his part, Moray seems to have been trying to ingratiate himself with his sister while at the same time putting his old adversary Bothwell firmly in his place. Mary was manipulating both men for her own purposes, and the issue of whether Maitland was returned to favour or not was purely incidental. On 28 August the erstwhile Secretary was allowed to come to Stirling to make his peace with the Queen. A week later Mary left Stirling and returned to Edinburgh. By 20 September Maitland could report to Cecil that he had been reconciled to Bothwell by Mary in the presence of Argyll and Moray and had now resumed his old duties.[12]

Mary had come to Edinburgh to confer with her accountants regarding her own household and arrangements for the guardianship of Prince James at Stirling Castle, under the Earl of Mar, with Lady Reres as wet-nurse. There was nothing out of the ordinary in this arrangement, Stirling Castle having been the royal nursery for generations. The arrangements for the baby prince were elaborate and costly, with his solid gold potty, brocaded cradle and exquisite layette. Five hundred arquebusiers accompanied the cavalcade of lords and ladies who conveyed the heir to the throne to his new abode.

At the end of September there was yet another ugly scene between Mary and Darnley, this time in front of a large assembly of noblemen and including the French ambassador, Philibert du Croc. The Earl of Lennox had written to the Queen on 29 September saying that his son felt so humiliated at his loss of status that he intended going abroad. As a result of this extraordinary missive, Mary decided on a showdown the following day. According to Du Croc, Mary made her husband a 'pretty strong harangue', asking him how she was supposed to have offended him. The nobles took up the chorus, more or less asking Darnley how they had offended him, and Du Croc added his denier's worth with the loud observation that if he went abroad it would be an offence to Her Majesty's honour. Faced with such concerted opposition, Darnley flounced out of the audience chamber without kissing his wife, his parting shot that she would not see him again for a long time. Interestingly, in light of later allegations that Mary and Bothwell had already embarked on an affair by this time, neither Darnley nor his father raised the matter of Bothwell's relations with the Queen during the course of this long and acrimonious meeting. Had there been any substance to these allegations, made with the benefit of hindsight, something of the sort would surely have been cast up by the venomous Darnley on this occasion.

It was later alleged by George Buchanan that it was while Mary was staying at the Exchequer House in Edinburgh that Bothwell, on his own admission, succeeded in having carnal relations with her. Evidence supporting Buchanan's sensational statements apparently came from a confession by a tailor named George Dalgleish, allegedly an eye-witness to these events, but if Dalgleish ever made such an extraordinary confession it has not survived in any original document. Buchanan also averred that Mary confessed her adultery with Bothwell to her brother Moray and to his mother, the Lady of Lochleven. There is no corroboration of Buchanan's story, other than the statement of Claude Nau that Mary gave birth to still-born twins when she was later incarcerated in Lochleven. In fact, Mary miscarried about 20 July 1567 and from the size and condition of the foetuses she could not have conceived any earlier than April that year, after she and Bothwell had got married. A pregnancy in April 1567, of course, does not preclude the possibility of sexual inter-course six months earlier. These stories were only seized on by Buchanan to discredit the Queen, and although some credence for them lingered on well into the twentieth century,[13] they have generally been discredited, or ignored altogether, by later writers.

It has well been said that Mary's fate was bound up with Bothwell from the day she fled to Dunbar. He was the one who had aided, abetted, comforted and protected her at the lowest ebb in her career, when her crown, her liberty, even her life itself, were in jeopardy. Thereafter she was bound to him by ties of deepest gratitude, and her only hope of future security was inextricably dependent on his help. Mary felt betrayed and alone and in these circumstances was peculiarly vulnerable. She mistook his coarse manner for blunt, straightforward honesty, a commodity she had found to be in short supply among the Scottish nobility so far. At twenty-four, she was still a young woman, passionate, highly emotional and susceptible to the charms of such a brave, virile and experienced blade; and Bothwell, just turned thirty, was very much in the prime of life, with a long track record of amorous encounters combined with an unscrupulously amoral attitude towards women of all ages and all degrees. The two were frequently alone together, dealing with affairs of state. It would have been surprising, therefore, had these affairs not veered towards the heart eventually. The wonder is that it took so long to come to that.

After his precipitate departure from the council chamber on 30 September, Darnley did not go abroad as he had threatened. Instead he travelled west, to cool his heels and nurse his grievances on the Lennox estates in the vicinity of Glasgow. Meanwhile, Mary herself left Edinburgh in the first week of October to hold an assize at Jedburgh. On 7 October Bothwell was wounded in the Borders during an encounter with the notorious reiver Elliot of Park. The Queen had got as far as Borthwick when she received news of the affray. A week later Mary, accompanied by Moray and a large entourage, rode from Jedburgh to Bothwell's stronghold of the Hermitage in Roxburghshire to commiserate with him as he recovered from stab wounds to his head, hand and body. The royal cavalcade returned to Jedburgh the same evening, a round trip in excess of sixty miles over very rough terrain. The Queen's Well at Bonchester Bridge and the Queen's Mire between Priesthaugh and the Hermitage derived their names from this epic journey.[14]

Mary was a superb horsewoman, habitually accustomed to hard riding all day on the hunting field, so it is unlikely that this feat so greatly taxed her strength that a day or two later she fell violently ill. It is probable that her illness was psychosomatic rather than purely physical. This is confirmed by Maitland who wrote to Archbishop Beaton in Paris that the Queen's illness was due entirely to her squabbles with her husband: 'He misuses himself so far towards her that it is a heartbreak for her to think that he should be her husband.'[15] This combination of physical and mental stress now manifested itself in violent and prolonged vomiting, 'more than sixty times', which reduced her to unconsciousness. For some time it seems that her life hung in the balance, her speech and eyesight were affected and she was subject to fits. She began to recover slowly, then had a relapse on 25 October and rapidly became comatose. As Mary stiffened into the coldness of death, prayers were recited in the churches of Edinburgh and preparations were made for her funeral. While her tearful servants opened the windows in her sickroom Moray scurried about, grabbing rings, jewellery and silver plate in a most unseemly manner.

At that point Mary's French physician Arnault detected a slight movement in one of her arms. Quickly he bandaged her limbs very tightly, then forced open her mouth and poured wine down her gullet. This brutal treatment was rounded off with a large herbal and wine enema which induced violent purging and vomiting of corrupt blood. This desperate remedy had the desired effect, and Mary afterwards began to recover slowly. Characteristically, Buchanan (who was once her tutor but who had now turned violently against her and become a staunch supporter of Moray) described in the most lurid detail Mary's madcap ride to the Hermitage to slake her illicit passion as soon as she knew of Bothwell's injuries, followed by God's punishment for her fornication, and the ludicrous tale that she had Bothwell moved from the Hermitage and installed in Jedburgh in an adjoining chamber, so that they could gratify their lust for each other during their mutual convalescence. This extremist Protestant version of the events would be utterly risible were it not for the fact

that, writing so soon after they occurred, Buchanan provided ammunition for subsequent generations of character assassins.

In truth Bothwell was nowhere near Jedburgh all through this
crucial period. When she was still coherent, but felt that she was
dying, Mary had summoned Moray and other leading nobles into
her chamber so that she could give precise instructions for the
settlement of her kingdom. She made it perfectly clear that the
succession must go to Prince James and not King Henry. Indeed,
Darnley was singled out expressly on account of her fear that he
might try to seize the throne to which he laid claim by right. And it
was specifically to Darnley that she referred when she spoke
sorrowfully of those 'whom I have advanced to a great degree of
honour and pre-eminence above others; who, notwithstanding, has
used . . . ingratitude towards me, which has engendered the displeasure that presently most grieves me, and is also the cause of my
sickness'.[16]

Darnley had been hunting and hawking in the west of Scotland
and was unaware of Mary's illness until 27 October. He immediately
set off for Edinburgh, and reached Jedburgh the following day. There
he received some sort of snub, though not (as stated by some
nineteenth-century writers) because Bothwell was occupying the
apartments which should have by rights been his. It is more
probable that he was chagrined that no attempt had been made to
inform him of his wife's illness, and that he had heard of it by merest
chance. At any rate he rode off in high dudgeon back to Edinburgh,
and thence to Stirling. The breach between Mary and Darnley now
seemed complete.

After Mary had recovered and was well enough to travel she set
off in a vast column of a thousand horse, led by Moray and Bothwell.
Mary herself rode in a litter and made a leisurely journey eastwards
via Kelso as far as Berwick-upon-Tweed where the English gun
batteries fired a royal salute and she had an interview with the
deputy-governor, Sir John Forster. Thence she journeyed north-
wards, via Coldingham and Dunbar to Craigmillar on the southern
outskirts of Edinburgh, arriving on 20 November. At Kelso, some
letters from Darnley had caught up with her, and though the
contents are not known it is obvious that they were not to her liking,
for they triggered off a recurrence of tearful anger and despondency,
so severe that her courtiers feared she would have a relapse. When
she was greeted at Craigmillar by Huntly and Maitland, she

immediately and violently unburdened herself to them, screaming that she would give anything to be rid of her husband. Du Croc reports that Mary was in a state of extreme anguish, crying, 'I wish I were dead,' over and over again. Afterwards she recovered her composure, but the direct outcome of this incident was a meeting at Craigmillar in order that the vexed question of what was to be done about Darnley should be thoroughly debated. There was no one present at this council who was prepared to say a good word for Darnley; everyone, it seems, had his own reasons for detesting him.

At first the consensus was that he should be removed from the political scene by means of a divorce. This was a very rare course of action, though it had become more fashionable, in royal circles at least, since Henry VIII set the precedent. At first Mary favoured this expedient, but because she feared that a dispensation, papal or otherwise, declaring the marriage with Darnley as null and void might affect the legitimacy of Prince James, Mary soon changed her mind. It seems extraordinary, in the religio-political climate of the time, that the views of the Pope should still be taken into account, but under the rules of canon law the Pope remained the final arbiter in matters of royal divorce. It was precisely because he wished to disregard the Pope that Henry VIII had instituted his own brand of Reformation in order to divorce Katherine of Aragon and marry Anne Boleyn, but only when every appeal to Rome had failed. That the views of the Pope still counted for something in Scotland was also due to the fact that Catholics, in England as well as Scotland, were still a force to be reckoned with. Darnley himself must have had a premonition of this sort, for several weeks previously he had himself written at great length, airing his grievances, not only to the Pope but also to the rulers of France and Spain and the Cardinal of Lorraine. In these he alleged that Mary was 'dubious in the faith'. This was a typically fatuous remark, but Mary took it seriously enough to counter with a series of letters strongly rebutting the insinuation.[17] Nevertheless, Darnley's action had seriously undermined any attempt on her part to approach Pope Pius for an annulment.

At Craigmillar a document was drawn up by the Queen in which she stated that the idea of a divorce was apparently initiated by Moray and Maitland who then discussed it with Argyll. All three consulted Huntly and finally Bothwell, before the proposal was put to Mary; but it seems more probable that the idea originated with the

Queen herself, who then suggested to Maitland that he might consider the matter. When Mary realised that a divorce was out of the question, Maitland assured her that some other way would be found of getting rid of Darnley, and that Moray would 'look through his fingers thereto, and will behold our doings saying nothing to the same'. Mary agreed on condition that nothing should be done that would besmirch her honour and conscience. Maitland replied evenly that if she would allow her council to guide the matter among themselves, she would 'see nothing but good and approved by Parliament'.[18] The purpose of preparing this document, known to posterity as the Queen's Protestation, was to absolve Mary of any guilty foreknowledge of the plot to murder her husband. And this may well have been done in good faith, for Mary may not have known, at that juncture, that what Maitland and Moray had in mind was the removal of Darnley by death, although it has to be said that she would have been naïve to suppose that there was any other effective method of getting rid of such a troublesome individual.

The plan originally hinged on the feasibility of seizing Darnley and bringing him to trial on a charge of high treason because of his complicity in the plot to seize Mary at the time of Riccio's murder. There was certainly some justification for such a course, which had the advantage of some semblance of legality; but it was apparently thwarted by the premature arrival of some foreign dignitaries for the baptism of Prince James, a sumptuous state occasion for which parliament voted the staggering sum of £12,000, to be raised by taxes. Nothing could be done about Darnley until this state occasion was over, and so the plan to deal with him was postponed for several months. Darnley himself turned up unexpectedly at Craigmillar just as these deliberations threatening his very existence came to an end. Thinking that Mary's hostility towards him would by now have abated, he demanded a restitution of his rights, both kingly and conjugal. He appears to have received satisfaction on neither count, although there were rumours that marital relations were briefly restored. Mary, for her part, refused bluntly to see him or have anything further to do with him.

The baptism of Prince James took place at Stirling on 17 December amid great pomp, circumstance and Catholic ritual. John Hamilton, Archbishop of St Andrews, the illegitimate brother of Châtelherault, led the procession of Catholic prelates, their costly vestments presenting a dazzling spectacle. One part of the traditional ritual, when the officiating priest spat into the baby's mouth, was omitted at the Queen's request; and rightly so, for Archbishop Hamilton was riddled with syphilis.

The Protestant lords absented themselves although they had now no objection to Mary having her own way in the matter. As it happens, this would be the last public Catholic observance in Scotland for many years. The Comte de Brienne, as proxy for King Charles of France, held the six-month-old baby, while Du Croc deputised for the Duke of Savoy. The baby's godmother, Queen Elizabeth, could not be present but made up for her absence by sending a gold font weighing twenty-eight pounds. Elizabeth's emissary, the Earl of Bedford, being a staunch Puritan, his place as proxy godmother was ably filled by the baby's aunt, the Countess of Argyll. Mary kitted out the leading noblemen in sumptuous raiment at her own expense: Moray in green, Argyll in red and Bothwell in blue, others in cloth of silver or gold. The Queen, recalling the splendid pageantry of the French court, took a personal interest in the plans by her valet Bastien Pages who organised some of the spectacular entertainments, the firework displays, bonfires, banquets, theatrical tableaux, masked balls and other festivities which accompanied the ceremony and continued for several days, although her concern over what was to be done about her husband undoubtedly marred her enjoyment of the celebrations. When the prolonged festivities were over, a nervous reaction set in and Mary became despondent and melancholy. When Du Croc visited her on 22 December he found her lying across her bed 'weeping sore'.

The cause of Mary's depression was, of course, her husband – or rather, how to resolve the problem which had recently been aired at Craigmillar. During the baptism Darnley was actually sulking in his own apartments within the castle precincts but pointedly stayed away from the ceremony. It has been argued that he boycotted this glittering occasion because Queen Elizabeth, still angry at his marriage, had ordered Bedford not to recognise him as King of Scots. No such orders have ever been found and in any case this seems a very feeble excuse. Du Croc was probably nearer the mark when he surmised that Darnley shrank at the humiliating idea of the English visitors witnessing the contempt in which he was now universally held. Du Croc himself had thrice refused Darnley an audience on the very morning of the christening, because King Charles had expressly forbidden him to have anything to do with Mary's husband.[19] A few days later, his quarrel with Mary unresolved, Darnley packed his bags and left Stirling without warning, and headed back for his power base in the Glasgow area. Here, Lennox commiserated with his son who aired his hare-brained schemes for raising a rebellion, kidnapping his son and seizing the reins of government in the baby's name. Doubtless Lennox heard him out, though he at least could have had no illusions regarding the sheer impossibility of these pipe dreams ever being realised.

It would be surprising had some inkling of Darnley's boastful rantings not got back to the Queen. Certainly vague rumours of a Catholic insurrection, with Darnley at its head, were circulating in London, for the Spanish ambassador De Silva dutifully passed them on to King Philip; but whether there was any substance to this Catholic plot in Darnley's mind remained to be seen, and the alternative notion, that the rumour was deliberately started by Darnley's enemies to discredit him even further, cannot be ruled out. On 23 December, probably the very day that Darnley abruptly left Stirling, Mary restored Archbishop Hamilton to his consistorial jurisdiction with full powers to hold courts under canon law. This extraordinary act, which in ordinary circumstances might have immediately triggered off a Protestant uprising, was dictated solely by Mary's desperate desire for a divorce. After an uneasy Christmas in Edinburgh, however, Mary changed her mind and revoked her decision by 9 January. After that date, divorce seems to have been no longer an option; some other solution to the Darnley problem would now have to be sought. While Mary may have expressed this in some vague, general terms, much as Henry II had asked rhetorically if someone would rid him of that turbulent priest Becket, all the subsequent events leading up to the murder and its immediate aftermath point to Mary having no knowledge of any actual plan to kill her husband.

Soon after Christmas she took the very wise precaution of removing Prince James from Stirling Castle and bringing him back to Edinburgh on 14 January 1567, where he was safely ensconced in her own apartments at Holyroodhouse. Stirling was uncomfortably close to the Lennox country, and as rumours of a plot centred on Darnley escalated, Mary was galvanised into action. Morton, Lindsay and others implicated in the murder of Riccio were allowed to return from exile. The order granting the recall was issued by Mary on 24 December. The timing of this seems significant; having taken a drastic step towards obtaining a divorce, Mary slept on it and the very next day swithered towards the alternative solution. Through the mediation of Morton's kinsman Archibald Douglas, Mary at first granted a pardon to the conspirators on condition that they continued to remain abroad for two years. Only Ker of Fawdonside and the Postulate of Arbroath were expressly excluded, on the grounds that they had personally threatened the Queen's life.

This compromise was apparently worked out in order to placate Bothwell, but the Earl got the bit between his teeth and argued for a full and unconditional pardon. The notion of Bothwell acting in such a friendly manner towards his old adversary Morton seems unlikely at first glance; but already Bothwell was hatching a scheme whereby Morton, who had had no compunction about slaying Riccio, might be induced to assassinate his kinsman Darnley whose double-dealing had forced him to flee the country.

The recall of Morton also suited Moray, for this would restore the balance between the Moray and Bothwell factions and, at the same time, considerably boost the Protestant cause which had suffered such hard knocks lately. Morton, for his part, was well aware that he was being used by both factions, but he was far too experienced a master of intrigue to let either side get the better of him. Some time after he recrossed the border on 10 January, he received a visit from Moray and Maitland at Whittinghame, his brother's seat. At this meeting Bothwell urged Morton to undertake the assassination, whereupon Morton coolly asked him to produce the Queen's warrant authorising the killing. The meeting broke up and the visitors rode off, but Morton sent Archibald Douglas to accompany them back to Edinburgh and sound them out further in the matter. As the answer was evasive, Morton felt free to bide his time without further involvement. He later stated that if the Queen herself had offered him a full pardon on condition that he murder her husband, he would have rejected these terms and chosen to go back into exile rather than agree to commit such a crime. Having been let down by Morton, Bothwell had no alternative but to undertake the project himself.

Before the old year was out, however, it seemed as if fate might intervene, when Darnley was struck down by a serious illness. The *Diurnal of Occurrents*, a diary compiled anonymously by someone who seems to have occupied an official position, merely stated that King Henry was stricken with 'a great fever of the pox',[20] but in the context of the period this could only mean syphilis, a view confirmed by the pitting on Darnley's skull (now in the possession of the Royal College of Surgeons, London) which indicates a fairly advanced secondary stage of the disease. If left to take its course, syphilis would reach its horribly disfiguring tertiary stage, followed by general paralysis of the insane, and death – but that might well be many years in the future, and neither Mary nor Bothwell could afford to wait. On news of Darnley's illness Mary, with characteristic concern, sent her personal physician from Edinburgh and then, on 20 January, set off for Glasgow in order to visit him herself. On that very morning, however, she wrote a long letter to Archbishop Beaton at Paris in which she made no attempt to conceal how much she despised her husband. Beaton, who had heard rumours of a pro-Darnley plot, immediately replied, urging her to patch up her quarrel with her husband, but this letter did not reach Mary until Darnley was dead. The chief purpose of Mary's journey was to bring her sick husband back to Edinburgh in a litter. Ostensibly the reason was her concern for his well-being, and in Edinburgh she could personally superintend his convalescence. This was oddly at variance with the cold contempt for Darnley expressed in Mary's letter to Beaton, which seems to suggest that, subconsciously at least, Mary was placing her husband in a vulnerable position, well away from Lennox and his kinsmen.

Bothwell convoyed the Queen on her outward journey as far as Callendar House near Falkirk, the seat of Lord Livingston, and then went back to Edinburgh. Mary made leisurely progress, and did not reach Glasgow till 22 January. She and her husband were re-united the following day. The sight of him lying in his sickbed, a taffeta mask concealing the hideous eruptions that covered his once-beautiful face, seems to have rekindled a spark of tenderness in Mary. An alleged memento of this idyll is Queen Mary's Tree in the vicinity of Darnley House on the south-western outskirts of Glasgow where, legend has it, Mary and her husband picnicked. Quite apart from the questionable likelihood of such *al fresco* dalliance in the depths of a Glasgow winter, the tree itself (a giant sycamore) is at least a century too young.

Darnley had been apprised of the fact that the nobles at Craig-millar had approached the Queen with a document plotting his downfall, but he was comforted by the knowledge that Mary had refused. Now, as he luxuriated under her tender ministrations, he was confident that this essentially gentle creature would never do him harm. In this frame of mind, therefore, he eventually consented to return to Edinburgh with her. Once before, Mary had won him over with soft words and the promise of future rewards, when they had escaped from Holyrood after Riccio's murder. Now, the weak-willed Darnley would be seduced again by hints of future happiness.

The only matter on which they disagreed was the proposed convalescent home. Mary wanted to install him in Craigmillar Castle, but with overtones of the recent plot against him, he shuddered at the prospect as the royal cortège approached that stronghold. Instead, on the spur of the moment, he proposed that he should reside at Kirk o' Field, just inside the walls of Edinburgh. Darnley could not have initiated this suggestion, and it is more likely that the idea was put to him as one of several alternatives. He himself thought that he was being conveyed to Hamilton House within the precinct of the ancient collegiate church of St Mary-in-the-Field, now simply known as Kirk o' Field, and he was rather put out to discover that he was to be installed at the Old Provost's Lodging instead. This house, on the southern outskirts of the town (where the university quadrangle now stands), was only ten minutes' walk from Holyrood. The house had formerly been the lodge of the provost of the collegiate church but now belonged to Robert Balfour, Sir James's brother. Across the quadrangle was the imposing three-storey mansion of the Duke of Châtelherault, one of Darnley's deadliest enemies, but currently occupied by Archbishop Hamilton.

The Old Provost's Lodging stood on an eminence overlooking the Cowgate and from its own garden a gate in the thick city wall led on to an orchard and the open fields which had given the church its name. It was, by all accounts (except Buchanan's, which stated that it was ruinous), a spacious and comfortable house, on two levels. Darnley's bedroom was on the upper floor, while a second bedroom, occupied by Mary herself, was immediately below. The house had commodious public rooms as well as a suite of vaulted cellars below. While Darnley was being made as comfortable as possible in his own chamber, Mary sent instructions to Holyrood, summoning a vast quantity of furniture and equipment for her husband's lodgings. Much of this furniture, ironically, came from the Strathbogie hoard confiscated in the autumn of 1562. Darnley's bed, however, had formerly belonged to Mary of Guise, and had been given by Mary to her husband in August 1566. A bath, for the daily ablutions necessary to Darnley's treatment, was placed alongside his bed, one of the doors being taken off its hinges and used as a lid when the bath was not in use. Darnley's bedroom had two windows, one overlooking the courtyard and the other in a gallery that jutted out over, and was supported by, the city wall itself. In contrast to the sumptuous draperies and furnishings of Darnley's chamber, the bedroom below was plainly furnished with a small bed for Mary's use, should she wish to stay overnight while ministering to her sick husband.

It was on Saturday, 1 February 1567, that Darnley settled in at Kirk o' Field. During his last week on earth he enjoyed a level of domestic felicity which he had probably never experienced before. Mary, confident that Darnley was powerless to scheme and plot here, so far removed from his father and kinsmen, relaxed and recovered her sunny disposition. She bustled and fussed brightly over the patient every day, and on Wednesday night she even slept over, in the little room below his. Mary herself later admitted that something approaching tenderness sprang up between them as they rediscovered their friendship. To Darnley it must have seemed like old times, a reprise of that happy period before their marriage when Mary had nursed him through his previous illness. By Friday evening Darnley was sufficiently emboldened by this new phase in their relationship to warn Mary that he had heard rumours of plots against her, and in terms more touching than hypocritical for once, he begged her to be on her guard against certain people who were trying to make trouble between them. According to the Earl of Lennox, it was on that very evening that his son wrote to him saying how much his health had improved as a result of the kind treatment of 'such as hath this good while concealed their good will, I mean my love the Queen, which I assure you hath all this while and yet doth use herself like a natural and loving wife'.[21]

During the day there was continual coming and going at Kirk o' Field, Mary or various courtiers being constantly on hand to converse with the patient, entertain him with music or play cards. Mary worked tirelessly and sincerely to create an atmosphere of sweetness and light, reconciling one faction with another and her husband with everyone else; but this new-found air of cordiality and harmony was superficial. Lord Robert Stewart, Mary's half-brother, was acutely aware of the building tension and finally blurted out to Darnley that it would cost him his life if he did not get away at once. Extremely agitated by this warning, Darnley confronted the Queen who, quite genuinely concerned, broached the subject with Lord Robert, but he immediately clammed up, afraid that the plotters would take their revenge on him if he revealed their intentions.

That Darnley had to be got rid of is not in doubt, nor can it be doubted that Bothwell and others were implicated, with or without the approval of the Queen. What is puzzling is the method apparently intended to murder Darnley. The preferred methods of assassination in the sixteenth century were the dagger and the rope, less often (because far less reliable) the firearm; but to kill someone by blowing them up was unheard of at that time. Gunpowder was still at a relatively primitive stage in its development and it took large quantities of it to achieve the purpose the assassins had in mind. To organise the delivery of so many barrels of powder and to pile them up in the cellars seems so impractical that it even gave rise to the theory that it was Darnley who procured the gunpowder with the intention of blowing up the Queen while she was alone in the building, and that it was detonated accidentally, so that Darnley was hoist with his own petard.[22]

A variant of this is that Bothwell, having discovered this plot against the Queen, ignited the explosives himself in order to give Darnley a taste of his own medicine.[23] In view of the fact that Darnley was still confined to his sickroom, with none of his own supporters at hand and only a few servants in attendance, in a house where the Queen, Bothwell and their supporters came and went all the time, such a notion of a Darnley plot is preposterous. Almost as fanciful is the notion that both Darnley and Bothwell were intended victims; that while Bothwell was planning and executing the murder of Darnley a separate sub-plot was being engineered by Morton and his kinsman Archibald Douglas to murder Bothwell simultaneously. It is more probable that Morton, having refused to take part in Bothwell's plan, held a watching brief and had his own Douglas henchmen on hand to ensure that the death of Darnley was accomplished.

The Kirk o' Field incident has been endlessly debated for more than four centuries. Contemporary accounts are coloured by the political viewpoint of their authors, and even primary sources, such as the depositions of witnesses (many of whom were tortured to extract confessions), are notoriously contradictory and unreliable. The subject has spawned a substantial literature of its own, events being interpreted for partisan purposes. If we stick to the incontrovertible facts, however, the following picture emerges.

Paris, formerly servant to Bothwell but now in Mary's service, attended upon her at Kirk o' Field and later deponed that his old employer had called on the Wednesday or Thursday before the murder. Bothwell was suffering a recurrence of dysentery and while relieving himself in a convenient garderobe, told Paris that he planned to kill King Henry. Furthermore, he named Maitland, Argyll, Huntly, Morton, the young Lord Ruthven (whose father had succumbed to his terminal illness three weeks after the Riccio murder) and Lindsay as his accomplices. Moray, it will be noted, was not mentioned – for the simple reason that, by the time this deposition was taken, he was Regent of Scotland. Bothwell browbeat Paris into handing over the house-keys – a factor that indicates the Queen's innocence, for had she really been a party to the murder Bothwell could have obtained the keys from Mary herself. On Saturday Paris got hold of the keys and delivered them to Bothwell at Holyrood.

Darnley, now greatly recovered, was scheduled to leave Kirk o' Field the following Monday morning. For Mary and her Catholic friends, 9 February, the last Sunday before Lent, was a day for merry-making, made doubly joyous on account of the marriage that morning of the Queen's favourite valet, Bastien Pages, to Christian Hogg. The wedding breakfast took place in Holyrood at midday and Mary was present. At four o'clock that afternoon the Queen attended a more formal occasion, a farewell dinner given by the Bishop of the Isles at his house in the Canongate for Moreta, the Savoyard ambassador, who was about to leave Scotland. Bothwell, Argyll, Huntly and Cassilis were in attendance, but Moray was conspicuous by his absence. He had left Edinburgh hurriedly that morning on receiving the news that his wife had miscarried and he had to rush to her side.

After the bishop's dinner, Mary and her friends rode off to Kirk o' Field to entertain Darnley with the day's doings. Huntly rolled dice, someone played the lute and others sang. All in all, it was a very jolly evening, but about ten or eleven o'clock Mary, who had planned to spend the night there, was reminded by a courtier that it was now the time of Bastien's wedding masque which she had promised to attend. So the entourage set off back to Holyrood, leaving Darnley in a fit of pique at being thus deserted. Mary brushed aside his petulance good-naturedly, giving him a ring as a pledge of her goodwill. Downstairs, in the cobbled courtyard, Mary was about to mount her horse when she was startled by the sight of Bothwell's former retainer. 'Jesu, Paris!' she exclaimed, 'How begrimed you are!'[24]

Paris stared back guiltily but said nothing. Mary studied him quizzically for a moment, but without further ado she mounted her steed and rode off.

Darnley, deserted by his wife and her friends, snapped at his valet William Taylor for a fresh bottle of wine, then gave orders that his horses should be prepared for departure at five o'clock the following morning. There was a bit of a sing-song, then Taylor snuffed the candles and settled down for the night on his palliasse, on the floor of Darnley's chamber. The rest of Darnley's staff – Bonkil the cook, the servants Thomas Nelson and Symonds, Taylor's page-boy and two grooms, McCaig and Glen, were already asleep in the gallery overhanging the city wall.

By the time Mary and her retinue had returned to Holyrood the jollification was almost over, but they were just in time for the merry ritual of putting the bride and groom to bed. It was well after midnight before Mary retired to her own quarters, but she had already been asleep for some time when she was awakened about two in the morning by a deafening explosion that shook the city. Mary sat bolt upright and cried out to her attendants, thinking it was gunfire. By now the palace was awake and people were running and screaming. Amid the clangour and confusion, Bothwell was the man of the moment. In his capacity as Sheriff of Edinburgh it was his duty to investigate the commotion, and he promptly sent out messengers to find out what had caused the tumult.

The townspeople, who had been abed for hours, were now up and rushing around, some partially clothed. Those living near Kirk o' Field beheld a ghastly scene. Where the Old Provost's Lodging had been there was now no more than a pile of rubble. Approaching the scene with bated breath they suddenly heard a hoarse cry. There, on the parapet of the city wall, stood the blackened, tattered figure of Nelson, Darnley's manservant. By some freak of the explosion he had been thrown clear and suffered only minor injuries, bruises and burns. This fearful apparition broke the spell, and now people rushed forward and began digging at the rubble with bare hands, impervious to the pitch darkness and the biting cold wind. Eventually they dug out two mangled corpses who proved to be servants. Feverishly they delved deeper into the fallen masonry but of King Henry there was no sign. Some time later, perhaps an hour or so after the blast, somebody happened to walk into the orchard beyond the city wall and there stumbled upon a gruesome spectacle. Beneath a tree lay the body of Darnley, clad only in his nightshirt. Alongside was the corpse of his valet, Taylor. What gave this scene a macabre twist, however, was a chair on which sat a dagger, some rope and a cloak which, according to eye-witnesses, were neatly and deliberately laid out. On the other hand, a sketch of the scene which was sent to Cecil soon afterwards (and is now in the Public Record Office, London) shows the semi-nude bodies of Darnley and Taylor with the dagger, chair and articles of clothing scattered nearby.

What was even more astonishing was the lack of obvious injuries on Darnley and Taylor, no signs of burns, far less loss of limbs and other maiming associated with the victims of explosions. Likewise the chair and clothing were unmarked by fire. The bodies of Darnley and his valet were carried into one of the nearby houses and examined soon afterwards by doctors who found that both men had been strangled.

10. BOTHWELL

February – June 1567

Wantons marry in the month of May
   Translation of a Latin placard on the gate of Holyroodhouse

The dust from the explosion at Kirk o' Field had hardly settled when rumours of plot and counter-plot spread like wildfire. Because of the subsequent turn of events it became fashionable to lay the blame squarely on Mary herself, aided and abetted by Bothwell, and this simplistic version of events is widely held to this day, even though Mary's complicity in the deed has been discounted by most modern scholars and historians.

That Bothwell was the arch-perpetrator, however, cannot be in doubt, although within months he would become the scapegoat while others evaded opprobrium for their part in the crime. The authorised version of events, purporting to come from statements made by the conspirators after their arrest, is that Bothwell's porter, William Powrie, brought the gunpowder from Holyrood in two trunks. He rode through the streets of Edinburgh quite openly, but it was not clear whether he had made one trip with two horses, or two trips with one horse. Bothwell was alleged to have brought the gunpowder from Dunbar Castle and stored it, in one large barrel, in his private apartments at the palace for some time prior to the murder, though no one questioned why, how or when he had done so. The powder, in trunks, was then transferred to bags which Powrie heaved over the wall of the Blackfriars Monastery and finally tipped out on to the floor of Mary's bedchamber while the Queen and her entourage were partying in Darnley's room upstairs. In the evening Powrie, assisted by Pat Wilson, took the empty trunks back down the Canongate to Holyrood. Finally, Bothwell himself stole out in the dead of night to ignite the explosive.

This tale is so palpably false that it is a wonder anyone was taken in by it for a moment. Two trunkfuls of gunpowder would have been quite insufficient to demolish a stoutly built stone structure, assuming that the explosive had been properly packed tight into a confined space, but loose powder would only burn with a flash and no explosive effect. To do the damage that was sustained at Kirk o' Field would have required a cartload of barrels, packed tightly in the cellars of the building. Within days, indeed, Sir William Drury was reporting to Cecil that James Balfour had spent £60 Scots on gunpowder. As Balfour and his brother owned both the Old Provost's Lodging and the adjacent New Provost's Lodging, it seems probable that the cartload of barrels containing the explosive was conveniently stored in the latter building, and transferred to the cellars of the older house on Sunday. The task of manhandling the barrels from one building to the other, during the afternoon when Mary and her entourage were attending the wedding and the farewell dinner and the house was at its quietest, was apparently carried out by eight of Bothwell's henchmen. In addition to William Powrie and Pat Wilson, there were John Hepburn, John Hay of Talla and the Ormiston brothers, James and Hob, all kinsmen of Bothwell, together with his tailor George Dalgleish and his former servant Paris.

The reference to heaping loose powder on the floor of the Queen's bedroom was a clumsy attempt to implicate Mary herself; but apart from the impracticality of placing gunpowder in such a manner, it must be remembered that the Queen, and probably others of her party, must have spent some time in that room later that afternoon when they returned from the bishop's dinner. And Mary herself, by all accounts, had planned to spend the night there. It was only when a courtier reminded her of her promise to attend Bastien's masque that she changed her mind. Some accounts state that the mindful courtier was none other than Bothwell himself. After Bastien and Christian had been put to bed amid the usual bawdy teasing, the Queen had gone to her own quarters where she had a long conversation, until midnight, with Bothwell and John Stewart of Traquair, captain of the palace guard. This is intriguing, but as no record of their conversation was preserved we can only guess at its content. Certainly we may be sure that Bothwell did not divulge his intention of slipping off to Kirk o' Field in the wee small hours to blow up King Henry. Had he done so, there is a distinct possibility that Mary would somehow have prevented his deadly mission, raised the alarm or otherwise wrecked his plans. It cannot be seriously imagined that, despite her contempt for Darnley, Mary would have cold-bloodedly given Bothwell the go-ahead. With her well-known squeamishness, innate gentleness and new-found tenderness towards her wretched husband, she would never have sanctioned such a revolting deed. Furthermore, Mary could not have retired for the night so calmly had she been apprised of what was now afoot.

Bothwell left the unsuspecting queen, went to his own apartment, changed out of his black-and-silver carnival costume into a canvas doublet and, wrapped warmly in his drab riding cloak, set off with the reluctant Paris on his deadly errand. We may dismiss the fanciful tale, based on some of the depositions of the lesser criminals, that Bothwell and Paris marched boldly along the Canongate in full view of the night watch, answering their challenge of 'Who goes there?' with the ingenuous cry 'My Lord Bothwell's men'.[1] It is more probable that they slunk along the alleys and back streets to Kirk o' Field where they were met by their accomplices. Meanwhile, lurking silently in the shadows, were Archibald Douglas and some of his supporters. Though related to Darnley they were Morton's men and were bent on revenge against the man who had betrayed them over Riccio's murder the previous year. There was some nonsense about Archibald wearing black velvet slippers, one of which was accidentally dropped at the scene of the crime, but the truth is that on such a bitterly cold night, with a powdering of snow on the ground, Douglas and his men were stoutly shod, and heavily armed as well. They skulked in the east garden adjoining the house and effectively sealed off the building from its neighbours.

The only account of Darnley's last hours was later provided by his father, Lennox, who was not there. The picture of his 'innocent lamb' reciting the Fifth Psalm with his servant – 'My voice shalt Thou hear in the morning, O Lord' – is as ludicrous as some of the accounts of the conspiracy itself. Nelson, the sole survivor, later testified that Darnley was drinking heavily and that he refused to play his lute, though they settled for 'a merry song' before retiring for the night.

Outside, in the perishing cold wind, the two distinct bands of conspirators, Bothwell's men probably ignorant of the Douglas party, waited till all was quiet. According to his cousin, John Hepburn of Bolton, Bothwell himself slipped into the building and ignited the fuses, then exited hastily to watch the explosion from a safe distance. The train of powder did not 'take fire so quickly as the Earl had expected', says Hepburn, so his impatient master approached the house again. 'Thereupon the train suddenly emitted fire,' adds Hepburn who only managed to pull Bothwell back under cover in the nick of time.[2] Immediately afterwards, according to various depositions, Bothwell and Paris rushed back to Holyrood, giving the same brazen answer to the challenge of the night watch as they went. The keys to the house were thrown down a well the following day.

Well satisfied with his night's work, Bothwell drank some wine, slipped into bed, and waited until he was roused shortly afterwards by George Hacket with the dreadful news that the King's house had been blown up. Crying, 'Fy! Treason!', Bothwell got up, swiftly dressed again and left his room where he was joined by Huntly. The two men went off to break the shocking news to the Queen. Afterwards, Bothwell assumed his role as Sheriff, mustered a squad of soldiers and went back to Kirk o' Field to check his handiwork, blissfully unaware that he had bungled the job. The likeliest scenario is that Darnley, perhaps awakened by some noise on the cobblestones, looked out of his window, saw Bothwell and his ruffians, and panicked. Accompanied only by his faithful valet, Darnley escaped from his upper room by means of a chair suspended from a rope, a drop of only three and a half metres to the alleyway outside the city wall. In his cowardly haste to escape he did not alert the rest of his staff, so that all but Nelson perished in the explosion. Not even pausing to dress, other than to grab his cloak, Darnley, with Taylor at his heels, fled towards the orchard. The barefoot figures in their white nightshirts were easily intercepted by the Douglas men and strangled on the spot, perhaps even with their own rope, though Moreta relayed the information that Darnley had been strangled with the sleeves of his nightgown.[3] His informants were Barbara Mertane and May Crokat, living in houses on the alley running alongside the orchard, who claimed to have overheard Darnley crying out to his captors, 'Pity me, kinsmen, for the sake of Jesus Christ, who pitied all the world!' even as they choked the life out of him. In this miserable manner perished Henry, King of Scots, in the twenty-first year of his short, unhappy life.

Mary, of course, had been rudely awakened by the deafening explosion, and long before Bothwell put in his appearance she had been informed by messengers of the doleful news. Bothwell later reported to Sir James Melville that he found the Queen 'sorrowful and quiet'. When Darnley was brought to Holyrood she had to undergo the ordeal of formally identifying his body, which she did 'without any outward show or signe of joy or sorrow'.[4] The plain truth is that, no matter how much Mary had despised her husband and wished to be rid of him, the suddenness and gruesome nature of his murder left her speechless with shock. Probably this was also compounded by guilty feelings as she recalled all the bitter, unkind things she had said or thought about the wretched boy. Mary was also horrified to think that, had she not changed her plans at the last moment and decided to remain at Holyrood that night after Bastien's masque, she would have been blown to bits in her bedroom at Kirk o' Field. A long letter to Archbishop Beaton, penned on the morning of Monday, 10 February, reveals the state of Mary's mind within hours of the atrocity. Her grief for Darnley is rather stilted and perfunctory, but the dominant theme was her belief that the plot had been aimed at herself. Significantly, she said that Darnley had been killed by the blast which had reduced the building so that nothing remained, 'not a stone above another'. She added that, although the perpetrators had not yet been identified, with 'the diligence our Council has begun already to use . . . the same being discovered . . . we hope to punish the same with such rigour as shall serve for example of this cruelty to all ages to come'.[5] And she concluded that she herself had escaped death, not by chance but by divine intervention.

Later that day, the post-mortem examination revealed the true cause of the deaths of Darnley and Taylor and now tongues began to wag. The Council, for all the diligence promised by Mary, seems to have been singularly lax in its questioning of the immediate eye-witnesses, the manservant Nelson, a surgeon John Pitcairn and Barbara Mertane and May Crokat, whose testimony was immediately dismissed as mere floating gossip. Their evidence, bandying about the names of the greatest in the land, was disregarded for purely political reasons. Darnley's corpse was brought back to Holyrood, embalmed by an apothecary and a surgeon, and after lying in state in the Chapel Royal for several days, was taken at dead of night and interred in the vaults below. Mary ordered her court into mourning and purchased £150 worth of black cloth for this purpose. By custom and tradition she should have spent the next forty days in strict seclusion in a darkened room, but her physical debility and overwrought mental state were so painfully obvious that her advisers urged her to cut short this period of mourning and withdraw to the country for fresh air, a change of scene and the opportunity to restore her strength. From the outset, however, Mary flouted the mourning convention. Within twenty-four hours of Darnley's murder she was in public again, attending the marriage of John Stewart and Margaret Carwood, her favourite lady of the bedchamber, on whom she had lavished a wedding dress costing £125, an enormous sum for the period. Needless to say, Mary was heavily criticised for attending the wedding so soon after her husband's death, but either she felt deeply obligated to such a valued servant and confidante, or was still too much in shock to appreciate that her actions would be misinterpreted.

Even the hard-bitten gentlemen of the Council could see that the Queen was on the verge of a nervous breakdown, and fearing a recurrence of the dreadful illness which had brought her to the brink of the grave the previous autumn, they urged her to take a holiday. Mary needed no second prompting, but went off, within days of Darnley's murder, to Seton where she spent three days. Later her detractors would claim that she had spent those days in amorous dalliance with Bothwell, although both he and Huntly were in Edinburgh the entire time, guarding Prince James and exerting themselves in damage limitation; for by now the identity of Darnley's killers was being openly bruited. On 12 February the Council, in the Queen's name, issued a proclamation offering a reward of £2,000 and a free pardon to anyone providing the identities of the murderers. That very night, the citizens of Edinburgh resorted to placarding, an extremely effective method of spreading propaganda. Overnight, handbills were affixed to the door of the Tolbooth, walls and trees, naming the murderers as Bothwell, James Balfour, David Chalmers and Black John Spens. Two days later other placards, frankly xenophobic, blamed Bastien Pages, a servant called Francisco Busso, John of Bordeaux and Joseph Riccio (the eighteen-year-old brother of the murdered David, and his successor as foreign secretary to the Queen), but as the days passed the majority of these little posters laid the blame at Bothwell's door. By the end of February they were quite scurrilous, with crude pictures that linked Bothwell and Mary, and suggest a well-orchestrated campaign by person or persons unknown, though one suspects the hand of Moray or his agents in this as he had the most to gain by implicating his sister and Bothwell.

Acutely aware of this propaganda campaign, Mary herself probably confronted Bothwell and demanded to know the truth. What answer he gave her is not known; but by March speculation concerning Bothwell's part in the murder had spread as far as Paris, Madrid and Venice. Both Catherine de' Medici and Queen Elizabeth wrote to Mary urging her to take swift and ruthless action. Someone had to pay for such a heinous crime; better to make an example of an innocent man than to let the crime go unpunished altogether. As more and more placards appeared as if by magic, and voices were raised in unison in the dead of night, chanting 'Bothwell! Bothwell!' as the murderer, Mary should have been galvanised into positive action; but she was overcome by nervous lassitude which prostrated her, and in this weakened, debilitated condition she was in no fit state to deal with the routine business of government, far less grapple with the mystery of Darnley's death. Had she had loyal, disinterested advisers, she might have been able to cope, but just when she needed them most she had no one reliable to whom she could turn.

At times like this, her natural ally and helpmeet should have been her half-brother, Moray, but he was almost certainly implicated in the murder and thought it prudent to withdraw to England for a time. Immediately after the murder he had gone to St Andrews on the pretext of nursing his sick wife. On 13 March he wrote to Cecil, vehemently declaring his innocence and requesting a passport that would enable him to travel to London. Just when his sister needed him most, therefore, Moray deserted her for his own selfish ends, partly to keep out of Bothwell's clutches and partly to ingratiate himself with Elizabeth. On 10 April he took an emotional farewell of his sister who wept and said that she wished he were not 'so precise in religion'. After a brief stay in London, he went to Italy, touring Venice and Milan while his sister was careering towards self-destruction.

All the other nobles, from Bothwell and Maitland downwards, seem to have been involved in the plot to a greater or lesser extent, and in the circumstances could hardly be relied upon to pursue the matter of Darnley's murder with any enthusiasm, much to the disgust of Lennox who, from his Glasgow stronghold, clamoured for justice and retribution. Instead, the only positive action was the prosecution on 14 March of James Murray of Tullibardine for defaming and slandering the Queen by means of 'certain painted papers' which he had affixed to the door of the Tolbooth.

On 19 March Argyll and Huntly escorted Prince James back to Stirling. At the same time the Prince's guardian, Mar, was formally appointed governor of Stirling Castle which effectively robbed him of the much more important position as governor of Edinburgh Castle, a duty which he had discharged loyally and conscientiously since August 1565. Bothwell now briefly installed his own hench-man, Sir James Cockburn, before conferring the appointment on none other than Sir James Balfour, his accomplice in the murders. At the end of February and in early March the Countess of Bothwell was dangerously ill. For several days she hovered between life and death and though she eventually recovered, the cause of her mysterious ailment was never revealed. The possibility that Bothwell had tried to poison his wife cannot be ruled out. Prudently, Countess Jean, as soon as she was able, readily assented to a separation, swiftly followed by a divorce in which Earl James was named the guilty party on account of his adultery with a servant, Bessie Crawford. Long before matters were thus resolved by due process of law, however, Bothwell was taking matters into his own hand.

On 23 March the forty-day period of mourning for King Henry came to an end with a Requiem Mass. The following day Mary wrote to her father-in-law, agreeing that he should be allowed to take out a private process before parliament against Bothwell as the killer of his son. The process was set in motion five days later by an Act of the Privy Council and was scheduled to take place on 12 April. By late March, however, Mary's health was deteriorating again, Sir William Drury reporting to London that the Queen was prone to fainting fits and seemed very melancholy. On the eve of the trial Lennox, at the head of a formidable army numbering three thousand men, set out from Glasgow, but at Linlithgow they were told that only Lennox himself, and no more than six supporters, would be permitted to enter the capital. Not surprisingly, Lennox declined to put in an appearance under these conditions, having been warned that Edinburgh was thronging with thousands of Bothwell's men. Bothwell himself rode along the Canongate that day to answer the charge. He was clad in his most flamboyant costume, his charger richly caparisoned, and he had Morton and Maitland at his shoulder, with hundreds of his spearmen marching behind. This gallant cavalcade was witnessed from a window at Holyrood by the Queen, accompanied by one of her Maries – Mary Fleming, who had married Maitland in January. A courier from London arrived at this juncture with an urgent plea from Elizabeth to delay proceedings till Lennox could attend, but the envoy was peremptorily denied access to the Queen.

The trial lasted from midday till seven in the evening, the Council solemnly going through the motions of examining the evidence; but in default of any accusations by Lennox, Bothwell was inevitably acquitted by his peers. The *Diurnal of Occurrents* drily noted that Bothwell was 'made clean of the said slaughter, albeit that it was heavily murmured that he was guilty thereof'.[6] Bothwell celebrated his acquittal by sending a crier round the town proclaiming the verdict, and had placards headed by his arms posted all over Edinburgh, offering to defend his innocence by personal combat. That night a rash of placards covered the city, an anonymous champion picking up the gauntlet on behalf of the Scottish people. The following Wednesday Mary rode in heavily armed procession to parliament, Bothwell bearing her sceptre, Argyll the crown and Crawford the sword. This parliament, packed with Bothwell's adherents, affirmed the verdict of his trial. The lieges were ordered to live at peace regardless of their religion, but the most significant business was the conferment of the lands pertaining to Dunbar Castle on Bothwell. At the same time Huntly and four of his Gordon kinsmen were formally restored to their estates, though unofficially they had been enjoying them for at least two years.

When this session of parliament ended on Saturday, 19 April, Bothwell and his cronies adjourned to Ainslie's tavern in the High Street. Towards the end of a lavish meal at Bothwell's expense, he produced a lengthy document. The preamble reaffirmed his innocence in the murder of Darnley, but went on to state that the Queen was now 'destitute of a husband, in which solitary state, the commonwealth may not permit her to remain'.[7] Bothwell went on to suggest that if 'the affectionate and hearty service of the said Earl, and his other good qualities' commended themselves to the Queen, he was ready to offer himself to her as a new husband. Well aware that the young widow might soon be the target of continental princes, he suggested that he was best qualified for the role as 'one of her native-born subjects'. Having plied his fellow nobles with drink, Bothwell persuaded them to put their names to the document, ever afterwards known as the Ainslie Bond, promising their support in promoting his marriage proposals. No fewer than nine earls, eight bishops and seven barons, including Argyll, Cassilis, Glencairn, Huntly, Morton, Maitland, Sutherland, Rothes, Seton, Sinclair, Boyd and Herries, subscribed to this preposterous manifesto. To be sure, some signatories were less enthusiastic than others, and one can hardly imagine that Morton and Maitland, for example, had any great relish at the prospect of Bothwell as king-consort. But stupefied by strong liquor and intimidated by the daggers of Bothwell's retainers, they signed the bond anyway.

With this precious paper in his pocket, Bothwell, accompanied by Maitland and Patrick Bellenden, went to Seton, whither Mary had gone earlier that day. According to Mary herself, it was there that Bothwell first broached the subject of her remarriage, and put himself forward as the candidate selected by her nobles. Nau put it succinctly: 'This poor young princess, inexperienced in such devices, was circumvented on all sides by persuasions, requests and importunities; both by general memorials signed by their hands, and presented to her in full council, and by private letters.'[8] Poor Mary was utterly taken aback at Bothwell's bare-faced effrontery, but Maitland smoothly told her that it had become absolutely vital that some remedy be provided for the disorderly state into which public affairs had fallen for a want of strong leadership. He reiterated that the proposal had the complete backing of the chief nobles and concluded that Bothwell was 'a man of resolution well adapted to rule, the very character needed to give weight to the decisions and actions of the council'. Mary refused these blandishments point blank on the grounds that there were too many scandals surrounding her husband's death, even if Bothwell had been absolved by parliament. Mary's reaction to the proposal, well-documented in contemporary accounts, has usually been conveniently overlooked by her detractors, preferring instead to lend credence to the statement (reported by Kirkcaldy of Grange in a letter of 20 April to the Earl of Bedford) that the Queen intended taking Prince James out of Mar's safe-keeping and transferring him to Bothwell whom 'she would follow to the world's end in a white petticoat ere she left him'.

On that very day, indeed, Mary set off for Stirling, arriving there on Monday, 21 April. She spent the whole of Tuesday playing with

Prince James, now ten months old, blissfully unaware of the fact that she would never see him again. From Stirling she wrote to the former papal nuncio, now the Bishop of Mondovi in Savoy. In this curious letter she reasserted her devotion to Scotland, to the Pope and the Holy Catholic Church. The bishop, reporting this to the Pope, shrewdly observed that unless His Holiness gave her his wholehearted support she might rush into marriage without sufficient thought, and even singled out Bothwell as a possibility on account of him ever having 'been the Queen's most trusty and obedient adherent'.[9]

On Wednesday, 23 April, Mary and her retinue set out on the journey back to Edinburgh. Despite Kirkcaldy's speculation, Prince James was not in the Queen's entourage. The trip to Stirling was of an unofficial nature and Mary had only Maitland, Huntly and James Melville, with about thirty horse, for company. On the journey back to the capital, Mary was doubled up by violent abdominal pain and had to rest at a wayside cottage before travelling on as far as Linlithgow where she spent the night. The following morning, she and her cavalcade resumed their journey, but at the Bridge of Almond, six miles west of Edinburgh, she was intercepted by Bothwell at the head of eight hundred men. He spurred forward and seized the Queen's bridle, explaining his impetuous action by saying that her life would be in danger if she continued on to Edinburgh. Instead, he proposed to take her to Dunbar Castle where she would be safe. Some of the Queen's men reacted violently to Bothwell but Mary calmed them down, saying that she would rather go with the Earl than be the cause of blood-letting. Faced with such a large army, Mary knew that resistance was hopeless. Preserving her dignity and putting a brave face on it, she allowed Bothwell to lead her horse on a forty-mile ride, giving Edinburgh a wide berth.

Mary's detractors would later maintain that her willingness to fall in with Bothwell's wishes showed that they were already lovers. Others, while not putting it quite so strongly, point out that she made no attempt to alert passers-by to her plight; but in truth she was helpless to resist. She could only manage to despatch one of her attendants, James Borthwick, to warn Edinburgh of possible trouble. To his credit, the provost of Edinburgh sensed that Mary was in danger and had the alarm bell rung, calling the citizens to arms; but by the time the lieges were mobilised Mary was firmly ensconced in Dunbar, and a rescue attempt would have been futile.

The abduction of the Queen was typical of the outrageous acts of which Bothwell had previously shown himself capable. Never the man to do anything by halves – as the explosion at Kirk o' Field testified – Bothwell now compounded his felony by an even greater one. No sooner was Mary installed in her bedchamber in the castle than Bothwell entered the room and raped her. James Melville, who had accompanied the Queen to Dunbar and was not allowed to leave till the following day, testified that 'the Queen could not but marry him, seeing he had ravished her and lain with her against her will'.[10] Mary's own version of the rape was given in a letter to the Bishop of Dunblane two weeks later: 'Albeit we found his doings rude, yet were his words and answers gentle.'[11] Mary now gave way to his full-frontal proposal of marriage, but Bothwell, not content with the initial rape, continued relentlessly and forcefully to assault her sexually so that Mary wearily submitted. Significantly, Mary's contemporaries, both her supporters and her detractors, firmly believed that the abduction was a put-up job, and that the Queen had only made a token resistance to save her face. Drury reported to London within three days that while the manner of the Queen's seizure might seem to have been forcible, it was known to be otherwise.

It was also common knowledge that Bothwell had completed his actions by having sexual intercourse with her, but that this was probably against her will. Whether, as has sometimes been claimed, Bothwell gave Mary sexual fulfilment is pure speculation. It is more likely that Mary gave way for reasons of state. The profligate Bothwell was, by all accounts, an experienced lover, well versed in all the arts of seduction. A street ballad, published after Bothwell's downfall, contained the couplet: 'Such beastly buggery Sodom has not seen, As ruled in him who ruled Realm and Queen.'[12] This does not imply homosexual leanings, as some writers have asserted, though it fully accords with the image of a man who practised the black arts and whose vicious tastes ran the entire gamut of depravity.

Mary's reaction to her seduction certainly seems out of character, but in mitigation it should be remembered that she was in a pretty debilitated state of mind and body at the time. Her confessor, Mameret, later avowed to the Spanish ambassador in London that, until her marriage to Bothwell, he had never encountered a women of greater virtue, courage and uprightness. From his intimate knowledge of her, acquired in the confessional, he was convinced that she had only given way to Bothwell to settle the religious question in Scotland.[13] Mary, in fact, had two good reasons for accepting Bothwell: he was the strong man who would give Scotland stable government, and he had obviously secured the support of the nobility. He seemed to be the one man who could guarantee power, and power was what Mary now craved above all else, being willing even to sacrifice her body and reputation in the process. Besides, he had now had carnal knowledge of her, and she felt that she could not now renegue on her promise to marry him.

There was, of course, the minor problem that Bothwell was still married to Lady Jean Gordon, though she seems to have agreed to the divorce readily enough. Arising from the rumours surrounding her recent illness, Bishop Leslie avers that her husband offered her the choice of divorce or a cup of poison. Her marriage to Bothwell had been solely dictated by political expedience, and what affection she might have had for him must surely have been sorely tried by his continued infidelities. By the end of March it was rumoured that her brother, Huntly, had agreed to the deal. On 3 May Lady Bothwell was given judgment against her husband in the new-fangled Protestant commissary court which had supplanted the old consistory courts in matrimonial disputes, but just to be on the safe side Lady Jean, a devout Catholic, had the marriage formally annulled on 7 May by Archbishop Hamilton on the specious grounds that she and James had not obtained a papal dispensation in the first place, required to overcome the bar to marriage on grounds of consanguinity. After all, Bothwell's great-great-grandfather had married a Gordon. In point of fact, a papal dispensation *had* been granted, and by Archbishop Hamilton, no less. Although this divorce went through with indecent haste it was not quick enough for the ever-impatient Bothwell who had the canon of Dunbar collegiate church, John Manderstoun, threatened with mutilation if he did not expedite matters.

On 6 May Bothwell brought the Queen back to Edinburgh, riding in procession along with the pliant Huntly and the dutiful Maitland by the West Port to the castle. The great guns of the castle fired a salute in her honour, but the *Diurnal of Occurrents* sourly observed that Bothwell led the Queen's majesty by the bridle, as though she were a captive.

Even as Mary and Bothwell were approaching their marriage, powerful forces were combining against him. Hitherto, opposition had been confined to placarding and street muttering, but on 1 May the nucleus of an opposition met at Stirling and signed yet another bond whose aims were the liberation of the Queen, securing Prince James and bringing the dictatorship of Bothwell to an end. Ironically, the ringleaders included Morton, Argyll and Atholl who, a few days earlier, had calmly signed the Ainslie Bond. Kirkcaldy of Grange asked the English ambassador, Bedford, to write to Moray in London, begging him to return to Scotland as soon as possible, while Robert Melville wrote directly to Cecil, urging English military intervention, and hinting that if this were not forthcoming he would have no compunction in writing to France along similar lines. The dissident lords even got a message to Mary herself, pledging their support against Bothwell. Mary, who seems to have been cocooned by Bothwell in a little dream world, could not believe that her new lord and master was less than all-powerful, and therefore would not countenance the opposition.

So far, opposition was directed against Bothwell, and there was still considerable support and sympathy for the Queen herself. But by pressing ahead with her marriage plans – or at least allowing herself to be swept along by the tide-race of events – Mary began to alienate opinion. When John Craig, minister in the parish church of Edinburgh, refused to publish the banns of marriage without the written consent of the Queen, Mary wrote to him immediately via the Justice Clerk, saying that she had neither been raped nor held against her will. When Craig did make the announcement from his pulpit on 9 May, he gratuitously added a broadside against Bothwell, before a congregation which included the Privy Council:

> I laid to his charge, the law of adultery, the ordinance of the
> Kirk, the law of ravishing, the suspicion of collusion between
> him and his wife, the sudden divorcement, and proclaiming
> within the space of four days, and last the suspicion of the
> King's death which her marriage would confirm.[14]

Bothwell threatened to hang Craig, but the minister was doing no more than courageously enunciating what the ordinary people of Edinburgh were now saying. Day by day, they were increasingly disillusioned by their beautiful young Queen; she, whom they had idolised, now seemed tarnished by Bothwell's opportunism. Mary, blind to the growing resentment of the citizenry, put her imprimatur on her choice of third husband; on 12 May she created her lusty paramour Duke of Orkney and Lord of Shetland, in allusion to his great-grandfather, the first earl, who had connections with the northern isles. At a brief ceremony Mary herself placed the ducal coronet on his head. On the same occasion she knighted four of Bothwell's henchmen, including James Ormiston of the Kirk o' Field plot. Two days later she formally pardoned the nobles who had signed the Ainslie Bond.

On Thursday, 15 May, twelve days after Bothwell's divorce and thirteen weeks after Darnley's death, Mary and her duke were married in the Council hall at Holyrood, Huntly and Maitland being among the witnesses. The upholder of the Catholic religion now pledged her troth in a Protestant ceremony. Bothwell's crony, Adam, Bishop of Orkney, presided over the event, preaching a sermon in which he announced that Bothwell had now repented of his former evil and wicked life. After this brief ceremony, there was none of the pageantry or merrymaking which had marked all previous royal marriages. A few close friends and supporters sat at a long table, with Mary at the head and Bothwell at the foot, and ate their wedding breakfast in subdued silence. While Darnley had received many costly gifts from the Queen on the occasion of their wedding, Mary's only present to Bothwell was some genet fur for his dressing-gown – and even this was second-hand, having been recycled from a cloak belonging to Mary of Guise. Whereas her own previous marriages had been glittering affairs, in which she had spent lavishly on her trousseau, this time round she contented herself with having an old yellow gown relined with white taffeta, an old black dress decorated with gold braid, and a black taffeta petticoat refurbished. The tawdriness of these preparations indicates that Mary, far from having something to celebrate, was already deeply ashamed of the whole wretched business. As if to underscore the folly of this enterprise, placards appeared all over Edinburgh that night, quoting a line of Ovid – *Mense malas Maio nubere vulgus ait* – which the douce burghers, with their classical education, would readily understand as signifying 'Wantons marry in the month of May'. The Scots, like the Romans, had a superstition against May marriages.

Eye-witnesses noted the absence of merrymaking at this wedding. When Du Croc (who absented himself from the ceremony but visited the couple later that day) commented on the unusual formality between bride and groom, Mary drew him up sharply with the response that she had no wish to be merry. Later on, however, she broke down in tears before Bishop Leslie, repenting of her recent actions, and her Protestant wedding most of all. Although Pope Pius was duly informed of her repentance, he responded on 2 July that 'it was not his intention to have any further communication with her'.[15] This was certainly a mark of disapproval, although well short of the excommunication hinted at by some historians.

In fact, immediately after her marriage, Mary was quite suicidal. Only two days after the ceremony Huntly and Melville happened to be standing outside the Queen's closet and heard Bothwell and Mary screaming at each other. Mary was heard to call for a knife that she might kill herself, and the following day her equerry Arthur Erskine heard her threaten to drown herself. It has been suggested that her hysterical state had been induced by some wedding-night confession of Bothwell about his hand in Darnley's murder, but this can hardly have come as a surprise to her by that time. It is more likely that the enormity of her moral lapse, in marrying Bothwell, and the consequent effect on her reputation, now unnerved her.

The marriage lasted four weeks, during which Mary was frequently reduced to tears by Bothwell's unreasonable behaviour. Too late, she found herself shackled to a dour, saturnine individual, increasingly paranoid and given to sudden fits of rage if Mary so much as looked at another man. He accused her of being frivolous and pleasure-seeking, and to appease him Mary gave up golf, card-playing, hunting, hawking and music-making – all those harmless pursuits which, not so long ago, had brought her so much happiness. Bothwell now revealed himself as an uncouth boor who seemed to delight in humiliating his wife in public. Bothwell's language was so obscene that courtiers, not usually noted for their squeamishness, hurried from his presence. Tongues wagged as far afield as London and Paris when it leaked out that Bothwell was maintaining his ex-wife in Crichton Castle, and that the Queen was wracked by jealousy.

In public, however, some semblance of harmony and proper behaviour was maintained. Mary and the Duke of Orkney, as he was now known, were often seen together on horseback. On public occasions Bothwell treated Mary with considerable respect; indeed, he could be unduly deferential, going bareheaded in her presence when he alone had the right to remain covered. On several occasions Mary herself took hold of his bonnet and placed it fairly and squarely on his head. In private, or, rather, in the relative privacy of the inner circle of courtiers, Bothwell was often quite indifferent to his wife, or spoke to her coarsely. The Queen may have been passionate and impulsive, but her feelings towards her new husband cannot have been anything like 'the warmth of infatuation for the strong desperado who had made her his obedient slave'.[16]

Domestic infelicity was now exacerbated by political troubles. The nobles who had formed a bond at Stirling at the beginning of May reacted violently to the Queen's marriage. By the end of the month they had mustered a formidable army and advanced on Edinburgh. Holyrood was indefensible, and even the seemingly impregnable castle would become a trap if the citizens of Edinburgh joined forces with the insurgents. Consequently, Mary and Bothwell slipped out of the city on 6 June and headed for Borthwick Castle with a company of loyal troops and a few cannon. Here they hoped to rally Bothwell's supporters in the Borders while Huntly and the Hamiltons raised the north-east and south-west on their behalf. At this juncture, however, Maitland deserted Mary's cause and went over to the dissidents. On 10 June a large body of cavalry under Lord Hume surrounded Borthwick Castle, but Bothwell managed to make good his escape. The following day Mary, in men's clothing, booted and spurred, mounted her horse and rode off to meet Bothwell at a pre-arranged rendezvous at Black Castle, stronghold of Bothwell's henchmen, the Wauchopes. Mary travelled light, abandoning all her feminine finery in the castle. From Black Castle she and Bothwell rode together to Dunbar which was infinitely better able to withstand a siege. Here she changed out of her male garments, but the only female apparel she could borrow was a humble dress, including 'a red petticoat, sleeves tied with bows, a velvet hat and a muffler'.[17]

The following day, after issuing a mobilisation order, Mary and Bothwell set off with sixty horse and two hundred arquebusiers to Haddington where they were joined by another six hundred horsemen. By the time they reached Seton their army had swollen to over 1,600 well-armed men. Meanwhile the nobles had issued their own proclamations at the mercat crosses of Scotland and mustered an army of comparable size. On 15 June, they marched out of Edinburgh and took up their positions on the slopes of a hill facing the Queen's forces who were already drawn up on Carberry Hill on the opposite side of the valley near Musselburgh. Both sides were in strong positions, but whoever attacked first would have to descend the slopes and cross the valley, where they would be exposed to the gunfire, arrows and spears of the enemy. During the resultant stand-off, the insurgents brandished a huge banner on which had been painted the corpse of Darnley below a tree. In front of him knelt his son Prince James with the caption 'Judge and avenge my cause, O Lord'. In charge of this standard was Captain Andrew Lambie, the same Leith merchant who had been so hospitable to Mary the day she returned to Scotland.

It was a very hot day; horses fretted and men sweated profusely with the heat and apprehension. On Carberry Hill, Bothwell overcame his natural impulse to rush down and charge the enemy, knowing that Hamilton and Huntly reinforcements were on the way and that this would tip the balance in his favour. Then a solitary horseman rode out from the opposing side and trotted gingerly towards the Queen's camp. It was Du Croc, the French ambassador, whom the rebels pressed into service as their mediator. Du Croc informed Mary that if she would abandon Bothwell, the lords would restore her to her rightful position. Mary rejected this offer vehemently. Were not these the very lords who, by the Ainslie Bond, had persuaded her to marry Bothwell in the first instance? Just because they had now changed their minds there was no reason for her to do likewise. Du Croc rode back to the rebel lines with the message.

Both sides continued to glower at each other for some time, then the lords came up with a solution to the impasse. Why not settle the matter in time-honoured fashion by single combat? Archbishop Beaton later claimed that this idea had originated with Bothwell,[18] but no matter who thought of it first, it was perfectly agreeable to Bothwell, and the challenge was eagerly taken up by Patrick, Lord Lindsay of the Byres; but Mary vetoed the proposal, so once again the opposing sides postured and glowered at each other across the valley. So the afternoon passed and dusk approached, but there was still no sign of the Hamilton forces. Anxiously Mary scanned the horizon, but her apprehension mounted when she realised that many of her supporters, responding to blandishments shouted across from the enemy side, were slipping across the valley or simply running off in the opposite direction.

At this crucial moment, Kirkcaldy of Grange made a last appeal to Mary to accept the lords' offer. Realising that her situation was helpless, she finally caved in. If the rebels would restore her to her proper place, she would dismiss Bothwell and come over to them of her own accord. Bothwell was loath to go, but she eventually persuaded him that it would be more prudent for him to save himself. He should make himself scarce until parliament had had the chance to meet and enquire impartially into Darnley's murder. If he were, indeed, innocent, then she promised 'nothing would prevent her from rendering to him all that a true and lawful wife ought to do'.[19] On the other hand, if he were found guilty, 'it would be to her an endless source of regret that, by their marriage, she had ruined her good reputation, and from this she would endeavour to free herself by all possible means'.

The lords were more than happy to go along with this; the last thing they wanted at this point was Bothwell alive and in their hands; for they knew only too well that he would not be slow in implicating many of them in the murder. Although the Queen's forces were now completely surrounded by the insurgents, Bothwell was permitted to escape, to save embarrassment all round. It was at this very moment that Bothwell pressed into Mary's hand a piece of paper. It was the Craigmillar bond signed by Morton, Maitland and others agreeing to murder Darnley. Swearing that anything he had done had only been for the good of the country, acting on the advice and persuasion of those very lords who now opposed him, he urged her to keep this document safe, and rode off.

Mary then surrendered herself to Kirkcaldy, saying, 'Laird of Grange, I render myself unto you, upon the conditions you rehearsed unto me, in the name of the Lords.'[20] She offered him her hand to kiss, then he took her bridle and led her down the hillside towards the insurgent lines. Dishevelled and perspiring though she was, Mary advanced imperiously on the rebel generals, expecting to be given the courtesy due to her rank, but she had not reckoned on the hatred which she had by now engendered among the rank and file who screamed insults and cries of 'Burn the whore! Burn the murderess of her husband!' as they pushed and jostled her. Mary never flinched; if anything, this treatment merely steeled her; she gave as good as she got, threatening to hang and crucify them all for their impudence. To Lindsay, who had dared to challenge her husband, she swore by his right hand held in hers, 'I will have your head for this and therefore assure you!'[21]

To the leader of the rebel lords she cried indignantly. 'How is this, my Lord Morton? I am told that all this is done in order to get justice among the King's murderers. I am also told that you are one of the chief of them!'

'Come, come,' he replied hastily. 'This is not the place to discuss such matters!' Then he scurried off, leaving the Queen to further taunts and insults from his men. Eventually Kirkcaldy and a few others, ashamed of the way the Queen was being mistreated, drew their blades and ordered their unruly troops to desist, under pain of death. The rabble drew back, and a sullen silence descended on their ranks. The atmosphere remained tense on the ride back to Edinburgh. Mary had to suffer the further humiliation of being closely guarded by two of the most surly ruffians who bore aloft between them, fastened to their spears, the insulting banner showing Darnley and Prince James. Poor Mary, now almost two months pregnant as a result of the rape, fatigued and distressed by the day's events, kept fainting and with great difficulty remained in the saddle, but she quickly recovered her composure and snapped back at those who continued to insult her. It was about ten o'clock at night when the rebels re-entered Edinburgh with their royal captive.

What a sorry sight she presented, her hair unpinned and falling in loose strands about her grimy, tear-stained face. The humiliating ride from Carberry Hill, however, was as nothing to the terrifying ordeal which she faced on entering the city. An immense throng filled the streets and jeered and howled wildly at her as she passed through their ranks with such difficulty that even her escort feared for their lives. She was not taken to Holyrood, but was lodged for the night in the house of the provost, Simon Preston of Craigmillar (Maitland's brother-in-law), in the High Street opposite the Cross. Inside, the rebel lords were just sitting down to dinner and invited Mary to join them but she declined, saying that they had given her supper enough. She was then locked into a small upper room, very sparsely furnished. Not only were guards posted outside the bedroom door, but two men remained seated in the room all night. Even in such dire straits Mary began exerting her charm and womanly guile on her guards whom she eventually persuaded to smuggle out some letters on her behalf. Only then, partially undressed, did Mary collapse on to the bed in search of sleep. The mob draped their hateful banner outside her window so that she would be constantly confronted with the deed in which she was now firmly implicated.

One can imagine what a terrible night she must have had. Certainly by morning, far from having regained her composure, Mary appeared at the window extremely distraught, wildly hysterical, partially dressed and hair dishevelled, calling piteously to passers-by to help her.[22] When Maitland appeared shortly after-wards, she appealed to him to speak to her, and remonstrated with him for having parted her from her husband. Maitland, whose hatred of Bothwell was as powerful as Bothwell's detestation of him, spitefully informed the Queen that letters had been discovered from Bothwell to his ex-wife letting Lady Jean know that he still regarded her as his true wife and the Queen merely as his concubine. Mary did not believe this for a single moment, and coolly suggested that she and Bothwell might be shipped off together into exile. Maitland actually thought that this might well be the best solution to what otherwise might prove an extremely embarrassing situation.[23] One of the brief letters Mary had written the previous night was addressed to Sir James Balfour, Bothwell's man, who was holding out in Edinburgh Castle whither he had been appointed on 8 May. In this she asked him to 'keep a good heart of her, and wherever she was convoyed or past, that he rendered not the Castle to the Lords'.[24]

'Though her body be restrained,' wrote Drury, 'yet her heart is not dismayed; she cannot be dissuaded from her affection to the Duke, but seems rather to offer sooner to receive harm herself than that he should.'[25] Although many writers have tried to play this down, if not deny it altogether, all the evidence bears out the fact that, at this juncture, Mary remained steadfast to Bothwell although he did nothing to secure her release. Immediately after the débâcle at Carberry Hill he had ridden off to Dunbar; but, swiftly realising that the situation was impossible and that his support had evaporated, he took ship for the north. By now Huntly had disowned him and the Gordons offered him no succour, so he sailed on to his dukedom where he gathered some men and a few vessels, intent on harrying shipping. Kirkcaldy of Grange was despatched thither with nine powerful warships and broke up this nest of pirates. Bothwell himself only narrowly escaped by a superior feat of seamanship and sailed off to Scandinavia where he hoped to find sanctuary; but in the country where Christopher Throndsen, the father of his discarded mistress, was admiral, he got short shrift. Shortly after going ashore at Karmoysund he was apprehended by Throndsen's men and clapped into prison at Bergen on 2 September. By the end of the month he had been transferred to Copenhagen Castle where Frederik, King of Denmark and Norway, appreciating the potential value of the husband of the Queen of Scots, held him as a useful pawn in international politics. During the relatively comfortable Copenhagen period Bothwell wrote his memoirs, later published under the title of *Les Affaires du Conte de Boduel*, an apologia for his actions with which he hoped to secure his release. Although the Scots pressed for his extradition, and Bothwell himself wrote to the King of France for help, Frederik kept a tight grip of his captive who spent the rest of his life in a succession of Danish prisons, each more vile than the last, until his death in 1578. Latterly he had been incarcerated in the grim fortress of Dragsholm in conditions of unspeakable cruelty, chained to a pillar and unable to stand upright, and fed slops through a tiny aperture. It is small wonder, therefore, that Bothwell went mad in the end. His mummified corpse is now on display in the crypt of Faarvejle Church near Dragsholm, a gruesome tourist attraction.

Mary's vehement loyalty to her fugitive husband dismayed and embarrassed the men who were now effectively in power. It is pointless to speculate on what might have happened had she given way, acceded to the wishes of the rebel lords, denounced Bothwell as Darnley's murderer and repudiated her late marriage. Some compromise might then have been worked out whereby Mary could have retained the throne. Uppermost in the mind of Morton and his cronies was the fact that Mary, if put on trial, would give damning evidence of their complicity in Darnley's murder. It was therefore essential to keep her in some remote place until they could figure out what to do with her. At this Kirkcaldy demurred, having promised her that she would not lose the throne. Now, however, Morton produced his trump card, a love letter, allegedly written by Mary to Bothwell the previous night. Addressing him as 'Dear heart', she swore to stand by him. No trace of any such letter can now be found, not even a transcript, even if the purported contents are known. The consensus nowadays is that it was a forgery, hastily prepared for the purpose of winning round waverers like Kirkcaldy. It demonstrated that the Queen was not prepared to keep her side of the bargain, and thus Kirkcaldy was absolved of his promise.

That Monday evening Maitland paid Mary a brief visit. When she demanded a parliamentary enquiry into Darnley's murder, confident that this would vindicate her, he smoothly told her that the lords would never agree to this. All the while, he averted his gaze and Mary noted, with contempt, that though his words were bold he did not dare look her in the eye when he spoke. Presently, about nine o'clock, Morton himself came to her room and peremptorily ordered her to get ready to depart immediately for Holyrood. Mary's heart soared, and she was in excellent spirits by the time she reached the palace and was joyfully reuinited with her household, including Mary Seton and Mary Livingston (now Lady Sempill) who quickly prepared the first meal she had taken since her surrender – the stress of the past thirty-six hours had robbed her of her appetite, apart from the fear that her captors might try to poison her. With Morton hovering impatiently behind her chair the whole time, she ate heartily. Suddenly, in the middle of the meal, Morton turned to one of the servants and asked if the horses were ready. Then he abruptly ordered the table to be cleared and told Mary to get ready to mount up. Alarmed and confused at this sudden turn of events, Mary asked him where they were taking her. Morton gave her to understand that she was being moved to Stirling where she could be with her son. Accompanied by only two chamberwomen, and with little luggage except a silk nightdress, Mary rode off. With Lord Ruthven (the son of Riccio's murderer) on one side and the thuggish Lindsay on the other, she was escorted to Leith as night fell. On the road somebody whispered to her that the Hamiltons would try to rescue her, and to this end she tried to lag behind, but Ruthven and Lindsay flogged her horse on.

They rode through the night, but when they turned off at Kinross, Mary realised to her horror that they were not going to Stirling after all.

11. LOCHLEVEN AND LANGSIDE

June 1567 – May 1568

But when we in our viciousness grow hard,
O misery on't! – the wise gods seal our eyes;
In our own filth drop our clear judgments; make us
Adore our errors; laugh at's while we strut
To our confusion.
Shakespeare, *Antony and Cleopatra*

It was still dark when Mary and her boorish escort reached the shores of Lochleven, the stretch of water at the centre of the former county of Kinross. The loch has a circumference of about nine miles and in parts attains a depth of eighty-four feet. On the largest of the seven islands in the loch stands the castle, now in ruins, where Queen Mary was imprisoned for nine months. Although Castle Island lies about a mile from the shore, it was connected with it by means of a submerged causeway. The choice of this stronghold was governed partly by its isolation and partly by the fact that it belonged to Sir William Douglas, a nephew of Mar, a cousin of Morton and a half-brother to Moray, being the son of Mar's sister Margaret Erskine by her husband Robert Douglas. This redoubtable lady, a former mistress of King James V, was the chatelaine. Silently Mary was rowed across the windswept waters of the loch. She was admitted to the castle without ceremony and taken to the laird's chamber. There had been no time to warn Lady Margaret of the Queen's imminent arrival, so no preparations had been made to receive her and the room was almost entirely empty of furniture. A rudimentary bed was hastily made up for her, and here Mary sank down in a state of shock compounded by pregnancy, nervous tension and deep depression. She remained in a catatonic, trance-like state for about two weeks, neither speaking nor eating the entire time, until her gaolers began to fear for her life.

Gradually Mary snapped out of her depression, but her surroundings must have been anything but congenial to her. As well as the dour Sir William who took his duties very seriously, there was his mother, a woman in her fifties who regarded Mary sourly as the person who had got the throne which, by rights, should have gone to her son James Stewart instead. The only person to lighten the gloom was Margaret's youngest son, George, known familiarly as Pretty Geordie on account of his slender beauty, the antithesis of his half-brother Moray in appearance and character. The castle was not unfamiliar to Mary. She had resided there during hunting trips, and it was here that, in the spring of 1563, she had had a discussion with the charmless John Knox on the subject of Old Testament justice. In the sixteenth century the level of the loch was much higher than it is today, with the result that the water lapped right up to the foundation walls. The castle itself was dominated by a large square keep, five storeys high, where the Douglas family and their retainers lived; but in the courtyard there was a smaller round tower, and it was here that Mary was eventually lodged. From her window she had a dismal view of the loch, with a bleak, windswept landscape stretching away to the Lomond Hills. Even in the height of summer, when Mary was consigned to this fortress, the view presented a chilling prospect, in which the chances of ever making an escape seemed remote.

On 16 June the Privy Council executed the warrant for the Queen's detention. It was signed by Morton, Glencairn, Hume, Mar, Atholl, Graham, Sanquhar and Ochiltree and of these the first three had put their names to the Ainslie Bond only weeks earlier. The warrant gave as the reason for Mary's imprisonment the fact that instead of showing a willingness to apprehend Darnley's murderer she 'appeared to fortify and maintain the said Earl Bothwell and his accomplices in the said wicked crimes' and that to allow her 'to follow her own inordinate passion, it would not fail to succeed to the final confusion and extermination of the whole realm'.[1]

The principal goal of her captors was to persuade her to agree to a divorce, but when Mary demurred, on the grounds that she was now seven weeks pregnant, they decided as an alternative:

to put in execution the coronation of the young Prince, with the Queen's consent, promising her, if so, that they mean to neither touch her in honour nor life, neither to proceed against her judicially by way of process; otherwise they are determined to proceed against her publicly by such evidence as they can charge her with.[2]

No sooner had Mary been whisked off to her island prison than the lords who had sent her there began the systematic despoliation of her private property. The furnishings of her private chapel were stripped as a matter of policy, of course, but her personal belongings, her clothing, jewellery, gold and silver plate, were ransacked. Moray collared Mary's fabulous collection of jewels, most of which, under her will of the previous summer, was to have been settled on the Scottish crown in perpetuity. Both Catherine de' Medici and Elizabeth coveted the better pieces, including Mary's famous black pearls. In the end Elizabeth outbid her rival, and Moray sold them to her. Twenty-seven large pieces of silver plate were subsequently sent to the Edinburgh mint to be converted into coin. When news of this thievery reached Mary her heart sank, for it gave the lie to the promise by the lords that they only intended to free her from Bothwell's domination and would restore her in power and status as soon as possible. Later she heard that her husband, having failed to respond to a summons of the Council on charges of murdering Darnley, abducting the Queen and marrying her by force, had been outlawed on 17 July, with a price of a thousand crowns on his head. When Bothwell was formally stripped of his estates, titles and offices, resistance to the lords crumbled. Huntly withdrew into his vast northern estates, while his sister Jean hurriedly vacated Crichton Castle and went back to her mother at Strathbogie. Even Seton and Fleming, two of Mary's closest friends and staunchest supporters, now seemingly deserted her.

By contrast with the initial inaction following Darnley's murder, the lords now pursued with vindictive ruthlessness those of Bothwell's minions who had had a hand in the affair. This business continued throughout the remaining months of 1567, and was deliberately publicised in order to distract the populace while Morton, Maitland and Balfour, the real perpetrators of the crime, consolidated their power. The first victim of this purge was William Blackadder. He had merely run out of a tavern near Kirk o' Field on hearing the explosion to see what all the commotion was about, and had immediately been apprehended by the night watch. This poor wretch may not have been entirely innocent of everything but curiosity – he was, after all, the captain of that vessel which had conveyed Mary to Alloa and a notorious henchman of Bothwell – and at the time of his arrest he was nearly stoned to death by a mob of women and boys. Now he was excruciatingly tortured to wring a confession out of him, and then publicly hanged and quartered, his head and limbs being stuck up on the gates of the principal towns.

William Powrie came next, but after furnishing two contradictory statements, he was merely hanged. Bastien Pages and Francisco Busso, two of the foreigners named in the placards, were imprisoned in the Tolbooth. John Spens, one of Bothwell's closest henchmen, was spared after he turned over Bothwell's treasure chest. John Hepburn of Bolton and John Hay of Talla were captured and executed on 3 January 1568 after something approximating a show trial. Nevertheless, on the scaffold Hay cried out to the assembled multitude that Huntly, Argyll, Maitland and Balfour had signed the bond for Darnley's murder. Those still in Edinburgh at the time hurriedly departed when the public clamoured that they, too, should be brought to justice.

Paris, the servant whom Bothwell had bullied and beaten so mercilessly, was not apprehended till a year later, but his deposition was the most damning of them all. When Cecil requested the man's extradition so that he could be interrogated in London specifically regarding Queen Mary's involvement, the Scots promptly hanged him instead. Sir James Ormiston was hanged in 1573 after making a very suspect confession to a priest. His brother Hob, as well as Pat Wilson, escaped retribution.

On 19 June 1567, as Morton and Maitland were dining, they were told that three of Bothwell's men from Dunbar had entered the castle to retrieve their master's belongings. A search was immediately ordered but they had already left the castle. One of the three, Thomas Hepburn of Oldhamstocks, got clean away. The second man, Cockburn of Skirling, was caught but released as nothing was found on him. After a prolonged search the third man was run to earth in a house in the Potterrow. This was Bothwell's tailor, George Dalgleish. Interrogated under threat of the thumbkins and the boot, Dalgleish, the following day, blurted out that he had retrieved from the castle a small silver box containing a quantity of personal papers which he had hidden under a bed in the Potterrow house. In this manner the notorious Casket Letters, which were to figure so prominently in the Queen's condemnation, made their début. Morton later deponed that the casket was brought to him and opened on 20 June in the presence of Atholl, Mar, Glencairn, Hume, Sempill, Sanquhar, the Laird of Tullibardine and Maitland. Significantly, although the fact was recorded that the contents were perused, no details were given regarding these papers at that time. There was no reference to letters, far less that they were in the Queen's hand. Morton had the casket sealed, and thus it remained in his possession.

In hindsight it is remarkable that no mention of the casket, or its contents, was made until December 1568, when it was trotted out at the Westminster conference. The casket was not referred to in July 1567, for example, when the Council publicly enumerated the various specific charges against Bothwell. Both then and for some time thereafter, the lords were putting all the blame for the Queen's disgrace on Bothwell. So far as any blame attached itself to Mary herself, it was in her refusal to disown her husband. There was certainly no suggestion at that time that she was involved in Darnley's murder. As the lords were determined to keep Mary in close confinement, it is unimaginable that they would not have seized on such incriminating evidence had it existed at that time. It is also significant that so little importance was attached to the silver casket at the time when Dalgleish revealed it that he was never questioned on the subject, and he himself went to the scaffold in January 1568, long before there was any attempt to reveal the nature of the contents. Eleven months later, of course, the casket would be alleged to have contained a series of love-letters and impassioned poetry from Mary to Bothwell, revealing that they had been having a serious affair since late 1566, when Bothwell was supposed to have seduced the Queen in her counting-house. This put the affair well in advance of Darnley's death and therefore, instead of almost being a victim of Kirk o' Field herself, Mary was shown to be deeply implicated in the plot to murder her husband.

Even at the time when these scandalous matters were being revealed there was considerable controversy surrounding the Casket Letters. Mary was never shown them, and steadfastly maintained that they were forgeries. Posterity has no way of checking, since the actual letters themselves have not been seen since the 1580s and are now known only as transcripts. If the famous 'Dear heart' letter of June 1567 were a forgery, might not this entire cache of eight letters and a long poem (actually a string of sonnets) have been similarly fabricated? The most damning letter of all, number two in the bundle, may well have been cobbled together from a letter, or letters, from Anna Throndsen which Bothwell may, indeed, have preserved in the casket. The long poem totalling 158 lines, with its curious theme of 'the other woman', was not only disjointed but in such bad French that Ronsard and Brantôme rubbished it immediately. Here again, it is more probable that it was composed, in whole or part, by Anna Throndsen. Scholars for four centuries have endlessly argued over the style and phraseology of the alleged letters. They constitute the single most important, and damning, piece of evidence against Mary on moral and criminal grounds. If genuine, they would justify all the opprobrium that has been heaped on her head. If not, the judgment of posterity on the unfortunate Queen of Scots must be very different.

The original letters only came to light publicly eighteen months after Mary's downfall. She herself was never permitted to examine them and although they were allegedly in her handwriting the fact that Mary wrote in the newly fashionable Italian round-hand would have been very easy to imitate. Nowadays the authenticity of the Casket Letters has been almost universally repudiated, especially as modern computerised methods of checking word patterns suggest that not only are the letters not the work of Queen Mary but are not even the work of the same writer throughout. It must be pointed out that without the originals, this method cannot be relied upon completely, as much would also depend on the accuracy of the translations. Nevertheless, as late as the 1960s, there were still historians prepared to swear, in print, that some at least of the letters were genuine, particularly the damning Letter Two, while one recent writer has gone full circle and has argued forcefully that the letters must have been genuine all along. Why else, so the argument goes, would King James have destroyed them in 1584? Had they been forgeries he would surely have trumpeted the fact.[3] There were probably many other reasons for their suppression, however, especially as Mary was still alive at the time.

Of the eight letters, only the first, dated from Glasgow, may have been genuine. The others were either garbled versions of genuine letters, or fragments of genuine letters interpolated with fabrications, or outright forgeries. The French versions, supposedly transcripts of the originals, are replete with grammatical errors and inconsistencies which Mary would never have perpetrated. At best they can only be regarded as clumsy imitations of Mary's style.

If Mary did not write them, who did? Suspicion has fallen mainly on Maitland who, on his own admission to the Duke of Norfolk, was able to imitate the Queen's handwriting – a fact which Mary herself corroborated in her instructions to her commissioners on 9 September 1568. Archibald Douglas, the Postulate of Arbroath, is another likely contender. He had lived in France and presumably had some knowledge of French. Furthermore, he is known to have forged letters from Bishop Leslie to Esmé Stewart and others in 1580–81. He was Morton's right-hand man and, of course, the leader of the plotters who actually murdered Darnley.

When news of what was afoot in Scotland reached London, Queen Elizabeth was immediately concerned on two counts: she was horrified that any anointed monarch could be subjected to such rough treatment as Mary was enduring; and, secondly, she was naturally interested to see what advantage to herself there might be in this startling turn of events. Accordingly she despatched Throckmorton to Scotland to assess the situation. Maitland informed him that the lords intended to crown the young Prince James, with the Queen's consent if they could obtain it. To induce Mary to take such a drastic step, the lords promised to spare her life. Indeed, they were prepared not to proceed against her judicially. If she refused, of course, they would have no compunction about bringing her to trial on three charges. Throckmorton summarised these as:

> (1) Tyranny, for breach and violation of their laws and decrees of the Realm, as well as that which they call Common Laws as their Statute Laws. (2) Incontinency as well with the Earl Bothwell as with others. (3) The Murder of her husband, whereof (they say) they have as apparent proof against her as may be, as well by the testimony of her own handwriting, which they have recovered, as also by sufficient witnesses.[4]

This appears to be the earliest reference to the Casket Letters, 'sufficient witnesses' being the hapless servants of Bothwell who were now in custody undergoing brutal interrogation.

John Knox had by now returned from temporary exile in England and was whipping up the populace into a white-hot frenzy against the luckless queen. Knox and his henchmen pulled out every stop in their rhetoric, demanding the immediate execution of this scarlet woman, this whore of Babylon, this red-haired bitch. The lords turned a deaf ear to this immoderate language, but at the same time they ignored the remonstration of Elizabeth that 'as a sister sovereign their Queen cannot be detained prisoner or deprived of her princely state'.[5] Elizabeth threw out a hint that if the lords could not deal 'by advice and counsel' with Mary then perhaps they could hand her over to Elizabeth herself, as Mary's 'next cousin and neighbour'. The lords ignored this. Even if they had been convinced of Elizabeth's sincerity and good will towards them, Mary and Scotland, they had now gone too far; there would be no turning back.

What goaded them into action was Elizabeth's suggestion that little Prince James should be handed over to her as his guardian. Elizabeth would then place him in the safe-keeping of his grandmother, the Countess of Lennox. Considering that Lady Lennox was still languishing in the Tower at the time, as punishment for her son marrying Mary, this was barefaced cheek, to put it mildly. It did not fool the lords for a moment, but it showed that the only course of action now open to them was to proclaim James king at the earliest possible opportunity.

Throckmorton, alarmed at the violent antagonism against Queen Mary which he encountered on all sides, at every level, was convinced that her life was in danger, and begged to be allowed to see her. Although this was consistently refused, he did eventually manage to communicate with her, smuggling a note to her concealed in a sword-scabbard. His worst fears were confirmed when he got word from her about 18 July that she was in daily fear for her life. Her mood of utter despair he dutifully conveyed to London in due course. He added that Mary would not agree to divorce Bothwell because she was seven weeks pregnant (her words); but a few days later, in deep depression and suffering acute distress, she miscarried. A day or two afterwards, Robert Melville and Lord Lindsay were on the spot with the instrument of abdication (three documents she had to sign), and on entering her bedroom found her lying on her bed, very pale and weak after a massive haemorrhage. Instead of feeling any compassion for her, Lindsay took the opportunity to deliver a brutal tirade. Melville managed to speak to the terrified woman alone and adopted a gentle approach: sign the documents and get it over with. After all, a signature obtained under duress would never be regarded as binding. Thus was Mary induced to sign three documents sent from the lords. By the first she resigned the crown to Prince James on the grounds that she was 'so vexed, broken and unquieted' by the responsibility of queenship that she could carry on no longer. By the second document she named her brother Moray as regent, and the third arranged for the Earl of Morton and his colleagues to form a provisional government, pending Moray's return from abroad.

By this time Mary was too far gone to care about anything. Without a second glance at the papers, she signed them where Lindsay indicated, but as she did so she said repeatedly, in front of everyone who was then in her bedchamber, that she was doing so under duress, and therefore could not be bound by the contents of the documents.

Five days later, on 29 July 1567, James VI was solemnly crowned in Stirling's parish church. Morton took the oath on the baby's behalf, while a triumphant Knox preached an appropriately fiery sermon. If the ceremony itself was low-key, the celebrations were widespread. Throckmorton records that there were almost a thousand bonfires in Edinburgh alone, accompanied by 'great joy, dancing and acclamations,'[6] while the guns of Edinburgh Castle fired a celebratory salute. At Lochleven, Sir William Douglas sang lustily in his garden and danced a jig, though he refused at first to tell his captive what he was celebrating so wildly. When he asked laughingly why she, too, was not celebrating her son's coronation Mary wept aloud, calling on God to avenge her.

In the immediate aftermath of Mary's downfall the Hamilton family had accepted the situation; but they were pointedly excluded from the coronation, and as they themselves had aspirations towards the throne, from that moment the rift with the Douglases (as represented by Morton) was renewed.

For several days after her abdication Mary was at a very low ebb, both physically and mentally. After Lindsay's departure with the signed documents, she had a relapse, her body began to swell up, her skin turned yellow and she developed an ugly rash. Although there have been theories that this serious condition was brought on by poison or a liver complaint, it is more likely to have been psychosomatic or a form of puerperal fever resulting from the miscarriage. Leeches were applied, and Mary was given a cordial; in spite of this treatment she gradually recovered.

By now her personal charm was beginning to take effect on the Douglas household. Even that doughty harridan Lady Meg was softening her attitude towards her royal prisoner. Fearing that she was weaving her spell over her captors, however, the lords had her removed from the main castle and kept under much more rigorous confinement in the old round tower across the yard. This decision appears to have been triggered off by Lindsay. When he threatened to drag her out of the house if she refused to sign his documents, young George Douglas had intervened, persuading the castle servants to support him in his defiance. Lindsay backed down, but neither forgot nor forgave Geordie. Although her new quarters were less comfortable, in some respects conditions improved. Belatedly some of her clothing and personal effects were sent from Holyrood. Eventually, she was even permitted to exercise in the castle gardens. As she recovered her equanimity, and became resigned to her surroundings, Mary took up her old pastimes, sewing, playing cards, even singing and dancing occasionally.

The Earl of Moray returned to Scotland on 12 August and was formally proclaimed regent ten days later. In an interview with Throckmorton soon after his return, Moray expressed doubt as to how to proceed. While he professed to abhor Darnley's murder, he commiserated with his sister; but soon Throckmorton learned that Moray concurred with the lords, 'yea and as seriously as any one of them'.[7]

Some time that month, Moray went to Lochleven to speak to his sister. Later he gave a full account of their meeting to Throckmorton who reported back to London: 'Sometimes the Queen wept bitterly, sometimes she acknowledged her unadvisedness and misgovernment, some things she did confess plainly, some things she did excuse, some things she did extenuate.'[8] The initial interview did not go well. Mary was disagreeably surprised to find her brother being addressed obsequiously as 'Your Grace', a form at that time reserved for kings and queens. Moray was dour and hostile and in a hectoring mood. The meeting was terminated abruptly when Mary said that she was opposed to him accepting the regency, and he left her coldly 'in hope of nothing but God's mercy'.[9] Having slept on it, however, Mary bowed to the inevitable, and when she met her brother again the following morning she greeted him warmly, hugging and kissing him, and telling him to accept the regency with her good wishes. Moray kept up his end of the charade, with a great show of reluctance to take on this onerous responsibility. He let her know that he was only doing this as a great favour to her, and certainly not for his own benefit. They embraced warmly and parted company on good terms, although, according to Nau, Mary delivered a warning to him. If she, a born queen, was rebelled against by her people, how much more would the people rebel against him, a bastard by birth and origin, and she quoted the aphorism: 'He who does not keep faith where it is due, will hardly keep it where it is not due.'[10]

With Moray firmly in place as regent and Bothwell in prison in Denmark, Scotland settled down to a period of comparative calm. Throckmorton returned to England early in September, without realising his plan to interview Mary personally. On his departure Moray offered him a silver plate in the name of King James, but Throckmorton declined it, saying that he had been instructed by Queen Elizabeth that he could not recognise Mary's abdication or Moray's regency. Despite this negative attitude from England, Moray's régime was secure, and Mary's supporters completely cowed and demoralised. By mid-October Moray was writing confidently to Cecil saying that the country was quiet.

On Lochleven, conditions were relaxed again, and in September some of Mary's ladies-in-waiting, including Mary Seton, were permitted to join her. After Moray's visit in August, various parcels were delivered, containing clothing, foodstuffs and other comforts. By the end of the year she was being treated with all the respect due to a royal lady, according to Drury, being waited on by five or six ladies and a couple of chamberwomen. The sum allowed for her meals was ten pounds a day, the same as King James and half that allocated to Regent Moray himself. The Venetian ambassador at Paris learned from England in January 1568 that conditions had become so relaxed that Mary was even allowed to go hunting,[11] under guard, of course, but this story has never been corroborated and must be treated with caution. When Moray next visited her, towards the end of October, he found her 'as merry and wanton as any time since she was detained'.[12]

On 8 December 1567 Mary celebrated her twenty-fifth birthday, traditionally a time for Scottish sovereigns to take back any grants of land made during their minority. As Morton and several other leading nobles stood to lose considerably if Mary revoked their rights, a parliament was hastily convened. On hearing that parliament had been summoned, Mary wrote a long letter to her brother, begging to be permitted to appear and clear herself of all charges levelled against her. Moray's refusal was brusque and contemptuous. In fact he showed his brotherly concern for her by pushing through an Act of parliament on December 15, declaring that the conduct of the lords against Mary had been fully justified by her own actions 'inasmuch as it was clearly evident both by her letters, and by her marriage to Bothwell, that she was privy, act and part, of the actual device and deed' of Darnley's murder. By renouncing the throne Mary had saved her life, but by this Act she was declared guilty. She had lost not only her liberty, but her honour as well. Hitherto the lords had merely condemned her for marrying Bothwell; but now she must bear the burden of guilt for Darnley's death as well.

News of this political manoeuvre upset Mary, but now she realised that her life was in danger once more, so she had a letter smuggled out of her island prison. Addressed to Catherine de' Medici, it begged her to send a token force of troops. Mary was confident that her subjects would rise in great numbers to join them; that was all that was needed to overcome their awe of the rebel lords. She wrote to Elizabeth in similar vein, but neither queen sent help. As winter gave way to spring, Mary determined to escape from Lochleven. On 25 March 1568 she disguised herself in the clothing of one of the washerwomen who came over from the shore to attend to her laundry, but she was detected by the boatman who noticed her beautiful white hands. Wordlessly he turned his skiff back to the castle and put her ashore again, but at least did not betray her.

Having almost succeeded in this bold attempt, Mary was more intent than ever on getting away. Now she exerted her charm on Pretty Geordie. The dashing, debonair young man was by now hopelessly in love with Mary and he enlisted the help of his orphaned cousin Willie Douglas. According to Drury, Mary actually proposed marriage to George, and that when this proposal was relayed to Moray he reacted by ordering his half-brother to leave Lochleven immediately. This may have been no more than a ruse on Mary's part to engineer the removal of George from the island, so that he could organise her escape from the landward side. If this were the case, then Moray fell into the trap.

By now Mary was hearing of dissension in the ranks of the lords, and when Maitland, no less, sent her a ring engraved with the scene from Aesop's fable of the mouse gnawing the ropes of the captive lion, she took heart. When Moray returned from England he had barred Maitland from his counsels, and thereafter the two men were on increasingly bad terms, although Maitland, hedging his bets, never completely defected to the Marian side. Word also reached Mary that Lord Seton and the Hamilton family were openly declaring themselves willing to obtain her freedom, so Mary formed a plan to escape. Fate took a hand when Sir William's wife, who watched over the Queen like a hawk, gave birth to a baby and was confined to her own bedchamber. On 2 May Willie Douglas organised a May Day masque. Everyone joined in the revels, but by dinnertime Mary claimed that she was fatigued and retired to her room. As she lay on the bed, her heart pounding, she overheard some of the women gossiping in the adjoining room about a large party of men on horseback who had been seen in the village of Kinross that morning. Someone had recognised Lord Seton among the party.

Mary went downstairs and rejoined Sir William Douglas. At that moment he happened to look out of a window and saw his nephew Willie acting suspiciously among the boats beached on the shingle and cried out to him. Mary, knowing that Willie was immobilising the boats, created a diversion by swooning, and Douglas being alone in the room with her, was obliged to fetch her a cup of wine. By the time he had returned to the window Willie had vanished. Soon afterwards, a servant came to Mary with one of her pearl earrings which she said had been found in the castle. The Queen recognised this as a signal from George Douglas that everything was ready on the shore-side of the loch. Hurriedly going downstairs again, Mary disguised herself in an old red kirtle belonging to one of the servants then threw her cloak over it. Saying that she need a breath of fresh air, she went out into the gardens with Lady Meg. When the old lady spotted some horsemen on the far shore she became suspicious, but Mary deftly diverted her attention by launching into a long tirade against the regent, and of course Lady Douglas immediately sprang vehemently to her son's defence, in her anger forgetting all about the horsemen.

They went indoors for supper. Mary was always served before the others, Sir William himself waiting table. It was then the turn of Willie Douglas to serve his aunt and uncle and in so doing he purloined Sir William's keys from the table. What, one wonders, was Sir William thinking, leaving the bunch of keys on the table? Willie's clumsy subterfuge of dropping a kerchief over the keys and thus abstracting them beneath his uncle's nose, seems barely credible – unless Sir William himself was party to the escape. Drury suspected that Sir William was tired of playing the gaoler, and had become increasingly sympathetic to Mary's plight. In a letter to his kinsman Morton, Sir William confessed that 'there ran no vice in her'.[13]

Be that as it may, after the laird and his wife had retired to their own chambers, the Queen hurried upstairs, exchanged her own fine cloak for a shabby one belonging to one of the servants. At a signal from Willie, Mary, accompanied by her chamberwoman, Jane Kennedy, came downstairs again, silently crossed the courtyard and exited by the gate which Willie unlocked. Once they were through, he locked the gate and dumped the keys in the mouth of the cannon at the entrance. For a few moments the trio stood close by the castle wall, hardly daring to breathe lest the alarm be raised; but when they realised that they had got this far without detection they glided down the pathway to the boats. Mary clambered aboard the one which had not been rendered unserviceable and hid under the seat. To his consternation, Willie realised that they had been observed by a group of washermen, but he whispered to them to hold their tongues, and with that the boat was pushed out into the loch. As they neared the shore, Mary stood up in the boat and waved to the party of horseman who had gathered there. In a few minutes she had leaped ashore to be greeted warmly by George Douglas and Lord Seton who presently led the cavalcade across country to Niddry, his castle near Winchburgh. It was close to midnight before they reached their destination, but already rumours flew ahead of them, and people came out of their houses to wave and cheer as they saw their beloved queen once more.

Greatly heartened by this reaction, Mary was elated but exhausted by the time she reached Niddry. Before she went to sleep she dashed off a letter to Archbishop Beaton in Paris announcing her escape, and instructions to Hepburn of Riccarton to seize Dunbar Castle before sending a messenger to Denmark to secure the release of his kinsman Bothwell.

The following morning Mary rode west with her supporters to Hamilton. On this journey she was escorted by Lord Claud Hamilton (first Baron Paisley), on whom effective leadership of the family had apparently devolved, since his father, the Duke, had retired to his French estates, while his eldest brother, the titular Earl of Arran, was now confined as a madman. It has been speculated that had she ignored Lord Claud's advice, and insisted on going to Dumbarton instead, the course of history might have been altered. Dumbarton Castle had continued to hold out in Mary's name ever since her downfall. Here, it will be remembered, she had taken ship to France when she was a little girl, and it would have been possible for her to take ship for France again should the political tide turn against her. But, against her better judgment, Mary was persuaded to go to Hamilton instead. Here she was met by Archbishop Hamilton who helped her to draft a proclamation reasserting her lawful sovereignty and condemning 'the ungrateful, unthankful and detestable tyrants and treasonable traitors' who had deposed and imprisoned her. She revoked her abdication and proclaimed the Hamiltons as heirs to her throne after her son James. Mary's anger and bitterness comes across vividly in the very pithy Scots language. Its more noteworthy clauses reserved her especial venom for those whom she had raised up, only to show their gratitude by making her the scapegoat for her husband's murder. Moray, for example, was held up as 'a spurious bastard, promoted from a religious monk to earl and lord', while Maitland was castigated as that 'mischent unworthy traitor William Maitland, whom from a simple unworthy page, our dearest mother and me did nourish and bring up to perfection'. These two men, together with Riccio's killers, were lumped together as 'godless traitors, common murderers and throatcutters, whom no prince, nor the barbarous ethnic, the Turk, for their perpetrated murders could pardon or spare'. This proclamation was not published at the time, but its tenor and context reveal how much Mary was now effectively in the hands of the Hamiltons, who hoped to use her solely for their own ends. Cynically they had, after Carberry Hill, been as loud in their condemnation of Mary as the fiery John Knox, and just as ready to demand her execution. But now, with their adversary Moray the most powerful man in the kingdom, Queen Mary was of far greater value to them alive than dead.

As early as August 1567, when Moray was still contemplating

acceptance of the regency, the Hamilton faction were planning that, in event of Mary divorcing Bothwell, she should marry Lord John Hamilton, titular Abbot of Arbroath. In furtherance of this plan, they held a family council in September, at which they appointed three regents: Lord John, deputising for his father Châtelherault, Argyll (an implacable enemy of Lennox) and Huntly (the deadly foe of Moray). The stated aim of this confederacy was the pursuit of Darnley's murderers, despite the fact that Argyll and Huntly themselves were implicated. Where they differed radically from Moray's faction was that while they professed loyalty to Prince James, they would not accept him as their king. Their immediate objective was to release Mary from Lochleven. Once she was in their hands, they would be in a very much stronger position to deal with Moray and Morton. They began mustering an army. Argyll provided five thousand men, by far the largest contingent, and this entitled him to be named as Lieutenant of the Kingdom, effectively commander-in-chief of the loyalist forces. By contrast, the Hamiltons, Huntly, Herries and Crawford each contributed about a thousand men, while Fleming, Livingston and other lesser nobles mobilised several hundred men.[14] This coup was abortive and Regent Moray had no difficulty in suppressing it, but now the confederates, inspired by Mary's dramatic escape, rallied to her.

On 8 May, less than a week after her escape, Mary's principal supporters signed a bond to which no fewer than nine earls, nine bishops, eighteen barons and many lairds put their names. Mary had been told that she could only regain the throne by recourse to parliament or battle. Emboldened by the support that was growing from day to day, she chose the latter course. Instead of heading for Edinburgh, where her cause might have been advanced by constitutional means, she led her army in a westerly direction, with the avowed intention of relieving Dumbarton Castle and consolidating her hold on the west of Scotland. She had the advantage both of superior numbers and surprise. Moray had been in Glasgow the day she escaped and when news was brought to him he was 'sore amazed'. Sir William Douglas tried to make amends for letting his captive escape by falling upon his dagger, but his suicide attempt was bungled, and within days he was doing his utmost to rally troops in support of the regent.

Mary tried to reach a political solution, and offered to negotiate with her brother, but Moray rejected this overture. By 13 May two opposing armies were in the vicinity of Glasgow. Moray's forces, numbering about six thousand, were drawn up on the Burgh Muir near the hamlet of Langside (now a district of Glasgow) whose main street, running east and west, was defended by Kirkcaldy's hagbutters armed with tripod culverins. Mary's troops, numbering about twice as many as their opponents, intended skirting to the south of Glasgow, but found their line of advance blocked by the regent's forces in and around Langside. Moray himself took up a commanding position on the summit of Langside Hill in order to direct the movement of his troops. What they lacked in numbers Moray's men made up for in the experience of their generals, Kirkcaldy of Grange, Morton and Moray himself. The battle opened with a royalist artillery barrage from the ridge of Cathcart Hill, under cover of which the cavalry commanded by Lord Claud Hamilton charged recklessly towards the enemy lines. Morton, who had overall command of the regent's army, stood his ground while Kirkcaldy with his hagbutters and archers skilfully took up positions in the village, so that they could enfilade the royalist troops as they tried to advance along the main street. The Border horse, under Lord Herries, put up a gallant fight, while Lord Claud's men made steady progress; but at a crucial stage in the conflict the main body, under Argyll, failed to press forward. Afterwards it was claimed that Argyll had either fainted or taken a seizure at the precise moment when he should have ordered his troops to advance. Now Kirkcaldy's hagbutters struck the Hamilton contingent from the flanks and without the back-up of Argyll's men they were swiftly cut off. Argyll's troops, seeing the tide of battle going against them, turned and fled from the field. So energetic was Kirkcaldy's conduct of the battle that only one man was killed on the regent's side, though Hume and Ochiltree sustained wounds in the mêlée; but over a hundred of the Marian troops were killed and several hundred were captured, including Lord Seton and Lord Ross, Sir James Hamilton, the Masters of Montgomery and Cassilis and the Sheriff of Ayr as well as many minor members of the Hamilton family.

Mary watched the horrifying progress of the battle from a nearby eminence. According to John Beaton, her personal servant, at one stage Mary herself had charged into the thick of the battle to rally the waverers, but to no avail. To her disgust and alarm she found her troops bickering among themselves, heedless of her eloquence and more intent on exchanging blows with each other than in attacking the enemy.[15] Accompanied by only a handful of retainers, Mary turned and rode from the field as fast as she could. Dumbarton Castle, the obvious refuge, was cut off by Moray's men and the adherents of the hostile Lennox faction, so this left Mary no alternative but to head south. Led by Lord Herries, with Lord Fleming, Claud Hamilton and half a dozen horsemen, Mary rode over the roughest terrain, towards Galloway, a district which had remained strongly Catholic and which, under the feudal sway of Herries and Maxwell, could be relied upon to give her refuge. Writing in June 1568 to the Cardinal of Lorraine, Mary described her nightmare journey:

> I have endured injuries, calumnies, imprisonment, famine, cold, heat, flight not knowing whither, 92 miles across the country without stopping or alighting, and then I have had to sleep upon the ground and drink sour milk, and eat oatmeal without bread, and have been three nights like the owls.[16]

Mary and her small entourage rode southwards to Cumnock, then through the remote passes of the Glenkens and along the west bank of the River Ken. At the head of the Tarff valley they rested at a place now known as Queen's Hill, then crossed the Dee near Tongland where her escort destroyed the bridge to delay pursuit. It was near here, at Culdoach, that Mary received the bowl of sour milk from an old woman who was afterwards rewarded by Herries who granted her and her family the freehold of their croft in perpetuity. Heading east by way of the Herries stronghold of Corra (now a picturesque ruin four miles north-east of Dalbeattie) the party finally came to a halt at Terregles, on the western outskirts of Dumfries.

For the moment, Mary was safe, but it would not be long before the vengeful Moray caught up with her. Opinion was fiercely divided among Mary's supporters as to what she should do next. Some argued that she should lie low in the remote fastnesses of Galloway while her scattered forces regrouped for another attack on Moray; but others thought it more prudent for her to leave the country for the time being. From the Solway coast she could have taken a ship to France where she had wealth and status as well as powerful friends and relatives. From there she could have mounted a counter-attack against Moray when the time was right. This was the soundest advice of all, but for some unfathomable reason Mary did not heed it. Not for the first time in her turbulent life she turned her back on logic and reason and chose a course of action which would ultimately lead to her death. She decided to put herself at the mercy of England, a country where she had no money, no estates, no friends and no relatives, other than her former mother-in-law, Lady Lennox, who loathed her as the murderer of her son Darnley, and Queen Elizabeth, the cousin whom she had never met, the cousin whose position as queen she had challenged a few short years previously. In hindsight, Mary's decision to cross the Solway into England seems the very height of folly. Perhaps her long confinement at Lochleven and the events of the past few days had clouded her judgment.

Realising that the Queen was adamant, and nothing he could do would persuade her to abandon her plans, Herries bowed to the inevitable and wrote to Lord Lowther, the deputy governor of Carlisle, seeking permission for the Queen of Scots to take refuge in England. Without waiting for a response, Mary made her way westwards from Terregles to the Abbey of Dundrennan, one of the most picturesque spots on the Solway Coast. On Sunday afternoon, 16 May, the Queen walked down to the mouth of the Abbey Burn. There, in sight of the Cumbrian hills three miles to the south, she boarded the little fishing smack that was to bear her off into exile. Herries, Maxwell, Fleming and Claud Hamilton accompanied her, together with about sixteen soldiers and servants. During the four-hour voyage to Workington, Mary's supporters entreated her to sail on to France. Tradition maintains that, at the last moment, Mary changed her mind, but by that time the winds and current were bringing her relentlessly closer to the Cumbrian coast.

At seven o'clock that evening Mary stepped ashore. As she did so, she stumbled and fell forward, involuntarily kissing the English soil. Her supporters took this as a good omen, a sign from God that she would one day take possession of the English throne.

12. FIRST TRIAL

1568–69

I was the Queen o bonie France,
Where happy I have been;
Fu lightly rase I in the morn,
As blyther lay down at e'en:
And I'm the sov'reign of Scotland,
And monie a traitor there;
Yet here I lie in foreign bands
And never-ending care.

    Robert Burns, *Lament of Mary Queen of Scots*

While Mary rested and had a meal after her voyage, Lord Herries sent word to his old friend Sir Henry Curwen at Workington Hall that he had come from Scotland with a young heiress whom he hoped to marry to Sir Henry's son. Sir Henry was in London at the time, but in due course a message came back saying that Herries and his ward were welcome to make use of the hall and its staff. Meanwhile, Workington buzzed with excitement. Due to her height and beauty, the identity of the Scottish lady was guessed almost immediately, and this was soon confirmed by one of Curwen's servants, a Frenchman, who told Lord Fleming that he had seen her in happier times.

The following morning Richard Lowther, forewarned by the letter from Herries, arrived with four hundred horse. His superior, Lord Scrope, was likewise absent in London, but on his own initiative Lowther decided to move Mary to Carlisle, gallantly providing the cash and horses for the journey. Mary told him that she had come to England to enlist her cousin's aid in putting down a rebellion. Before leaving Workington, Mary wrote again to Elizabeth, her third letter in a week. At Cockermouth the next day she lodged with Henry Fletcher, a haberdasher, who kindly presented his royal guest with a bolt of cloth with which to make up some new clothes. By 18 May the fugitive queen was taken to Carlisle Castle. Along the way she ran into Villeroy de Beaumont, the French ambassador to Scotland, on his way back to France after having his baggage train looted by Moray's men. His up-to-date intelligence on what was happening in Scotland, as the regent's forces mopped up pockets of Marian resistance, did nothing to dispel Mary's growing sense of gloomy foreboding.

Until he received instructions from London, Lowther was at a loss to know how to treat his unexpected visitor. Was she to be regarded as a political prisoner or an honoured guest? Lowther decided to take the latter option, and accorded Mary every courtesy; but at the same time her movements were rather restricted and she was closely guarded, as much for her own safety as for state security. Mary herself, in a letter to the Earl of Cassilis two days after her arrival in Carlisle, stated that she was being 'right well received and honourably accompanied and treated', adding confidently that she expected to return to Scotland 'about the fifteenth day of August' at the head of an army, French if not English.[1]

If Lowther was nonplussed regarding the proper treatment to be meted out to the Queen of Scots, Elizabeth and her advisers were extremely apprehensive about this dramatic intrusion. Mary had come to England of her own free will, specifically in search of assistance against her rebellious subjects – a point which Mary would often reiterate over the ensuing years and, with especial bitterness, at her trial in 1586. Clearly she had not given any consideration to the wider implications of her foolish impulse. By setting foot on English soil, unannounced and without permission, she immediately posed a threat as well as an embarrassment to Elizabeth. On account of her religion, she was, whether she liked it or not, a potential rallying point for English Catholics, then enjoying a period of relative tolerance. While Elizabeth may have felt that there should be solidarity among sovereigns, there was no way in which she could lend her support to a Catholic monarch against a Protestant régime. Her dilemma was that if she turned Mary down, the Scottish queen would almost certainly seek military intervention from France, and that was a prospect which Elizabeth found abhorrent. For that reason alone, it was quite out of the question that Elizabeth should grant her cousin a safe-conduct pass to travel through England *en route* to France.

Passing from the general to the specific, Elizabeth debated whether her cousin should be summoned to London, to be received at court with the honours due to her exalted status. That something of the sort was originally considered seems to be borne out by the report of the Venetian ambassador in Paris that a palace in the London area was being prepared for Mary,[2] but this idea must have been rapidly dropped, as the full implications sank in of having a rival to the throne so close to the seat of power. In the end, masterly inactivity seems to have been the watchword. While Elizabeth waited for clearer reports on the situation in Scotland, she decided that her cousin should be detained in the north. As she could not allow her to roam at will over England, or cross to France, the obvious solution was to deport Mary back to Scotland. There was no way that Elizabeth was going to restore Mary by force of arms and consequently she now put out feelers to the Scots, enquiring on what terms they would be prepared to take back their queen. That seemed the best solution to a knotty problem, especially if there was some advantage for England to be wrung out of the negotiations.

The immediate and most pressing problem was what to do with Mary in the meantime. In the end Elizabeth decided that Mary should remain in the north, as far from London as possible, not exactly a captive but not exactly at liberty either. On 20 May orders from the Council were sent to Lowther to use the Scottish queen and her company honourably, 'as the Earl of Northumberland should appoint'; but significantly he was also enjoined to let none of them escape. The Earl of Northumberland wished to remove Mary to Alnwick Castle, but in spite of a great deal of threats and cajolery Lowther refused to budge. Again, we can only speculate on what might have happened had Mary gone to Alnwick. Within days of her arrival in England, she was being visited by noblemen from different parts of the country, and to them she spoke eloquently and persuasively of her campaign against the Scottish lords, raising considerable sympathy and support as a result, although she was always at pains to utter no word that might incite disloyalty towards Elizabeth, from whom she was daily expecting a positive response to her pleas for help.

In due course, however, Mary was told in no uncertain terms that as Elizabeth intended to help her, any attempt on Mary's part to enlist the aid of France, Spain or any other foreign power would be regarded as an unfriendly act. Furthermore, Elizabeth pointed out that Mary was in a very weak position, having arrived in England under a cloud. The unresolved scandal of Darnley's murder and Mary's hasty marriage to the chief suspect was sufficient reason for not inviting her to court. Indeed, Elizabeth magnanimously offered her services as arbitrator in the case between Mary and her nobles.

In putting these rather delicate proposals to Mary, Elizabeth selected one of her most experienced diplomats, Sir Francis Knollys. On 25 May the Council sent a directive to the Earl of Northumberland not to interfere with Mary's removal until after Knollys had interviewed her and reported back to London. On 28 May Mary received Knollys, accompanied by Scrope, who tendered Elizabeth's congratulations on her escape and her condolences on her 'lamentable misadventure and inconvenient arrival'. Although Knollys was a leading Puritan, and therefore likely to be prejudiced against her on religious grounds, Mary made an immediately favourable impression on him. In due course he reported back to London that Mary had 'an eloquent tongue and discreet head' and from her doings it seemed that she had 'stout courage and liberal heart adjoined thereto'. But when she took Knollys and Scrope into her bedroom for greater privacy 'she fell into some passion with the tears in her eyes', complaining that Elizabeth had sorely disappointed her by not promptly inviting her to her court.[3]

Mary pointedly reminded her cousin that it had been at Elizabeth's request that she had allowed the lords who had previously rebelled against her to return from exile in England. Mary now proposed that, if she could not go to London herself, she would send Lord Herries to explain the position to Elizabeth and clarify any matters of which she was in doubt. At the same time, she hinted that she would send Lord Fleming to France on a similar mission. Guzman de Silva, the Spanish ambassador, reported to Madrid that Elizabeth was inclined to permit Mary to come to court, but that she had been talked out of this by her Council.[4] And the French ambassador, De la Forrest, opined that if Mary were allowed to go to London the two queens would not remain on friendly terms for more than eight days.[5] Sadly, this was never put to the test. Elizabeth, it seems, was merely indulging in one of her characteristic pretences in order to lull Mary into trusting her while, at the same time, deterring France and Spain from helping her. In pursuance of this policy, therefore, Elizabeth wrote to Mary on 8 June, assuring her that there was 'no creature living' more anxious than herself to lend a sympathetic ear to Mary's plight. But much as her personal interest inclined her to do so, she could never be careless of her own reputation – a dig at Mary who, by inference, had been too careless of hers – and then, assuming that Mary had entrusted her with 'the handling of this business', she assured her cousin that she would be as careful of Mary's 'life and honour' as Mary herself could be. She concluded by saying that it would be one of 'her highest worldly pleasures' to receive her, once she had been acquitted of this 'crime' – acquitted, of course, by judges of Elizabeth's own choosing.

On the same day Elizabeth wrote to Moray accusing him of his 'very strange' doings against a sovereign prince (i.e., Mary) who was now seeking her aid and 'is content to commit the ordering of her cause to us' – a rather sweeping assumption on Elizabeth's part. Elizabeth was willing to hear his side of the matter, so long as Moray suspended all further action against Mary's supporters. In this astounding manner, therefore, Elizabeth gave herself the right to arbitrate in a quarrel between Mary and her subjects. There is little to be said by way of justification for this high-handed approach. Mary, it is true, had appealed to her for help, but Mary rejected that help because of the strings Elizabeth attached to it. Elizabeth's behaviour, in fact, must have given both Mary and Moray a sense of *déjà vu*: here was the latest in a long line of English monarchs from Edward I onwards claiming suzerainty over Scotland. The Scots had always repudiated this notion, and in this case Elizabeth had absolutely no right to meddle in the domestic affairs of another sovereign nation.

The *realpolitik*, however, was that Scotland only owed its continuing independence to the mutual jealousy of England, France and Spain, and it was always prone to interference by one of these powers whenever a favourable opportunity presented itself. Moray was acutely aware that if Elizabeth intervened on Mary's behalf, his own position would be untenable; while he depended on Elizabeth's protection against intervention from France. Shrewdly he judged that Elizabeth's protestation against the wrongs suffered by Mary was not to be taken too seriously. Nevertheless he had no option but to humour her as best he could. Accordingly, he replied that he was reluctant to take further action against the 'queen mother of the king our sovereign' and he wished to know what Elizabeth intended to do, in the event that he proved the case against Mary. He hoped that Elizabeth would leave matters in Scotland as they were. Regarding the case against Mary he proposed that when the judges were selected to try the matter, they should first read copies of the letters which had been found in the casket in the hope that once they had perused the contents the case would be sufficiently proved. In other words, the Casket Letters alone should convict Mary, and there would therefore be no need for a trial. In any event, he could not possibly consent to a trial unless he had some sort of guarantee that its outcome would be based solely on the evidence produced, and not on some whim of Elizabeth's.[6]

Some inkling of the person Elizabeth would have to deal with was furnished by Knollys when he reported back to Cecil, and as it is the most perceptive character sketch of Mary ever written it is worth quoting at length:

> This lady and princess is a notable woman; she seemeth to regard no ceremonious honour beside the acknowledging of her estate regal: she showeth a disposition to speak much, to be bold, to be pleasant, and to be very familiar. She showeth a great desire to be avenged of her enemies, she showeth a readiness to expose herself to all perils in hope of victory, she delighteth much to hear of hardiness and valiancy, commending by name all approved hardy men of her country, although they be her enemies, and she concealeth no cowardice even in her friends. The thing that most she thirsteth after is victory, and it seemeth to be indifferent to her to have her enemies deminished either by the sword of her friends, or by division and quarrels raised among themselves: so that for victory's sake pain and peril seem pleasant unto her: and in respect of victory, wealth and all things seem to her contemptible and vile. Nowe what is to be done with such a lady and princess, or whether such a princess and lady be to be nourished in one's bosom? or whether it be good to halt and dissemble with such a ladie, I refer to your judgment.[7]

A few days later Knollys got a response from London. Indeed, he was to dissemble with Mary as this was the most favourable political expedient. Furthermore, he was instructed to tell Mary that she could not be received at court until she had been acquitted of her husband's murder and that this could only be achieved by submitting herself to Elizabeth's judgment. Mary's reaction to this proposal was predictably passionate. When the matter was put to her she burst into tears of anger and vehemently pointed out that both Morton and Maitland were implicated in the murder, although now they were chief among the prosecutors of the supposed murderers. Knollys was very impressed by Mary's indignant sincerity and wrote to Elizabeth saying that Mary had already convinced everyone in the north of England of her innocence. It would be better, he argued, to offer Mary the choice of remaining in England, to be cleared by Elizabeth of complicity in the murder, or returning to Scotland of her own free will. The worst that could happen was that Mary might then try to go to France (in which case Moray could surely prevent that happening). Elizabeth, however, had now latched on to the question of Mary's honour, apparently so besmirched that Mary could not be released until it was formally investigated by judges appointed in England. Knollys was ordered to remain at Carlisle until he had managed to get Mary to agree to submit herself to this process.

On 30 May Mary and Knollys met again to argue on the vexed question of Mary's enforced abdication. When Mary railed against Moray's conduct, Knollys quietly pointed out that if princes could be deposed on grounds of insanity, they could also be deposed for committing a felony like murder. The more Mary howled and wept at the remembrance of this outrage, the more Knollys quietly persisted: her only course now was submission to her cousin so that she could be properly purged of her crimes.[8]

Knollys also reported to London at some length regarding the conditions in which Mary was being held at Carlisle. She had about forty persons in her retinue, including menials, but lacked proper ladies-in-waiting. Among her gentlemen was George Douglas who had accompanied her into exile and would, with cousin Willie, be among her most faithful aides to the end of her life. When Montmorin, the ambassador of Charles IX, visited her late in June, he was appalled to discover that Mary occupied a gloomy room in the great Border fortress, lit only by a heavily barred casement and entered via three other rooms all guarded and occupied by hagbutters. Her servants and domestics, except three women in attendance on her, slept outside the castle. Mary was permitted to attend football matches organised by her retainers on the castle green – Knollys noted with surprise that the Scots played 'very strongly, nimbly and skilfully without foul play'. But whenever Mary went out walking – only as far as the town church – she was invariably accompanied by a guard of a hundred armed men. On one occasion she had gone hunting after hares, but this was deemed to be far too great a security risk, so it was never repeated.

The want of suitable ladies was supplied to some extent by the arrival of Mary Seton, the only member of the Four Maries as yet unmarried. Not only was her company much appreciated, but she was also an expert hairdresser, a talent that the Queen valued very highly. After Langside, Mary had cut her hair short to facilitate male disguise if need be, and thereafter she frequently had it cropped in an attempt to mitigate the severe headaches to which she was increasingly prone. As a result, she relied more and more upon wigs and hairpieces to remedy the deficiency. Clothing continued to be a major problem for several months. An appeal to Elizabeth for a few cast-offs from her very extensive wardrobe yielded a meagre haul of old duds fit only for the lowliest servants, much to the embarrassment of Knollys who had the unenviable task of making the present to Mary. Moray was scarcely less niggardly, eventually sending down three trunks of her clothing, containing mostly cloaks and saddle-cloths and only one old taffeta dress. In July her personal chamberlain, Servais de Condé, sent down from Lochleven a large quantity of trinkets and accessories, including ear-muffs to drown out the sound of the soldiery in the adjoining ante-chambers when Mary tried to sleep.

Important as such matters of dress and hairstyling undoubtedly were, they took second place to Mary's determination to meet her cousin face to face. Between her arrival at Workington and the end of 1568 Mary wrote at least a score of letters to Elizabeth on this subject. Most of these were long, well-written and soundly reasoned arguments as Mary elaborated her case for restoration to her rightful throne with Elizabeth's help. She was even inspired to write a long poem in French, addressed to her *chère soeur*, the theme of which was the mixture of pleasure and pain which the subject of their meeting induced in her, swayed now by hope and then by doubt. Other matters which occupied her letters were the harsh persecution of her followers in Scotland by Moray and the outrageous nature of the rebellion against her. At the same time she was carrying on a voluminous correspondence with Catherine de' Medici, Charles IX, the Duke of Anjou and the Cardinal of Lorraine, emphasising that she was suffering on account of the true religion, though a recurring theme was the desperate need for cash, which was owing to her anyway from the revenues of her French estates.

On 8 June Mary had a visit from Henry Middlemore, Elizabeth's envoy to Scotland, on his way north. He handed Mary a letter from Elizabeth who promised to restore her to her throne if she would permit Elizabeth to hold an enquiry in order to establish her innocence. Mary reacted violently and later he reported her immediate response: 'She had no other judge than God, neither none could take upon them to judge of her: she knew her estate well enough.' And she made the telling point that there were things she would reveal to Elizabeth but only face to face. This could only have been as full an account of the Darnley murder from the facts as Mary knew them, and which would have implicated Maitland and Morton, if not Moray himself. Indeed, Mary urged Elizabeth to summon Maitland and Morton to London and let them debate the matter with her in Elizabeth's presence. Middlemore, who seems to have conducted the interview in a tactless manner, had a parting shot for the Scottish queen: Elizabeth meant to bring her nearer to her, where Mary would have more pleasure and liberty and be utterly out of danger of her enemies. Middlemore made the gaffe of presenting this as a decision of Elizabeth, not merely a suggestion. Mary pounced on this blunder and asked him sharply whether she was to go as a prisoner, or 'at her own free choice'. What happened next is uncertain, but the meeting ended in a violent quarrel – 'a great conflict' is how Middlemore subsequently described it. In the end Mary gave way resignedly: 'Alas, it is a small piece of comfort to me (nay rather is it a hurt to me) to be removed hence, and not to be brought to the Queen my good sister; but now I am in her hands, and she may dispose of me as she will.'[9]

In Scotland, Middlemore found that the regent and his supporters stressed Mary's culpability for the murder of her husband, the redoubtable George Buchanan being then employed in compiling his *Book of Articles* as a propaganda exercise to blacken Mary's character. It was hoped that this in itself would suffice to keep her securely locked away in an English prison. The last thing Moray wanted was Mary at liberty, a pawn in Elizabeth's game to gain control over Scotland. To Moray, his sister's moral turpitude was the one thing that would guarantee his own survival. For this reason he was prepared to go much further than the English, and in this he succeeded so well that the assassination of Mary's character has endured to this day. The collusion of Elizabeth and her government in this was all the more reprehensible in view of the fact that Mary had gone to England of her own volition, trusting in her cousin's frequent promises of help. Mary had been tried and condemned by her own subjects without being given an opportunity to defend herself, but now she was being denied the same opportunity to defend herself before Elizabeth in person. In denying her cousin a basic human right, the English queen never acted in a more devious and selfish manner. In mitigation, it should be noted that Moray took good care to keep Elizabeth fully informed of his findings against his sister, and as early as 24 May, only eight days after Mary fled to England, his emissary John Wood was in London, poisoning the Queen's mind against the fugitive. Shortly afterwards Wood was furnished with Scottish translations of the Casket Letters (the originals being in French), so that Elizabeth might have conclusive proof of her cousin's viciousness.

On 22 June Moray replied to Elizabeth's request that he should justify his actions against his sister. His response was cagey to say the least. In effect, he sought an assurance that if Mary were brought to trial in England she would be found guilty, but that whatever the outcome of the trial there must be no question of Mary being restored to her throne. Of course there was no way that Elizabeth could be seen to agree with such preposterous proposals, but Cecil drew Wood aside and told him, off the record, that no matter what Queen Elizabeth said publicly, in order to lure Mary into accepting her arbitration, there was no intention of putting Mary back on her throne, whatever the outcome. Moray received some sort of verbal assurance by the end of June, and thereafter fell in wholeheartedly with the proposal of an English trial.

Even at this late juncture Elizabeth continued to lure Mary with the prospect of restoration. Through the agency of Lord Herries, Elizabeth promised that, notwithstanding the alleged reasons of the Scottish lords, she would restore Mary to her 'seat royal on condition that her Lords and subjects should continue in their state and dignity' (whatever that may have meant). But Elizabeth also laid down three specific conditions: Mary must renounce her title to the

English throne, she must abandon her alliance with France and enter into a league with England, and she must give up the Mass, 'receiving the common prayer after the manner of England'.[10] Mary was now so desperate that she readily agreed to these demands. She had previously been denied a Catholic priest, Scrope having told her flatly that there was none anywhere in England; but now she quite meekly submitted to the ministrations of an Anglican chaplain to whose denunciation of Popery she was said to have listened 'with attentive and contented ears'.[11]

While Herries was in London conferring with Cecil and Elizabeth, Mary was suddenly transferred from Carlisle to Bolton Castle near Leyburn in Yorkshire. Carlisle was far too close to the Scottish border for comfort and the wonder is that it took the English so long to have her transferred to a more secure location. In fact, almost from the moment she landed at Workington, there had been considerable discussion in government circles over the selection of a place of really secure confinement, but the delay arose largely from the fact that Mary was not technically a prisoner. Although she had accepted Middlemore's hint that she might be moved, when the actual time came she ranted and raved tearfully, giving vent to a terrifying anger which probably released all the pent-up frustration at the way she had been treated so far. It required all the skill and tact of Knollys to calm her down and get her to acquiesce in the move.

The journey took two days, with the first night at Lowther Castle and the second at Wharton, north-east of Beetham in Westmorland. On arrival at her destination in remote Wensleydale, Knollys noted with relief that Mary was very quiet, tractable and 'void of displeasant countenance'.[12] In fact, she soon had much to displease her, for her new abode was extremely isolated, forty miles from York and fifty from Carlisle. The castle was virtually unfurnished and furniture and tapestries had to be hastily borrowed from the mansion of Sir George Bowes some miles distant. Whether Bolton was more comfortable and less rigorous than Carlisle was questionable; as to Mary now being nearer Elizabeth, that was a palpable lie. The move to Bolton began the long period, lasting nineteen years, in which Mary was effectively cut off from the political and intellectual world outside.

Thither came Lord Herries at the end of July with Elizabeth's proposals of a restoration, subject in the first instance to a form of judicial enquiry. Whatever the outcome, Elizabeth promised to restore Mary to her throne, the only stipulation being that, if she were found guilty, the rebel lords could not then be punished for their actions. Mary was so certain of being vindicated that she even sent word to her supporters in Scotland, urging them to suspend operations against the regent's forces, on condition that the latter did likewise. In fact, at a session of the Scottish parliament on 16 August, Moray declared the forfeiture of Lord Fleming, the Bishop of Ross and sundry Hamiltons.

On 20 September Elizabeth wrote to Moray assuring him that whatever promises had been made to Mary, Elizabeth would not restore her to her throne if she were found guilty. No provision for action in the event of Mary being proved innocent was mentioned. Moray, of course, took the hint, and redoubled his efforts to blacken his sister's character with fabricated evidence. At this juncture the Queen's 'privy letters' moved centre stage. The English translation of Buchanan's *Book of Articles* was far more explicit than the Latin original, and in place of an ambiguous reference to a letter or letters there was now a long appendix devoted specifically to the subject. Mary's supporters, now aware of the emphasis being placed on the letters, met at Dumbarton and publicly announced that the letters contained nothing to convict her, even if they were genuine, which they firmly believed were not. Meanwhile Mary herself was blissfully unaware of the gravity of the situation, naïvely placing her trust in her cousin to set her free whatever the outcome.

The judicial enquiry at York opened in October 1568 under the chairmanship of Thomas Howard, Duke of Norfolk. Both Mary and Moray were permitted commissioners; Moray's consisted of himself and Maitland, but Mary (who was not allowed to attend) was represented by the Bishop of Ross and Lords Livingston, Boyd and Herries. At Bolton, her hopes of freedom rising day by day, Mary whiled away the time by learning to write English under the supervision of Knollys whose own letters betray him falling under the charm of his beautiful captive. When Knollys left Bolton for two or three days, Mary wrote her very first English letter to him. For a first effort it was quite execrable, ending with the words 'Excus my ivel vreitn thes furst tym'.[13]

Much has been made of Mary's apparent conversion to Anglicanism at this time, usually held up by her detractors to show her inconstancy in religion, as in so much else. While it is true to say that the Puritan Knollys, an essentially good and sincere man, probably did more than any English man of the cloth to inculcate the Protestant faith in Mary, this is not saying much. Mary was eager to learn what motivated men, while reserving judgment in regard to her own private beliefs. Moreover, she was acutely aware that everything she said and did was being assiduously reported back to London by Knollys. If Mary could create a good impression on Sir Francis, might not this put her in good favour with Queen Elizabeth? Rumours that Mary had abandoned her old faith inevitably reached the Catholic community, which was particularly strong in Yorkshire, and this precipitated an extraordinary showdown, late in September, when Mary appeared before a large assembly of local Catholics in the great hall of the castle, and publicly re-affirmed her faith. Afterwards she excused herself to Knollys, saying that she could not be expected to lose France, Spain and her foreign allies by seeming to change her religion, and yet still not be certain that Elizabeth was her assured friend. In November she wrote to King Philip of Spain saying that, even if her close relationship to Queen Elizabeth precluded her having the services of a Catholic priest, this did not mean that she had given up the beliefs and practice of her religion.

The York conference was marred by confusion in the aims of the protagonists and in the promises of Queen Elizabeth to both sides. Moray alone was ruthless in his determination that, come what may, Mary must never be set free, and for this reason he was prepared unreservedly to incriminate his sister. Maitland, on the other hand, still had a union of the kingdoms uppermost in his mind, and did not rule out the possibility of a restored Mary playing some part in this. Conversely, Mary's commissioners were not as keen to prove her innocence as they might have been. They had endured the turbulent régime of Bothwell and were not utterly convinced that Mary had been Bothwell's unwilling tool. Thus they went into battle more than half-convinced that Mary would be found guilty, and already setting their sights lower, at some sort of deal which would allow Mary to return to Scotland without necessarily regaining her throne. The panel of three judges consisted of the Duke of Norfolk, Sir Ralph Sadler and the Earl of Sussex. Norfolk, a widower and nominally a Protestant although many of his family were still Catholics, was being suggested as a possible fourth husband for Mary, although she was not yet divorced from Bothwell. In the circumstances, therefore, it would be expected that Norfolk could be biased towards Mary.

Proceedings opened in a rather leisurely fashion and seemed to be going round in circles at first, but on 11 October Moray decided to cut the Gordian knot by secretly circulating copies of the Casket Letters to the panel of judges. Maitland leaked this to the Marian commissioners (who had not seen the letters themselves), for they rode over to Bolton Castle the following day to deliver this bombshell to Mary. Norfolk was horrified at the contents of the letters and sought further instruction from Queen Elizabeth, saying that he did not see how the conviction of Queen Mary could be avoided. Elizabeth responded by ordering that the conference be terminated forthwith and provision made for it to resume examining the evidence in the calmer atmosphere of Westminster. On 16 October, before the proceedings at York ended, Maitland had a secret meeting with Norfolk in which he dangled the bait of marriage with Mary. Maitland's extraordinary conduct can only be explained in terms of seeing such a marriage as likely to promote his plans for a union of the kingdoms. It has been speculated that, at this meeting, Maitland divulged to Norfolk that the Casket Letters were forgeries and that the allegations against Mary as a murderess were not to be taken too seriously. How else would such a pillar of rectitude as the Duke of Norfolk have seriously contemplated marrying this woman?

The Earl of Sussex also seems to have shared these views. Were Mary herself allowed to testify at Westminster, he was convinced that she would deny authorship of the letters and that she would be believed. Consequently the judges would have no alternative but to declare her innocent and Elizabeth would have to set her free. Even if Mary were not permitted to appear, he felt that the matter could be fudged to save her honour, without exposing the Scottish lords as forgers. In this case Mary could be kept incarcerated. All things considered, therefore, he felt it advisable that Mary should not be allowed a personal appearance. With less cynicism perhaps, but coming to a similar conclusion, Knollys felt that it would be necessary to condemn Mary if she were to be kept in captivity. Elizabeth could not continue to detain her cousin with honour unless Mary were utterly disgraced before the world and the Moray faction clearly vindicated. His solution to the problem was to marry Mary off to his wife's nephew, George Carey, who, through the Boleyn connection, was a cousin of Queen Elizabeth. Mary had met this personable young man at Bolton in September when he was going north to join his father, Lord Hunsdon, the governor of Berwick.

The commission reconvened at Westminster on 25 November, the panel of judges now enlarged to include both Cecil and the Earl of Leicester. When Mary learned that Moray had had frequent audiences with Elizabeth, she ordered her own commissioners to boycott the proceedings unless she were accorded similar privileges, but unfortunately this negative stance merely weakened her own position further. Moray opened the onslaught on 29 November with a recital of his accusations, together with a personal allegation by Lennox implicating Mary in his son's murder. Two days later Mary's commissioners made their first protest, arguing that Mary should be allowed to appear in person on the same basis as Moray, and speak in her own defence, in front of the assembly of the English Council and foreign ambassadors. Elizabeth vetoed this on the specious grounds that no proof had so far been adduced against Mary and there was therefore no point in her appearing at this juncture. Besides, there was snow on the ground and Bolton was 250 miles away. It would not be fair to subject the Queen of Scots to several days' hard riding, when it might not be necessary anyway. Now Mary's isolation seemed greater than ever, and her well-meaning commissioners, unable to take instructions from her, acted on their own initiative and began some form of plea-bargaining.

On 7 December Moray produced his trump card. With a fine sense of the dramatic, he exhibited the actual silver-gilt box decorated with the crowned monogram of King Francis II, first husband of Mary. Two marriage contracts were then produced, though they had nothing to do with the Casket Letters as such, and the session ended that day with the production of the first two letters from the casket. The following day, Mary's twenty-sixth birthday, the remaining contents of the casket were revealed. The panel of judges now had copies of the letters made for their own purposes and at Moray's request returned the originals to him. Moray then presented the documentation in the cases of Bothwell's henchmen, Hepburn, Hay, Powrie and Dalgleish.

On 9 December, while Mary's commissioners loudly protested against this travesty of justice which did not even permit them to attend the hearing, the tribunal continued to examine the copies of the letters and sonnets, now in English translation. Included was a supplementary declaration by Morton about the finding of the casket, and transcripts of evidence from Darnley's servant Thomas Nelson as well as Thomas Crawford, one of Lennox's men, were also produced. It was now decided to enlarge the tribunal still further by including other leading English nobles, such as Northumberland, Westmorland and Shrewsbury. The enlarged tribunal met at Hampton Court on 14 December and heard a summary of the proceedings so far. Meanwhile Elizabeth had written to Mary at Bolton, offering her three choices: she could answer the charges through her commissioners, in writing herself, or verbally to some English nobles sent to Bolton for that specific purpose. Mary indignantly rejected all three, saying that she could hardly be expected to answer accusations based on evidence she was not allowed to examine, or surrender the traditional right of the defendant to face her accusers. Elizabeth coolly retorted that if Mary refused these three options it would be 'thought as much as she were culpable'.[14]

Only now did Mary begin to realise, with mounting horror, the terrible trap into which she had unwittingly stumbled. Distraught by this ominous turn of events, she dashed off a letter to her old friend, the Earl of Mar, begging him to guard her son well at Stirling, and not permit him to be sent by agreement to England or abducted, and she reminded him of his promise never to surrender the boy without her express consent. On 19 December Mary drew up her own list of charges against Moray, and this was presented on Christmas Day. In this she countered her accusers with a long tirade against the lords who had murdered Riccio and would fain have killed her also, with the unborn babe in her womb. She concluded with a general attack on the illegality of Moray's regency. These accusations were never given any serious consideration and in spite of Mary's repeated requests to be shown the writings on which the charges against her were based, the proceedings were wound up on 11 January 1569 without Mary or her commissioners being given a sight of the incriminating letters.

The verdict was as ambivalent as the rest of the process, and it was decided that neither party had had anything sufficiently proved against them. Mary had not proved that her lords had rebelled against her, but, on the other hand, the detailed inspection of the Casket Letters had failed to convince the tribunal of Mary's guilt. Neither party had lost, and neither party had won. The only difference at the end was that Moray was free to return to Scotland (with a subsidy of five thousand pounds from Elizabeth) whereas Mary was still detained at Bolton, and plans were now in train to move her to an even more secure prison. Belatedly Elizabeth offered Mary copies of the incriminating evidence, provided she would answer the charges. Mary's commissioners woke up and pointed out that as Moray had now departed it was too late for Mary to rebut his allegations. Mary's commissioners were permitted to return to Scotland on 31 January. Thus ended the most peculiar case in British legal history, with a verdict of not proven on both sides but very different treatment accorded to the parties involved. Never was a double standard in British justice more cruelly demonstrated. The Casket Letters, which so singularly failed to impress the tribunal at the time, later became the subject of endless debate and a considerable literature arguing every conceivable aspect: phraseology, textual anomalies, usage of language, orthography, theories of authorship, problems of interpolation and, most recently, word patterns. Among those who had the opportunity to examine the purported originals, Norfolk was so undismayed by their murderous revelations that he seriously considered marriage with Mary, while Maitland, who knew the contents of the letters more intimately than most, subsequently became one of Mary's most valiant protagonists. Despite contemporary contempt for the letters, countless generations of scholars and historians have argued for and against acceptance of the letters as genuine, although it has to be said that even the most resolute champions of their authenticity were only prepared to argue that *some* were genuine. Argument on both sides was subjective to a greater or lesser degree, up to the present time when scientific methods, using computer technology to establish word patterns and detailed comparisons of known letters of Mary with the Casket Letters, should resolve the matter fairly conclusively and prove that the Casket Letters are forgeries, and clumsy forgeries at that.

Dr Jenny Wormald apart, no one today would continue to argue the contrary, despite the problem that has faced every scholar and historian since 1584, when the original letters were last seen. Moray took the casket containing the letters back to Scotland in January 1569 and handed them over to Morton on 22 January 1571. Copies were taken again at this juncture but they vanished almost at once. After Morton's execution the letters passed to the Earl of Gowrie, but following his execution in 1584 the letters disappeared and have never been seen since, despite strenuous efforts by Queen Elizabeth to obtain them. The little casket appears to have come into the hands of a Catholic family which cherished it as a relic of the ill-fated Queen of Scots. Some time after 1632 the Marchioness of Douglas purchased it. After her death her plate was sold by her daughter-in-law, Lady Anne Hamilton (later Duchess of Hamilton in her own right). She subsequently repurchased it and at her husband's behest had the Hamilton arms engraved on it. Today it is one of the chief exhibits in the museum at Lennoxlove, a mutely eloquent reminder of calumny and perfidy.

Ironically, Lennoxlove itself has indirect connections with the ill-fated Mary. Formerly the estate of Lethington, it was in the possession of the Maitland family from the fourteenth century, but in 1682 the one-time home of William Maitland was purchased by 'La Belle Stuart' – Frances, Duchess of Lennox and Richmond, the mistress of Charles II who modelled for the figure of Britannia on the coinage. The name was controversially changed to Lennoxlove in 1704 to symbolise the amorous propensities of the later Stuarts. Even more ironically, it later passed to the Hamiltons, once the implacable enemies of the Lennox Stewarts.

13. CAPTIVITY

1569–84

Stone walls do not a prison make
Nor iron bars a cage;
Minds innocent and quiet take
That for an hermitage.
  Richard Lovelace, *To Althea, from Prison*

On 20 January 1569 Mary was informed that Elizabeth was preparing to move her to another location 'more honourable and agreeable' to her.[1] The reason for the move was given that Mary's commissioners had communicated with Elizabeth that their queen was desperately unhappy with Bolton; but the real reason was that, having got the judicial enquiry out of the way, Elizabeth was determined to keep Mary in captivity, and to this end required something of a more permanent nature. Knollys was becoming unduly sympathetic while Elizabeth suspected Lord Scrope (whose wife was Norfolk's sister) of intriguing with the Catholic Earl of Northumberland. On 5 February, after a terrible journey made even more rigorous by the severity of the weather, Mary arrived at Tutbury Castle, about four miles north-west of Burton-on-Trent in Staffordshire. This grim pile, parts of which dated back to Anglo-Saxon times, would be demolished eighty years later, in the course of the Civil War. During the nightmare journey from Wensleydale, Lady Livingston took ill and had to be left behind; then Mary herself, suffering from a gastric ulcer, collapsed on the road between Rotherham and Chesterfield and there was a further delay while she recovered sufficiently to continue. In the midst of all this trouble Knollys's wife died, casting further gloom over the little cavalcade.

The slow progress of Mary's entourage was exacerbated by frequent changes in plans. Tutbury being not yet ready to receive her, orders were given that Mary be taken to Sheffield House, residence of her new gaoler George Talbot, Earl of Shrewsbury; but it had already been denuded of furniture to supply Tutbury, so the party were obliged to travel on to the original destination after all.

If Carlisle had been oppressive and Bolton downright uncomfortable, Tutbury was loathsome in the extreme. This vast, sprawling fortress, perched on heights with commanding views of Staffordshire and Derbyshire, had been in a ruinous condition for many years and, in spite of some feeble attempt at repairs in 1559, had been virtually uninhabitable for some time. The choice of such a prison, and the lack of attention to such details as furniture, betray the callous indifference of Elizabeth and her ministers towards their royal captive. The timber and plaster apartments where Mary was lodged were barely weather-proof and suffered from rising damp. Moreover, just beyond the castle walls was a vast swamp from which marsh gas rose to poison the atmosphere. The sanitary arrangements were primitive in the extreme, offering the worst humiliation that Mary ever had to endure. For someone in Mary's poor health, compounded by the strain of the recent trial and general depression over her increasingly harsh treatment, Tutbury could not have been a worse choice. It was small consolation to Mary that her new gaoler, Shrewsbury, was one of the English nobles more sympathetic to her cause. Indeed, it was said that he was specifically chosen for the job because he favoured Mary's succession to the English throne.

This was more than counter-balanced by his meanness. He was given an allowance of forty-five pounds a week for the care of his prisoner; any additional expenses had to come out of his own pocket. Although he was one of the richest men in England, with vast estates and many fine mansions across the midlands, he was constantly preoccupied with the minutiae of the bills incurred in looking after Mary. A nervous, fussy little man, scared of putting a foot wrong, he guarded Mary rigorously rather than conscientiously. He was also very much under the thumb of his second wife, the much-married Bess of Hardwicke, eight years his senior. Almost twice Mary's age, Bess was the most formidable businesswoman of her era, and now applied her qualities of flinty masculinity and utterly selfish arrogance to the care of her prisoner. Two people more diametrically opposed in character could not be imagined than Bess and Mary.

In fairness to Shrewsbury, he had proposed that his royal charge be lodged at his principal residence, Chatsworth, which Bess had brought to the marriage, but Queen Elizabeth vetoed that plan, no doubt on grounds of security. As if to add insult to injury, Mary was told that her personal staff would have to be considerably reduced, and she, now virtually destitute, was in no position to argue. Mary's commissioners were allowed access to her and she was also permitted to have visitors so long as their names were submitted in advance. Later she had a good stud of horses and no restraint was placed on outdoor pursuits, so long as she was closely accompanied by guards at all times.

Mary's chief occupation was sewing, a pastime in which she found common ground with Bess. Together they would sit in Bess's boudoir sewing with Agnes Livingston and Mary Seton, and their joint efforts may be admired to this day in the magnificent embroideries at Oxburgh and Hardwicke Hall.[2] After a few weeks in this ramshackle medieval pile, even the Earl and Countess of Shrewsbury could stick it no longer, and as a result it was agreed that they could transfer their prisoner to the much more salubrious Wingfield Manor near Alfreton in neighbouring Derbyshire. By this time Mary's health had deteriorated and she was suffering a recurrence of abdominal pain. Shrewsbury, with a fair degree of accuracy, described this stress-induced ailment as 'grief of the spleen'. Wingfield, however, produced no beneficial results and by late April Mary suffered a sharp decline after hearing of the barbaric treatment of her principal supporters in Scotland, who were hunted ruthlessly and put to death. Her face swelled up and she was prone to sudden fits of weeping. When she was moved to Chatsworth in May so that Wingfield could be spring-cleaned, she was so ill that the two doctors summoned to her bedside feared for her life. Shrewsbury himself was very ill that summer with gout and 'the hot ague', but whereas his illnesses were short-lived, Mary would be plagued by chronic ill-health for the rest of her life. A catalogue of illnesses becomes the recurring theme of her correspondence from now on.

Queen Elizabeth's chief aim then, and for the remaining years of Mary's life, was to render her rival politically harmless, and that was the chief reason for immuring her in the midlands, far from Scotland and equally distant from London and the royal court on which Mary had set her heart. The treatment she received from George and Bess Talbot, in the early phase at any rate, was as kind as could be expected in the circumstances, but later this deteriorated when the Earl and Countess drifted apart, and eventually Bess showed her fangs when she scurrilously denounced her captive. For Mary, prisoner though she was, still possessed the power to charm. Nicholas White, Cecil's envoy to Ireland, visited Mary at Tutbury *en route* and though, like John Knox before him, he professed to be impervious to her charm, he had to concede that 'She hath withal an alluring grace, a pretty Scotch accent, and a searching wit, clouded with mildness'. And he warned Cecil, 'Fame might move some to relieve her, and glory joined with gain might stir others to adventure much for her sake.'[3]

These were perceptive words indeed. The death of Lady Knollys – Elizabeth's cousin Catherine Grey and the main Protestant candidate for the English throne – suddenly made the Queen of Scots more attractive to the Duke of Norfolk. Ever since his conversation with Maitland in December 1568 he had nourished the ambition of marrying Mary, despite the uncertainty of the judgment and Mary's continuing captivity. Elizabeth herself had once considered Norfolk a suitable husband for Mary, before the latter had chosen Darnley instead. Just who initiated the latest scheme is not known for certain, but it appears that John Leslie, Bishop of Ross, and Maitland himself made the first moves. The idea seems to have been generally well received in Scotland, even Moray himself giving it his guarded approval initially, though he later resisted it strenuously when the possibility of his sister's restoration grew stronger as a result. By this time opposition to the dictatorial régime of Moray was growing but had not yet crystallised into rebellion. Similarly, in England, there were many nobles who resented the often arbitrary power of Cecil, and who therefore regarded the union of Mary and Norfolk as a potential counterweight. Mary's part in the ensuing plot was purely passive. She and 'My Norfolk' (as she addressed him) exchanged increasingly affectionate letters, but never met, though he did send her a huge diamond as a token of his affection. He was then aged thirty-three and a widower. What he lacked in good looks he made up for in other ways. He was the most powerful magnate in England and the only person of ducal rank. He had shown himself a wise and able administrator and military commander in the northern counties, and in the recent tribunal had acquitted himself well in the most difficult of circumstances.

Even before judgment in the case was given, Mary was taking alternative steps to secure her release. As early as 8 January 1569 she got a message to Guerau de Spes, the Spanish ambassador, to the effect that if King Philip helped her, she would be Queen of England in three months, and Mass would be said all over the country.[4] Devout Catholic though he was, Philip was even more devoted to his own interests, and at that juncture the last thing he wanted was a foreign adventure in England, whose outcome was by no means as certain as Mary suggested. In fact the predominantly Catholic northern nobility of England were heavily involved in this scheme, which envisaged setting Mary free to marry a husband of Philip's own choice, Don John of Austria being now the front-runner. As late as 15 June, Lord Dacre told Philip that if he sent a Spanish army to England, 15,000 select troops mustered in the north would be at his disposal.[5] But Philip vacillated, and the northern earls had to modify their plans, merging them with the proposal to link Mary and Norfolk in marriage.

The co-ordinator of the two distinct schemes which eventually became one was Maitland, partly to atone for his role in implicating Mary in Darnley's murder, and partly to deflect further enquiry into his own part in that crime. Beyond these immediate motives was his enduring vision of the union of the kingdoms in the person of Mary or her son. Lady Scrope and his own wife, the former Mary Fleming, also worked on him, constantly reminding him of all that Mary had done for him in the past, and hinting that she might yet do very much more for his advancement. Apart from any clandestine manoeuvring, Norfolk was also openly negotiating with Moray on 8 July to secure the annulment of Mary's marriage to Bothwell, in order that he could marry her and unite 'this land into one kingdom in time coming',[6] while Bishop Leslie brokered a deal whereby Elizabeth agreed to recommend that Mary be appointed co-regent, with Moray, in the name of King James. Both proposals were put before a convention of the Scottish Estates at Perth on 28 July, but were rejected. Considering that the reason that Mary had been imprisoned in Lochleven was her refusal to give up Bothwell, it is ironic that her desire to divorce him was now so summarily dismissed. Mary was understandably upset when apprised of this decision, but now she realised that there was absolutely no hope of an accommodation with her brother. Thereafter more serious consideration was given to her restoration by armed force.

Bishop Leslie now pressed forward with his plans to foment an uprising of the English nobility, with Norfolk at their head. Briefly this plan aimed at liberating Mary and recognising her title to the succession in England in exchange for the establishment of the Anglican form of Protestantism in Scotland. By this extraordinary compromise, a combination of Protestant and Catholic nobles of such influence was formed that on 27 August the Privy Council in England passed a resolution for the settlement of the succession to the crown on the royal captive, provided that she agree to marry Norfolk. Within months of the conference at Westminster and Hampton Court, in which these nobles had declared that Elizabeth could not permit Mary to come into her presence 'without blemish of her own honour', a majority of the Council was now declaring Mary to be the most fit and proper person to become Elizabeth's successor. It must be remembered that, at this point, Norfolk was professing his zeal for the Protestant religion. How far he was also implicated at this juncture in the plot by Catholic nobles to liberate Mary, by force if necessary, and to install her as a Catholic sovereign over England, is a matter for conjecture; but in August De Spes was informed that Norfolk, Arundel and Pembroke were promoting this venture with the support of Northumberland, Cumberland, Westmorland, Derby, Exeter, Montague and others, and that if they succeeded 'religion' would be restored.[7] Two months previously, Arundel and Lumley assured the ambassador that they would convert Norfolk to Catholicism.[8]

Mary herself assured King Philip, towards the end of August, that if she were set free she would hand herself and her son over to him. For the moment, however, she must sail with the wind, though she hastened to assure him that she would never depart from his wishes in religion or other things.[9] Meanwhile she continued her courtship by correspondence, and the warmth and affection in her letters undoubtedly turned Norfolk's head. Norfolk was no Bothwell – vain, well-meaning, insipid, timid, spineless and colourless are some of the adjectives which have been applied to him – and he was so far lacking in courage that he could not even bring himself to broach the subject of his proposed marriage, until Elizabeth (informed by Leicester of Norfolk's intentions) tried to draw him out. When she failed, her impatience exploded and after a terrific scene Norfolk was forced to withdraw from her presence. He fled to Andover, whence he wrote a placatory letter to Cecil on 15 September. Nine days later he wrote along similar lines to Elizabeth herself, saying that he had retired because he had learned that some intended his overthrow and imprisonment. This letter crossed with one from Elizabeth, ordering him immediately to report to her at Windsor.

This contretemps with Norfolk had an unfortunate outcome for Mary. As soon as Norfolk left the court, Elizabeth, still shaking with rage, gave orders to the Earl of Huntingdon to remove Mary to Tutbury again, under his special charge. Interestingly, Mary took this news calmly, boldly retorting that as Elizabeth would do nothing for her, she would see what other princes would do.[10] She was expecting an insurrection in her favour at any time, and promptly sent a message to Norfolk urging him to be bold and resolute. Sadly, Norfolk lacked Bothwell's qualities of the hero or desperado. Using the fact that Mary was now closely guarded by Huntingdon as an excuse, he wrote to Northumberland advising him to call off the planned uprising. To Elizabeth he made his excuses for not coming immediately to Windsor, saying that he was abed with the ague. Elizabeth promptly summoned him, on a litter if need be, so he had no alternative but to put aside his feigned illness and submit to her wishes. Predictably he was arrested on his way from London to Windsor and consigned to the Tower on 8 October, but as no conclusive evidence could be found against him he was never put on trial.

In November the northern nobles raised the standard of rebellion and marched south with a considerable army in order to liberate Mary. As soon as Elizabeth got wind of the uprising she had Mary suddenly sent to Coventry, a place which would subsequently become a byword for ostracism or social exclusion.[11] It had been intended to incarcerate her in Coventry Castle, but this was in an even more dilapidated condition than Tutbury, and had not been habitable since the Wars of the Roses. Accordingly, Huntingdon lodged her at the Black Bull Inn in Smithford Street, in the town centre. Elizabeth was incensed when she discovered this, since it implied something approaching a normal social life for Mary. Huntingdon was then ordered to transfer her to the upper floor of Caesar's Tower adjoining St Mary's Hall. From here Mary wrote an impassioned plea to Elizabeth on 17 December, denying complicity in the uprising which had now collapsed farcically. Mary was appalled when she heard of the plot and wrote to Northumberland imploring him to call it off, not only because it would cause unnecessary bloodshed but would not do her cause any good.

It has been alleged that in November 1569 a papal bull stated that the Bothwell marriage was null and void on the grounds that, in the eyes of the Church, he was still married to Countess Jean at the time. Moreover, he had obtained Mary's consent only by raping her. If this were true, this papal action meant that Mary was now free to marry again. In point of fact no trace of such a document has ever been found to substantiate this claim, and it may be significant that not till rumours of Bothwell's death reached her in 1576 did Mary again seriously contemplate matrimony. The rumours, of course, soon proved to be unfounded, as Bothwell lingered on for a further two years.

Further impassioned letters to Norfolk, as he languished in the Tower, were written on 9 December and 31 January 1570, and on 19 March Mary declared that if his mind did not shrink at the prospect she was ready to live and die with him.[12] Meanwhile her new gaoler, Huntingdon, was pressing the suit of his brother-in-law, none other than Robert Dudley, Earl of Leicester, on the grounds that as Elizabeth was now contemplating marriage herself, with the Duke of Anjou, this left Leicester free to marry Mary. Relaying this information to Norfolk, Mary told him angrily that Huntingdon then had the cheek to add that his own claims to the English throne should be recognised after those of Mary and James.

The growing rift between Moray and Maitland had climaxed early in September 1569 when the regent learned of the latter's intrigues with Norfolk and induced Thomas Crawford, a servant of Lennox, to testify that Maitland had been 'of counsell, foreknowledge and device' in the murder of Darnley. Maitland was arrested and imprisoned, but while he was awaiting trial, he was freed by Kirkcaldy of Grange and spirited off to Edinburgh Castle of which he was then governor. After the collapse of the rebellion of the northern earls of England, Moray wrote to Elizabeth saying that his sister was 'the ground and fountain from whom all these tumults and dangers flow' and that she should be handed over to him for safe-keeping. Before this deal could be finalised, however, fate intervened. On 11 January 1570, as he rode through Linlithgow, Moray was gunned down by an unknown assailant. Later the myth would develop that the regent had been killed by a poor man whose wife he had driven out into the snow, but in fact the assassin was James Hamilton of Bothwellhaugh who acted apparently with the connivance of Archbishop Hamilton. Bothwellhaugh had fought for

Mary at Langside and had subsequently been captured and sentenced to death but reprieved on the intercession of John Knox. As his lands were forfeited, and his wife forcibly ejected from her house, there may well be a grain of truth in the tale of the woman driven insane by her brutal eviction.

Mary wrote to Beaton at Paris soon afterwards, smugly satisfied that she was all the more indebted to the assassin in that he had acted without any instigation of hers.[13] Later, she arranged that the killer should receive a pension. Mary was not alone in supposing that Moray planned to make himself king; to this end he had tried to have his mother's union with James V legalised retrospectively. Under Moray Scotland was less stable and less ably governed than it had been under Mary; but with his death Scotland would be subject to intermittent civil war as the various factions jostled for power, and a stream of regents briefly held uneasy sway.

If Mary imagined that Moray's death promised an improvement in her personal fortunes, she was soon disillusioned. About the time of Moray's death Mary wrote her son a rather touching letter to accompany a hackney pony complete with its equipage, along with a pony from the Earl of Shrewsbury which she entrusted to two of her servants, James Lauder and Sandy Bog. Neither letter nor ponies were ever delivered, their transmission being vetoed by Elizabeth. In any case, young James was now so thoroughly brainwashed into believing that Mary had murdered his father that there was never any hope of kindling affection between mother and son.

By May 1570 Mary was back in the comparative comfort of Chatsworth. Elizabeth was now going through the motions of restoring her cousin, but these negotiations came to a halt abruptly on the publication of Bishop Leslie's pamphlet, *In Defence of Queen Mary's Honour*. Matters were not improved either, when Pope Pius V published his bull *Regnans in Excelsis*, ritually excommunicating Elizabeth and releasing her Catholic subjects from loyalty to her. A copy of this inflammatory document was mysteriously nailed to the door of the Bishop of London, and although it had nothing to do with Mary, indirectly it would have a serious impact on her future. Such was the English hold on Scottish affairs by this time that it was Elizabeth who graciously gave her permission for the Earl of Lennox to take over the regency in July, six months after Moray's death. With the accession to power of her former father-in-law, now one of her most implacable enemies, Mary must have realised that her chances of restoration were slimmer than ever. By midsummer 1570 she had been moved again, this time to Sheffield Castle, where Shrewsbury delegated her to Sir Ralph Sadler, the same Sadler who had inspected Mary as a baby almost three decades earlier.

In the autumn of 1570, bowing to diplomatic pressure from France and Spain, Elizabeth resumed her pretence of liberating Mary, but after months of prevarication the mask dropped when Elizabeth, on 23 March 1571, flatly told Mary's commissioners that she could go no further in the matter. About this time George Buchanan, at the behest of his feudal superior Lennox, published his grossly vituperative pamphlet *De Maria Scotorum Regina*, a scurrilous litany of Mary's alleged crimes. A Scots version appeared soon afterwards with the title of *Ane Detection of the Doinges of Marie Quene of Scottis*.

Meanwhile, Norfolk, who had been released from the Tower in August 1570, was intriguing with the Duke of Alva, Philip of Spain and the Pope with a view to raising a foreign expedition in aid of an English uprising. In April 1571, however, Charles Bailly, a servant of Bishop Leslie, was apprehended at Dover with coded despatches from Roberto Ridolfi, the Florentine banker employed by Norfolk as his go-between. Cecil's intelligence officers soon broke the code and revealed the extent of the Ridolfi Plot. Leslie himself was captured and interrogated; under threat of torture he blabbed everything. In his haste to make a full confession Leslie denounced his queen in terms only slightly less immoderate than Buchanan, leading his interrogator, the Master of Requests, Dr Thomas Wilson, to exclaim, 'Lord what a people are these, what a Queen, what an Ambassador.'[14] On the very same day (8 November) Leslie had the nerve to write sanctimoniously to Mary, saying that the hand of providence had exposed her and that this should teach her and her friends a sharp lesson against seeking relief by such means in the future. Leslie's life was spared, though he remained a prisoner until 1575.

Norfolk was re-arrested on 7 September 1571 and brought to trial the following January. He paid the supreme penalty on Tower Hill on 2 June 1572 and when Mary was informed she wept bitterly and took to her bed. The Earl of Shrewsbury had gone to London to participate in Norfolk's trial, so the responsibility for breaking the bad news to Mary was willingly undertaken by the hard-bitten Bess of Hardwicke. Both houses of parliament petitioned that Queen Mary should likewise be executed; but Elizabeth, touched by the ardent expressions of loyalty to herself in which the parliamentary petition was couched, was inclined on this occasion to be magnanimous. Turning down the petition, she said that 'she could not put to death the bird that had fled to her for succour from the hawk'.

Though her life was spared, Mary was now enduring much harsher conditions than previously. On his return from London, Shrewsbury, convinced that the 'passion of sickness' induced by news of Norfolk's execution was no more than pretence, tactlessly informed her of the proceedings in parliament by which a bill of attainder had been passed, stripping her of her right of succession to the English throne, and letting her know, in no uncertain terms, that if she were caught plotting again, she would be subject to a trial by peers (that is peers of the realm, not her own peers, her fellow monarchs). Soon afterwards, the news that the Catholics of France had gone on the rampage, murdering Huguenots on St Bartholomew's Day (24 August), inflamed popular opinion against the hapless Mary more than ever.

Ironically, though her own movements were restricted, Mary at least held on to her life, unlike so many of the major players back in Scotland. On 5 September 1571 Lennox was assassinated by Hamilton agents, and in due course was succeeded as regent by the Earl of Mar. Shortly afterwards, Elizabeth sent her envoy Henry Killigrew to Edinburgh to discuss with the new regent what was to be done with Queen Mary. Elizabeth proposed to hand Mary over to the Scots, on formal petition from them, so that they could have the responsibility of putting her to death themselves. Mar, who had not so long before been a true friend of the Queen, now coldly responded that Mary's execution was 'the only salve for the cures of this commonwealth'. When this proposal was put to Morton, however, he took the view that this expedient would not be a good idea, unless Elizabeth was prepared openly to avow the same responsibility for it as the Scots, and this was something that Elizabeth was not prepared to do.

Mar's attitude, in fact, shows how far the Scots (or at least those with power and influence) were now totally alienated from Mary. Even the death of John Knox on 24 November 1572 did nothing to alleviate the situation. Following the death of Mar on 29 October 1572 at Stirling the regency passed to Morton, who persecuted Catholics more ruthlessly than any of his predecessors. Morton also showed considerable energy in reducing Edinburgh Castle which, under Kirkcaldy of Grange, continued to hold out until 29 May 1573. With Kirkcaldy dangling from a gibbet at Edinburgh Cross died Mary's hopes of liberty and restoration. Maitland would have suffered the same ignominious fate had he not succumbed to malnutrition and natural causes (some sort of wasting disease that left him paralysed) shortly after the castle surrendered. It was a sad end, nevertheless, for one who had once risen so high in the trust of both queens and whose long-term ideals had been so lofty. Whatever she felt, when told of Maitland's death, Mary kept to herself, though Shrewsbury reported to London that 'She makes little show of grief, and yet it nips her near'. Whatever his past transgressions, Maitland had tried to make amends in his latter years, tirelessly intriguing on Mary's behalf. Under the brutal dictatorship of Morton, the warring factions were cowed into submission and Scotland enjoyed a decade of relative tranquillity.

Mary herself was now resigned to her role as Elizabeth's prisoner. With no prospect of release, far less restoration, she settled down to make the best of a poor situation. Elizabeth's arrangements for her comfort were about as liberal and generous as could be expected in the circumstances, but from time to time, during periods of national crisis, restrictions were placed on her movements. Nevertheless, her custodial régime was reasonably relaxed. She had a household of forty-one attendants and servants, including Lord and Lady Livingston, Mary Seton, Jane Kennedy and John Beaton (her master of the household). The grooms of the chambers included the resourceful Bastien Pages, her English secretary was Gilbert Curle and her usher was Willie Douglas. Augustine Raullet, her foreign secretary, died in August 1574 and was, after a considerable delay, replaced by Claude Nau from Lorraine. His brother Charles had earlier been in her service and he himself was highly recommended by Mary's Guise relatives. It was to Nau that Mary increasingly confided her memories, which enabled him to write one of the more useful contemporary accounts of her life and times.

There were four officers of the pantry and three of the kitchen, and Mary maintained a large stable with its own complement of three grooms and a farrier. Shrewsbury now had an allowance of fifty-two pounds a week for Mary's maintenance, but in 1575 this was suddenly, and for no reason, cut to thirty pounds. Shrewsbury, in fact, was spending up to thirty pounds a *day* on his royal prisoner and was almost ten thousand pounds a year out of pocket; yet, despite his frequent complaints to London, Elizabeth turned a deaf ear, and it was often with extreme difficulty that Shrewbury wrung the official allowance from an increasingly parsimonious government, despite warnings from Cecil's protégé Sir Francis Walsingham to his master that this was false economy: 'I pray God the abatement of the charges towards the nobleman that hath custody of the bosom serpent, hath not lessened his care in keeping her.'[15]

After being returned to Chatsworth in August 1573 the situation improved for a time, and in the following February Mary wrote to Elizabeth, assuring her that she had no desire to establish any secret relations in England. All she wanted now, she said, was to be allowed to leave the country and retire to her estates in France. Had she left it at that, Elizabeth might have felt obliged to release her, but Mary foolishly added the alternative, about re-establishing her authority in Scotland, and that was something which Elizabeth could never tolerate. Elizabeth enjoyed an even cosier relationship with Morton than she had had with Moray, and she had no wish to disturb this ideal arrangement. Elizabeth turned aside Mary's pleas, but a positive outcome of this was a further relaxation in Mary's detention. Within days of her return to Chatsworth Mary was allowed to go off to Buxton for a month's bathing in its curative waters. After her return to Chatsworth late in September, Mary asked the French ambassador, La Mothe Fenelon, to tell Elizabeth that the waters had worked wonders on her rheumatism and the chronic pain in her side. She hoped that a much longer visit to Buxton the following year would effect a complete cure.[16] This request was duly conceded, and thereafter Mary took the waters every summer up to 1584.

While these annual visits to Buxton undoubtedly did much good, it has to be admitted that Mary's health in captivity was generally poor. Severe pain in her right arm may have been arthritic, but a fall from her horse in 1580 resulted in a painful spinal injury which plagued her till the end of her life. Gastric influenza in 1581 and again in November 1582 severely weakened her constitution. The pain in her side was almost certainly the kidney disease of nephritis, while the rheumatism induced by the cold, damp climate produced such excruciating pain in her legs that by the time of her trial and execution she was virtually a cripple. By the 1580s, when Mary was barely forty, she was commonly regarded as an old and sickly woman. Tragically, Mary's frequent profession of ill health was usually dismissed as a ploy to obtain more frequent visits to Buxton, and when her physical condition was so wretched that it could not be entirely neglected, it was usually ascribed airily to hysteria. Recent examinations of Mary's various ailments have resulted in the verdict that Mary suffered from porphyria, the hereditary disease which also afflicted George III.[17]

The even tenor of her life in captivity, however, was punctuated by alarums and excursions. In November 1573, for example, she was again transferred to Sheffield as a precaution against some plot, real or imagined, which caused momentary concern in London. By the beginning of 1574 this panic had abated and she was restored to the comparative comfort of Chatsworth.

About this time Mary gave up all pretence of flirting with Protestantism, and demanded facilities for the exercise of her own faith. So convincing had been her profession of the reformed religion, especially at the time when she was cultivating Norfolk, that her guardians were sceptical about this apparent change of heart. It will be remembered that even the local Catholic community had been convinced that Mary had abandoned the true faith. Now she pleaded with La Mothe Fenelon: 'I do not joke at all in regard to so serious a matter.' The Protestant clergy in Scotland and England had been baying for her blood. Besides, after the specimens of Protestant opinions she had listened to, she had been only the more confirmed in her own faith, 'for, in truth, the only point of importance on which she had found the Protestant clergy in agreement, was in their attacks on the Pope and the Catholic princes'.[18] On 29 March 1575 Mary wrote to Archbishop James Beaton in Paris, saying that she had got hold of a French Book of Hours, corrected by the Pope, and she wished to know whether, as it was in the vulgar tongue, special permission might in the circumstances be granted for the servants to use it in their private devotions. The one practice of religion they had was the reading (Mary herself was probably the reader) of some sermons of M. Picard, to which they all assembled.[19]

Her demand for improved religious facilities was tacitly conceded, when various Catholic chaplains, disguised as servants, were allowed access to her. Sir John Moretoun and a French priest named Préau were followed by the celebrated Ninian Winzet, nominally employed as her Scottish secretary but actually her confessor. In the 1580s a Jesuit named Samerie made a number of fleeting appearances, disguised variously as a valet or a physician. It should be noted that the religious climate in England progressively deteriorated during the years of Mary's captivity. Catholicism, barely tolerated at the beginning of this period, was increasingly proscribed, and after the excommunication of Elizabeth, Catholics were harried and persecuted mercilessly. The practice of the Catholic faith became, in effect, a subversive act, subject to ruthless punishment, and it speaks volumes for Mary's tenacious adherence to her faith, not to say her courage, that she continued to flout the law in this way to the end of her days.

In the late 1570s Mary had been able to go out hunting, with the ever-watchful Shrewsbury at her elbow, but after her riding accident she was more and more housebound. Embroidery, in which she possessed considerable skill, was one pastime which gave her immense pleasure in her later years. Another was the collecting of birds and little animals whose antics were an unending source of pleasure and amusement. On one occasion she wrote to Archbishop Beaton asking for some turtle doves and Barbary fowls which she hoped to breed in England. In the same letter she mentioned that she was collecting all kinds of small birds to rear in cages. A few months later she wrote again to Beaton asking him to get her uncle, the Cardinal, to procure her a pair 'of pretty little dogs', for almost her only pleasure, besides reading and sewing, was in her small menagerie of animals.[20]

Beaton was also importuned to send to her Jean de Compiègne from Paris with dress patterns and samples of the latest fabrics. In the same letter she requested news from Italy of the latest styles in head-dresses, veils and ribbons.[21] In May 1575 Mary completed for Elizabeth the elaborate embroidery of a skirt of crimson satin in silver lace. Elizabeth duly thanked her, and expressed her admiration of the present.[22] Thus encouraged, Mary deluged her cousin with her handiwork – head-dresses, network, bracelets, tablets and cushion-covers – as well as luxury items such as French confectionery, in the pathetic hope that Elizabeth's gratitude would eventually result in her release. Elizabeth gradually became more sparing in her expressions of gratification, and finally informed Fenelon that he should remind Mary of the difference in their years, and that persons who began to grow old were accustomed to take with two hands and give with only one finger.[23]

A recurring fear of Mary's in the early years of her captivity was that Elizabeth would get her hands on her son and have him groomed as her eventual successor. Mary fervently wished that her Guise relatives would take the boy over to France where he could be raised as she had been herself. Then some day, when he was grown to manhood, he could lead an expedition against England and set her free. This was no more than a dream, but Mary cherished the thought, blissfully unaware of reality. In the spring of 1575, through George Douglas, she got in touch with Cunningham of Drumwhassel, master of James's household at Stirling Castle, with a view to transferring the boy to Dumbarton whence he could be got away to France. Unbeknown to Mary, however, Cunningham obediently revealed her plans to his patrons Argyll and Atholl who intended to keep James in Scotland, the better to serve their own interests. They and other nobles, in fact, were finding Morton's rule increasingly irksome, and used Cunningham as a means to open negotiations with Mary herself. In this lay the seeds of the intrigue that would eventually lead to the downfall of Morton.

While this plotting and intriguing was going on, Charles IX of France died in May 1575. Since his marriage, in November 1570, to Elizabeth of Austria, his interest in Mary (whom he had once adored) had diminished. With the accession of his brother Henry III, the situation promised to improve. As Duke of Anjou, he had been regarded as a friend of the Guise family and, notwithstanding Elizabeth of England's diplomatic flirtation, first with him and then his brother, the Duke of Alençon, Mary had high hopes that he would do something to help her. But as time passed, and King Henry showed little enthusiasm for her cause, Mary began to look elsewhere, and opened tentative negotiations with Spain.

In 1577, when King James was ten, Mary made a new will in which she expressed the pious hope that he would embrace the true religion and marry a Spanish princess. Indeed, it was widely rumoured that James would marry King Philip's eldest daughter, and that Mary herself would marry Philip's illegitimate half-brother, Don John, whose decisive victory over the Turks at Lepanto in 1571 had made him the darling of Christendom. It was rumoured that his next exploit would be the defeat of the English Turks (the Protestants) and his marriage to the Scottish queen so that they could reign over a united Catholic Britain. This notion was fondly nurtured by Mary herself, especially after the death of the Cardinal of Lorraine made hopes of a French deliverance even more remote. In 1577 Don John was appointed governor of the Spanish Netherlands, and the death of Bothwell in 1578 cleared the way for Mary to pursue matrimony yet again. Don John had all the masterful qualities which had endeared Bothwell to her, without any of Bothwell's faults and failings. Mary's courtship of Don John was far more brisk and businesslike than had been her pursuit of Norfolk. No letters from Mary to Don John are extant, and her frequent references to him in other correspondence are surprisingly reserved. This episode ended abruptly when Don John died of typhoid at the siege of Namur on 1 October 1578. On receipt of this latest blow, Mary took to her bed and refused food for two days.

But a Spanish connection, if not for herself, then certainly for her son, became for a time Mary's dearest wish. By inclination and upbringing, however, James was extremely unlikely to comply with his mother's wishes, but it reveals how divorced from reality Mary had become in captivity. From time to time she did receive the odd snippet of news of her son, but invariably carefully edited by the bringer of the glad tidings that he was growing up a fine boy, remarkably intelligent and precocious for his age. Fondly nurturing an image of him as a tender, loving boy who, whenever he was able, would put pressure on Elizabeth to let his mother go free, Mary probably never knew that if James ever thought of her at all it was with studied indifference. He had been brought up to believe that she was a very wicked woman who had been responsible for his father's murder, an adulteress who had abandoned him for her lover and the champion of a false, heretical religion. Eventually he saw through the wicked libels of Knox and Buchanan, and in 1584 procured the condemnation of Buchanan's writings in parliament; but long before that time the damage had been done. A succession of guardians and regents had robbed him of a normal childhood, but knowing nothing different it can hardly be wondered at that James had no tender feelings towards his mother.

Morton enjoyed the longest tenure of any of the regents during the minority of King James, but in March 1578 he was forced by a revolt (led by Argyll and Atholl) to relinquish office. Before Mary and Archbishop Beaton could exploit the situation, the young Earl of Mar seized Stirling Castle on Morton's behalf, and full-scale civil war was only averted when the various factions effected a compromise in August, whereby a council of regency was established, under Morton's chairmanship. Having had her hopes raised one moment and dashed the next was too much for Mary who wrote to Beaton on 25 September bewailing her abandonment by the Pope and France, her neglect by Spain and the evil plotting of Catherine de' Medici.

With the death of Atholl on 5 April 1579 in suspicious circumstances, Morton was once more in the ascendant, and Mary's hopes were correspondingly wrecked. In desperation she sent Claude Nau to Scotland with gifts and a letter for James, but as she addressed this to Prince James rather than King James, Nau was denied an audience, and the letter was never delivered. Nau, however, used his visit to cement relations with various nobles and make the acquaintance of others who might be helpful or sympathetic to Mary's cause. At this juncture a new player came on to the Scottish stage.

Esmé Stewart, Lord of Aubigny in France, was the third son of the third Earl of Lennox, younger brother of the late regent and thus a first cousin of Lord Darnley. Charles Stewart, Darnley's younger brother, had recently died, leaving a daughter, Arabella, by his wife Elizabeth Cavendish, herself a daughter of Bess of Hardwicke by a previous marriage. King James had conferred the earldom of Lennox on his Uncle Robert, second son of the third earl. As Robert was childless, the heir to the earldom was Esmé Stewart, who was married and had children. The death of Atholl gave Stewart the opportunity to become leader of the Scottish Catholics, but soon after he landed in Scotland it suited him better to become a Protestant.

The forfeiture of the Hamilton family, involved in one of the recent plots, thrust Esmé Stewart into the limelight as the next in line to the throne, after King James himself. At one stage Mary had toyed with the idea of using Esmé, but in her long letter to Beaton in September 1578 she advised against this, partly because she did not entirely trust the man, and partly because she did not wish to give offence to the friends of the infant Arabella, to whom she herself was devoted.[24] Whether Esmé had any real devotion to her interests or not, he was regarded as being pro-French rather than pro-Spanish, but beyond that he was, first and foremost, out for himself. On 8 September 1579 he landed at Leith and warmly congratulated his cousin James on his acceptance of the government, and he was prominent among those who greeted the King at his state entrance to Edinburgh. In a very short time he had become James's closest confidant, and decided to take up permanent residence in Scotland.

Had Esmé been devoted to her cause, Mary could hardly have wished for a better mentor for her son, but she did not trust him, and while she let him think that she countenanced him as a go-between in a proposal to marry James to the Princess of Lorraine, Mary intrigued instead with Philip of Spain, reviving the scheme to place herself and her kingdom under his protection, and marry James to some Spanish princess. This plan was tangled up with a plot involving the notorious Sir James Balfour, then in command of the Scottish troops fighting alongside the English contingent on behalf of the Dutch Protestant rebels against their Spanish overlords. Balfour was supposed to negotiate with the Spaniards to promote the Spanish match for King James. The whole thing seems wildly implausible, yet Mary was so dazzled at this prospect that she did not realise how she was being duped by the various participants, serving their own ends. In any case, the nobles who were now regrouping in opposition to Morton would never agree to let King James leave the country, recognising that his physical presence was vital to their success. The plain fact of the matter was that the cause of Queen Mary was, to them, a matter of relatively minor importance.

On 5 March 1580 Esmé Stewart became Earl of Lennox, his uncle having given up the title. About the same time, Sir James Balfour let it be known that, if he were permitted to return to Scotland from the Netherlands and resume the estates which had been declared forfeit by Morton, he would provide the evidence incriminating the regent in the murder of Darnley. Considering that, next after Bothwell himself, Balfour was probably the person most deeply implicated in that crime, it seems ironic that Balfour of all people should have been the means of bringing the regent to book for a crime which he had taken care to avoid committing himself. Compared to Balfour, Morton had been a mere onlooker in the Darnley affair. Some time before 18 March, Balfour's hints as to Morton being implicated reached the ears of Mary herself, for on that date she wrote to Beaton asking him, if possible, to get hold of Balfour's evidence, especially details of the bond which Morton had signed for the murder of her husband.[25] Balfour sent her what documentary evidence he had, which was not much, and Mary, writing again to Beaton on 20 May, suggested that Balfour should be played along, though she questioned the wisdom of attempting any venture in Scotland.

At any rate, the picture now emerging was that Bothwell's plot to murder Darnley had been aided and abetted by the Protestant lords. Balfour, after a great deal of preliminary negotiation as to the terms of his pardon, arrived at Edinburgh on 12 December 1580 and had an audience with the boy-king soon afterwards. As a result, it was arranged that Morton should be denounced by Captain James Stewart of the king's bodyguard. He was the son of Lord Ochiltree (and thus the brother-in-law of the late John Knox). Morton was duly arrested and whisked off to Dumbarton Castle to await trial. Archibald Douglas, Morton's close kinsman, was also to have been seized, but he got wind of the regent's arrest and promptly fled to England. Archibald's flight weakened the case against Morton but, nothing daunted, Balfour and the prosecutors did their best to fabricate their case. In furtherance of this, Balfour wrote to Queen Mary on 30 January 1581 asking her to produce an affidavit concerning all she had known about the Darnley murder. This, of course, was intended to nail Morton, but it was an extremely delicate matter to put to someone who was firmly believed to have been deeply involved herself. Mary supplied as much as she cared to reveal. Certainly she made no mention of the bond which Bothwell had slipped into her hand as he fled from Carberry.

On 2 June 1581 Morton was decapitated at the Cross of Edinburgh; ironically he was beheaded by the Maiden, an early form of guillotine which he himself had introduced. At the age of fifteen, James assumed the reigns of government, putting his trust in Esmé Stewart whom he now created Duke of Lennox. This man, the first in a long line of royal favourites on whom James relied throughout his life, was raised a Roman Catholic, and his appointment gave Mary once again the hope that she would soon be released; but Esmé Stewart was a convert to Protestantism, and with all the zealotry of the convert he backed James in his new National Covenant which denounced 'the usurped authority of that Roman Anti-Christ'. Even this did not satisfy the Protestant extremists led by the Ruthven family who, on 22 August 1582, kidnapped James and forced Lennox to flee to France where he died shortly afterwards. On 27 June 1583 James escaped from his captors at Falkland and made for St Andrews where he re-established his authority. The Protestant lords were ruthlessly hunted down but many of them managed to take refuge in England.

James was now under the spell of a new favourite, Captain James Stewart, his protector at St Andrews, whom he created Earl of Arran, despite the fact that the holder of that title, Queen Mary's erstwhile suitor, was still alive though insane. Another rebellion was nipped in the bud and its chief instigator, the Earl of Gowrie, who had been one of the kidnappers in the Ruthven raid of 1582, was executed. These intrigues, together with the revelations at the trial of Morton, softened James's attitude towards his mother, and he even began negotiations with the Duke of Guise and even the Pope in a bid to secure his mother's freedom. Mary, of course, welcomed this change of heart, proposed an Association (joint sovereignty of herself and James) and enlisted the support of Patrick, Master of Gray, an intimate of Archbishop Beaton and a friend of the Guise family, who visited Scotland on several occasions between 1582 and 1584 on diplomatic missions. In the autumn of 1583, for example, he had gone to Scotland with a vast quantity of Catholic vestments as part of a programme to spread the old religion. In November 1583 he had brought Esmé Stewart's son, the young Duke of Lennox, to Scotland from Paris. Understandably, the opportunist Gray ingratiated himself with King James and betrayed many of Mary's secrets to her son. Mary, unaware of this, continued to trust Gray, and fondly imagined that James would take seriously her Association project. For a time James played along with this idea, because it suited his plans, but it is doubtful whether he ever seriously entertained such a notion.

In 1583 the Duke of Guise was party to a plot to liberate Mary. This entailed the landing of foreign troops in England, to be joined by a strong force of supporters from Scotland and the north of England. The go-between in this plot was Sir Francis Throck-morton, brother of Sir Nicholas, the quondam English ambassador in Scotland, but he was betrayed by a double agent named Charles Paget. Throckmorton broke down under torture and confessed enough to implicate King Philip and the Duke of Guise, as a result of which England broke off diplomatic relations and expelled the Spanish ambassador, Bernardino de Mendoza in January 1584. This was a big enough setback for Mary, but on top of this came a scandal that threatened to blacken her character still further. At the heart of it was the unseemly wrangle between Shrewsbury and his wife Bess, the latter alleging that her husband was having an affair with his royal prisoner. The issue was further complicated by the rivalry between Mary and Bess for the affections of Arabella Stewart, and Bess sought, by her vile slanders, to deny Mary access to the little girl. There was no truth in the calumnies but Mary tried continually, through the French ambassador Castelnau, to bring pressure from France to bear on Elizabeth to take legal action against the Countess of Shrewsbury and her two sons by an earlier marriage, Charles and William Cavendish. Mary threatened to reveal all the salacious slanders of Bess against Queen Elizabeth, the malicious tittle-tattle which she had passed to Mary during those long years when the two ladies had sat together over their embroidery.[26] To this end Mary wrote a long letter to Elizabeth on 22 July detailing all the scandalous remarks attributed to Bess. This remarkable document was intercepted by Cecil, who wisely decided that it was better for all concerned that Elizabeth should not see it. Instead, he forced Bess and her sons to recant publicly, so Mary's honour was preserved without the need for a judicial enquiry. Mary, however, was the loser since she was taken out of Shrewsbury's relatively benevolent care and transferred, on 6 September, to Wingfield Manor where she found herself once more under the charge of the elderly diplomat, Sir Ralph Sadler.

That summer Mary had other, weightier matters on her mind. Delighted by her son's victory over the rebel lords, in July Mary sent Fontenay (Nau's brother-in-law) to Scotland to procure the punishment of Lindsay to whom, it will be remembered, Mary had sworn as he roughly led her from Carberry that she would have his head. James agreed that Lindsay should have exemplary punishment, but left him in possession of his head, merely incarcerating him in Tantallon Castle. James assured Fontenay that he would always have his mother's best interests at heart, though Fontenay was surprised that at no time did James enquire after Mary's health or the treatment she was receiving.

Late in October 1584 Patrick Gray was sent to London as James's ambassador, with the task of obtaining the extradition of the rebel lords who had fled to England after the failure of the Gowrie conspiracy.[27] More importantly, he was to propose a defensive league between England and Scotland, and as an earnest of his good faith, he disgorged full details of plotting on Mary's behalf. Mary, on the other hand, was under the impression that Gray was labouring mainly on her behalf. In this atmosphere of double-dealing, the final act was about to unfold.

14. THE FINAL ACT

1585–87

But, as for thee, thou false woman,
My sister and my fae,
Grim vengeance yet shall whet a sword
That thro thy soul shall gae!
　　Robert Burns, *Lament of Mary Queen of Scots*

On 13 January 1585 Mary was transferred to Tutbury, of all her prisons the one she loathed the most. In April the role of gaoler fell to Sir Amyas Paulet, a harsh Puritan who hated everything that Mary stood for. Having heard that she possessed immense powers to charm everyone with whom she came into contact, he had made up his mind in advance that this charm would have no effect on him. His first act was to rip down the royal cloth of state, above and behind Mary's chair which, as tangible evidence of her majesty, had always meant so much to her. Paulet justified his action by saying that, as the cloth had never been officially sanctioned, it had no right to be there. Paulet belonged to the no-nonsense school of prison governors who believed that 'There is no other way to do good to this people than to begin roundly with them.'[1] Paulet's father had been governor of Jersey and he himself had been English ambassador in France for three years, but his career to date had not been outstanding. His only qualification for his present appointment was his dour, uncompromising Puritanism. Whereas Mary had managed to establish a rapport with Knollys, Shrewsbury and Sadler, she never succeeded in penetrating Paulet's flinty, blinkered antagonism.

Paulet's orders from Sir Francis Walsingham were explicit: Mary was to be subjected to the strictest régime. She was no longer allowed to walk out of doors, the reason being that her habit of giving alms to the poor and other little acts of kindness had endeared her to the common people. Hitherto Mary had managed to smuggle in and out letters and messages, but now Paulet rigorously cut off even the flimsiest strand of communication. The only letters she was now permitted to receive were from the French ambassador, and of course Paulet read these first and refused to deliver them if he considered their contents improper. Throughout 1585 Mary's contact with the outside world was almost entirely broken. Those visits to the baths at Buxton, which in previous years had been so eagerly anticipated, were now terminated. When Mary complained to Elizabeth about Paulet and his harsh treatment, Elizabeth blandly replied that, as Mary had so often claimed to be ready to accept whatever served Elizabeth best, she would surely accept Paulet.[2] Paulet imposed the same harsh régime on Mary's attendants and servants, mainly to prevent illegal correspondence, but inevitably this put the Queen's household under considerable strain. Paulet also had the number of retainers reduced.

Mary's health suffered grievously under these increased privations, but Paulet was without sympathy or compassion, merely lecturing her that her ill-health was just retribution for her sins. In the matter of Mary's religious beliefs, Paulet showed himself in the worst possible light, possessing not just the dour, unreasoning bigotry of someone who refuses to acknowledge the right of people to hold sincerely convictions other than his own, but a strong element of sadism, taking a positive delight in destroying a parcel of 'abominable trash', religious trinkets which a Catholic well-wisher had sent Mary from London.

By October, word of this harsh treatment had percolated through to the French court which now brought pressure to bear on Elizabeth to have Mary transferred to a more salubrious location. Eventually Chartley Hall, about six miles north-east of Stafford and twelve miles from Tutbury, was selected. This moated manor-house was the property of the Earl of Essex who protested vigorously against this decision, with the result that the move was delayed until Christmas. Predictably, Mary went into a total decline as soon as she arrived there, and even the hard-hearted Paulet, suddenly concerned for her health, obtained for her the down mattress which she requested. Almost nine weeks elapsed before Mary was well enough to leave her bed, but with the onset of spring she gradually recovered.

Arising out of the Throckmorton Plot, in 1584 Cecil and Walsingham pushed through parliament an Act of Association, the nub of
which was that it was not necessary for Mary to be implicated in a
plot to be guilty of treason; it merely required a plot to be engineered
on her behalf, even if she had no knowledge of it herself. Having
secured this useful piece of legislation, Walsingham now began
putting together the conspiracy that would inevitably lead Mary to
the scaffold. This started out as two quite separate plots, to
assassinate Elizabeth and to liberate Mary. To achieve these ends
some sort of foreign intervention was vital, and it became a central
plank of Walsingham's plans that his agents should convince would-
be conspirators that such foreign aid was forthcoming. Conversely,
the English and Scottish Catholics in exile were duped into
believing that the subversive groups at home were much larger and
far better organised than in fact they were. Communication between
the plotters, at home and abroad, was entirely in the hands of
Walsingham's agents, many of them Catholics suborned by English
gold.

Central to Walsingham's plans were the cousins Gilbert and
George Gifford, a failed priest named John Savage and an ordained
priest named Ballard, the last-named being in close contact with
Thomas Morgan, a veteran intriguer and double agent domiciled in
Paris, who had been implicated in an assassination plot by a Dr
Parry, himself an *agent provocateur* of Cecil and Walsingham. Gilbert
Gifford had been expelled from the English College in Rome and
travelled all over Europe for some time before joining the English
College at Rheims. A man of considerable charm and a skilled
linguist, he was the ideal person to advance the Catholic cause. Soon
after landing in England in December 1585 he was arrested and
brought before Walsingham who promptly 'turned' him. Thereafter
Gifford worked directly for Walsingham; as a result Walsingham had
full details of every conspiracy almost before the conspirators
themselves.

Shortly afterwards Gifford visited the French embassy in London
and claimed that he would be able to get letters to Queen Mary. This
was a godsend, and the fact that he was lodging with Thomas
Phelippes, one of Walsingham's principal agents, was overlooked. As
a result, a package of letters – the first she had received in more than
a year – was delivered into Mary's hands on 16 January 1586. She
was then informed that the same ingenious device – a leather pouch

concealed in a beer-barrel from the local brewer – could be used to smuggle letters out of Chartley. The brewer took the cask back to Burton where Gifford received the packet and promptly took it back to Paulet, either for Phelippes to decipher on the spot, or to be forwarded to Walsingham in London. Mary's despatches were in cipher, but a skilled cryptologist like Phelippes soon cracked the code. The packet was then resealed and handed back to Gilbert Gifford who would deliver it to the French embassy as arranged. Through diplomatic channels the packet would reach Paris about eight weeks after Mary had despatched it. Incoming despatches were processed in the same way, though long before Mary received them they would have been deciphered and digested by Walsingham. This arrangement suited everyone; Mary got the latest intelligence from her supporters, Paulet's prejudices against his deceitful prisoner were confirmed, Walsingham was able to manipulate the conspirators, and even the Burton brewer was paid by both sides, thereby placing on a sound financial basis the brewery which flourishes to this day.

To be sure, there was a germ of a genuine assassination plot against Elizabeth and to the extent that she was aware of it and gave it her approval, Mary was culpable; but neither she nor any of the exiles were aware that they were being monitored and manipulated at every stage by Walsingham. At this point the separate conspiracy of young Catholics became enmeshed in the assassination plot. This plan, named after Sir Anthony Babington who was the alleged ringleader, was a rash adventure designed to liberate Queen Mary who, by this time, was regarded on the Continent as a living martyr for the faith, a symbol of the Counter-Reformation. Memories of Mary's flirtation with Protestantism had faded and her Protestant marriage to Bothwell was long forgotten. The beautiful but rather headstrong young queen had acquired an air of sanctity with the passage of the years. In maturity she had developed a philosophic attitude, piously resigned to hardship and injustice on account of her steadfast adherence to the true religion. By the late 1570s writers like Adam Blackwood and Nicholas Sanders were already engaged in what can only be described as exercises in public relations which laid the foundations for the vast Marian literature that poured forth after her death.

In this heady atmosphere, sympathy for the Scottish queen inevitably took a tangible, if incurably quixotic, form. Babington, barely twenty-five, was typical of the dashing young cavaliers who were drawn into the bold plot to liberate Mary and place her on the throne. In the spring of 1586 Babington made contact with Ballard and the continental plotters and thereafter both conspiracies became inextricably locked together, with Walsingham and his *agents provocateurs* pulling the strings. Mary was first made aware of Babington's plans in June 1586, through Fontenay (Nau's brother-in-law) and, independently, through Morgan in Paris. Mary's first letter to him, written on 25 June, was addressed vaguely to 'Master Anthony Babington, dwelling most in Derbyshire at a house of his own within two miles of Wingfield, as I doubt not you know for that in this shire he hath many friends and kinsmen.'[3] Despite such an imprecise address, Walsingham's efficient agents made sure that this letter reached the addressee on 6 July.

Babington responded with a very long and incredibly indiscreet reply, which gave comprehensive details of his plans, including the fact that the assassination of 'the usurping Competitor' was to be carried out by six of his closest friends. At that precise moment, Babington himself, with a hundred picked men, would release Mary from Chartley. Mary received these glad tidings on 14 July, after Walsingham himself had perused them. To his disappointment, Mary merely acknowledged receipt of this letter, but his patience was rewarded three days later when Mary wrote an equally long letter to Babington endorsing his plans, although she emphasised that their success hinged on sufficient help from Spain. When Phelippes read this extremely damaging letter he gleefully drew a gallows on the cover before forwarding it to Walsingham. So sure was Sir Francis that Mary would fall into this trap that he had actually written to Leicester in the Netherlands on 9 July – a week earlier – that the Scottish queen would soon be caught out in practices that would condemn her. Before sending Mary's letter on to Babington, Walsingham or his minions forged a postscript asking Sir Anthony to furnish the names and particulars of the six gentlemen detailed to assassinate Elizabeth.

Just why Mary should have committed such folly at this juncture has puzzled generations of historians and exercised the minds of apologists down the centuries. It can only be said, by way of mitigation, that Mary was at the end of her tether, both physically and mentally. Knowing that the Act of Association had virtually signed her death warrant anyway, she probably felt that she had nothing to lose in giving her approval to this hare-brained scheme. It must be remembered that she had been in almost total isolation for a year, suffering under the petty sadism of the bigoted Paulet, and was now goaded into action. It is probable that Paulet had been deliberately chosen by Walsingham to provoke Mary into rash action, so out of character with her previous caution. The last straw was the news that her son and her cousin had at long last signed a treaty of mutual defence, at Berwick on 6 July (only eleven days before Mary began writing to Babington). The treaty between James and Elizabeth completely ignored Mary and she was utterly devastated by this news. Henceforward, her intense bitterness against Elizabeth, who it seemed had now robbed her of her son's affection, was more than Mary could bear. Now, freedom was uppermost in her mind, and if this could only be accomplished through the death of Elizabeth, then so be it.

The incriminating letter reached Walsingham on Tuesday, 19 July; the following day Gilbert Gifford, his work completed, skipped the country. On 29 July Babington received the letter and a day later deciphered it with the help of his friend Chidiock Tichborne. On 3 August Babington wrote to Mary acknowledging receipt of her instructions. By the beginning of that month, however, William Wade, one of Walsingham's agents, was already at Chartley, conferring with Paulet on how best to arrest Queen Mary. On 4 August Ballard was apprehended; Babington fled but ten days later he, too, was arrested and promptly consigned to the Tower. At midnight, the bells of London pealed in triumph at the smashing of the conspiracy. After four days of torture, Babington broke down and confessed all, reconstructing every minute detail of the plot, and if he inadvertently overlooked some point, there was always Phelippes at his elbow to prompt him.

On 8 August Paulet told Mary that Sir Walter Aston had invited her to a stag hunt at his estate of Tixall. Due to bad weather, the hunt was postponed till 16 August. In the interim, we may imagine Mary's elation and anticipation of a good day out, as she made preparations to be suitably attired to meet the local gentry. Nau, flamboyant as ever, was magnificently dressed for the occasion. They were joined by Gilbert Curle, Mary's Scottish secretary, and her physician Bourgoing; Bastien Pages carried her cloak, and her groom, Hannibal Stewart, her bows and arrows. It was a beautiful day and Mary was in fine fettle, galloping ahead of the throng about a mile before she realised that Paulet was trailing far behind. Recalling that he had been ill recently, she considerately waited for him to catch up. Presently, as they rode across the moor, Mary spotted a group of riders galloping towards them. Her hopes soared as she imagined that Babington's young men were about to rescue her, but she was very sharply brought down to earth when their leader, Sir Thomas Gorges, addressed her coldly: 'Madam, the Queen my mistress finds it very strange that you, against the agreement which you made together, have undertaken against her and her estate, what she never would have thought of if she had not seen it with her own eyes.'[4]

Mary, completely taken unawares, blustered and protested her innocence, but Gorges silenced her, saying that her own servants were immediately to be taken away, because some of them were also guilty. Mary was convinced that she would be despatched on the spot; desperately she turned to Curle and Nau for help, but they were disarmed and dragged off, and Mary never saw either of them again. Only the ever-faithful Bourgoing was allowed to stay with her as she was taken to Tixall. When she suddenly realised that they were not returning to Chartley Mary tried to resist; she dismounted and collapsed in tears on the bosom of Elspeth Curle, her lady-in-waiting. For some time she refused to budge, and only remounted her horse when Paulet threatened to drag her off by force in his carriage. Mustering as much dignity as she could, Mary eventually got up, and prayed under a tree for deliverance. Bourgoing tried to comfort her, but at length she gave in when Paulet showed her his orders, signed by Elizabeth herself.

At Tixall Mary was closely confined for over a week. Bourgoing returned to Chartley the following day, but two of Mary's chamber-women and an equerry were sent to her, with some changes of clothing. Meanwhile Paulet and Wade went through Mary's papers and belongings at Chartley; the inventory compiled by Paulet shows how Mary, once renowned for her fabulous collection of jewels, was now reduced to a few pathetic trinkets and portrait miniatures.

On 25 August Mary left Tixall for Chartley. The local beggars clamoured outside the gatehouse, hoping for alms, but Mary called out, 'Alas, good people, I have nothing for you, for I am a beggar as well as you.' On returning to Chartley Mary found that her personal effects had been scattered and plundered. She did her best to comfort her weeping servants. When she found that Barbara Curle had given birth in the absence of husband Gilbert, now imprisoned in London, Mary herself baptised the infant, much to Paulet's indignation. The only thing which had not been seized was the quantity of cash which Mary kept in a cupboard to pay her servants, but on Tuesday, 13 September, this was taken by Paulet and a local magistrate, Richard Bagot. These gentlemen burst into her bed-chamber and were unmoved when Mary painfully clambered out of bed and hobbled across in her bare feet to plead with them to leave the money which she had intended for her obsequies. As Paulet left, she told him haughtily that she now had only two things left to her, and these he could never take away – her royal blood and her Catholic religion.[5]

Meanwhile, Walsingham had revealed the extent of Mary's perfidy to Elizabeth who was thrown into blind panic, unaware of the extent to which the plot was of his manufacture. Later she wrote effusively to Paulet: 'Amyas, my most faithful and careful servant, God reward thee treble fold in three double for the most troublesome charge so well discharged' in dealing with 'your wicked murderess' who would, in due course, get 'her vile deserts'.[6] In mid-September the Babington plotters were tried and condemned. Mary's name was not mentioned during the brief proceedings, not to save her any embarrassment but to stop anyone else getting ideas about assassinating Elizabeth. The conspirators, in two batches, were barbarously done to death: 'They were all cut down, their privities were cut off, bowelled alive and seeing, and quartered,' says the historian Camden. Babington delivered a Latin prayer, Tichborne made a heroic speech which moved spectators to pity, and the rope hanging Savage broke, so he had not lapsed into unconsciousness before the executioner disembowelled him. The other conspirators, Bellamy, Charnock, Dunn, Gate, Jones, Salisbury and Travers, were dragged to the scaffold on hurdles the following day but were not cut down to be drawn and quartered until they were actually dead, an act of mercy attributed to Elizabeth herself.

Nau and Curle were interrogated at length, browbeaten and cajoled into admitting the authenticity of Mary's letter to Babington. Curle, confronted with what he took to be the Queen's letters in his own fair hand, could not deny the deed. Babington had, in fact, destroyed the incriminating letters before his arrest, but Walsingham had copies, and it was a relatively simple matter to make passable forgeries of them which Curle, in his petrified state, imagined were in his handwriting. Nau and Curle saved their own skins by incriminating their mistress, a matter which mortified Mary intensely, but in the circumstances it is difficult to see how they could have avoided this. Later the story got around that Nau had sold out his mistress for seven thousand pounds and lodged in relative comfort in Walsingham's own house before being sent back to France a few months later. Back in France, Nau convinced the Guise family that he had merely bowed to the inevitable. Twenty years later he even applied to King James to have his good character vindicated. Curle fared worse, being kept in prison for a year.

During her confinement at Tixall, Mary had had time to ponder her fate and come to terms with the dire situation she found herself in. At no time had her religion meant more to her than during those terrible days, but at the end she had gained an inner strength. Realising that Elizabeth now wished her dead, Mary determined to make the most of it. At first she was afraid that her captors would poison her; surely Elizabeth would not make the mistake of bringing her to trial. But as the prospect of a trial and execution grew in her mind, Mary's hopes soared. By the time she was removed from Chartley on 21 September this conviction had grown, so that she positively looked forward to the opportunity of her martyrdom. Up to now, her life seemed to have been a succession of calamities, many of them, to be sure, of her own making; but now, as death seemed inevitable, she would transform her personal tragedy into something glorious and triumphant, something which would be remembered long after she and her rival were consigned to the history books.

At eleven o'clock on Wednesday, 21 September, under a guard of two hundred local Protestants, Mary was spirited away from Chartley by Sir Thomas Gorges and his henchman Stallenge, the Usher of Parliament. Paulet gave her no clue as to her destination, and her servants imagined that she was being taken to London. In fact her eventual destination was the great sprawling castle of Fotheringhay in Northamptonshire overlooking the River Nene. The journey took four days, and on the first night Mary was lodged at Burton in Staffordshire. The following morning, after a lengthy harangue from Gorges, Mary's anxious journey resumed. That day the cavalcade travelled barely seven miles, to Hill Hall near Abbot's Bromley. On 23 September they managed fifteen miles, Mary being put up for the night at the Angel Inn in the outskirts of Leicester. Although the corporation presented Paulet with some wine, it is significant that the ordinary townspeople gathered in murmuring sympathy for Queen Mary, and Paulet was obliged to post three armed men as a guard on his coach to prevent it being wrecked by the demonstrators. On 24 September they departed at ten o'clock and after a hard day's riding arrived late in the evening at the Rutland manor of Roger Smith.

On Sunday, 25 September, the grim cavalcade reached its destination. Built shortly after the Norman Conquest, Fotheringhay had been a Yorkist stronghold and in 1452 the birthplace of the future Richard III. In Tudor times it was exclusively used as a state prison, and Katherine of Aragon had been held there, pending her divorce. Mary was locked up in a small chamber where her terror of clandestine assassination came back to assail her; but she was mightily reassured when her servants told her that the empty staterooms were being hastily refurbished. From this she drew the conclusion that this was to be the place of her trial, and she was positively exultant at the prospect of her day in court, at long last. When Paulet came to her on 1 October to tell her that she was about to be interrogated, and that it would be best if she admitted her sins and begged for pardon, he was taken aback to find a dramatic change in her appearance and demeanour. There was a serenity about her which he found oddly disconcerting. She even managed to poke fun at him, deflating his pomposity by saying he was behaving like an adult reproving children. A portent of how she intended to conduct herself at the trial was her dignified statement:

> As a sinner, I am truly conscious of having often offended my Creator, and I beg Him to forgive me, but as Queen and Sovereign, I am aware of no fault or offence for which I have to render account to anyone here below . . . As therefore I could not offend, I do not wish for pardon; I do not seek, nor would I accept it from anyone living.[7]

On Thursday, 6 October, Mary was considerably heartened by the arrival of her steward Andrew Melville and her irrepressible valet Bastien Pages, together with his daughter Mary who was the Queen's god-daughter. Paulet asked the Queen if she would receive his own daughter. Much astonished, Her Majesty agreed. Three days later, however, she noted grimly that Paulet had now dismissed five of her male servants, including her coachman, Sharp. Clearly her travelling days were at an end.

On 8 October the commissioners appointed to try Mary met at Westminster and read transcripts of the evidence, including the Babington correspondence and the depositions of Nau and Curle. It was solemnly resolved that Queen Mary should be brought to trial under the Act of Association which provided that a commission of twenty-four peers and privy councillors might be appointed to investigate any conspiracy or attempt to hurt Elizabeth by any person pretending to the title of the crown of the realm. The punishment consisted of the forfeiture of any right to the crown, followed by execution. The commissioners were duly appointed. Shrewsbury was one of them, and when he tried to stand down, he was sharply reminded by Cecil that his failure to take part would confirm the rumours that he had been unduly lenient to his prisoner. Sir Thomas Bromley, the Lord Chancellor, unpleasantly warned Shrewsbury not to absent himself.

Even without the damning evidence, Mary realised that there was no chance of an acquittal under the terms of the Act of Association, and it was obvious to her that this would be an open and shut case. But just to make absolutely sure, the commission refused to allow the defendant any counsel, or indeed any witnesses for the defence. She was not even allowed a clerk to keep notes or help her prepare her own case. She would stand alone, a poor, helpless, defenceless woman, chronically infirm and a foreigner, ignorant of England, its laws and customs and barely understanding its language, and pitted against the best legal brains.

The trial itself was illegal, of course, for there was no precedent in national or international law for the sovereign of another country to be tried for treason. Where that sovereign had been held against her will in the first place, the just solution would have been to deport her back to her own country, but that remedy was never even contemplated. The trial also flew in the face of the basic fundamentals of English law which gave every person the right to be tried by his peers. Elizabeth alone was competent to try the case, and no amount of earls or privy councillors could be legally substituted. At the time, English lawyers tried to justify their actions by some vague reassertion of the feudal suzerainty of England over Scotland which had been claimed, with varying degrees of success, from William I to Henry VIII, but which neither the Scots nor Mary herself would ever countenance. Nearer the present day, some apologists for Elizabeth (notably the historian James A. Froude) tried to justify the trial on the ground that Mary's place in the English succession automatically conferred on Elizabeth legal rights over her, but this argument is completely undermined by the fact that at no time did Elizabeth ever acknowledge Mary's place in the succession. Significantly, this was never an argument put forward at the time of Mary's trial.

Realising that whatever semblance of legality the trial had hinged on the Act of Association, Cecil went to extraordinary lengths to bolster it. Parliament was in recess at the time and was not due to be recalled till November. In order to ensure that the Commons sat during the time of the trial, the old parliament was dissolved and writs for a new one issued on 14 September. The Commons, with a deeply engrained hatred of Mary, could then be relied upon to endorse the verdict of the commission and obscure the innate illegality of the proceedings in the eyes of the world.

The commissioners and their staff, about fifty in all, arrived at Fotheringhay over the weekend of 11–12 October. Only the most important were accommodated in the castle itself while the others lodged in the village or at the farms of Monde, Mardelemat and Nayde. Mary was given a copy of the commission which had summoned them and on Sunday, 12 October, a deputation of commissioners headed by Sir Walter Mildmay and Edward Barker, Elizabeth's lawyer, called upon her to persuade her to appear in person and acknowledge the legality of the proceedings. A letter from Elizabeth was also handed to her. In this Elizabeth argued forcibly that as Mary was in England she was subject to the laws of the country. Mary drew herself up to her full height and replied to this impudence:

> I am myself a Queen, the daughter of a King, a stranger, and the true kinswoman of the Queen of England. I came to England on my cousin's promise of assistance against my enemies and rebel subjects and was at once imprisoned . . . As an absolute Queen, I cannot submit to orders, nor can I submit to the laws of the land without injury to myself, the King my son and all other sovereign princes . . . For myself I do not recognise the laws of England nor do I know or understand them as I have often asserted. I am alone,

without counsel, or anyone to speak on my behalf. My
papers and notes have been taken from me, so that I am
destitute of all aid, taken at a disadvantage.[8]

The following morning Mary's lunch was interrupted rudely by
Sir Thomas Bromley who told her that whatever she might protest,
she was subject to the laws of England, whether as a sovereign or as
a captive, and that if she did not appear in person she would be tried
in absentia. Mary indignantly replied that she was no subject, and
that she would rather die a thousand deaths than acknowledge
herself one, as to do so would betray the majesty of kings and
virtually concede that she was bound to submit to the laws of
England even over religion. She offered to appear before parliament
itself and answer questions, rather than submit to commissioners
who, she suspected, had already condemned her unheard. Defiantly,
through her tears, she cried, 'Look to your consciences and
remember that the theatre of the world is wider than the realm of
England.'[9] She was brusquely interrupted by Cecil himself, sensitive
to the innuendo that he was sympathetic to her, on account of his
grandson William's recent visit to Rome and conversion to Catholicism, a source of immense embarrassment to Elizabeth's chief
minister. 'Will you therefore hear us or not? If you refuse, the assembled Council will continue to act according to the Commission.'
Even then, Mary would not give in, and discussion over whether
she would submit dragged on until 14 October when she finally
backed down, in order to answer personally to the single charge that
she had plotted against the person of Queen Elizabeth. In the
interim, Mary received another letter from Elizabeth, more in sorrow
than in anger as she reproached her cousin for her ingratitude,
reminding her hypocritically, 'I have maintained you and preserved
your life with the same care which I use for myself.' The letter ended
on a curiously hopeful note, 'But answer fully, and you may receive
greater favour from us.'[10] It is a matter for conjecture whether this
hint tipped the balance and decided Mary in the end to give way. In
fact, she must have been sceptical about receiving any clemency, far
less a pardon, from Elizabeth; but Mary had now reached a fatalistic
stage. They were going to execute her come what may, and it behove
her to make such a noble impression that this would be remembered
for all time. This would be her last chance to present herself for
posterity in the best possible light, given the circumstances.

Many writers have criticised Mary for changing her mind about appearing before this illegal court, but there is no doubt that, by this time, her overriding concern was to have her say at last. Her majestic deportment throughout the actual proceedings, and above all the brilliant speeches she made there, determined how future generations would regard her. Mary was not merely addressing the assembled commissioners, nor even the absent Elizabeth herself, but a much wider audience. As she stood before the bar of humanity the martyr queen never assumed a more heroic stance. By succeeding in delivering a devastating account of the ills and injustices she had endured for nineteen years, shaming her audience to the point of tears, she was able to divert attention away from the damning evidence of the Babington correspondence. She may have compromised her sovereignty by appearing there at all, but she immeasurably enhanced her image for posterity.

Mary's trial began the following morning, Wednesday, 15 October, in a large chamber immediately above the great hall. Detailed plans, drawn up by Cecil himself, show exactly where everyone was seated throughout the proceedings. At the far end was a dais, complete with a throne surmounted by the royal arms of England. Opposite the vacant throne was one of Mary's own crimson velvet chairs with a matching cushion for her feet. The chamber was partitioned by a low wooden barrier. On one side were long benches on either side of the room where Lord Chancellor Bromley, Lord Treasurer Cecil and the earls sat. In front of them sat the two premier judges and the High Baron of the Exchequer. On the left sat the barons and knights of the Privy Council, including Walsingham and Sadler, with four other judges and two doctors of civil law in front of them. A large table in front of the throne was provided for the crown officials, including the Attorney-General and the Solicitor-General, assisted by the notary Barker who arranged the mountain of documents in the case. Beyond the partition the room was occupied by the spectators, including the commissioners' servants and the ordinary people of the neighbourhood.

At nine o'clock Queen Mary was brought in under military escort. She was clad in a dress and mantle of black velvet, relieved by her white head-dress and a long white veil. Her maid, Renée de Beauregard, carried her train, but Mary was now so crippled that she had to be helped along by Melville and Bourgoing. Behind came her surgeon Jacques Gervais, her apothecary Pierre Gorion, an elderly retainer Balthasar Huylly and three of her chamberwomen, Jane Kennedy, Elizabeth Curle and Gillis Mowbray. The commissioners respectfully uncovered their heads and bowed as she passed. There was a brief awkward moment when Mary exclaimed, 'I am a queen by right of birth and my place should be there under the dais!' but she quickly recovered her composure and took her seat on the velvet chair, with Paulet and Stallenge standing guard behind her. To Melville Mary observed wryly as she gazed around the room, 'Ah! here are many counsellors, but not one for me.'[11]

Bromley opened the proceedings with a speech outlining the reasons for this trial. Mary defended herself eloquently, much as she had done before, saying that she denied the jurisdiction of the court over a queen. She also reiterated forcibly the circumstances in which she had come to England, and that she had only agreed to appear before the court in order to assert her innocence of the particular charge of conspiring against Elizabeth's life. Bromley then countered, denying that Mary had arrived in England under any promise of help, and brushing aside as futile her protests against the court's jurisdiction. The commission to try her was formally recited in Latin, and Mary again riposted that she did not approve this commission or its constitution, being based on new laws made expressly against her.

Sergeant Gawdy then narrated the events leading up to Mary's arrest, including the capture of Babington and the six assassins. Mary interjected that she had never met Babington, had never trafficked with him and knew nothing of the six men. Copies of Babington's confession and the depositions signed by Nau and Curle were then circulated. Again Mary vehemently repudiated this evidence and demanded to see the originals of her letters to Babington. As they could not be produced, she refused to accept the validity of the copies. Infirm though she may have been physically, Mary had never been more alert, dealing intuitively with the prosecutors and keeping a cool head throughout. She made a clear distinction between reasonable actions to secure her liberty and actual participation in a plot to kill Elizabeth which she vehemently denied. Rhetorically she asked the tribunal: 'Can I be responsible for the criminal projects of a few desperate men, which they planned without my knowledge or participation?'

The rest of the day was taken up with a recital of the correspondence, depositions and confessions. The prosecutors, in making

their case, indulged in long speeches addressed to the commissioners rather than Mary herself. The evidence was presented at
random, the prosecutors reading or speaking non-stop, and Mary
had no warning of what was coming next as she had not been given
the courtesy of seeing copies of the documents. In spite of these
considerable handicaps she gave a masterly account of herself,
although the strain in constantly keeping her wits about her must
have been appalling. When the question of England's ancient
suzerainty over Scotland was raised, as justification for this case,
Mary rose nobly to the occasion. To admit such suzerainty would
dishonour the memory of her own ancestors. But she conceded that
almost twenty years in captivity and failing health had robbed her of
the will to rule:

> My advancing age and bodily weakness both prevent me
> from wishing to resume the reins of government. I have
> perhaps only two or three years to live in this world, and I do
> not aspire to any public position, especially when I consider
> the pain and desperance which meet those who wish to do
> right, and act with justice and dignity in the midst of so
> perverse a generation, and when a whole world is full of
> crimes and troubles.[12]

Cecil then went off at a tangent, upbraiding Mary for never
ratifying the treaty of Edinburgh thirty years previously and accused
her of always coveting the English throne. Mary responded with a
long, well-argued speech which showed that this was a matter on
which she had given considerable thought. The main thrust of her
argument was that she had never wished to usurp the throne while
Elizabeth lived; but, on the other hand, she never had any 'scruple
of conscience in desiring the second rank as being the legitimate and
nearest heir'. There then followed a very moving passage when Mary
expressed her personal philosophy:

> I do not desire vengeance. I leave it to Him who is the just
> Avenger of the innocent and of those who suffer for His
> Name under whose power I will take shelter. I would rather
> pray with Esther than take the sword with Judith.

Then she went on to attack Walsingham whom she condemned

for inventing the ciphers and manufacturing the whole plot. As to her own letter to Babington, she repudiated it utterly. When Cecil claimed that no Catholic had been put to death for religion alone, but only for treason against the Queen, Mary engaged in a verbal duel with him, giving as good as she got. Walsingham, provoked by Mary's withering condemnation of him, defended himself with the telling sentence: 'God is my witness that as a private person I have done nothing unworthy of an honest man, and as a Secretary of State, nothing unbefitted of my duty.' Thus the distinction between public and private morality was nicely put.

Concerning the evidence of Nau and Curle, Mary angrily demanded that the two secretaries be produced as witnesses, so that she could question them directly. In the end she commented:

> For my part, I do not wish to accuse my secretaries, but I see plainly that what they have said is from fear of torture and death. Under promise of their lives and in order to save themselves, they have excused themselves at my expense, fancying that I could thereby more easily save myself, at the same time, not knowing where I was, and not suspecting the manner in which I am treated.

She also made a fine distinction between the two men, both of whom she had known so well. If Curle had done anything wrong, she argued, then he must have been forced into it by Nau whom he was afraid of displeasing. And she reiterated her demand that they be produced: 'If they were in my presence now, they would clear me on the spot of all blame.' On the face of it, the fact that her own secretaries had testified against her was very damning, but Mary strove valiantly to put this in perspective. According to Bourgoing, the trial now degenerated into total chaos as prosecutors, judges and commissioners joined in a babel of accusation and condemnation. As this hubbub rose, Mary remained in repose. Afterwards she confided to her servants that this unedifying scene had reminded her of the passion of Jesus Christ, for her accusers had treated her just as the Jews had treated Him, with shouts of 'Away with Him! Crucify Him!'. She was certain, however, that some of those present pitied her and did not say what they thought.

Many of those present the following morning would later comment on the deathly pallor of Queen Mary as she entered the courtroom. Her spirit was as strong as ever, and she immediately intimated that she wished to address the assembly personally. For many reasons, Mary was truly a legend in her own lifetime. Few present that fateful morning had seen her previous to the trial and all were curious to hear what she had to say for herself. The lords sat bareheaded, as a mark of respect, and listened very attentively to her speech.

She began by passionately denouncing the deplorable treatment she had so far received, referring scathingly to the importunity of advocates who behaved with all the chicanery of small-town lawyers. Under such circumstances she concluded, 'There is not one, I think, among you, let him be the cleverest man you will, but would be incapable of resisting or defending himself were he in my place.'[13] The morning was spent on a recapitulation of the main points from the previous day. In the afternoon some consideration was given to Mary's communication with 'Christian princes', notably Philip of Spain. Mary interrupted the court imperiously, telling them that it was none of their business even to consider the affairs of princes. When Cecil asked her how she would have acted, had a Spanish invasion been mounted, she simply replied, 'I desired nothing but my own deliverance.'

Other accusations now rained down on her, some so trivial and irrelevant as to appear ludicrous, if the overall matter had not been so serious. Through all these harangues, Mary remained calm, almost detached, as if she were a spectator at some strange perfor-mance. At an appropriate moment she reminded her audience that she herself had been blamed for being so tolerant of Protestants. 'It has been the cause of my ruin,' she said sadly, 'for my subjects became sad and haughty and abused my clemency; indeed they now complain that they were never so well off as under my government.' Warming to her theme, she declared that she had cared only for her own freedom, the Catholics and the kingdom of God, 'desiring the deliverance of the former and the defence of the latter'. She was growing old and infirm and was unlikely to live long. She did not pose a threat to anyone. As to her son James, he belonged to her and the Queen of England, and the latter could do what seemed best to her. She deplored the fact that Elizabeth had driven a wedge between her and her son, and made a telling point about the subsidies with which Elizabeth ensured his loyalty.

With that she rose gracefully from her chair and in her grandest manner, her voice ringing out through the chamber, she pardoned them for what they had done. As she passed Walsingham she conversed briefly with him, to his discomfiture, then turned again and rebuked the commissioners for their rude behaviour. Her last words, as she limped out of the courtroom, were delivered with a rueful smile: 'May God pardon you and keep me from having much to do with you.'

This brought proceedings to an end. The commissioners returned to London, to reconvene ten days later in the Star Chamber at Westminster. Mary was returned to her cramped quarters. She had had her day in court and, on the whole, she could regard it as a minor triumph. Paulet, reporting to Walsingham on 24 October, had a different view, alleging that the Scottish queen was 'never more odious than when displaying the full counterfeit charm of her character'. A few days later, when Mary was confined to her bed, Paulet wrote again: 'I deny that I have any time left the lady in her passionate speeches, but I confess I have often left her in her superfluous and idle speeches.' Impartial observers, however, would express their admiration for the courageous manner in which Mary had faced her accusers.

On 25 October the commissioners met in the Star Chamber. Now Curle and Nau appeared in person and affirmed that they had given their evidence 'frankly and voluntarily'. The commission then pronounced Mary guilty of 'compassing and imagining since June 1st diverse matters tending to the death and destruction of the Queen of England', the sole dissenting voice being that of young Lord Zouch. King James was formally dissociated from his mother's guilt and both houses of parliament now presented a petition to Elizabeth calling for the execution of the Scottish queen. Elizabeth responded with a long and ambiguously worded speech, the nub of which was that it was one thing for parliament to demand Mary's death but quite another, for Elizabeth, a fellow-sovereign, to con-cede it. Twelve days later, Elizabeth asked parliament to see whether some solution could be found, whereby the life of the Scottish queen might be spared without prejudice to her own safety. The only way out of this impasse was a royal act of clemency, but that would only be possible if Mary admitted her guilt and begged forgiveness. Successive attempts by Paulet to get Mary to confess her crimes and appeal for mercy fell on deaf ears.

On 16 November Elizabeth, after considerable soul-searching, drafted instructions to Lord Buckhurst concerning the death sentence on her cousin. On the same day Elizabeth wrote to Paulet letting him know that she was sending Buckhurst to interview Mary in the forlorn hope of wringing that vital confession from her. Three days later Buckhurst, with Robert Beale, a Clerk of the Council, came to Fotheringhay and told Mary bluntly that it was considered impossible that both she and Elizabeth should continue to live. Although Elizabeth had still not given her consent for the execution, Buckhurst urged Mary to repent, and offered her the services of the Protestant Dean or Bishop of Peterborough. Mary quietly told them that she was now ready to shed her blood for the Catholic faith. Buckhurst retorted that she would die as a traitor and not as a saint or martyr, but Mary could see that things were going exactly as she had hoped. Paulet retaliated by again removing the royal cloth of state over her chair, rudely telling her, 'You are now only a dead woman, without the dignity or honours of a Queen,' and he added insult to injury by remaining seated in her presence with his head covered. The following day he had second thoughts and offered to restore the dais and royal cloth, but Mary reproved him coldly, pointing to the crucifix which she had installed in its place. Her queenship no longer mattered to her, but her role as a martyr for the faith meant everything.

The next few weeks passed in relative tranquillity, though Mary never knew whether the next day would be her last. Much of this period was therefore spent in prayer, reading religious works and in quiet contemplation of the life to come. Mary wrote at great length to the Pope. She had done her best to live up to the ideals of her religion; now she would have the supreme opportunity, as the last representative of the Catholic faith in the royal house of Scotland and England, to make a sacrifice 'for my sins and those of this unfortunate island'.[14] On 23 November she wrote to Bernardino de Mendoza, now Spanish ambassador in Paris, assigning her rights to the English throne to King Philip if her son refused to embrace the true faith. She recommended to him her servants, charitably including Bishop Leslie, whom she had heard was now wholly destitute. As a token of their old friendship she bequeathed to Mendoza the great diamond which the Duke of Norfolk had given to her.

On the same day she wrote to her cousin Henry of Guise who, since James had betrayed her, she now regarded as her closest blood relative. She begged both Henry and Mendoza to listen carefully to the testimony of 'my poor servants', for she was afraid that Elizabeth's propagandists would try to suppress the truth of her death.

There was an element of urgency in these letters. Mary could hear the clatter of the carpenters in the great hall as they fashioned her scaffold. 'They are at present working in my hall, erecting the scaffold, I suppose, whereon I am to perform the last act of this tragedy,' she wrote to Mendoza. As it happens, a further eight weeks would pass before the final act was played. The reason for the inordinate delay was Elizabeth's anguished inability to take the ultimate decision, despite the fact that parliament had publicly announced the death sentence on 4 December, before being prorogued till the spring of 1587. Quite apart from an instinctive repugnance at the judicial murder of a fellow sovereign and close relative, Elizabeth was now greatly exercised over world opinion. Relations with Spain were now at an all-time low, and Elizabeth needed all the friends she could get; but the death of Mary might provoke France into action against her, and who could say how the Scots themselves might react.

In particular she was concerned at James's reaction. When news of his mother's arrest reached him, however, he cynically commented that she should 'drink the ale she had brewed'. Far from raising a howl of protest at the way Elizabeth was treating his mother, James now seized the opportunity to broach the subject of marriage between himself and Elizabeth, despite the fact that she was now in her fifties and at least thirty years his senior. Although Elizabeth quite properly rejected this grotesque idea, James let it be known that he approved of her actions. So far as he was concerned, his mother could be consigned to the Tower, so long as her life was not forfeited. Only after the trial and sentence was James made aware that if he opted to fight for his mother's life he would jeopardise the new-found Anglo-Scottish alliance (which was, of course, a prerequisite to his succession to the English throne).

James's reaction was neatly described by Robert Stewart, writing to the Commendator of Pittenweem from Linlithgow on 27 November. He reported the King's reaction verbatim:

His opinion apparently was 'that she had done worse evil, and far beyond her honour and duty, and he could in no wise excuse her for that conspiracy'. He added, 'She is my mother, and I love her as well as any man may do his natural mother, albeit I must hate her actions deadly.'[15]

Significantly, Stewart reported that nobility and common people alike were 'all in a miserable state' over this wretched affair. Ironically, while Elizabeth wept as never before, James remained quite dry-eyed throughout this painful period. Public opinion in Scotland was daily mounting in opposition to the execution of the once-beloved queen. All the animosity and opprobrium which had once been heaped on her was swept aside as Scottish sympathy for the unfortunate Mary increased by leaps and bounds. This was partly due to a natural feeling for a wretched woman in dire straits, and partly due to resentment that the old enemy had the temerity to meddle with Scottish sovereignty. Even James, the wisest fool in Christendom, became acutely aware of public feeling when he wrote to Elizabeth, 'Guess ye in what strait my honour will be, this disaster being perfected, since before God I already scarce dare go abroad, for crying out of the whole people.'[16]

James could easily have saved his mother by breaking off diplomatic relations with England. This was the one step which terrified Elizabeth, aware of mounting hostility abroad and growing animosity at home; but James was far more concerned about his own succession rights than his mother's life. In the telling phrase of Sir Alexander Stewart, 'he would somehow digest his mother's death'. Once Elizabeth had the assurance that, no matter how James might bluster, he would take no action to jeopardise the alliance, she was free to go ahead and authorise the execution. The garrison at Fotheringhay was augmented by seventy spearmen and fifty archers. A letter by Mary to Elizabeth dated 19 December was couched in such restrained but reproachful language that Paulet dared not send it, for fear that it would move Elizabeth to commute the sentence. He deliberately held it up, hoping that the execution would be carried out before Christmas. But the New Year came and went and still Elizabeth had not made up her mind. On 12 January 1587 Mary again wrote to Elizabeth, this time begging her to put her out of her misery, not so much for herself as for her servants on whom the strain was having a devastating effect. In the final paragraph she tantalised her cousin by asking in all innocence to whom should she confide her deathbed secrets. It seemed as if this was her last desperate throw of the dice to secure that interview with Elizabeth that had so long eluded her.

By 20 January, however, hopes were beginning to rise again. Three months had elapsed since the trial and with every day that passed it seemed less likely that Elizabeth would take the fatal decision. But the following day Paulet brutally announced that Mary's servants were to be sent away. Mary feared that Paulet meant to poison her and conveyed this to her gaoler through Bourgoing. Paulet replied indignantly that he would not take such dishonour upon himself as to exercise such cruelty or 'behave like a Turk'. In the next few days Paulet subjected Mary to further petty humiliations because she was no longer a queen but merely 'an attainted, convicted and condemned woman'.

During the night of Sunday, 29 January, the sky was lit up by a great ball of fire, which everyone took as an ill omen. The appearance of the comet did, indeed, portend Mary's death, for three days later, at Greenwich, Elizabeth sent for the senior Clerk of the Council, William Davison, with the death warrant. Davison shuffled it among other papers requiring her signature so that the Queen should not tremble at the very act of appending her name to the fatal document. Even so, Elizabeth teased him, asking if he was distressed to see her give the famous signature after so long. Davison tactfully replied that he preferred to see the death of a guilty person rather than an innocent one. Sending Davison off to the Lord Chancellor to get the Great Seal appended before taking it to Walsingham, Elizabeth joked, 'I fear the grief thereof will go near to kill him outright!' Then she instructed Davison that the execution must not be outdoors in public but within the great hall at Fotheringhay. Dismissing the clerk, she stipulated that she had no desire to hear anything more of the matter until after the execution.

Even then, Elizabeth hoped that some patriotic person would save her the embarrassment of the execution and would secretly take Mary's life. Elizabeth even insisted on this point being put to Paulet who, man of honour that he was, immediately wrote back indignantly, ending with the ringing words 'God forbid that I should make so foul a shipwreck of my conscience, or leave so great a blot on my poor posterity, to shed blood without law or warrant.'[17] When Elizabeth received this letter she howled with rage at Paulet's 'daintiness'.

The matter was now resolved by the Council; with the warrant signed and sealed, there was no need for further delay. It was entrusted to Robert Beale, a Clerk of the Council, and he, accompanied by Shrewsbury and the Earl of Kent, went to Fotheringhay on 5 February.[18] Meanwhile Walsingham dealt with the minutiae of the execution, arranging for the hire of the executioner Bull at a fee of ten pounds. Bull was despatched to Fotheringhay with his headsman's axe concealed in a trunk. Beale notified the justices of the peace as well as the Sheriff of Northampton, just to keep everything nice and legal. On Tuesday evening, 7 February, the arrival of Shrewsbury, Kent and several other prominent people at Fotheringhay threw Mary's depleted retinue into total despair.

Mary had already gone to bed when the earls and their officials arrived with their grim news. The task of telling the Queen was deputed to Shrewsbury, her old gaoler, and then Beale formally read out the warrant. At the end Mary said calmly and with regal dignity, 'I thank you for such welcome news. You will do me great good in withdrawing me from this world out of which I am very glad to go.' Placing her hand on a New Testament she solemnly protested her innocence, and when Kent objected that it was a Catholic version of the Bible, Mary said, 'If I swear on the book which I believe to be the true version, will your lordship not believe my oath more than if I were to swear on a translation in which I do not believe?'

Even at this late stage her captors would not countenance any Catholic observance. She was told that the Dean of Peterborough would be at her side to the end to rid her mind of 'these follies of popery and abomination', and when, after a heated exchange, Mary asked that her chaplain Préau be sent back to her, only to have the request turned down, Kent added, 'Your life would be the death of our religion, your death would be its life.' Mary derived some crumb of comfort at the thought that her death was regarded as so crucial in religious terms. When she asked at what hour she was to die, Shrewsbury, in a voice shaking with tears, said, 'Tomorrow morning at eight o'clock.' Mary commented that they had left her little time, and made several requests, all of which were rejected. The deputation then left hurriedly.

Mary asked for some supper, to be served as quickly as possible as she had much to do. It was a poignant meal, her remaining servants vying with each other in performing this last menial duty as best they could. In the absence of Melville, Bourgoing waited on table, the tears streaming uncontrollably down his cheeks. Mary toyed with her food, seemingly in a daze. At the end of the brief repast she asked her servants to join her in a cup of wine. As they knelt to toast her health, their tears mingled with the wine.

The Queen spent her last night going through her few meagre possessions, making up pathetic little packets which she labelled with the names of the recipients. Then she drew up her last will and testament, naming Henry of Guise, Bishop Leslie, Archbishop Beaton and Du Ruisseau, her French chancellor, as executors. Curle was to receive his marriage portion, which had never been paid, and even Nau was to get his pension, so long as his innocence could be proved. Deprived of her chaplain and unable to make a last confession, Mary dealt with this vital matter in the form of a letter to him. Her very last letter was written to her brother-in-law, King Henry III of France. This was more of a political testament, averring that her death was on account of her religion, coupled with her place in the English succession. She hoped he would get a true account of her trial and execution from her servants, and begged him to secure a benefice in France for Préau where he could end his days in prayer for his dead mistress. Just after two in the morning Mary signed and dated this letter, Wednesday, 8 February 1587.

She lay on her bed fully clothed and made no attempt to sleep. Her women were gathered around, already clad in black. Jane Kennedy read aloud the story of the good thief who ended up on the cross alongside Jesus, provoking from Mary the comment, 'In truth he was a great sinner, but not so great as I have been.' Then she closed her eyes and said no more. Sleep was impossible; apart from the ominous banging from the great hall, there was the incessant tramp, tramp, tramp of Paulet's soldiery, marching up and down outside the Queen's chamber all night, to foil any eleventh-hour attempt to rescue her.

At six o'clock, while it was still dark, Mary got up, handed over her will and distributed the packages. She embraced each of her women in turn and offered her hand to her male servants to kiss. In her tiny oratory she prayed alone, before breakfasting on bread and a little wine served to her by Bourgoing. The day dawned surprisingly sunny, with a hint of spring in the air. Shortly before nine there was a loud knock on the door, and a messenger called out that the lords were waiting for her. Quietly Mary asked for a moment to finish her prayers. Fearing that he would have to drag her, kicking and screaming, to the block, the Sheriff of Northampton, Thomas Andrews, burst into the chamber, but there found Mary kneeling in prayer before her crucifix.

Mary's groom Hannibal Stewart took down the cross and bore it in front of her as she was led to the great hall. Calmly Mary limped into the place of execution. There was an anxious moment at the antechamber when her servants were held back and Mary was told that, by orders of Elizabeth, she must die alone. At this Melville burst into tears and fell on his knees crying, 'Oh Madam, it will be the sorrowfullest message that I ever carried when I shall report that my Queen and dear mistress is dead.'

Mary brushed aside her own tears and said quietly, 'You ought to rejoice and not to weep for that the end of Mary Stewart's troubles is now done. Thou knowest, Melville, that all this world is but vanity and full of troubles and sorrows. Carry this message from me and tell my friends that I died a true woman to my religion, and like a true Scottish woman and a true French woman.' She urged Melville to go to King James and tell him that her dearest wish was to see England and Scotland united.

Mary earnestly requested Paulet and the lords to allow her servants to be with her at the end as witnesses of her courage, her constancy, her piety and firmness to her religion. Kent said this could not be granted because her servants were sure to cry out and upset the Queen herself, as well as disquieting the company. Besides, they might dip their napkins in her blood for relics, and that would never do.

'My Lord,' said Mary, 'I will give my word and promise for them that they shall not do any such thing as your Lordship hath named. Alas poor souls, it would do them good to bid me farewell.'

Her impassioned plea was finally and reluctantly rewarded, when the lords agreed that she could have six of her servants with her. Melville, Bourgoing, Gervais and Didier (an aged retainer who had been with Mary for many years), were allowed to accompany her, along with Jane Kennedy and Elspeth Curle. Mary presented a miniature portrait of her son to the governor of Fotheringhay, Sir William Fitzwilliam, who, unlike Paulet, had at all times behaved courteously towards her.

The little procession now entered the great hall itself. About three hundred pairs of eyes were fixed on the tall, majestic figure who, finding some hidden reserves of strength, progressed slowly and painfully across the floor to the scaffold. Eye-witnesses differ sharply in their descriptions, one noting that she was corpulent, flat-faced and round-shouldered, while another was charmed by 'the most beautiful princess of her time'. Mary wore a long-sleeved black satin dress with a long white veil. Her shoes were of black Spanish leather but her stockings were clocked and edged with silver and her petticoat was of crimson velvet. Two rosaries hung from her waist; round her neck was a pomander chain and an *agnus dei*. Her lustrous auburn hair peeped out below her starched white head-dress and long gossamer veil edged in lace. To the very last, Mary was every inch a queen.

In the middle of the hall stood a black-draped wooden stage, two feet high and twelve feet square. Two stools, for Shrewsbury and Kent, were placed near the back. Nearby, also draped in black, was the block, about two feet high, and a small cushioned stool on which Mary would sit while her gentlewomen disrobed her. She was escorted up the three steps on to the stage and sat inscrutably while the commission for her execution was read out. The first sign of emotion came when Dr Fletcher, Dean of Peterborough, came forward to harangue the Queen according to the Protestant rites. Mary cut him short and they argued vehemently in defence of their respective faiths.

At a sign from the earls, Fletcher knelt on the scaffold steps and began praying out loud and long. Mary ignored him and, turning to one side, began to pray aloud in Latin from her own prayerbook, involuntarily sliding off her stool on to her knees as she did so. When Fletcher wound up his peroration, Mary switched suddenly to English and prayed in ringing tones for the afflicted English Catholic Church, for her son and for Elizabeth, that she might serve God in the years to come. Kent interposed rudely: 'Madam, settle Christ Jesus in your heart and leave those trumperies!' Mary ignored this interruption and continued praying. Then she kissed the crucifix and, crossing herself, ended: 'Even as thy arms, O Jesus, were spread here upon the cross, so receive me into Thy arms of mercy, and forgive me all my sins.'

As tradition demanded, the executioners asked her to forgive them in advance for causing her death. Mary replied: 'I forgive you with all my heart, for now I hope you shall make an end of all my troubles.' Then the executioners, assisted by Jane Kennedy and Elspeth Curle, helped Mary to undress. In a red satin bodice, crimson petticoat and red sleeves, Mary knelt on the cushion. Bull made to grab the Queen's last remaining pieces of jewellery as was his perquisite, but Jane protested and Mary herself interceded, saying that Bull would be amply recompensed in cash. As the rough hands of the executioner and his assistant stripped her of her last jewels Mary remarked ruefully that she had never had such grooms of the chamber to make her ready. At this the two women began to weep and muttered Latin incantations, but Mary calmed them, saying quietly in French: 'Ne criez point pour moi. J'ai promis pour vous . . .' She bade them rejoice for her, not mourn, and then she turned to her menservants, standing on a bench alongside the scaffold, weeping and praying in French, Scots and Latin. Mary smiled and comforted them, but asked them to pray for her to the very last.

Jane Kennedy bound Mary's eyes with a white chalice veil embroidered in gold and wound it round her head like a turban so that her neck was left bare. Then the women left the scaffold. Without the slightest sign of fear, Mary knelt down again on the cushion, recited the Latin psalm In te Domino confido (In you Lord is my trust) and then felt for the block. Carefully she laid her head down upon it, positioning her chin with both hands. Then, stretching out her arms and legs, she cried out, 'In manus tuas, Domine, confide spiritum meum' (Into your hands, O Lord, I commend my spirit) several times. When her body was still at last, Bull's assistant put out his hand to steady her for the blow. Nevertheless, the first strike missed the neck and the axe bit deep into the back of Mary's head. She was heard to whisper, 'Sweet Jesus!' Bull tried again, and the second blow severed the neck, all but one sinew which he cut deftly with a sawing motion. It was a minute or two before ten o'clock on Wednesday, 8 February 1587, that Mary Queen of Scots, aged forty-four, passed from this to the next world.

Bull picked up the severed head and cried out, 'God save the Queen!' Impressionable eye-witnesses maintain that Mary's lips continued to move for fifteen minutes after death. As if this gruesome manifestation were not weird enough, the auburn tresses came away in the executioner's hand and the head fell to the floor. The auburn hair was, in fact, a wig, and now everyone saw that Mary's own hair was grey and close-cropped – 'verye graye and near powled [bald]' is how Robert Beale described it.[19] This had quite an unnerving effect on the spectators, who fell silent. Dr Fletcher alone broke the stillness as he called out, 'So perish all the Queen's enemies,' echoed by Kent with 'Such be the end of all the Queen's and all the Gospel's enemies.' By contrast Shrewsbury, who had once known Mary so well and had been more than half in love with her, sobbed silently. As the executioners began stripping the corpse before handing it over to the surgeons for embalming, one of those little animals in which Mary had taken such delight, a Skye terrier, crawled out from under her petticoat. Now it crouched beside the severed head of its mistress and howled piteously.

The gates of Fotheringhay were barred so that no one could leave. The distraught servants were escorted back to their quarters and held under lock and key. The corpse, now wrapped unceremoni- ously in the baize of the Queen's billiard table, was laid in the antechamber. The blood-spattered block and all Mary's clothing were burned and the scaffold scrubbed and scoured so that not a single bloody splinter might be left as a precious relic of the martyr queen. Even the little dog was repeatedly washed; afterwards he would not eat and wasted away. The few personal items which the executioners purloined were promptly confiscated and destroyed. So rigorous was the destruction of all potential relics, it was as if the English government were determined to erase Mary's memory altogether.

Shortly after the execution a plaster mask was taken, for future use in modelling effigies of the dead queen. A cast from this death- mask, beautifully made up by a skilled cosmetician, and crowned with an auburn wig, is displayed in Queen Mary's House at Jedburgh and gives us a tolerable impression of the still glamorous queen at the time of her death. At four o'clock Mary's heart and other organs were surgically removed and handed to the sheriff who had them buried deep within the bowels of the castle. The physician from Stamford examined the body before he embalmed it; he found the heart to be sound and the other organs satisfactory, thus con- founding Cecil's optimism that Mary would have died soon anyway. On Walsingham's instructions, the body was wrapped in waxed cloth and placed in a heavy lead coffin. Although Cecil had ordered that the coffin should be kept on an upper shelf in Fotheringhay Church it was merely left in the castle, unburied.

Only Lord Talbot, Shrewsbury's son, was allowed to leave the castle. At one o'clock he galloped off to London to break the news to Elizabeth and reached Greenwich about nine the following morning. When informed what had happened, Elizabeth's immediate reaction was great anger, and then terrible distress, as she wept profusely and put on her mourning weeds. Then she turned venomously on the unfortunate Davison, threw him into prison for presuming to use the warrant which she had signed, and subsequently fined him ten thousand pounds for his temerity. Elizabeth kept up a great show of grief – presumably her conscience was tweaked – but the citizens of London rang bells, lit bonfires and held impromptu street parties to celebrate the death of the woman they had been brainwashed so long to hate.

Contrary to Mary's wishes, her servants were not permitted to return to France or Scotland but were held for several months in even more rigorous confinement than before.

Amyas Paulet was made a Knight of the Most Noble Order of the Garter for his services above and beyond the call of duty. All English ports were sealed for three weeks after Mary's execution, and it was not till early March that the French ambassador Châteauneuf could send the doleful news to King Henry who immediately ordered a requiem Mass in Notre-Dame and national mourning. Meanwhile, Mendoza had somehow received news from Mary's servants of her heroic death and this lost nothing in the retelling. There were spontaneous mass demonstrations in the Paris streets as the people called for her immediate canonisation.

When Mary's son was given the news, he is said to have remarked gleefully to his courtiers, 'Now I am sole King!'[20] The Scottish people, on the other hand, reacted with greater sympathy and spirit, smarting with humiliation at the affront to their independence. When James went through the motions of declaring a period of court mourning, the Earl of Sinclair appeared before him in a suit of armour. The King enquired whether he had seen the order for mourning, to which Sinclair retorted, 'This *is* the proper mourning for the Queen of Scotland!' Walsingham received disconcerting rumours from his agents that the Hamilton faction were raising a large army and intended to burn Newcastle as a reprisal. When Sir Robert Carey was sent north by Elizabeth to present her excuses, James refused at first to grant him an audience, but diplomatic relations were never severed and, so far as the new Anglo-Scottish alliance was concerned, it was business as usual.

Mary's wishes, that her body be interred in France, at Rheims or Paris, were ignored. Five months after the execution, her coffin was at last removed from Fotheringhay in the dead of night and taken to Peterborough, where it was interred in the Cathedral in a Protestant ceremony organised by the Garter King of Arms, who imported heralds, nobles and mourners (including a hundred black-veiled widows) from London. Queen Elizabeth picked up the bill for £321. Other than the ladies of Mary's household, no Scots were present at this belated funeral.

In October Mary's attendants and servants were repatriated and the farewell letters, written eleven months earlier, were finally delivered. Gorion gave Mendoza the Norfolk diamond, and Mendoza handed it over to King Philip who honoured Mary's memory by paying her servants' wages and settling her debts in France. Firmly believing the story that Mary, on the eve of her execution, had disinherited her own son and thus transmitted her claims to the English throne to himself, Philip II gave orders for the great invasion of England, popularly known as the Spanish Armada. Defeated by the English weather as much as by English seamanship, it would be the last great seaborne assault by an enemy power on England.

Jane Kennedy returned to Scotland and later married Andrew Melville, Mary's steward. In 1589 she was despatched by King James to bring back his bride Princess Anne of Denmark, but she was drowned when the ship was wrecked in a storm on the outward voyage. Gillis Mowbray also went back to Scotland where she married Sir John Smith of Barnton. Her mementoes of Queen Mary, as part of the Penicuik Bequest, are now preserved in the Royal Museum of Scotland. Her sister Barbara, who had given birth at Fotheringhay, was in due course reunited with her husband Gilbert Curle and together they lived with Gilbert's sister Elspeth in Antwerp. Gilbert died in 1609, but Barbara lived till 1616 and Elspeth till 1620. Elspeth Curle commissioned a life-sized portrait of Queen Mary at the time of her execution and bequeathed it to her nephew, the Jesuit Hippolytus Curle, who presented it to the Scots College at Douai. Elspeth and her friend Jane Kennedy appear on the right. The painting survived the French Revolution and is now preserved at Blairs College, Aberdeen. A joint memorial to Elspeth and Barbara Curle, incorporating a portrait of Queen Mary, may be seen in St Andrew's Church, Antwerp.

Fotheringhay Castle was never occupied again. As it gradually fell into decay its masonry was purloined by local masons and builders, though Sir Robert Cotton acquired the great hall intact and incorporated it into his own mansion at Connington in Huntingdonshire (demolished in the eighteenth century). There is absolutely no truth in the historian Camden's loyal statement that King James had Fotheringhay razed to the ground to avenge the shameful crime against his mother. All that can be seen today is a grassy mound where the keep once stood, and a solitary piece of masonry encased in railings bearing two small private plaques, installed in 1913 by the Richard III Society and the Stuart History Society and respectively commemorating the birth of Richard III and the death of Mary Queen of Scots, ironically two of the most maligned and least understood of all British monarchs.

In August 1603 James VI, King of Scots, now transformed into King James I of England, sent a velvet pall to Peterborough to be hung over his mother's grave. Having erected an elaborate monument to Elizabeth in Westminster Abbey, James bowed to the pressure of his court and commissioned a similar honour for his mother. In September 1612 her remains were brought from Peterborough and re-interred in Westminster in a magnificent tomb by Cornelius and William Cure, costing two thousand pounds. Cannily, King James insisted that the velvet pall be taken from Peterborough and re-employed in the new setting. Mary's armorial bearings in Peterborough were destroyed by Puritan iconoclasts during the Civil War, but her quarter of a century in Peterborough is today marked by a stone slab.

In Westminster Abbey the mortal remains of Elizabeth and Mary lie close together, united in death as they never were in life. Mary's tomb is surmounted by a recumbent effigy in white marble under a huge decorated canopy. The effigy is regarded as an excellent likeness, presumably based on the original death-mask, and the overall impression is one of serenity and majesty. Within a decade of her re-interment, pious Catholics were making a surreptitious pilgrimage to the tomb of the martyr queen and many miracles were being ascribed to this shrine. In 1867, during a search of the Abbey for the tomb of James VI and I, the vault under his mother's monument was opened. James's coffin was absent (it was, in fact, later found in the tomb of Henry VII), but alongside Mary's lead sarcophagus was an enormous heap of lead coffins, large and small, as well as funerary urns, cluttered haphazardly. Here, in fact, were many of Mary's descendants, including the first ten offspring of James VII and II, Queen Anne's eighteen still-born babies, as well as Elizabeth, the Winter Queen of Bohemia, and her son, the dashing cavalier Prince Rupert of the Rhine. Here lie Arabella Stewart and even a child named as Lord Darnley, apparently an illegitimate son of James II.[21]

She who never reigned in England has been the ancestor of all eighteen British monarchs through thirteen generations since 1603. The subject of violent polemical writing in her own lifetime, she has inspired white-hot controversy ever since, although the emergence of a more rational, balanced view in recent years has largely taken the heat out of the debate. If Mary has for far too long been the grindstone for many a religio-political axe, biased one way or the other, she has also attracted an inordinate amount of attention from poets, novelists and playwrights, from Pope Urban VIII to Liz Lochhead, from Friedrich Schiller to Hal Wallis. She has been endlessly reincarnated in many different media, from painting and sculpture to the cinema and television. Mary Stewart may not be as controversial a figure nowadays as she was even a century ago, but she continues to fascinate each new generation, not only in the land of her birth, but to the far corners of the globe.

As Scotland takes a step towards recreating its national identity, the life and times of Mary assume a new relevance. By the conscious decisions of who she married and when, Mary influenced the course of Scottish history. Had her marriage to Francis lasted and produced heirs, Scotland might have become a French appanage. A marriage with Frederik of Denmark or Erik of Sweden might have produced a Scoto-Scandinavian alignment stretching from Greenland to Pomerania. If she had relinquished her Scottish throne and remained in France, the Duke of Hamilton might today be the monarch of an independent Scottish kingdom. The present Duke himself has described these ifs as 'futile speculation',[22] but in any number of possible permutations and combinations of alliances and marital unions, there might never have been a Union of the Crowns in 1603 and certainly no Act of Union in 1707.

It has been Scotland's misfortune to share an island with a much larger, more populous and infinitely more powerful nation. But for the accidents of birth, marriage and death four centuries ago, Scotland might well be a very different place today. Today the Scots share with the Basques and the Kurds the unenviable distinction of being a nation without having a sovereign, independent state. Ironically, religion is one of those things that gives the Scots a separate identity: not only the Protestant Church which John Knox created, but a Catholic Church whose status is recognised by having its own cardinal, distinct from the authority of York or Westminster.

Mary Queen of Scots, whose own spirit of tolerance and ecumenism was so far ahead of her times, would surely have approved.

SELECT BIBLIOGRAPHY

Primary Printed Sources

Accounts of the Lord High Treasurer of Scotland, HMSO, 1916

Acts of the Parliament of Scotland (ed. T. Thomson), Edinburgh, 1814

Bannatyne Miscellany, Bannatyne Club, 1827

Blackwood, Adam, *Martyre de la Royne D'Escosse, 1588* (English Recusant Literature, vol. 391)

Bothwell, James Hepburn, 4th Earl of, *Les Affaires du Conte de Boduel*, Bannatyne Club, 1829

Brantôme, Pierre de, *The Book of the Ladies* (trans. Katharine Wormeley), London, 1899

—— *Oeuvres Complètes*, Paris, 1823

Buchanan, George, *Ane Detection of the Actions of Mary Queen of Scots*, London, 1721

Calendar of State Papers Domestic, 1547-1580 (ed. Robert Lemor), London, 1856

Calendar of State Papers Domestic, James I (ed. Mary Green), London, 1857

Calendar of State Papers Foreign, Edward VI (ed. W. Turnbull), London, 1861

Calendar of Letters and State Papers Relating to English Affairs (Rome), 1558-1587 (ed. J.M. Rigg), London, 1971

Calendar of State Papers, Foreign Series, 1566-1568 (ed. Allan J. Crosby), London, 1871

Calendar of State Papers Relating to Scotland and Mary Queen of Scots, 2 vols. (ed. Joseph Bain), Edinburgh, 1898, 1900

Calendar of State Papers Spanish (ed. M.A.S. Hume), London, 1892

Calendar of State Papers Venetian, vol. VII, 1558-1580 (ed. Rawdon Brown and G. Cavendish-Bentinck), HMSO, 1890

Camden, William, *Annales* (trans. Abraham Darcie), London, 1625

Diurnal of Remarkable Occurrents, Bannatyne Club, Edinburgh, 1833

Hamilton Papers (ed. Joseph Bain), Edinburgh, 1890

Herries, Lord, *Historical Memoirs* (ed. Robert Pitcairn), Abbotsford Club, 1836

Inventaires de la Royne Descosse (ed. Joseph Robertson), Bannatyne Club, 1863

Leslie, John, Bishop of Ross, *The Historie of Scotland* (ed. E.G. Gody and William Murison), 2 vols., Scottish Text Society, Edinburgh, 1895

Letters and Papers, Foreign and Domestic, of the Reign of Henry VIII (ed. James Gairdner and R.H. Brodie), vol. 18, HMSO, 1901-2

Nau, Claude, *The History of Mary Stewart* (ed. Joseph Stevenson), Edinburgh, 1883

Pitcairn, Robert, *Criminal Trials in Scotland, 1488-1624*, vol. I, Bannatyne Club, Edinburgh, 1833

Register of the Privy Council of Scotland, vol. I, 1545-1569 (ed. John Hill Burton), Edinburgh, 1877

State Papers and Letters of Sir Ralph Sadler (ed. A. Clifford), Edinburgh, 1809

Secondary Printed Works

Bingham, Caroline, *Mary, Queen of Scots*, London, 1969

—— *Darnley*, London, 1995

Blake, William, *William Maitland of Lethington, 1528-1573*, Studies in British History, vol. 17, Lampeter, 1990

Bowen, Marjorie, *Mary, Queen of Scots*, London, 1934

Breeze, David, *A Queen's Progress*, HMSO, 1987

Cowan, Ian B., *The Enigma of Mary Stuart*, London, 1971

—— *Mary Queen of Scots*, Edinburgh, 1987

Cowan, Samuel, *The Last Days of Mary Stuart*, London, 1907

Davison, M.H. Armstrong, *The Casket Letters*, London, 1965

Dickinson, W. Croft, Donaldson, Gordon and Milne, Isobel, *A Source Book of Scottish History*, vol. II, Edinburgh, 1958

Donaldson, Gordon, *The Scottish Reformation*, Cambridge, 1960

—— *Scotland: James V to James VII*, Edinburgh, 1965

—— *The First Trial of Mary Queen of Scots*, London, 1969

—— *Mary Queen of Scots*, London, 1974

—— *All the Queen's Men: Power and Politics in Mary Stewart's Scotland*, London, 1983

Drummond, Humphrey, *The Queen's Man: James Hepburn, Earl of Bothwell and Duke of Orkney 1536–1578*, London, 1975

Fleming, D. Hay, *Mary, Queen of Scots*, London, 1897

Forbes-Leith, W., *Narratives of Scottish Catholics under Mary Stuart and James VI*, Edinburgh, 1885

Franklin, David, *The Scottish Regency and the Earl of Arran*, Studies in British History, vol. 35, Lampeter, 1995

Fraser, Lady Antonia, *Mary Queen of Scots*, London, 1969

Gatherer, W.A., *Tyrannous Reign of Mary Stewart, extracts from George Buchanan's History*, Edinburgh, 1958

Gore-Browne, Robert, *Lord Bothwell*, London, 1937

Hamilton, Angus, Duke of, *Mary Queen of Scots: the Crucial Years*, Edinburgh, 1991

Henderson, T.F., *The Casket Letters*, London, 1890

—— *Mary, Queen of Scots*, 2 vols, London, 1905

Hosack, John, *Mary Queen of Scots and her Accusers*, London, 1874

Hume, Martin, *The Love Affairs of Mary Queen of Scots*, London, 1903

Knox, John, *History of the Reformation in Scotland* (ed. W. Croft Dickinson), Edinburgh, 1949

Labanoff, Prince A., *Lettres et Mémoires de Marie, Reine d'Ecosse*, 7 vols, London, 1844

Laing, David (ed.), *The Works of John Knox*, Edinburgh, 1895

Lang, Andrew, *Mystery of Mary Stewart*, London, 1901, revised 1912

—— *Portraits and Jewels of Mary Stuart*, Glasgow, 1906

Lee, Maurice, *James Stewart, Earl of Moray*, New York, 1953

Lindesay of Pitscottie, Robert, *The Historie and Cronicles of Scotland*, Edinburgh Text Society, 1899-1911

Linklater, Eric, *Mary, Queen of Scots*, Edinburgh, 1933

Lynch, Michael (ed.), *Mary Stewart: Queen in Three Kingdoms*, Oxford, 1988

MacCunn, Florence A., *Mary Stuart*, London, 1905

MacNalty, Sir Arthur S., *Mary Queen of Scots: The Daughter of Debate*, London, 1960

Mahon, General R.H., *Indictments of Mary Queen of Scots*, Cambridge, 1923

—— *Mary Queen of Scots: A Study of the Lennox Narrative*, Cambridge, 1924

—— *The Tragedy of Kirk o' Field*, Cambridge, 1930

Marshall, Rosalind K., *Queen of Scots*, HMSO, 1986

—— *Mary of Guise*, London, 1977

Melville, Sir James of Halhill, *Memoirs of his own Life*, Bannatyne Club, Edinburgh, 1827

Morris, John, *Sir Amias Poulet, Keeper of Mary Queen of Scots*, London, 1874

Morrison, N. Brysson, *Mary Queen of Scots*, London, 1960

Mumby, Frank A., *The Fall of Mary Stuart*, London, 1921

Phillips, James E., *Images of a Queen*, Los Angeles, 1964

Plowden, Alison, *Two Queens in One Isle*, Brighton, 1984

Pollen, J.H., *Papal Negotiations with Mary Queen of Scots*, Edinburgh, 1901

—— *Mary Queen of Scots and the Babington Plot*, Edinburgh, 1922

Read, Conyers, *Mr Secretary Walsingham*, 3 vols, Oxford, 1925

—— *Mr Secretary Cecil and Queen Elizabeth*, London, 1955

Ridley, Jasper, *John Knox*, Oxford, 1968

Sanderson, Margaret, *Cardinal of Scotland: David Beaton*, Edinburgh, 1986

—— *Mary Stewart's People*, Edinburgh, 1987

Strong, Roy and Oman, Julia, *Mary Queen of Scots*, London, 1972

Teulet, Alexandre (ed.), *Lettres de Marie Stuart*, Paris, 1859

—— *Relations politiques de la France et de l'Espagne avec l'Ecosse au 16e siècle*, Paris, 1862

Thomson, George M., *The Crime of Mary Stewart*, London, 1967

Turner, Sir George, *Mary Stuart, Forgotten Forgeries*, London, 1933

Wormald, Jenny, *Mary Queen of Scots: A Study in Failure*, London, 1988

Zweig, Stefan, *The Queen of Scots*, London, 1935

NOTES

Introduction
1. Friedrich Schiller, author of the play *Maria Stuart*

1. Rough Wooing, 1542–47
1. John Knox, *The History of the Reformation* (ed. W. Croft Dickinson), Edinburgh, 1849 (hereafter referred to as Knox), vol. I, p.28
2. Quoted by Gordon Donaldson, *Mary Queen of Scots* (1974), p.17. His book (pp.10-22) contains the best summary of the early years of Queen Mary, usually treated cursorily, if at all, by other writers
3. Robert Lindesay of Pitscottie, *The Historie and Cronicles of Scotland*, Scottish Text Society, 1899-1911 (hereafter referred to as Pitscottie), vol. I, p.394
4. Bishop John Leslie, *Historie* (hereafter referred to as Leslie), vol. II, p.259 gives 7 December, whereas Knox, vol. I, p.39 gives 8 December. The former had access to special records. It is probable that the date of birth was conveniently moved to 8 December, the feast of the Virgin Mary. MQS herself always believed that she was born on 8 December
5. Knox, I, p.38
6. Letters of Lisle to Henry VIII from Alnwick, 12 December 1542. Chapuys, imperial ambassador in London, to the Queen of Hungary, 23 December, quoted in *Hamilton Papers*, (ed. Joseph Bain), vol. I, p.328, and CSP Spanish, VI, p.189
7. *State Papers of Sir Ralph Sadler*, (ed. A.

Clifford), Edinburgh, 1809, vol. I, p.88
8. Knox, I, p.50
9. *Hamilton Papers*, II, p.33
10. Leslie, II, p.310
11. Sir John Dalyell, *Fragments of Scottish History*, Edinburgh, 1798: The Late Expedition in Scotland, despatches to Lord Russell, Lord Privy Seal, 1544
12. Archive di Stati di Napoli, Carte Famesiane, tascio 709
13. Pitscottie, II, p.84
14. This was part of a general French takeover of Scotland at this time. Effectively, Scotland became a French protectorate for the next 13 years
15. CSP Scottish I, p.157
16. Hamilton Papers II, p.618
17. W.M. Bryce, 'Voyage of Mary Queen of Scots in 1548', in *English Historical Review*, XXII (1907)

2. France, 1548–60
1. *Lettres de Diane de Poytiers*, (ed. G. Guiffrey), Paris, 1866 (hereafter referred to as Guiffrey), p.33
2. *Lettres de Catherine de Medicis*, (ed. M. de la Ferrière), Paris, p.liv
3. Pierre de Brantôme, *Oeuvres Complètes* (ed. Bouchon), Paris, 1823 (hereafter referred to as Brantôme), vol. II, p.135
4. Ibid., p.134
5. For conflicting accounts of this affair see A. Teulet, *Relations*, vol. I, pp.260-70, CSP Edward VI, p.97, and Francisque Michel, *Les Ecossais en France*, Paris, 1862, vol. I, pp.114-15.
6. Quoted in translation by T.F. Henderson, *Mary Queen of Scots*, Edinburgh, 1900 (hereafter referred to

as Henderson), vol. I, p.78
7. Brantôme, II, p.135
8. Guiffrey, p.10
9. Labanoff, Prince A., *Lettres et Mémoires de Marie, Reine d'Ecosse*, London, 1844 (hereafter referred to as Labanoff), I, p.42
10. Sir James Melville, *Memoirs*, hereafter referred to as Melville, p.21
11. Knox, *Works*, I, p.242. The original is in Scots and I have here rendered the text into English for the sake of clarity
12. CSP Venetian, VI, no. 552
13. A. Baschet, *La Diplomatie Venetienne*, Paris, 1862, p.486
14. *Acts of the Parliament of Scotland*, II, pp.504-19
15. Brantôme, II, p.136
16. For detailed accounts of the marriage ceremony and its attendant celebrations see *Discours du Grande et Magnifique Triomphe*, Rouen, 1558, reprinted by the Roxburghe Club, 1818; Teulet's *Relations*, I, pp.302-11 and CSP Venetian, 1557-8, no. 1216.
17. The English claim to the French throne, in fact, dated from the reign of Edward III (1327-77) by virtue of his descent from the Valois kings through his mother Isabella. It was quietly dropped at the end of the eighteenth century, a few years after Louis XVI had lost his head during the French Revolution, when Britain was giving sanctuary to the surviving Bourbons
18. For the text of this correspondence see Labanoff, I, pp.62-5
19. Alphonse de Ruble, *La Première jeuness de Marie Stuart*, Paris, 1891, pp.187-8
20. CSP Venetian, 1558-60, nos. 207, 209 and 211

3. Widowhood, 1560-61
1. CSP Venetian, 1558-60, no. 215
2. Labanoff, I, p.91
3. CSP Venetian, 1558-60, no. 233
4. Brantôme, II, p.136
5. CSP Scottish, I, p.427
6. Ibid., I, pp.511, 518. See also Hardwicke State Papers, vol. I (1778), p.174
7. CSP Foreign, III, no. 833 (5)
8. Knox, *Works*, II, pp.142-3
9. CSP Scottish, I, p.534
10. CSP Foreign, III, no. 1030 (23)
11. J.H. Pollen, *Papal Negotiations*, Scottish History Series, 1901 (hereafter

referred to as *Papal Negotiations*), pp.62-3
12. CSP Foreign, IV, no. 133
13. Labanoff, I, p.94
14. CSP Foreign, IV, no. 263 (3)
15. CSP Scottish, I, p.540
16. Ibid, p.541
17. British Library, Additional MSS 35,830 f.146
18. CSP Foreign, IV, no. 455
19. Knox, *Works*, II, p.264
20. Ibid., p.270

4. Mary and Elizabeth, 1561-62
1. Knox, *Works*, II, p.277
2. Ibid., p.288
3. *Diurnal of Occurrents*, hereafter referred to as *Diurnal*, p.67
4. Knox, *Works*, II, p.288
5. CSP Scottish, I, p.555
6. Edinburgh Town Council Records, 1557-71, p.215. The original text is in Scots which I have quoted in an English translation.
7. Knox, *Works*, VI, p.132
8. CSP Scottish, I, pp.322-3
9. Henderson, I, p.193
10. British Library, Additional MSS 35,125, f.8
11. Labanoff, I, pp.123-7
12. CSP Scottish, I, pp.609-10

5. Hamiltons and Gordons, 1562-63
1. Knox, *Works*, II, p.227
2. CSP Scottish, I, p.569
3. Ibid., p.597
4. Ibid., p.609
5. Knox, *Works*, II, p.325
6. Pollen, *Papal Negotiations*, p.154
7. French journal of James Ogilvy of Cardell, in Chalmers MSS, University of Edinburgh
8. CSP Scottish, I, p.651 contains Randolph's vivid, if badly spelled, description of MQS at Inverness
9. Ibid., I, p.656
10. Ibid., I, p.658
11. Ibid., I. p.665
12. Chalmers MSS, op. cit.
13. *Papal Negotiations*, p.156
14. CSP Spanish, 1558-67, p.270
15. Labanoff, I, pp.175-80
16. CSP Scottish, I, p.663
17. Ibid., p.666
18. CSP Spanish, 1558-67, p.263
19. CSP Scottish, I, pp.672-3
20. Knox, *Works* II, p.330

6. Marriage Prospects, 1563–65
1. CSP Spanish, 1558-67, p.314.
2. CSP Scottish, I, p.669
3. Knox, *Works*, II, p.368
4. According to Brantôme, II, p.148, who was not a witness. Widely circulated, this story appears in Knox, *Works*, II, p.369, whose version characteristically has its own insinuation: 'O cruelle Dame; that is, cruell mistress. What that complaint imported, lovers may divine'.
5. Teulet, *Relations*, V, p.5
6. CSP Scottish, II, p.2
7. CSP Spanish, 1558-67, p.422
8. Ibid., pp.339-40
9. Ibid., pp.332-3
10. CSP Scottish, II, p.30
11. Henderson, I, p.269
12. Knox, *Works*, II, p.381
13. Ibid., p.382. I have rendered the text in English as the original Scots is particularly difficult to follow. Knox's spelling tends to degenerate when he is unduly excited
14. CSP Spanish, 1558-67, p.315
15. CSP Scottish, II, pp.19-20
16. Ibid., p.23
17. Ibid.
18. CSP Spanish, 1558-67, p.371
19. CSP Scottish, I, p.59
20. Ibid., p.65
21. Ibid., pp.67-9
22. Melville, p.117
23. Ibid., p.129
24. CSP Scottish, II, pp.96-7
25. Ibid., II, p.118

7. An Ideal Husband, 1565
1. Melville, p.134
2. CSP Scottish, II, p.136
3. Henderson, I, p.310
4. CSP Scottish, II, p.40
5. Opinion is divided regarding Knox's age, various dates of birth from 1505 to 1514 having been suggested
6. Ibid., p.54
7. Nicol Burne, *Disputation concerning the Controversit Headdis of Religion*, Edinburgh, 1581
8. CSP Scottish, II, p.140
9. Ibid., p.151
10. Ibid. P.159
11. Ibid. p.172
12. T. Wright, *Queen Elizabeth and her Times*, London, 1838, I, pp.202-3
13. British Library Additional MSS 35,123 f.14

8. The Riccio Affair, 1565–66
1. See John Glen, *Early Scottish Melodies*, Edinburgh, 1900, for a careful examination of this claim
2. CSP Scottish, II, p.101
3. Labanoff, VII, p.298
4. CSP Scottish, II, p.223
5. Report of De Foix, 13 October 1563, in Teulet's *Relations*, II, p.243
6. CSP Scottish, II, p.216
7. Labanoff, I, pp.281-3; *Papal Negotiations*, pp.208-12
8. *Papal Negotiations*, pp.213-15
9. Labanoff, VII, pp.8-10
10. Teulet, *Relations*, p.267, as reported by De Foix
11. Melville, p.147
12. J. McCrie, *Knox*, Edinburgh, 1850, p.283
13. CSP Scottish, II, p.255
14. Ibid., p.258
15. *Maitland Miscellany*, III, pp.188-91. Several MS variants of this bond exist
16. CSP Scottish, II, p.265
17. Ruthven's *Narration* in MS Oo 7(47), Cambridge University Library
18. Randolph to Throckmorton from Berwick, 11 March 1566. British Library Additional MSS 35,831 f.261
19. Ruthven, op. cit.
20. Melville, *Memoirs*, p.150
21. Labanoff, I, pp.341-50
22. Claude Nau, *Memorials of Mary Stewart* (ed. J. Stevenson), Edinburgh, 1883 (hereafter referred to as Nau), p.31
23. Ibid., p.16
24. Ibid.

9. Birth and Death, 1566–67
1. *Diurnal*, p.94
2. CSP Foreign, VIII, No. 298
3. CSP Scottish, II, p.278
4. Melville, p.154
5. CSP Scottish, II, p.284
6. Melville, p.158
7. CSP Scottish, II, p.289
8. Henderson, I, p.401
9. J. Robertson, *Inventaires de la Royne d'Escosse*, Bannatyne Club, Edinburgh 1883, p.xxvi
10. George Buchanan, *Detection*, MS Dd 3 (66), Cambridge University Library
11. Ibid.
12. CSP Scottish, II, p.300
13. Henderson, I, pp.404-5
14. On 16 October 1966 a pageant was

staged to recreate Queen Mary's ride, on its 400th anniversary

15. Quoted by P.F. Tytler, *History of Scotland*, Edinburgh, 1841, II, p.400

16. Quoted by Lady Antonia Fraser in *Mary Queen of Scots*, London, 1969, p.277, but without stating the source

17. CSP Spanish, 1558-67, II, p.597

18. Quoted by Henderson, I, p.417

19. Quoted in R. Keith, *History of the Affairs of Church and State in Scotland down to 1567* (ed. J.P. Lawson), Spottiswoode Society, Edinburgh, 1844, I, p.xcviii

20. *Diurnal*, p.105

21. Nau, p.34

22. R.H. Mahon, *The Tragedy of Kirk o' Field*, Cambridge, 1930

23. Robert Gore-Brown, *Lord Bothwell*, London, 1937

24. Nau, p.34

10. Bothwell, February – June 1567

1. CSP Foreign, VIII, p.182

2. CSP Rome, II, p.273. Deathbed statement of John Hepburn to a fellow prisoner, Cuthbert Ramsay, who narrated it in 1576 in Paris at the hearing for the nullification of Bothwell's marriage to Mary

3. CSP Venetian, 1558-80, no. 384; Jenny Wormald, *Mary Queen of Scots: A Study in Failure* (1988)

4. Knox, *Works*, II, p.550

5. Labanoff, II, p.3

6. *Diurnal*, p.108

7. Keith, II, p.562

8. Nau, p.37

9. *Papal Negotiations*, p.386

10. Melville, p.149

11. Labanoff, II, p.31

12. Phillips, *Images of a Queen* (1964), p.48. The ballad, by Robert Sempill, was entitled 'An Declaration of the Lord's Just Quarrel', and is not untypical of the religio-pornographic balladry of the period

13. Andrew Lang, *Mystery of Mary Stuart*, Edinburgh, 1901, p.210

14. Hay Fleming, *Mary Queen of Scots*, Edinburgh, 1897, p.454

15. *Papal Negotiations*, p.387

16. Henderson, II, p.463

17. CSP Foreign, 1566-68, no. 1313; Teulet, II, p.303

18. Quoted in Laing, II, p.113

19. Ibid.

20. Ibid.

21. Recorded by Sir William Drury in a letter to Cecil of 18 June 1567, now in the PRO

22. Laing, op. cit., p.114

23. Teulet, II, pp.311-12

24. Laing, p.114

25. CSP Foreign, 1566-68, no. 1313

11. Lochleven and Langside, 1567-68

1. Laing, *The Works of John Knox*, Edinburgh, 1895, II, p.117

2. CSP Scottish, II, 354

3. See, for example, N. Brysson Morrison, *Mary Queen of Scots,* London, 1960, pp.166-8. Lady Antonia Fraser, in *Mary Queen of Scots*, London, 1969, pp.385-408, has conclusively demolished any argument favouring authenticity. M.H. Armstrong Davidson, *The Casket Letters*, London, 1965, provides the most detailed study of this complex controversy

4. R. Keith, *History of the Affairs of Church and State in Scotland down to 1567* (ed. J.P. Lawson), II, p.699

5. CSP Scottish, II, p.340

6. Ibid., p.370

7. Ibid., pp.380-1

8. Ibid.

9. Nau, pp.66-7

10. Ibid., p.49

11. CSP Venetian, 1558-60, p.406

12. CSP Foreign, VIII, no. 1778

13. Quoted in Robertson's *History of Scotland*, II, p.417

14. CSP Scottish, I, p.394

15. Brantôme, V, p.99

16. Labanoff, II, p.117

12. First Trial, 1568-69

1. *Historic Manuscripts Commission*, V, Appendix to 5th Report, p.615. Ailsa Muniments, folio 17

2. CSP Venetian, VII, p.416

3. CSP Scottish, II, p.416

4. CSP Spanish, 1568-79, p.36

5. Teulet, II, p.369

6. CSP Scottish, II, pp.441-2

7. Ibid., p.428

8. Ibid., p.420

9. CSP Scottish, II, pp.431-5

10. Ibid., pp.465-6

11. Ibid., p.509

12. Ibid., p.457

13. Ibid., p.494. Mary's letters to Elizabeth, for example, were written in French

14. W. Goodall, *Examination of the Letters said to be written by Mary Queen of Scots to James, Earl of Bothwell* (London, 1754), II, p.261

13. Captivity, 1569–84

1. CSP Scottish, II, p.605
2. For detailed accounts see Francis de Zulueta, *Embroideries by Mary Stuart and Elizabeth Talbot at Oxburgh Hall*, 1923, and M.S. Jourdain, *English Secular Embroidery*, 1910
3. *Calendar of the Manuscripts of the Marquess of Salisbury at Hatfield House*, Historical Manuscripts Commission, 1883, hereafter referred to as Hatfield, I, p.400
4. CSP Spanish, 1568-79, p.97
5. Ibid., p.167
6. Hatfield, I, p.414
7. CSP Spanish, p.183
8. Ibid., p.158
9. Ibid., p.189
10. CSP Scottish, II, p.677
11. The origin of the expression 'sent to Coventry' is not known. It is sometimes said to be derived from the Royalist prisoners sent thither from Birmingham during the Civil War, but I am inclined to think that the incarceration of MQS there is more likely
12. Labanoff, III, pp.5, 19 and 31
13. Ibid., p.354
14. Hatfield, I, p.564
15. Ibid., II, p.428
16. Labanoff, IV, p.428
17. Ida Macalpine and Richard Hunter, *Porphyria, a Royal Disease*, British Medical Association, London, 1968
18. Labanoff, IV, pp.94-8
19. Ibid., pp.129-30
20. Ibid., pp.183, 186 and 229
21. Ibid., p.186
22. Teulet, VI, p.122
23. Ibid., VI, p.393
24. Labanoff, V, p.61
25. Ibid., p.158
26. Ibid., VI, pp.36-42
27. Hatfield, III, pp.46-7

14. The Final Act, 1585–87

1. J. Morris, *Letter-Books of Sir Amias Paulet*, London, 1874, p.15
2. Ibid., p.6

3. Labanoff, VI, p.345
4. Bourgoing's journal, in M.R. Chantelauze, *Marie Stuart, son procès et son exécution*, Paris, 1874, p.467
5. Morris, op. cit., p.276
6. Ibid., p.267
7. Ibid., p.287
8. Labanoff, VII, p.36
9. Hon. Mrs Maxwell-Stuart, *The Tragedy of Fotheringhay, founded on the Journal of Bourgoing and unpublished MS documents*, Edinburgh, 1905, p.35
10. Agnes Strickland, *Lives of the Queens of Scotland*, Edinburgh, 1854, VII, p.428
11. Chantelauze, op. cit., p.513
12. Ibid., p.520
13. J.H. Pollen, *Mary Queen of Scots and the Babington Plot*, Scottish History Series, Third Series, Edinburgh, 1922, p.cxcii
14. Labanoff, VI, p.477
15. Text in Samuel Cowan, *The Last Days of Mary Stuart*, London, 1907, pp.120-1
16. Robert S. Rait and Annie Cameron, *King James's Secret: Negotiations between Elizabeth and James VI Relating to the Execution of Mary Queen of Scots*, Edinburgh, 1927, p.55
17. Morris, p.361
18. The actual execution warrant is no longer extant, although the letter from the Privy Council ordering the execution warrant exists with annotations by Robert Beale. It was sold at Sotheby's, London in December 1996 for £45,000, the purchaser being the Church of England. There was a considerable outcry from the Scottish National Party that neither the National Library of Scotland nor the National Museums of Scotland had shown any interest in the sale
19. MS account of the execution by Robert Beale; purchased by the Church of England for £6,900 at Sotheby's, December 1996
20. D. Calderwood, *History of the Kirk of Scotland* (ed. T. Thomson), Edinburgh, 1842, IV, p.611
21. Dean Stanley, *Memorials of Westminster Abbey*, London, 1867, Appendix p.507
22. Angus, Duke of Hamilton, *Mary Queen of Scots, the Crucial Years*, Edinburgh, 1991, p.115

INDEX